EAST ANGLIAN ARCHAEOLOGY

The Saxon and Medieval Settlement at West Fen Road, Ely: The Ashwell Site

by Richard Mortimer, Roderick Regan and Sam Lucy

with contributions by
Rachel Ballantyne, Paul Blinkhorn, Adrian
Challands, Natasha Dodwell, David Hall,
Lorrain Higbee, Anne Holton-Krayenbuhl,
Gwladys Monteil, Andrew Mudd, Sarah Percival,
Phil Piper, Ian Riddler and Robert G. Scaife

and illustrations by
Andrew Hall, Marcus Abbott and Matthew
Brudenell

East Anglian Archaeology
Report No. 110, 2005

Cambridge Archaeological Unit

EAST ANGLIAN ARCHAEOLOGY
REPORT NO.110

Published by
Cambridge Archaeological Unit
Department of Archaeology
University of Cambridge
Downing Street
Cambridge CB2 3DZ

in conjunction with
ALGAO East
www.algao.org.uk/cttees/regions

Editor: Ben Robinson
Managing Editor: Jenny Glazebrook

Set in Times New Roman by Trevor Ashwin using Corel Ventura™
Printed by Geerings of Ashford Ltd., Kent

ISBN 0 9544824 1 7

Funded by Ashwell Property Group Plc

East Anglian Archaeology was established in 1975 by the Scole Committee for Archaeology in East Anglia. The scope of the series expanded to include all six eastern counties and responsibility for publication was transferred in 2002 to the Association of Local Government Archaeological Officers, East of England (ALGAO East).

For details of *East Anglian Archaeology*, see last page

Cover illustration
Aerial view of the excavation area at West Fen Road, overlain by plan of all features (RC8 Kn BL214, *photography by Cambridge University Collection of Air Photographs*)

Contents

List of Plates

List of Figures

List of Tables

Contributors

Rachel Ballantyne, BA, MSc
Dept of Archaeology, University of Cambridge, Downing St, Cambridge CB2 3DZ

Paul Blinkhorn, BTech
60 Turner St, Northampton NN1 4JL

Adrian Challands, BA, MIFA
The Old School House, Glinton Road, Helpston, Peterborough PE6 7DG

Natasha Dodwell, BA, MSc
Cambridge Archaeological Unit, Dept of Archaeology, University of Cambridge, Downing St, Cambridge CB2 3DZ

David Hall, MA, FSA
Pinfold, Raunds Road, Hargrave, Wellingborough, Northants NN9 6BW

Lorrain Higbee, BSc, MSc
2 Knights Cottages, Knights Farm, Fitzhead, Somerset TA4 3JY

Anne Holton-Krayenbuhl, BA, PGCE
10 Marroway Lane, Witchford, Ely, Cambs CB6 2HU

Dr Sam Lucy, BA, PhD, FSA
Cambridge Archaeological Unit, Dept of Archaeology, University of Cambridge, Downing St, Cambridge CB2 3DZ

Gwladys Monteil, BA, MA, MPhil
School of History, Classics and Archaeology, Birkbeck College, University of London, Malet Street, London WC1E 7HX

Richard Mortimer
(Formerly CAU) Cambridgeshire County Council Archaeological Field Unit, Fulbourn Community Centre, Haggis Gap, Fulbourn, Cambridge CB1 5HD

Andrew Mudd, BA, MIFA
Senior Project Officer, Northamptonshire Archaeology, 2 Bolton House, Wootton Hall Park, Northampton NN4 8BE

Sarah Percival, BA, MA
Finds Specialist, Norfolk Archaeological Unit, Spire House, 13–15 Cathedral Street, Norwich NR1 1LU

Dr Phil Piper, BA, PhD
McDonald Institute for Archaeological Research, University of Cambridge

Roderick Regan
(Formerly CAU) Kilmartin House Museum, Kilmartin, Argyll PA31 8RQ

Ian Riddler, MA, FSA
Tatra, Diddies Rd, Stratton, Nr Bude, Cornwall EX23 9DW

Robert G. Scaife, BA, PhD
Visiting Fellow, Palaeoecology Laboratory, School of Geography, University of Southampton, Highfield, Southampton SO17 1BJ

Acknowledgements

The site and its publication was generously funded by the Ashwell Property Group Plc, and particular thanks go to Paul Thwaites for his support throughout, while the co-operation and understanding of Tim Bluff and Nigel McCreith of that company must also be acknowledged. The unexpected scale and obvious complexity of the site posed significant challenges to all involved. The willingness of the Ashwell Property Group to arrange the construction programme to accommodate the needs of the fieldwork — and also the innovative response by Simon Kaner of Cambridgeshire Development — were instrumental in the project, allowing what could have been a problematic excavation to be successfully resolved in a professional manner. Our appreciation also goes to the employees of Mervyn Lambert for stripping the site with care and speed in difficult conditions, and to the Breheny crew for their on-site co-operation.

Over the course of the assessment and excavations, many people worked on the site. Our particular thanks go to the main excavation team: Marcus Abbott, Natasha Dodwell, Steve Every, John Foulkes, Jon Hall, Lorrain Higbee, Duncan MacKay, Paul Masser, Becky Scott, and Paula Whittaker. Others participating, for lesser or greater lengths of time, were Joe Abrams, Nick Armour, Oscar Aldred, Emma Beadsmoore, Marc Berger, Phil Church, Graeme Clarke, Duncan Garrow, Andy Hall, Pip Patrick and Samantha Smith. We would also like to thank Wayne Davis, for his assistance with on-site metal-detecting. The project was managed by Christopher Evans.

The large finds assemblage was processed by Norma Challands and the CAU finds team, and thanks are also due to David Hall and J.D. Hill for spot-dating the pottery, to Professor Jenny Price and Jennifer Jones for help with the Roman glass and metalwork identification, to Jane Cowgill for the initial metalwork identifications, to Professor James Graham-Campbell for help with the Saxon brooch identification, to Brunella Flackett for information derived from the conservation of the armorial mount, and to Chantal Conneller for the flint identification. Unless otherwise stated, specialist reports are by the authors. Computer graphics were produced by Richard Mortimer, Andy Hall and Marcus Abbott; Andy Hall and Matthew Brudenell undertook the finds illustration.

We are also grateful to Andrew Mudd of Northamptonshire Archaeology for permission to reproduce plans of the excavations to the north of West Fen Road. Finally, we would like to thank those people who have commented on various versions of this text: Dr Catherine Hills; our editor, Ben Robinson, and the anonymous reader, all of whom assisted us greatly with their constructive comments.

Summary

Excavations by the Cambridge Archaeological Unit in 1999 and 2000 on a housing development site off West Fen Road, to the west of Ely city centre, produced abundant evidence for Mid and Late Saxon and medieval settlement. Established in the early 8th century the site saw continuous occupation, often within the same ditched property boundaries, for almost 800 years, until its eventual desertion in the 15th century. A detailed reconstruction of the settlement history of the site indicates a very stable, but gradually evolving settlement which probably provided food and other services, originally to the monastic settlement, then to the abbey, and subsequently to the bishops. The finds assemblage suggests that the occupants of the settlement did not enjoy a high-status lifestyle; a lack of imported pottery, of high-value metalwork, and an almost total absence of coinage all indicate that this site was somewhat removed from the ecclesiastical power centre to the east.

Résumé

Les fouilles entreprises par Cambridge Archaeological Unit en 1999 et 2000 à l'occasion de construction de logements au-delà de West Fen Road et à proximité du centre de la ville d'Ely, ont permis de mettre à jour d'importantes traces d'implantations datant de l'époque médiévale et des périodes saxonnes intermédiaire et tardive. Depuis le début du huitième siècle, le site a été occupé en permanence pendant presque 800 ans jusqu'à ce qu'il soit finalement abandonné au quinzième siècle. Cette occupation s'est souvent déroulée dans les mêmes limites territoriales qui étaient délimitées par un fossé. La reconstruction détaillée de l'histoire du site a permis de démontrer l'existence d'une implantation qui se caractérise à la fois par la stabilité et par une évolution progressive. Cette implantation fournissait sans doute de la nourriture et d'autres services qui étaient d'abord destinés au monastère du site puis aux évêques. L'analyse des objets découverts suggère que les occupants du site ne jouissaient pas d'un niveau de vie élevé et ne disposaient que d'un nombre limité de poterie importée et de métaux travaillés de grande valeur. Par ailleurs, on n'a pratiquement pas trouvé de pièces. Ces différents indices permettent de conclure que le site était quelque peu éloigné du centre du pouvoir ecclésiastique en direction de l'est.

(Traduction: Didier Don)

Zusammenfassung

Die Cambridge Archaeological Unit führte in den Jahren 1999 und 2000 in einer Wohnsiedlung unweit der West Fen Road nahe beim Stadtzentrum von Ely Grabungen durch, die zahlreiche Belege für eine mittel- und spätangelsächsische sowie eine mittelalterliche Siedlung erbrachten. Die Stätte war ab dem frühen 8. Jh. fast 800 Jahre lang durchgängig besiedelt, häufig innerhalb derselben Grundstücksgräben, bis sie schließlich im 15. Jh. aufgegeben wurde. Eine detaillierte Rekonstruktion der Siedlungsgeschichte der Stätte verweist auf eine höchst stabile Ansiedlung, die sich Schritt für Schritt entwickelte und wahrscheinlich zunächst die Klostergemeinde, dann die Abtei und zuletzt die Bischöfe mit Nahrungsmitteln und anderen Dingen versorgte. Der Fundkomplex deutet darauf hin, dass die Siedlungsbewohner keinen besonders hohen Status genossen. Das Fehlen importierter Töpferware und hochwertiger Metallobjekte sowie die fast vollständige Abwesenheit von Münzen sind Zeichen dafür, dass der Ort vom kirchlichen Machtzentrum im Osten weit entfernt war.

(Übersetzung: Gerlinde Krug)

Figure 1.1 The location of the site in relation to the built-up areas of Ely

1. Introduction and Background

I. The site history
(Figs 1.1–1.8)

Background
Recent housing development along the western fringe of the City of Ely now covers over twenty hectares of ex-agricultural land. At the heart of this development lie the three fields that are the subject of the excavations reported on here. The site, centred on TL 529808, is bounded on the north by West Fen Road, on the west by the A10 bypass, and on the east by the western suburbs of Ely (Fig. 1.1). The higher, eastern field, Area A, had been under pasture for some time, with visible remains of ridge and furrow, while the lower north-western field, Area B, and the large south-western field, Area C, had both seen recent arable cultivation (Fig. 1.2). Areas A and B were intensively excavated and produced a wealth of archaeological features, particularly of the Saxon and medieval period, while Area C was assessed by trial-trenching and was found, with the exception of a medieval trackway, to be archaeologically blank. Excavations were undertaken in 1999 and 2000 by the Cambridge Archaeological Unit (hereafter CAU) on behalf of the developers, Ashwell Property Group Plc.

Geology and topography
The city of Ely occupies one of the highest points on the largest of the 'islands' within the Cambridgeshire Fens. The high land at Ely became completely surrounded by wetland in post-Roman times, and remained an island until the large-scale post-medieval drainage schemes were implemented (refer to Hall 1996 for the general environmental background). The area under discussion here lies approximately 1km to the west of Ely Cathedral and the city centre and well beyond the urban core of medieval Ely, which centred around the Cathedral and down the east side of the island along the River Ouse (Figs 1.1–1.3). The intensively excavated part of the site (*i.e.* Areas A and B) lies close to the fen edge, on the downslope of the west side of the Isle of Ely, and slopes from *c.* 12m OD at the south-eastern corner to *c.* 6m OD at the north-western. The boundary between Areas A and B coincides with a significant change in the overall topography, with the eastern half of the site being more steeply sloping than the western half. The higher southern end of Area A is level, with the rest of the field falling away to the north and west. In contrast, the whole of Area B is relatively flat, with a slight depression running east–west across its centre. Area C covers some 7.4ha and slopes down from east to west, from 14.75m OD to 5.50m OD (Fig. 1.2).

The underlying geology of the area is Kimmeridge clay, with some pockets of Cretaceous sand and sandstone. Unlike other sites of the Late Saxon and medieval periods in Ely, which tend to be located where the Kimmeridge clay is overlain by Lower Greensand, the site reported on here lies on uncompromising pure clay

(Gallois 1988). The saturated ground at the high southern end of Area A indicated the presence of springs.

Archaeological background

Prehistoric
Previous archaeological work in the vicinity (Fig. 1.3), including an excavation to the north of West Fen Road (Gibson 1995), had demonstrated the archaeological potential of the area prior to the 1999–2000 excavations, and provides a wider context for the current project. Excavations in advance of pipelaying and water pumping station construction to the north of West Fen Road exposed part of a Late Iron Age site consisting of interconnecting ovoid enclosures which produced large amounts of pottery, animal bone and fired clay along with two decorated objects: a bone gouge and an unusual clay plaque (*ibid.*, 14–15). More recent excavations in the same area by Northamptonshire Archaeology have produced evidence for a concentration of Iron Age features (a probable house site surrounded by two concentric enclosure ditches), in the southern part of the excavated area (Mudd 2000; see p.4 below for a summary, and Chapter 2 for further discussion).

To the south two further fields — Trinity and Runciman Fields — have also now been investigated by the CAU, and the results of these works are presented elsewhere (Masser 2001). Excavations at these locations from December 2000 to February 2001, again on behalf of Ashwell Property Group Plc, revealed sporadic Neolithic and Bronze Age activity, followed by evidence of settlement activity in the Middle and Later Iron Age. The Late Iron Age settlement (1st century BC–1st century AD) consisted of ephemeral ring-gullies, shallow pits and spreads of midden deposits. In the late 1st or early 2nd century AD, two rectilinear ditched enclosures were laid out to the south, probably to mark out fields or control livestock. As at West Fen Road Area C, to the north of the road, there was no evidence of any Mid to Late Saxon settlement or of substantial medieval activity.

Further to the west, on a sand and gravel rise at the end of a peninsula projecting westward from the Ely ridge clays, lies the Late Iron Age/early Roman site at Hurst Lane (TL 52518141). Excavations by the CAU under extreme 'rescue' conditions in 1999 (the construction of a reservoir having side-stepped the normal development control procedures) recovered evidence for Iron Age house gullies and enclosure complexes (Evans *et al.* forthcoming). Elsewhere on the higher ground and removed from the fen edge, the Fenland Survey (commissioned by English Heritage to identify and map the extents of archaeological sites across the Wash fenlands of Lincolnshire, Norfolk and Cambridgeshire) revealed a scatter of Iron Age settlement sites, some associated with enclosure crop-marks, evidenced by occupational debris, fragments of animal bone and pottery sherds (Hall 1996, 35).

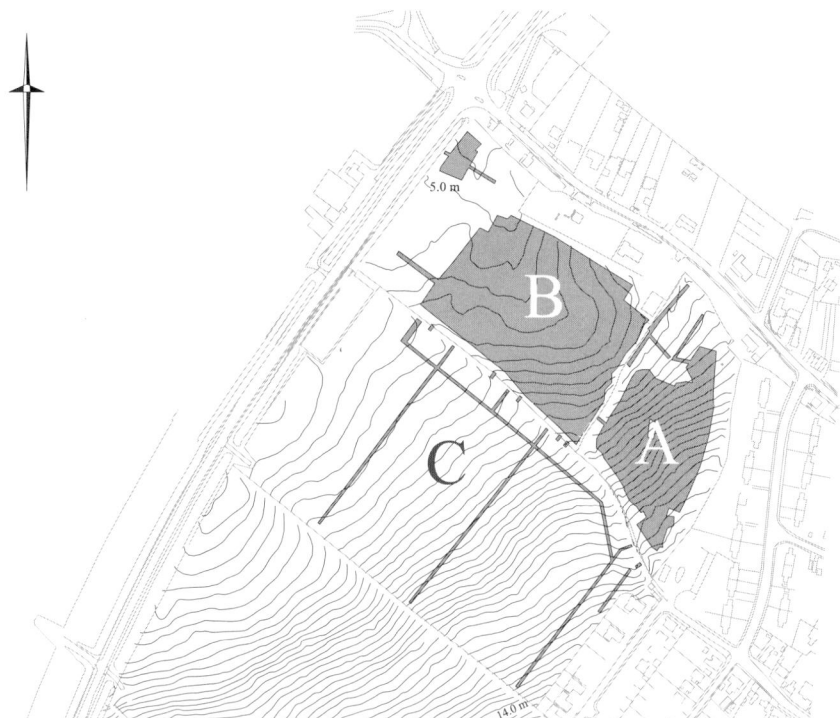

Based on the Ordnance Survey 1:2500 map
With the permission of the controller of Her Majesty's Stationary Office © Crown Copyright.
University of Cambridge Licence No. AL 550833

```
0                    200                   400
|======|======|======|======|======|======|      Contour intervals at 25cm
                    metres
```

Figure 1.2 The excavated areas and site topography

Roman

Little was known until relatively recently about Roman settlement west of Ely. The Fenland Survey recorded Roman and medieval pottery on the northern edge of the present site. These finds came from what was described as a dark 'greasy' area, with colour-coated wares and late grey ware sherds, hypocaust tile, St Neots ware and medieval sherds spread over an area of 0.25ha centred on TL 53018077; an aerial photograph suggested double-ditched and linear-ditched features and earthworks (Hall 1996). Before the current excavations, it was thought that these finds might be related to field system ditches recorded to the north of West Fen Road (Gibson 1995), but it is now apparent that they relate to the excavated areas directly to the south. Further to the east, the Fenland Survey also produced evidence for another ten sites of Roman date, including a Roman 'dock' at the edge of Stuntney island. Again, many of these are located on the higher ground (*ibid*., 36).

Saxon

Likewise, until 1990, little was known about the Saxon period in the area (the term being used here purely as a chronological indicator for the 5th–11th centuries AD), with the exception of a fragment of stone sculpture from one of the barn walls at St John's Farm (see below) which had been tentatively identified as part of a frieze of 8th-century date, and possibly a remnant of the first stone church at Ely (Cobbett 1934; Henderson 1997). Since 1990, however, a small number of excavations and other

archaeological interventions have produced evidence of Mid and Later Saxon activity and occupation west of Ely, and these results can help to set the current excavations in context (for discussion and synthesis, see Chapter 7). Archaeological work at Upherds Lane, *c*. 200m to the east of West Fen Road, identified elements of a Saxo-Norman enclosure/paddock as well as later ridge and furrow (Taylor-Wilson 1992), while small trenches at St Mary's Lodge (Robinson 2000), Chapel Street (Hinman 1996) and the former Red, White and Blue public house in Chief's Street (Kenney 2002) produced some Mid and Later Saxon material. A small number of Early–Mid Saxon sherds were also found in later features at 2 West End (Kenney 1999; see below for details). To the east of the Cathedral, trial trenching at the site known as The Paddock revealed Late Saxon ditches, which appeared to represent the boundaries of urban properties (Holton-Krayenbuhl 1988). Nearer to the Cathedral, south of the Lady Chapel, Late Saxon evidence suggestive of high-status activity has been observed (Regan 2001). Here, a large pit contained various fills yielding a substantial amount of pottery (the largest inland assemblage of Ipswich ware yet found — 89 sherds, weighing 2453g — along with some imported French wares) and animal bone.

Early Saxon cemeteries have been reported from Witchford aerodrome, to the south of the city (found during levelling work in 1947), while the construction of a housing estate to the north of Ely in 1959 exposed a second inhumation cemetery, probably of 6th-century

2

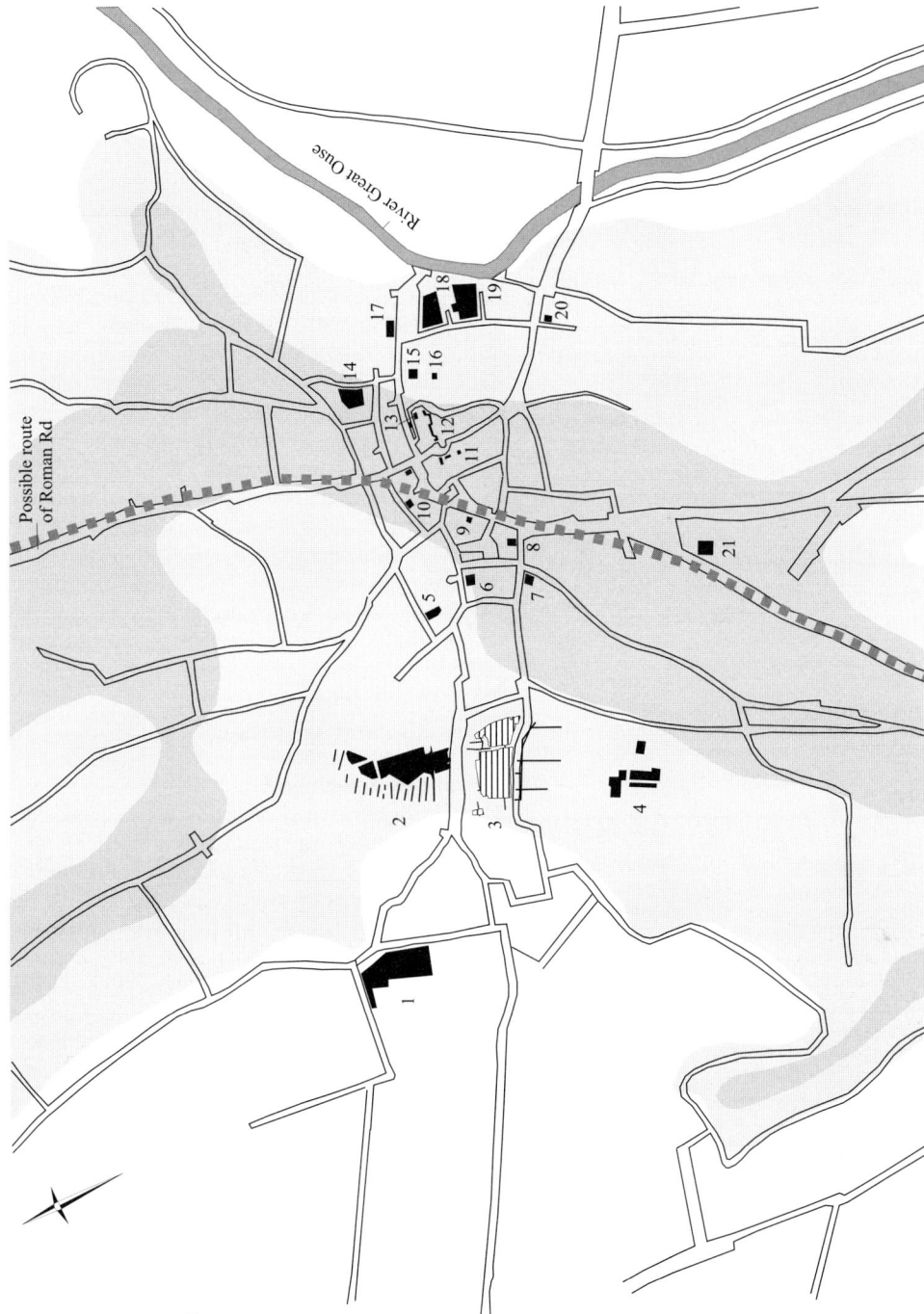

1 Hurst Lane
(Evans & Knight Forthcoming)
2 West Fen Rd. (Mudd 2000)
3 West Fen Rd. (this volume)
4 Trinity & Runciman (Masser 2001)
5 Upherds Lane (Taylor-Wilson 1992)
6 Chief's St. (Kenney 2002)
7 St. John's Rd. (Abrams 2000)
8 West End (Kenney 1999)
9 St. Mary's Lodge (Robinson 2000)
10 Chapel St. (Hinman 1996)
11 Old Bishop's Palace
(Alexander 1997)
12 Cathedral, South Choir
(Whittaker 1996)
13 Lady Chapel (Regan 2001)
14 Bray's Lane (Hunter 1991)
15 The Paddocks
(Holten-Krayenbuhl 1988)
16 Walsingham House (Hunter 1992)
17 Forehill (Alexander 2003)
18 Broad St., Tesco's
(Cessford et al. forthcoming)
19 Broad St., Jewson's Yard
(Cessford et al. forthcoming)
20 Potters Lane
(Spoerry unpublished)
21 Witchford Rd (Yates pers. comm.)

Figure 1.3 The location of main excavations in Ely, using the 1830s 1st edition Ordnance Survey road plan; higher ground (above 5m OD) shaded

date (Hall 1996, 36). In 2003, excavations between the two sites at Witchford Road, on the south-west outskirts of Ely, produced evidence for another possibly 6th-century cemetery, albeit heavily disturbed by sand extraction (A. Yates, *pers. comm.*; Fig. 1.3 No. 21). All these cemetery sites are found on raised ground, along the spine of the island, perhaps implying that Early Saxon settlement is to be found in similar geographical locations.

More recently, a large area around the pipeline to the north of West Fen Road has been excavated by Northamptonshire Archaeology, and this is briefly reported on here (see Chapters 2 and 7 for further discussion).

Excavations north of West Fen Road, Ely, 1999–2000: a summary
by Andrew Mudd

There was fragmentary evidence for earlier prehistoric occupation on the site. This included a pit containing sherds of an earlier Neolithic plain bowl and, from the western margin of the site, part of a probable Bronze Age Collared Urn. A small collection of worked flint from across the site all appears to have been residual, although supporting the suggestion of light activity in the earlier prehistoric period.

In the Iron Age a settlement was established, comprising substantial enclosure ditches (characteristically 1m or more deep) and probable eaves drainage gullies, with few other features. An outer oval enclosure, nearly 100m across at its widest, encircled an inner enclosure, which in turn surrounded a probable house gully. Another enclosure was attached to the south. A complete plan of the settlement was not exposed and it is difficult to be sure of its overall form, but two more peripheral western boundary ditches indicated an overall concentric pattern to the ditch layout.

Most of the Iron Age pottery falls into the later plain ware hand-made tradition, with a limited range of forms. Two enhanced precision radiocarbon dates indicate the main occupation to have been in the 3rd–2nd centuries BC, although wheel-made and Roman pottery from some of the upper ditch fills suggests that the site was not effectively abandoned until the 1st century AD. There was a limited quantity of later Roman material, and the site appears to have been marginal to settlement at that time.

The site was re-occupied in the Mid Saxon period, with a layout of relatively shallow ditched enclosures concentrated in the eastern central part of the site. There was also a scatter of pits, the deeper ones perhaps being water-holes, typically located in the corners of enclosures and on their edges. No obvious structures were identified, although groups of post-holes and small gullies might indicate the locations of buildings of some sort, probably in the backyards of house plots.

The Saxon pottery is almost exclusively Ipswich Ware, and indicates that occupation may have been confined to the period AD 725–850. Later Saxon pottery is limited to five sherds of St Neots Ware, suggesting that the site had been given over to other uses by this time. There was a small assemblage of Mid Saxon metalwork and other finds. The objects included a *sceatta* (AD 740–50), four dress pins, a fragment of a pair of tweezers and part of a bone comb. Textile manufacture is indicated by a number of bone pin beaters and annular loomweights, as well as an iron heckle tooth and a ceramic spindle whorl. Twelve blades were among the other iron objects.

Medieval
Also at 2 West End, Saxo-Norman and medieval pottery associated with probably domestic occupation was found during evaluation in advance of a small housing development (Kenney 1999). Further excavation in 2000 revealed evidence for six phases of activity spanning the Late Saxon to medieval periods; the earliest phases were associated with field systems and boundaries, with settlement and industrial activity evidenced on the site from the late medieval period (Abrams 2002).

Three buildings with medieval components survive at St John's Farm, to the south-east of the development area. Two are thought to have been chapels; these buildings were part of St John's Hospital formed by the amalgamation in *c.* 1240 of the two adjacent hospitals of St Mary Magdalene (recorded in 1162) and St John the Baptist founded by or before the early 13th century (Cobbett and Palmer 1935). Medieval hospitals were frequently located just outside urban areas, on major routeways. If this was the case here, it offers some indication that the West Fen Road site lay in a peripheral location in the medieval period (although it had not necessarily done so in Saxon times: see Chapter 7).

Ridge and furrow elements, and their associated headlands, were visible as earthworks and crop-marks over the development area and indicated medieval cultivation. The area was enclosed in 1844; some of the smaller fields created then have since been amalgamated for the purposes of modern agriculture (Gibson 1998, 7).

Regarding the overall development of medieval Ely, while the historical sources are reported on below by Holton-Krayenbuhl, recent excavations have produced abundant archaeological evidence. At Broad Street and the surrounding area several excavations, both large and small in scale, have offered the opportunity to examine the waterfront areas (Cessford *et al.* forthcoming). Here, some Late Saxon activity was followed in the 12th–13th centuries by relatively dense urban occupation within typically medieval building plots. Nearby, at Ely Forehill, excavations have revealed an even denser continuous building sequence from the 12th century onwards (Alexander 2003). These occupation sequences seem to tie in with documentary evidence (see below) for the reorganisation of the urban environment in Ely in the late 11th and 12th centuries.

The historical context
by Anne Holton-Krayenbuhl
The first appearance of Ely in the documentary record is in connection with the foundation of a monastery by Etheldreda (or Æthelthryth), daughter of Anna, the king of the East Angles *c.* 673 (Garmonsway 1972, 34–5; Sherley-Price 1968, 239). Etheldreda founded a double house for nuns and monks and she was the first abbess; the history of her monastery and of the Church at Ely until the 10th-century refoundation is described in Book I of *Liber Eliensis* (Blake 1962, 1–62), compiled between 1131 and 1174 by a monk of Ely. The Saxon monastery served as a central church, probably with responsibility for pastoral work within its territory (Blair 1988, 1). Saxon monasteries resembled large secular households and were endowed with family land; they could accommodate noble relatives of the (often royal) founder, and provided them with a place of burial (Stafford 1985, 101).

The compiler of *Liber Eliensis* recorded that Etheldreda established her monastery on a new site a mile away from an existing settlement at *Cratendune* where ancient objects and coins were still being found (Blake 1962, 3–4). *Cratendon* occurs in both 13th-century surveys of the bishop's demesne, listed after Gruntifenfield (BL Cott. Tib. Bii, 1; CUL EDR G3/27, 1); both of the bishop's 15th-century rentals refer to Bedwellhay in Gruntifenfield (CUL EDR D10/1/1; D10/1/2). *Cratendune* is therefore unlikely to be the site identified near Bedwell Hay Farm (*contra* Hall 1996, 36), some two miles (3km) south of Ely. It is important to note (*pace* Hall 1996, 39) that neither the *Liber Eliensis* nor Blake's preface state that Etheldreda had a church at Cratendune which was 'destroyed by fire in 673' (J. Fairweather, *pers. comm.*). It has often been assumed that the Saxon monastery stood on the site of the cathedral precinct, but this is still debated. Among the other possible sites are St Mary's church, whose medieval parish included the West Fen Road area, or the hospital of St John the Baptist, with its 8th-century sculpture fragment (Cobbett and Palmer 1935, 73–4). The latter site was clearly significant when the open fields were laid out; the Inclosure Map of 1844 shows two of the fields converging upon it (CRO 515). Identification of the site of Etheldreda's monastery must, however, remain tentative in the absence of firmer evidence (see Chapter 7 for further discussion).

The Danes conquered East Anglia and much of Cambridgeshire in 870 (Darby and Miller 1948, 379) and are said to have burnt the monastery at Ely (Blake 1962, 54). *Liber Eliensis* records, however, that secular priests provided continuity of religious life in Ely until 970 when they were expelled on the foundation by Bishop Ethelwold of a Benedictine abbey at Ely (still focused on the shrine to St Etheldreda), on land granted by King Edgar (*ibid.*, 74–5; Keynes 2003, 14–27); replacement of double houses by colleges of canons seems to have been common in the 9th and early 10th centuries (Blair 1988, 3). By purchase and gift, the refounded abbey built up an extensive estate on the Isle of Ely and well beyond, between *c.* 970 and *c.* 1020 (Miller 1951, 16–24; although not without challenge — see Keynes 2003, 26–7). The foundation of the abbey at Ely would have had a considerable impact on the lives of the local inhabitants. They had acquired a new landlord consisting of a community of monks and their dependants, with regular requirements for goods and services. This may well have been the stimulus for renewal of existing thoroughfares or establishment of new ones, to facilitate communications between the abbey and its manors.

The Norman Conquest affected Ely in several ways. Ely is famed for its association with Hereward 'the Wake', who used the island as a refuge and a base after joining the Fenland revolt against William in 1070–1, until the king laid siege and secured the surrender of the majority of the rebels (Keynes 2003, 29, 42–4). The subsequent introduction of the feudal system reduced all the abbey's dependants to the status of tenant whereas previously there had been a variety of classes, some of which had enjoyed considerable freedom (Miller 1951, 49–51). The peasantry suffered from the gradual increase in burdens imposed on it from the late 11th century onward (*ibid.*, 73–4). Domesday Book provides a picture of the manor of Ely in 1086. It was assessed at ten hides, half of which were in demesne, and the recorded population consisted of 40 villeins, 28 cottars and 20 serfs (Hampson and Atkinson 1953, 34).

The abbey's estates had already been confiscated once, as a result of Hereward's revolt. Although most of this property was recovered in the 1080s the abbey was to lose much of it again after 1109, when the See of Ely was created out of the southern part of the See of Lincoln and endowed with the greater part of the estate of Ely abbey (Darby and Miller 1948, 201–4, 384–5). The abbey became a priory; the abbey church, a monastic cathedral.

The earliest standing buildings in Ely date from the second half of the 12th century. These comprise the Norman cathedral (founded 1081) and a number of conventual buildings, including the prior's hall and the infirmary (Holton-Krayenbuhl 1997, 122–3). The bishop's palace complex stood west of the cloister, and his home farm south of Barton Square. The monastic enclosure stands on the east-facing slope, overlooking the River Great Ouse, the main channel of which had been diverted to Ely from a more easterly course in the 12th, or possibly the 10th, century (*ibid.*, 119–20). This was a significant episode in the development of the topography of the medieval town. The river provided the chief means of communication with the outside world, linking Ely with Cambridge, King's Lynn and the ports beyond, thus creating a new focus for activity in Ely.

Material and documentary evidence suggests that the topography of medieval Ely was established by *c.* 1200. The medieval pattern of settlement was established, with occupation concentrated north and east of the monastic precinct and oriented towards the river. The years after *c.* 1200 saw changes in agricultural organisation when manorial lords resumed direct exploitation of their estates, in order to increase profitability (Postan 1975, 110–11). This process occurred at Ely and the bishops' surveys of 1222 and 1251 provide evidence for the organisation of agriculture on episcopal manors. Once the bishop and monastery had reached some degree of agreement regarding ownership of land, they could engage more actively in maximising yields. There was expansion of arable from the woodland at Chettisham near Downham between 1222 and 1251 (CUL EDR G3/27, 1), and from the fens, as recorded by Matthew Paris in the mid-13th century (1854, 182). Two of the free tenants listed in the bishop's survey of 1222 held land described as encroachment (*purprestura*) (BL Cott. Tib. Bii, 2r, 2v), and this must have occurred elsewhere.

The 13th century had thus been an age of high farming and increased population, but this trend was reversed in the early decades of the 14th century. There were harvest failures and livestock epidemics in 1315–22; by the 1340s, at least 4870 acres had gone out of cultivation in Cambridgeshire, in part the result of flooding (Miller and Hatcher 1978, 59–61). The Black Death, reaching Ely in 1349, caused increased mortality (see Owen 2003, 63 for its effects on the monastic community). Much arable land was turned into pasture. The work burdens imposed on the unfree tenants in the 13th century were increasingly commuted to money payments, and there is 15th-century evidence for the reduction in the level of rents on some holdings. The move from arable to pasture continued into the 15th century when enclosure for sheep-farming became widespread. Enclosure also occurred at Ely but the area of West Fen Road does not appear to have been affected at this time (Palmer 1936, 373–8). Enclosures at Ely were usually small and probably used for dairy farming (*ibid.*, 372).

The most comprehensive picture of medieval Ely is provided by the 1417 survey. This records the rights and duties of bishop and monastery and lists all their free tenants, stating who the landlord was. It exists in five copies (BL Harley 329, fos 10–24v; BL Harley 329, fos 25–32; BL Cotton Claudius C XI, fos 327–332v; BL Cotton Vespasian A XIX, fos 76–98v; PRO C66/401). The tenants are listed, street by street, with references to abuttals or adjoining tenements in some cases. Most of these streets occur in 13th-century charters, suggesting that the later medieval town plan was already established by then. Holdings of monastery and bishop were not evenly distributed throughout Ely. Along Broad Street, the monastery owned 60 tenements and the bishop 21, whereas in the area between Downham Road and West End–Fieldside the bishop owned 43 tenements and the prior 23. These apparently extended as far as Chief Street or thereabouts. In the latter area, there are incidental references to a number of bishop's holdings with unfree status (*tenementum nativum* or *de bondagio*) (BL Harl. 329, 21–22v; BL Cott. Vesp. A19, 93–95v).

Evidence from the 1417 survey suggests that most of the area around West Fen Road had been awarded to the bishop, and that it included unfree holdings. Unfree holdings occur in the bishop's surveys of 1222 (BL Cott. Tib. Bii, 89v–92v) and 1251 (CUL EDR G3/27, 5–7) listing all the tenants of the bishop and recording the customary obligations attached to each holding. There were two categories of unfree men: the villeins, who were holders of full lands (eighteen acres) or subdivisions thereof; and the cottagers, each holding one acre. Such men were required to work one to three days per week on the lord's demesne, in proportion to the size of their holding, and depending on the time of year. Additional burdens were attached to these holdings. In 1222, there were 51 villeins and 98 cottagers on the bishop's manor of Ely, and about 180 free men. The location of the bishop's unfree holdings is not stated in the 13th-century surveys, but two rentals for 1436–37 (CUL EDR D10/1/1) and 1440–41 (CUL EDR D10/1/2) have occasional topographical references. The tenants are listed under the headings of *firma terre native* (rent of holders of full lands, *etc.*) and *firma cottariorum* (cottagers' rent), and some are recorded as holding land at or towards West Fen. The bishop's rental for 1436–7 records a drop in the rent payable for a full land at West Fen from 12/- to 4/-, while other reductions are slighter (CUL EDR D/10/1/1). It should be noted that there were unfree holdings elsewhere in Ely, *e.g.* Lisle Lane and Potter's Lane. There are references to field names in these two rentals; these have not yet been located, and may include fields adjoining West Fen Road.

Thus, by 1200 the West Fen Road area had become a peripheral one, despite the considerable increase in the population of Ely between 1086 and 1222 (BL Cot. Tib. Bii), and it underwent a further decline in the 15th century. The 1844 Inclosure Map shows six open fields around Ely. If this map reflects the medieval situation, West Fen Road formed a dividing line, with Downham field to the north and Little Debden Field to the south. The Inclosure Map shows the limits of Downham field in 1844, the modern road from Ely to Downham running through the middle. Another road, following West Fen Road and the fen edge along Hurst Lane, is likely to have been more important in the medieval period, linking the bishop's palace at Ely with his more favoured one at Downham. The northern end of Hurst Lane is marked Ely Lane on an undated map in the archives of Clare College, Cambridge (Acc. 1985/5, Box 3/2).

The dissolution of the monastery in 1539 had a lesser impact on Ely than did many similar dissolutions elsewhere, since the monastery was replaced by a college of Dean and Chapter in 1541, but the medieval framework for the life of the town came to an end when pilgrimage and the cult of the saints were abolished. The bishopric remained, but the eighteen-year vacancy after the death of Bishop Cox in 1581 marked a break with the medieval period. Post-medieval Ely became isolated from the centres of development, and the exceptional powers retained by the bishopric until 1836 stunted development. Ely remained a small market town for an agricultural hinterland until the 1960s.

The site

The area affected by the excavations had already been covered by the Fenland Survey, which had identified a dark soil-mark in its northern part complete with significant assemblages of Roman and medieval pottery (Hall 1996; see above). Prior to the housing development, a desktop assessment was carried out (Gibson 1998). Although this revealed no other known archaeological evidence from the development area, trial excavation was recommended due to the presence of known occupation in the immediate area and the possibility that surviving archaeological remains were somehow 'masked'. As Area A (Fig. 1.2) lay under 0.50–0.80m of remnant ridge and furrow, aerial and geophysical survey were of little value. Even in Area B, which had recently been ploughed, aerial survey was not very informative: archaeological features on clay subsoils can be difficult to detect from the air, unless seen under near-drought conditions (Palmer 1998). Moreover ridge and furrow, even when levelled as here, can mask pre-medieval features (Palmer 1996).

In March 1999, therefore, the CAU carried out an evaluation of the land on behalf of the developers, Ashwell Group Plc, using machine trenching (Knight 1999). Nineteen trenches, each 2.20m wide, were machine-excavated, twelve in Area B and seven in Area A. These produced background Iron Age material, as well as significant amounts of Roman, Saxon and medieval pottery suggesting intensive activity. In light of these findings, the decision was taken to carry out as full an excavation as possible of Areas A and B, although construction work was due to begin within just a few days (Plate I). (Working under the assumption that such low-lying wet clays would not have seen large-scale settlement, it had been assumed when scheduling construction work that trial excavations would be adequate.)

In contrast, assessment of Area C to the south produced very little evidence, indicating that this intensive settlement landscape did not extend this far. Four north–south trenches were machine-excavated in July 1999, and a further small trench along the northern boundary of the field located a trackway running east–west along this northern boundary (which still exists to the east in the form of a road known as Fieldside). To check these largely negative findings, three further trenches were excavated in January 2000. In total 850m of trial trench (3% of the available area, or 2125m²) was excavated, producing only sixteen discrete archaeological features; the majority of these were confidently dated to the 14th century and later (Regan 2000). The trackway consisted of a rough gravel surface running the whole length of the field from east to west, and severe rutting suggested that it was a rough, though heavily used, route. Its maximum exposed width was 1.80m, although it may originally have been wider. Pottery suggests a late 13th-century date for construction of the metalled trackway, although an unsurfaced track may have preceded it. The Ordnance Survey map of 1836–8 clearly shows a track still running along the north side of this field.

One further area of excavation is reported on here. An area of land between West Fen Road and the present northern edge of Area B was subject to an archaeological evaluation in advance of the building of a bungalow on a former garden between two existing properties (TL 55292808: Fig. 1.2). The aims of trial excavations in 2000 were to elucidate the relationship of the main site (Areas A and B) to West Fen Road itself, and particularly to investigate whether or not a 'street frontage' had existed here (Masser 2000). Three trenches of 18m–23.5m in length were excavated, and the results from them integrated into subsequent chapters of this report.

II. The excavations
(Figs 1.4–1.9)

The main excavations at Areas A and B were carried out by the Cambridge Archaeological Unit between April and November 1999 (Site Code WET99), with a further, smaller excavation in October 2000 taking place in an area in the far north-west of Area B prior to the installation of new sewer/storm drains (Site Code WET00). The excavation of Area A followed on almost immediately after the evaluation, with that of Area B immediately after that of Area A. In total, 2.12ha were excavated in Area B and 1.04ha in Area A, although it was not possible for large tracts to be opened simultaneously: the archaeological team had to deal with individual areas quickly, and in a somewhat piecemeal fashion (often working on individual planned houseplots), so that the building contractors would not be forced to delay work. The site's location on pure clay, coupled with wet excavation conditions, also created problems for the

excavation team. During wet weather (of which there was plenty), running water was common across the site, as was the accumulation of rainwater within excavated features, while on the (few) hot days the clay could become rock-hard and fissured.

Methodology and recording
The ridge and furrow earthworks within Area A were recorded prior to stripping, both in plan and section, and both areas were then metal-detected. Almost all earthwork/crop-mark features identified in, or adjacent to, the assessment area were ridges, furrows and associated headlands remaining from medieval cultivation. The ploughsoil (c. 0.30m deep) and the upper part of the subsoil (in parts up to 0.50m deep) were then removed by the developers using a box scraper. The remainder of the subsoil was removed under archaeological supervision by a tracked 360° excavator (Plate II). The site was base-planned at a scale of 1:100 (Area A) and 1:50 (Area B), with localised plans of complex areas and individual features produced subsequently at larger, more suitable scales. An arbitrary site grid was subsequently tied into the OS national grid using a total station.

When the topsoil and remnant ridge and furrow had been removed, a mass of negative features was revealed (Fig. 1.4). As well as an estimated 15–20km length of ditches and gullies, the site contained hundreds of pits, many wells and ponds, beam-slots and post-holes, gravel paths and roads, cobbled surfaces, and the remains of at least thirty structures. The great majority of the features dealt with were ditches, their fills consisting mainly of

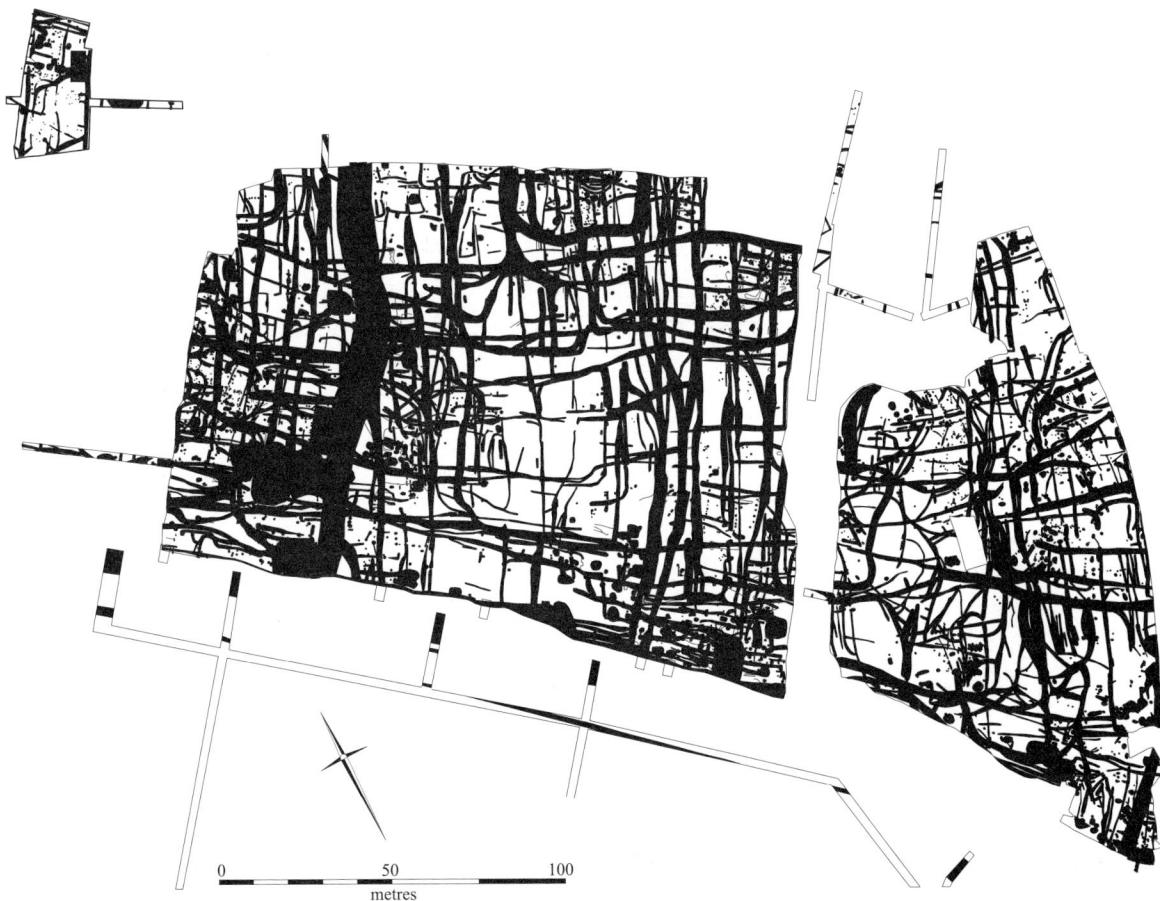

0   50   100
metres

Figure 1.4 Plan of all features

7

Figure 1.5 Locations of all recorded surface finds (predominantly pottery sherds)

Plate I View over the site during the excavations and construction work

Figure 1.6 Locations of all excavated slots and features (indicated in black)

Plate II View over the site from the west, showing the machine-scraped surface

Figure 1.7 Locations of all environmental samples, indicating the period of the context from which they derived

● IronAge/Roman - Phases 2-3

⬠ Anglo-Saxon - Phases 5-8

◻ Medieval - Phases 9-11

0   50   100
Metres

grey or slightly brown-grey clays, though many contained quantities of darker, more organic, occupation fills.

The surface was metal-detected again after stripping and, wherever possible, finds were related to underlying features (the site was, however, prey to illicit metal-detecting). In addition, after initial machining of each area, every sherd of pottery visible on the surface was collected, plotted on the base plans, and again where possible related to underlying features; throughout the excavation, as further sherds weathered or washed out, these too were collected and recorded in a similar manner (Fig. 1.5). The majority of the ditched features were then sample excavated using 1m slots, sited where possible (and when time allowed) at 10m intervals, with additional slots cut at salient junctions between them. The stratigraphic sequence was established by appraising a combination of feature relationships, where these were visible in section and/or plan, along with finds assemblages that had been assessed for residuality and intrusion (see below). Obviously, any changes to the accepted date span for the major pottery types collected will affect the durations of the phases presented here, but the sequence itself should not be altered by such developments. Clearly, what is presented in this volume is just one of a number of possible interpretations of the sequence of settlement and activity although every effort has been made, within the constraints of time and money, to present the most accurate sequence possible.

The majority of sections were recorded at 1:10. Non-ditch features such as post-holes were either half-sectioned or fully excavated if appropriate. Some surfaces, such as gravel surfaces, paths and roads, were recorded in plan before further stripping, while some were partially planned and partially stripped (Fig. 1.6). The written record throughout followed the CAU-modified version of the MoLAS single-context recording system (Spence 1990): all stratigraphic units — cuts, fills, layers and spot finds recovered from the surface of features during machining — were assigned individual context numbers. In the text these are shown in italics, while they have been grouped together for analysis where appropriate under feature numbers (prefixed by an 'F'). Small finds or groups of finds, such as animal bones from features, were assigned numbers from a separate sequence, which could also then be related to the context number from which they derived.

Environmental sampling

Bulk samples were taken from a variety of contexts, including post-holes, pits, ditches and layers, in order to ensure that all phases were represented: 108 samples in all were able to be processed (Fig. 1.7). These produced the macrofossil evidence reported on in Chapter 5, and also the bulk of the fishbone and small vertebrate remains. Pollen cores were taken from a variety of contexts across the site, but an arson attack on the site hut during the Area A excavations resulted in the destruction of several of these, and also of the bulk samples being stored there, although there was no major damage to the small finds or archive. Just three pollen cores could be processed: two from Roman contexts and one from a medieval context. To facilitate the identification of worked bone artefacts, all bone was sent for analysis to the faunal specialist, who then separated any worked pieces for further study. With the benefit of hindsight, further off-site pollen cores would have added to the environmental interpretation.

Problems of residuality and intrusion

The possibly residual nature of much of the pottery found within the features had significant implications for site phasing. On a complex and intensely-ditched site, a substantial amount of the material from the earlier phases will have become incorporated into later ones: for example, at least 40% of the Roman pottery assemblage was recovered from subsequent medieval features. That said, the pottery assemblages still offered the most reliable method of dating features, and the chronological sequence presented here has largely been based upon them.

Intrusive pottery, while somewhat less of a problem, may also distort the chronological picture. This is most obvious with the medieval ridge and furrow system, where the furrows coincide with the alignment of earlier features. The difficulty here was contamination by later pottery within what appeared to be the upper fills of earlier features which were, in fact, the ploughed-in lower fills of now-invisible furrows. As is often the case, animal burrowing along the sides of ditches throughout the site's history had also introduced intrusive finds material.

Figure 1.8 sets out the percentages of the major pottery groups that are intrusive, in-phase or residual. As is to be expected, it shows that in general the earlier the pottery type, the more likely it is to have been found as residual; the later the pottery, the more likely it is to have been in-phase. Figure 1.9 clearly shows that residuality was a major factor while intrusion was almost negligible; the only significant pottery type occurring as intrusive material was the 'other' (later) medieval wares, principally introduced through ploughing.

Dating and phasing

West Fen Road saw virtually continuous occupation from the later Iron Age through to the 15th century, and over 21,000 pottery sherds were recovered from the excavations. The pre-Saxon sequence is divided into *Phase 1* (Neolithic–Bronze Age), *Phase 2* (Iron Age) and *Phase 3* (Roman). Very few Early Saxon pottery sherds have been recovered from the excavations on either side of West Fen Road. While this suggests a presence in this period, perhaps nearby and/or transient, it does not indicate settlement here in the immediate post-Roman period, or through the 6th and 7th centuries. While some of the land may have been exploited in the Early Saxon period, through cultivation or as pasture, large parts of the area would have been covered with the earthwork remains of the extensive Iron Age and Romano-British settlement (this being demonstrated by the respect shown by the subsequent Mid Saxon buildings and ditches). The Early Saxon period, although poorly represented at the site, has been designated *Phase 4*, while the post-Roman sequence has been divided into eight separate phases (*Phases 5–13*), covering approximately seven centuries from c. 725 to 1400 AD (Tables 1.1 and 1.2). Most archaeological evidence belongs to the Late Saxon and earlier medieval periods. The chronological boundaries between one phase and its neighbours are not clear-cut, as the dating often relies upon pottery types for which we lack precise known start- or end-dates for production or importation. The major period changes are dictated by significant changes in these pottery types — the Mid–Late Saxon activity (Phases 5–7) indicated by the introduction of St Neots and Thetford wares, and the Late Saxon–medieval (Phases 7–9) by the introduction of the locally-made Ely wares. However, while a period pre-dating the introduction of a particular pottery type can always be identified, the wares that it replaced will often remain in use long after its introduction. The principles underlying the phasing are outlined here.

The period in which Ipswich ware was in use, broadly 725–850, has been termed Phase 5 (and is described as Mid Saxon), while Phase 6 covers the first half of the Late Saxon period, from the mid-9th century through to the late 10th/early 11th century. There are no firm dates available for the beginning of Phase 6, which begins with the influx of the wheelmade pottery forms — Thetford and St Neots wares — which eventually replaced the Ipswich wares. The speed with which this change took place is not known but the clear superiority of the new pottery, in terms of availability, size and form variation, would probably have ensured relatively rapid displacement.

It is not suggested here that any of these phase changes represent clear-cut archaeological events. Significant changes in the pottery repertoire current at the site need not have coincided with major changes in settlement morphology and dynamics, which might well have changed dramatically at different times and for different reasons. Phase 6 should be seen as the fluid continuation of Phase 5, with many of its features seeing their first use during Phase 5 and having a lifespan that took them beyond Phase 6 (and possibly even Phase 8, in the case of

Phase		Period	Dating evidence	
Phase 5		Mid Saxon	Ipswich ware	725–850
Phase 7	6	Late Saxon	Thetford ware;	850–c. 1000
	8		St Neots ware	c. 1000–1150
Phase 9		Medieval	Ely ware; Lyveden wares	1100–1200

Table 1.1 Summary of dating evidence for Mid–Late Saxon and Saxo-Norman phases

11

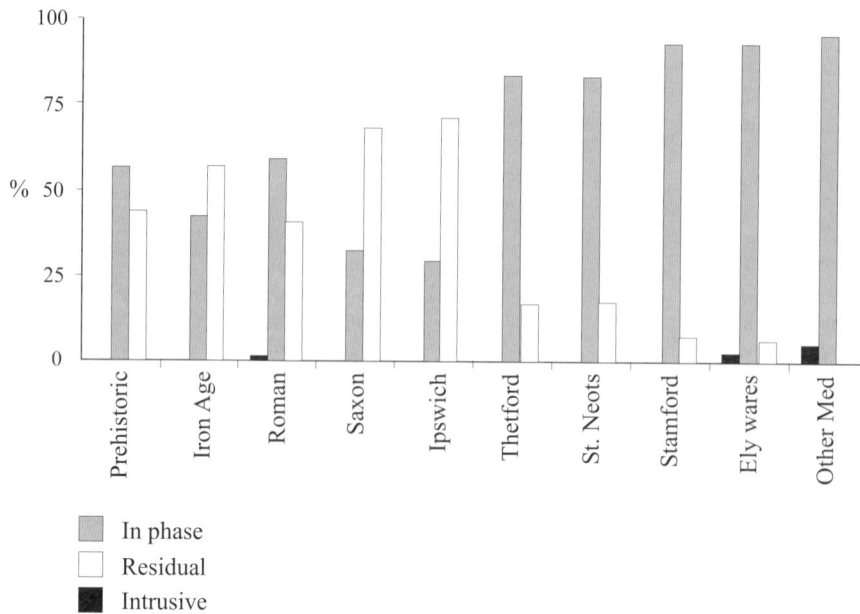

Figure 1.8 Ceramic residuality

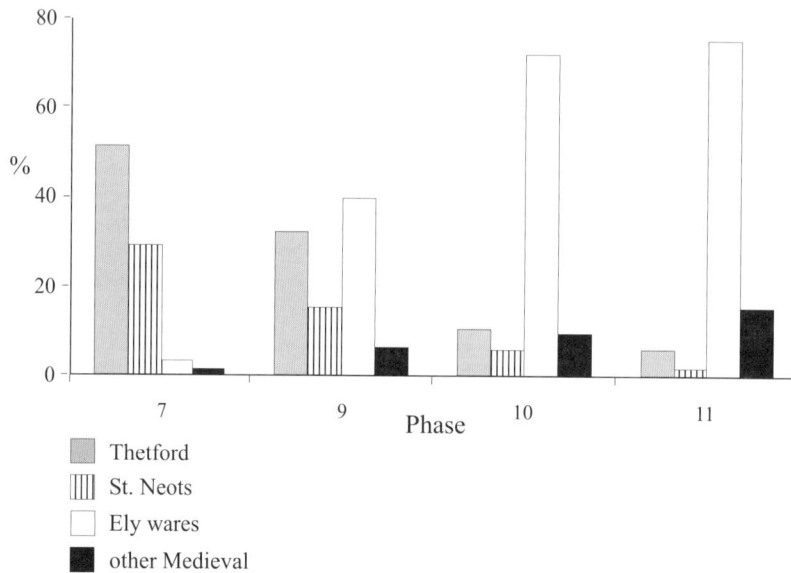

Figure 1.9 Percentages of the principal medieval pottery types found in contexts of each phase

major boundaries). The majority of features can only be dated by the latest pottery recovered within them, giving a closing date — an indication of when they were fully infilled or abandoned — rather than indicating when they were first in use.

Two factors combine to make it difficult to separate the Late Saxon evidence into clear 'early' and 'late' phases. One is the complex and fluid nature of the archaeological evidence itself, with intensive recutting of features and mixing of artefacts. The difficulty involved in judging what material may belong to which phase is compounded by the absence of much graphic change in the pottery forms during the period. While it is possible to identify certain sherds and even certain assemblages as either pre- or post-Conquest, it is not possible to do so with the majority of the assemblage. As a result, while it has been

possible to identify two fairly distinct phases using stratigraphic relationships and some of the pottery data, most of the Late Saxon and Saxo-Norman evidence has been incorporated within a single 'bulked' phase designation, Phase 7. Phase 6 and 8 are not intended to represent the pre- and post-Conquest periods respectively — the Conquest appears invisible in the archaeological record, and should be assumed to have occurred during the span of Phase 8.

A 'crossover' phase in more ways than one, Phase 9 marks not only the change from Saxo-Norman pottery forms to medieval ones, but also the beginnings of a characteristically 'medieval' farming practice and settlement pattern. The duration of this phase is difficult to assess, as it represents a transitional period that has been identified largely in terms of the replacement of Thetford

Phase	Period
1	Prehistoric
2	Iron Age
3	Romano-British
4	Early Saxon – *c.* 5th–late 7th century
5	Mid Saxon – *c.* early 8th–mid 9th
6	Late Saxon – mid 9th–10th/11th
7	Late Saxon – unphased
8	Late Saxon – 10th/11th–mid 12th
9	12th century
10	13th century
11	14th century
12	15th century
13	16th century and later
14	Unphased

Table 1.2 Summary of site phasing

Pottery type	West Fen Road	Ely Forehill
Prehistoric	99	0
Iron Age	808	0
Roman	2448	5
Ipswich	245	0
Thetford	4670	34
St Neots	2489	42
Stamford	128	18
Ely Ware	8516	4583
Other med. (Grimston, Lyveden, Blackborough End, Essex Reds *etc.*)	1175	3079

Table 1.3 Quantities of principal pottery types recovered from excavation and surface finds at the Ashwell site, West Fen Road, compared with the excavated assemblage from Ely Forehill (Alexander 2003)

and St Neots wares with new pottery forms. The clearest indicator is the introduction of the locally-made Ely wares (along with a few shelly Lyveden sherds and other sandy 12th-century wares). The timescale over which the new forms displaced the old is unknown. However, the time it would have taken for the new potteries to be producing enough to satisfy demand for the new wares must be taken into consideration, along with the quantities of the earlier pottery that remained in use, even when no more was being bought. Phase 9 *should* represent a period during which all three of these major pottery types — Thetford, St Neots and Ely wares — were in current use, from the production of the first Ely ware pot to the breaking and discard of the majority of the earlier wares. The make-up of the pottery assemblage at Phase 9 is approximately equally divided between Thetford/St Neots wares and Ely wares, with the former better represented by a couple of percentage points. However, by Phase 10 the market would have been dominated by Ely wares and any Thetford and St Neots sherds from these deposits should, barring the odd long-kept piece, be residual items.

Using what little evidence is available, this transition period may only be dated approximately to around the end of the 12th century. Dating the beginning of Phase 9 rests solely on the still very imprecise dating for the cessation of the production/use of Thetford and St Neots wares, traditionally put at around 1150. This does not allow for the duration of this phase to be any greater than 50 years; in all probability, it was considerably less. Even given this short time-span, as many as seven new buildings may have been constructed in this phase, and it produced more artefactual material than any other phase other than that within which much of the Late Saxon evidence was bulked. The heightened structural development may have reflected major reorganisation taking place within the settlement at this time, and the abundant pottery the increased production and consumption that occurred in the region in the 12th and 13th centuries. However, it is possible that the introduction of the locally-made Ely ware (and thus the cessation, or at least the decline, of the earlier wares), took place earlier than is generally thought. If so, this may push the beginning of Phase 9 back to *c.* 1100 and allowing the phase a span of closer to a hundred years — *i.e.* the entire 12th century.

The coin evidence also contributes to the dating of Phase 9. A Henry II Tealby Penny, minted *c.* 1160–80 and no longer in circulation after the mid 1180s, came from a mixed gravel make-up layer lying immediately above a road surface in Enclosure 16. A second coin, a Short Cross penny issued between 1207 and 1214, was found at the machine-stripped surface of the fill of the northern boundary ditch of Enclosure 1. The ditch was large and had silted up gradually, while the wear on the coin suggests that it had been in circulation for some time and may not have been lost till the 1230s or 40s. Given these factors, both of these coins have been allocated to Phase 10 — the first recovered from surface trample or a possible make-up for the next road surface (the coin maybe lost in the 1170s or 80s), and the second deposited by the time a Phase 9 ditch had been completely infilled and the area abandoned.

The dating of subsequent phases is less dependent on identifying the introduction of new pottery forms, though the medieval pottery sequence for the Ely area is fairly well-documented (Alexander 1998; 2003) and has proved valuable. Figure 1.9 represents the incidence of the principal pottery types by phase across the site and clearly shows the main 'crossover' period at Phase 9; it indicates the individual pottery types as a percentage of all pottery within that phase (*e.g.* from Phase 7, 51% of all pottery is Thetford ware). The Ely and other medieval wares within Phase 7 should be regarded as intrusive; the Thetford and St Neots beyond Phase 9, residual.

The only other large medieval pottery assemblage to have been studied from Ely is that from Ely Forehill (Alexander 1998; 2003); this has almost no Late Saxon component (76 sherds of Thetford and St Neots wares), but much 13th–14th-century and later material (*e.g.* over 4500 sherds of Ely ware). The expansion of that site coincides with the contraction of the West Fen Road settlement in Phase 11, and a comparison with the 13th–14th-century and 14th–15th-century pottery assemblages from Forehill is shown in Table 1.3. The contemporary Phase 11 assemblage is far closer to the earlier Forehill phase, perhaps indicating abandonment of the West Fen Road settlement in the 14th century. Alternatively, the different make-up of the assemblages could be linked more to the affordability of the imported Grimston and other medieval wares, with Forehill exhibiting significantly greater spending power.

Artefact distributional analysis

Study of artefact distributions featured strongly during analysis. Given the quantities of material involved, and the overall density of features (as well as the issues concerning residuality discussed above), in order to illustrate changing site-wide distributions the excavated material is shown in the phase plans in Chapters 2 and 5 in the form of shaded or sized dot densities for each 10m x 10m square. Within any category presented in this way, all the excavated and surface finds recovered from each individual gridded unit have been grouped *en masse*. When interpreting the resulting plots the density of the excavated features themselves must, of course, be considered. It is unlikely that areas with few archaeological interventions will produce large numbers of artefacts. Thus the artefact density plots should be viewed along with Fig. 1.6 which shows all the excavated features and ditch sections. This clearly shows the greater overall intensity of excavation across Area A, and the parts of Area B where excavations were focused, and clearly highlights the possibility of distributional bias — 'blank' zones on the distribution plots may in fact have seen no excavation. However, the distributions also reflect the intensity or 'cover' of features. This is particularly the case thoughout the central portion of Area B, where there was the lowest recorded density of features and a number of

10m x 10m squares coincided with no, or only very little, excavation. Despite this uneven distribution of excavation coverage, and of features, particular localised concentrations of artefacts can still be demonstrated, though these provisos should be borne in mind.

III. Aims and structure of the report

It should be emphasised that this report presents a synthesis of the available information, along with an interpretation of the significance of the results within a local, regional and national framework. The intention is not to present a detailed account of all excavated features; given that there were over 10,000 excavated contexts this would not be practical, nor (arguably) desirable. For those who wish to consult it, the full site archive is lodged with Cambridgeshire County Council under the Site Code WET99.

Although the main focus of this report is the Saxon and medieval occupation, the pre-Saxon background is covered in Chapter 2. Chapter 3 details the Saxon and medieval settlement sequence, and the buildings, pits, enclosures, wells and layers are discussed phase by phase. Chapter 4 discusses the artefacts and Chapter 5 the zoological and environmental evidence. Discussion of the nature of the site, and how it relates to its wider context, concludes in Chapters 6 and 7.

Figure 2.1 Distribution of Neolithic and Bronze Age finds

2. Period I: Pre-Saxon Activity and Settlement

I. Summary

While the main emphasis of this volume lies on the Saxon and medieval periods, this chapter presents the prehistoric and Roman background. The pre-Saxon evidence, representing pre-Iron Age visitation and a subsequent sequence of Iron Age and Roman enclosures, is not plentiful. The Mesolithic–Neolithic and Bronze Age activity indicates short stays on wooded heavy clay subsoils; in the Iron Age, the main settlement focus evidently lay to the north of West Fen Road (see below). Although the focus of the Roman enclosure complex clearly lay within Area B, the features were too severely truncated by subsequent occupation to warrant detailed presentation here.

Evidence for these early phases, however fragmentary, is important as it contributes to appreciation of the long-term (pre-)history of the West Fen Road complex as a place — episodic visits between the Mesolithic and the Early Iron Age giving way to Later Iron Age enclosures (Enclosures I–II), which themselves determined the layout of the ensuing Roman settlement (Enclosures III–IX), whose earthwork traces clearly influenced the axes and the enclosures of the Saxon and medieval settlement (Enclosures 1–21) in turn.

II. Phase 1: Mesolithic, Neolithic and Bronze Age
(Fig. 2.1)

Altogether 213 pieces of worked flint, attesting to limited prehistoric activity, were recovered from the site (Fig. 2.1). Overall densities (0–8 pieces per 10m square) were low. Moreover, the distribution of flint was sporadic and worked flint occurred in only *c.* 35% of the excavation squares. Though no discrete 'sites' as such are identifiable, a degree of clustering is apparent. This is most obvious in the central western side of Area A, where densities greater than four flints per 10m square occurred consistently across an area of 600m².

When studied by Chantal Conneller, three main horizons were identified within the lithic assemblage. While a scraper, crude flakes and multi-platform and denticulated cores attest to a later Bronze Age presence, most of the material would seem to be of later Neolithic–Early Bronze Age attribution. The latter includes a variety of knife-types, and both an oblique and a barbed-and-tanged arrowhead. Debitage characteristic of this period points, moreover, to on-site core reduction and tool manufacture. Later Mesolithic–Early Neolithic activity is also evident. While the recovery of a scraper and a leaf-shaped arrowhead, blades and a blade core in the eastern portion of the grid reflects some manufacturing activity on site, the recovery of a tranchet axe fragment, a truncation and blades (two serrated) as a cluster in the west of Area B rather suggests the importation of a mobile tool kit onto the site, since there is no indication of associated working debris.

The eastern lithic cluster (in Area A) corresponds with the location of two small pits from which sherds of Early Neolithic plain bowl pottery were recovered (*2888*, *2889*; 44 small sherds/145g in total from the cluster). However only four pieces of worked flint of Early Neolithic attribution were retrieved from this portion of the grid and most of this flint assemblage would appear to consist of later material (23 later Neolithic–Early Bronze Age pieces and nine of later Bronze Age date). Some of the latter material may, in fact, be Early Iron Age as this 'spread' also overlapped with a concentration of pottery of that date (see below). A flake struck from the butt of a ground stone axe was also recovered from the central northern part of Area B.

In general terms, the flintworking evidence suggests little more than prolonged visits, probably associated with hunting, foraging and, perhaps, pastoral usage. This interpretation would be further supported by the low frequency of burnt flint. Only 75 pieces were recovered in total, and these occurred in a ratio of 1:2.8 in relation to the worked pieces. When compared to the evidence for more sustained occupation nearby at, for example, Wardy Hill and the Soham environs sites (Evans 2003a; Edmonds *et al.* 1999), this can only suggest a very low intensity of activity. As well as the Neolithic pottery, 25 Bronze Age sherds were recovered. Occurring as surface material in the northern portion of Area A, this grog-tempered material probably derived from a single urn (S. Percival, *pers. comm.*). Another significant find was the broken hilt of a later Bronze Age rapier (see Evans 2002, 48, fig. 9.4). It was found by metal-detectorists within the machined spoilheaps and its exact provenance is unknown. An undated and unurned cremation (326g of bone) within a small pit, F36 (0.50m x 0.15m deep), was situated on the north side of the Area A flint cluster (and also within the area of the Early Iron Age distribution).

Discussion
There is no reason to think that the West Fen Road settlement was a particularly distinct 'place' prior to the later Iron Age. The large scale of excavation and the density of its subsequent features trapped the traces of broader usage. The other evidence for pre-Iron Age activity at Ely has recently been outlined by Evans (2002 and 2003a). In terms of range, the Mesolithic–Bronze Age material from West Fen Road is comparable with that from Wardy Hill, for example, or that from the Trinity/Runciman lands immediately to the south, and also that from other claylands elsewhere in the region (*e.g.* West Cambridge: Lucas forthcoming). The recovery of the rapier hilt fragment is important in the light of broader fenland/fen-edge Bronze Age metal distributions, which are discussed more fully discussed in Evans 2002. From a broader perspective, it seems possible that particular locales saw the deposition of metalwork during seasonal gatherings.

III. Phase 2: Iron Age
(Plate III; Figs 2.2–2.5)

As discussed by Percival below (see Chapter 4), the Phase 2 pottery divides into two distinct chronological groups — although it is largely of later Iron Age date (with contemporary activity being centred in the northern part of Area B) there is also a minor Early Iron Age component. As indicated, the latter was focused around the western side of Area A, beside and partially overlapping the main Phase 1 lithic scatter. (This raises the possibility that some of the 'later Bronze Age' flint there was actually of Early Iron Age date; it is conceivable that the cremation in F36 discussed above was also post-Bronze Age.) A circular ring of post-holes with an overall diameter of 9–10m, apparently associated with this cluster, may indicate a contemporary roundhouse (Structure 1: Fig. 2.2). Extremely truncated, and lacking the obvious definition of a surrounding eaves-gully, the identification of this building can only be considered tentative. Immediately to the south lay another cluster of post-holes, three of them containing Iron Age pottery. All may have related to minor structures — possibly a fence-line, a rack/frame or four-posters. A shallow pit, F651, lay to the north-west of Structure 1.

In the later Iron Age, a compound in the northern part of Area B (Enclosure I) was presumably contemporary with other enclosures and structures to the north of West Fen Road (Fig. 2.3). Thirty-five metres across from east to west, only its southern part extended into the excavation area; it is assumed to have been of sub-square plan,

however. In its primary form, the defining ditch circuit was fairly consistent in size and profile, measuring 2.00–2.80m across and 1.10–1.20m deep (F1573: Fig. 2.4). Its fill sequence suggested that a bank had lain immediately inside the circuit.

Towards the eastern side of the enclosure, and probably contemporary with it, was the re-cut gully of a roundhouse, Structure 2. This feature (F1491/F1487) was shallow, and no more than 0.15m deep. Pottery, bone and burnt clay were recovered from its fills, though the majority were small and abraded pieces suggesting secondary deposition. The exact size of the building remains unclear, as no internal post settings or full structural dimensions were recorded. Extrapolation of the arc of its eaves-gully would give a roof span of 9–10m; there is evidence, albeit slight, for the positioning of a doorway to the south-east.

The only other features dated to the later Iron Age within this enclosure circuit were pits F1529 and F2581 (2.00m and 1.50m in diameter). Pit F1529 contained a mixed assemblage of domestic waste, presumably from the nearby roundhouse. The other pit (F2581), although not fully excavated, cut into the upper fills of the enclosure ditch; it is dated by its pottery to the 1st century AD. A small pit, F1448, situated outside Enclosure I to the west contained a near-complete example of a pot in a pre-Belgic style. No associated cremation was evident and its significance is unclear.

A fragment of a human cranium from an older sub-/young adult was recovered from a later ditch cutting the west side of this enclosure (F1471 *6640*; another

Figure 2.2 Structure 1, possible Iron Age roundhouse (contemporary features in black, intruding later features in white overlay)

human cranium fragment was recovered from one of the Iron Age enclosure ditches to the north of the road: Mudd 2000) and six fragments of adult parietal (cranial) bone displaying old post-mortem breaks were found within the western circuit itself (F1573 *6872*). Disarticulated human remains were recovered from a Roman ditch inside the enclosure (F1396 *6358*): parietal fragments, a left and right proximal radius, proximal right ulna, distal right humerus and the mid-shafts of the right femur and fibula, along with fragments of phalanges, a lumbar vertebra and the sacrum. Also with old post-mortem breaks, the bones are all adult-sized and probably derive from the same individual. The robusticity and size of the radial head suggest that this individual was male, and the quantity of bone suggests that the ditch had cut through an earlier burial. Two inhumations lay *c*. 8m south of the compound. One, F1474, a possible adult male, was heavily disturbed and was only represented by a scatter of partially articulated bones. The second burial (F1450), again severely truncated and also an adult male, lay in a crouched position (Plate III). In the absence of grave goods, these are only possibly of Iron Age date; they are reported on in detail in Chapter 5.

In the centre of the site, straddling Areas A and B, was another sub-square compound, Enclosure II (F633). The enclosed area measured *c*. 31m north–south by 25–8m east–west, and was defined by a ditch of similar size and profile to that of Enclosure I. The absence of any domestic debris, such as pottery, ash/charcoal or daub, from the excavated segments indicates that it never saw sustained occupation — this view is also supported by the pottery distribution shown on Fig. 2.5. Perhaps it was connected with stock management. An Iron Age date is suggested because its plan was markedly similar to that of Enclosure I, while its east side had been re-cut by a Roman-period ditch.

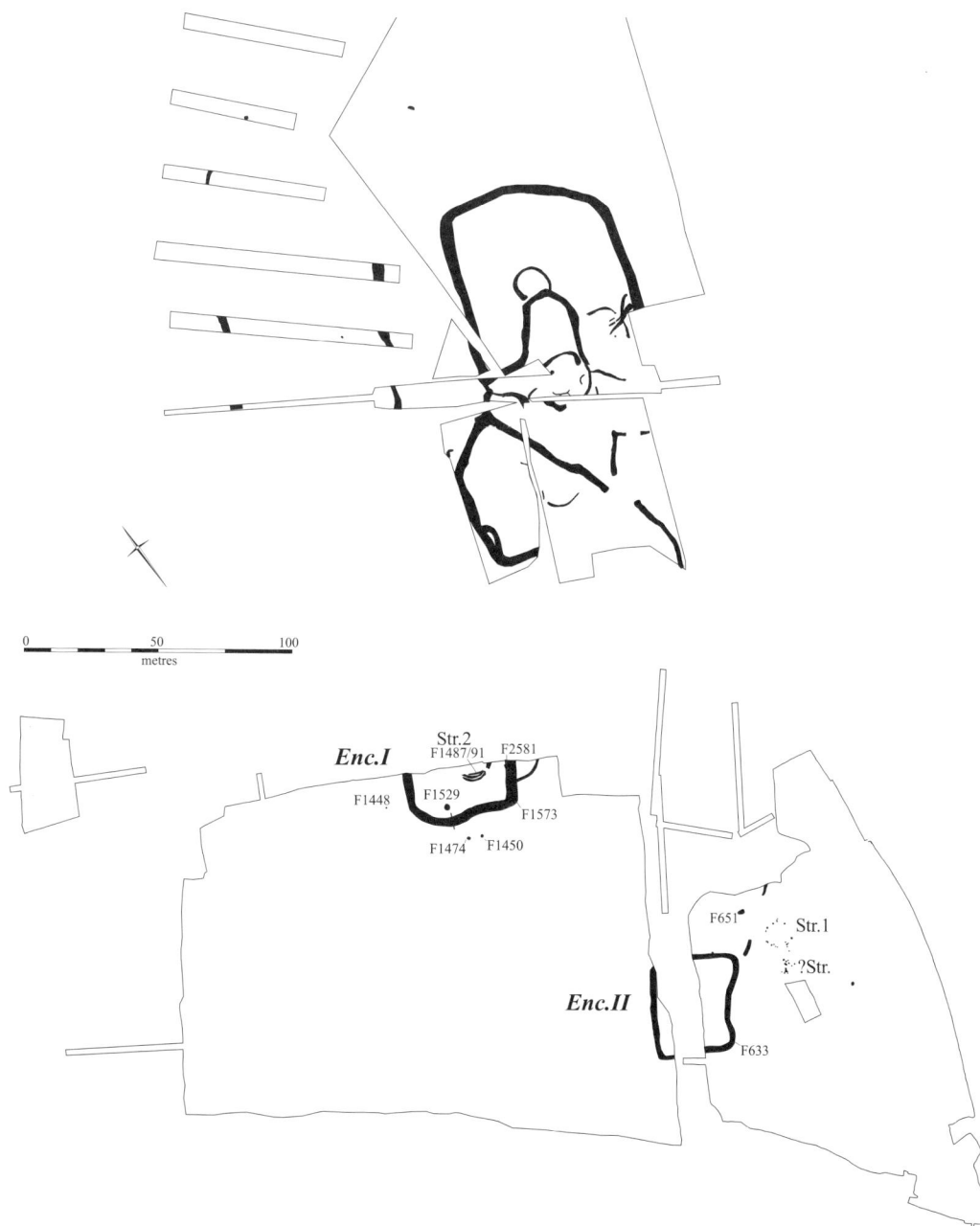

Figure 2.3 Phase 2 plan, showing excavated features of Iron Age date to the north (Mudd 2000) and south of West Fen Road

17

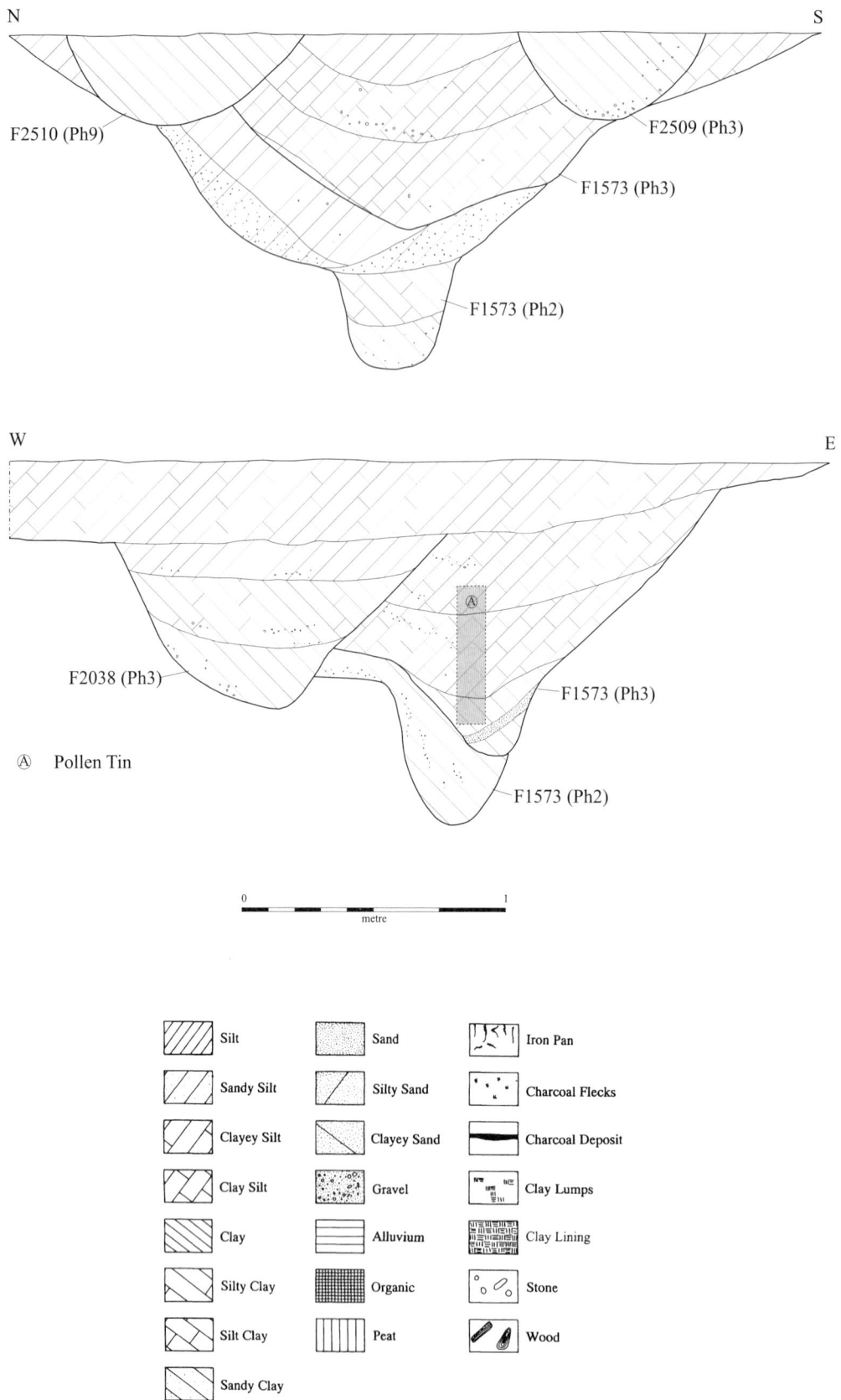

N   S

F2510 (Ph9)

F2509 (Ph3)

F1573 (Ph3)

F1573 (Ph2)

W   E

F2038 (Ph3)

F1573 (Ph3)

Ⓐ   Pollen Tin

F1573 (Ph2)

0   1

metre

Silt	Sand	Iron Pan
Sandy Silt	Silty Sand	Charcoal Flecks
Clayey Silt	Clayey Sand	Charcoal Deposit
Clay Silt	Gravel	Clay Lumps
Clay	Alluvium	Clay Lining
Silty Clay	Organic	Stone
Silt Clay	Peat	Wood
Sandy Clay		

Figure 2.4 Sections of Phase 2 and 3 enclosure ditches, Enclosure I; section illustration conventions

Figure 2.5 Distribution plot of Iron Age pottery, shown against Iron Age features

Number of sherds
100+
51-100
11-50
6-10
2-5

0   50   100
metres

Plate III Possible Iron Age crouched burial F1450

With regard to economic evidence (Chapter 5), only 136 animal bones from this phase were identifiable to species. Cattle and sheep/goat bones (and respectively-sized unidentified material) occurred in comparable numbers (43% and 44% respectively, in terms of Number of Identified Specimens per Species/NISP); otherwise there were only seven bones each of horse and pig (6% each), and a partly digested pike vertebra. The assemblage of plant remains is dominated by hulled chaff from spelt and emmer wheat. This probably attests to food preparation, with the grain being removed from storage and de-husked prior to consumption. Otherwise, cereals are poorly represented, but barley and free-threshing wheat were present; oats were also recovered. A later prehistoric bone awl from the east of the site, whose characteristics recall Sellwood's definition of class 2 awls from Danebury (Sellwood 1984, 387: I. Riddler, *pers. comm.*), also attests to activity in this period.

Discussion

The Iron Age occupation would appear to have begun with a small, open Early Iron Age settlement cluster, recorded in the central part of Area A, associated with a post-built roundhouse and possibly four-post settings. The fact that the house was not surrounded by an eaves-gully would make it typical of the period's domestic architecture (Pryor 1984) both in the region and beyond. This settlement was succeeded by two sub-square later Iron Age compounds, Enclosures I and II; a more substantial enclosure associated with further roundhouses was excavated to the north of the road by Northamptonshire Archaeology. The paucity of domestic debris associated with the more easterly enclosure, Enclosure II, would either suggest a somewhat earlier date than that of Enclosure I, or an ancillary function in relation to it. It is difficult to know how to interpret these compounds. On one hand their form is clearly typical of Mid–Late Iron Age farmstead settlements throughout the western fen-edge (*e.g.* Upper Delphs, Haddenham; Colne Fen, Earith and Werrington, Peterborough: Regan and Evans 1998, 2000; see Evans and Hodder forthcoming for overview). Against this, however, the scale of their ditching is quite slight, their enclosed areas relatively small, and the quantity of associated domestic remains relatively insubstantial. Therefore, rather than discrete household enclosures, these might be better thought of as 'offspring' of a main Iron Age settlement north of West Fen Road (see below). A similar pattern of peripheral enclosures surrounding the main settlement area is seen nearby at Hurst Fen (Evans *et al.* forthcoming).

The recovery of pre-Flavian material suggests continuity of settlement up to and beyond the Conquest period. However, the negligible wheelmade wares from the Area B excavations possibly suggests a decline in activity within the southern part of the settlement into the 1st century AD; some 1st-century AD pottery was found to the north, suggesting continued occupation here (Mudd 2000). The relative poverty of this settlement, at least within the confines of the immediate area of excavation, is noteworthy. Despite extensive metal-detecting, no Iron Age or Conquest/early Roman coinage or brooches have been recovered, aside from a solitary miscast Langton Down type, though this paucity of metal finds would now seem to be characteristic of Ely's later Iron Age settlements in general (see Evans 2003b, 257–8 for overview).

The human skull fragments from the ditch fills of Enclosure I are of particular note. Other disarticulated human remains were recovered from post-Iron Age features which cut the enclosure, and from both Roman and Saxo-Norman ditches, though at least some of the latter may derive from disturbed Romano-British inhumations (p.91, below). The recovery of disarticulated skeletal material, and more specifically skull pieces, is now known to be a feature of settlements of the period (Wait 1985; Hill 1995). Within the immediate environs 'loose' human remains have been found both at Hurst Lane and within the Runciman/Trinity fields (both Evans *et al.* forthcoming), at Wardy Hill (Evans 2003a) and, to the north, in the main West Fen Road settlement core (Mudd 2000).

IV. Phase 3: Romano-British
(Figs 2.6 and 2.7)

Early Roman occupation
(Fig. 2.6)

The CAU excavation site saw continued use into the Roman period, although much of the area to the north of West Fen Road had been abandoned by the early Roman period. In Area B, Enclosure I was subject to re-cutting and/or cleaning along its entire length early in this phase, although this re-use was perhaps only short-lived. Thereafter the picture is one of organic growth, with paddock and field systems developing south of the main settlement core (Fig. 2.6). The settlement would appear to have developed fairly rapidly; Enclosure I was quickly backfilled, the material for this probably coming from the cutting of an east–west enclosure ditch (F14) that formed the southern boundary of Enclosures III, IV and V.

Together with east–west ditches F1483 and F2038, these features represent an arrangement of three rectangular paddocks, possibly for stock and/or small horticultural plots.

A penannular compound (F958) added to the south side of these early enclosures enclosed a single adult male burial, F1509, and might represent a mortuary enclosure. This inhumation was further distinguished by its interment with a small coarse pottery vessel (dating to *c*. AD 70–150), placed to the side of the head; hobnails around the feet indicated footwear, and nails along the edges of the grave a coffin.

A large field, Enclosure VIII, was established to the south of the main settlement area, with a western boundary ditch F2062. Its southern limit was demarcated by an east–west trackway running the length of Area B (represented by linear features F1868/F2178 and F1908). This trackway appeared to terminate to the east within an open area or second large field, and to represent the southern limit of the settlement throughout the Roman period. The eastern boundary of Enclosure VIII was partly formed by the re-cutting of the eastern circuit ditch of Iron Age Enclosure II (F596); the new cut continuing beyond the enclosure to the north-east for a distance of 17m. After an interruption, it continued further northward beyond the edge of the excavated area. An associated early Roman ditch (F700) extending north-westward formed the corner of another enclosure that lay beyond the main excavation area.

The area lying north of the trackway and west of Enclosure VIII was divided into two 'fields', Enclosures VI and VII. The truncated remains of two burials, F1649 and F1687, were aligned along the western exposed length of the trackway within Enclosure VII. They produced no dating evidence and may belong to this or to a later phase of the Romano-British occupation. Other disarticulated human remains found within later features nearby suggest that a small cemetery once lay to the north of the trackway.

No structure could be firmly dated to this period, although the pottery density around the early Roman Enclosure I/IV suggests a building may have lain to the north beyond the edge of excavation. This is further indicated by the presence of two shallow drainage gullies (F1454 and F1455) running from the north into the re-cut ditch of the Iron Age compound.

Late Roman occupation
(Fig. 2.7)

The settlement did not expand beyond the boundaries already established in the earlier Roman period. The pottery suggests slight intensification of activity in the later 3rd and 4th centuries, although this may be a reflection of pottery becoming more readily available. A single sherd of 'Romano-Saxon' pottery and one later 4th-century coin may suggest that the occupation continued into the late 4th century. The principal changes visible in the later Roman phase are seen in the internal reorganisation of the early settlement core, principally within and around Enclosures III and IV, while further alterations took place within the north part of Enclosure VIII (Fig. 2.7).

The previously unoccupied north side of Enclosure VIII was affected by southerly settlement expansion beyond Enclosures III and IV. This effectively formed an internally divided annex-like compound (F1045, F1050,

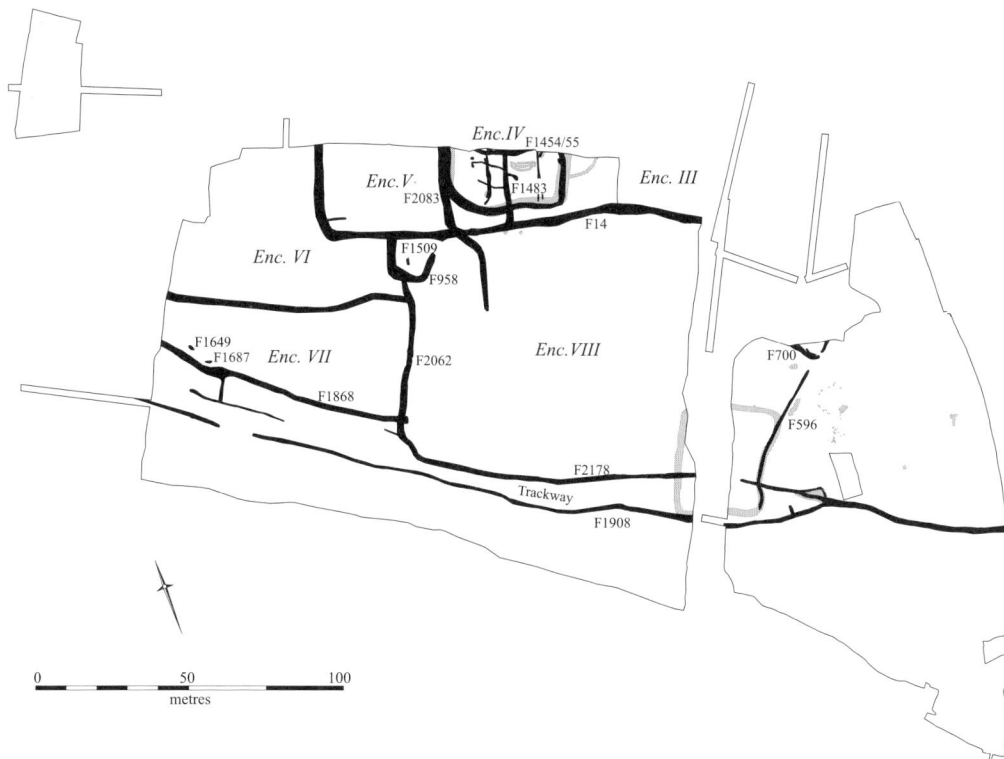

Figure 2.6 Phase 3 plan showing early Roman enclosures and features (earlier features in grey)

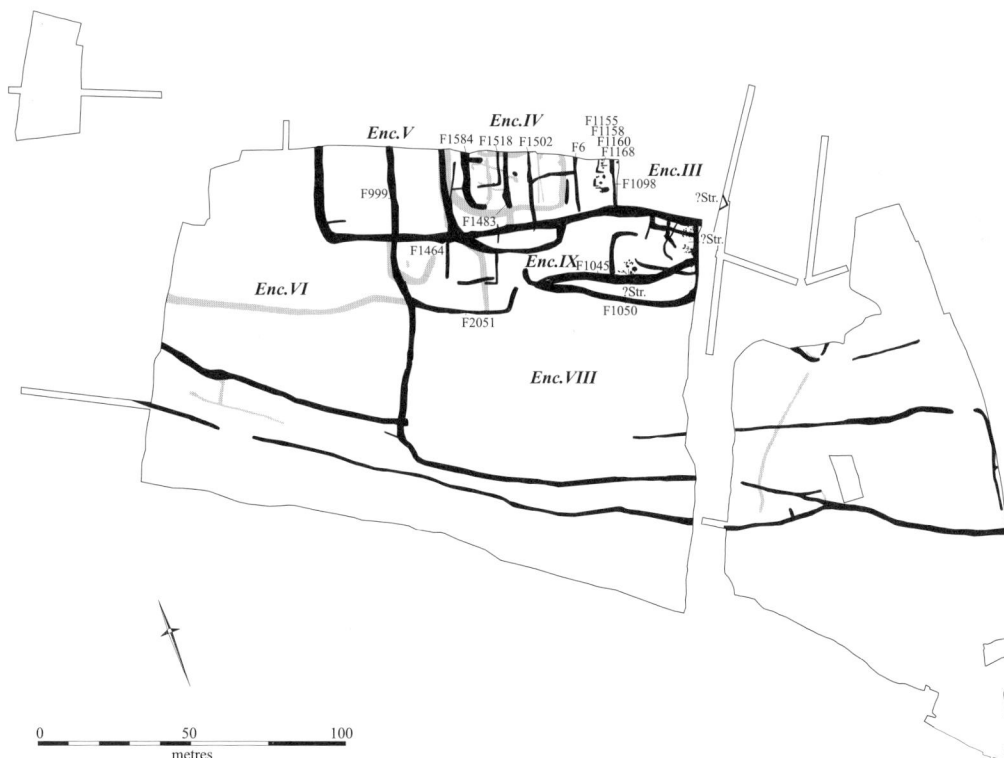

Figure 2.7 Phase 3 plan showing later Roman enclosures and features

21

F2051, Enclosure IX) which had an inturned entrance on its central southern side. This may indicate a substantial re-organisation of the compound system, for its west boundary (F999) appears to have sub-divided Enclosure V and probably marks the disuse of its western half. East of F999, as with the previous phase, the settlement is divided into a series of small rectilinear compounds or paddocks (F6, F1098, F1464, F1483, F1502, F1518, F1584). Two groupings of post-holes set within the eastern side of Enclosure IX may represent structures. The eastern group survived as a disparate cluster of 21 post-holes. If this represented a building, then it had been cut away on all sides by later features, the surviving parts of the eastern and southern walls suggesting a north-east–south-west alignment and an extent of *c.* 7.00m by 3.50m. The second western group also suggested a north-east–south-west aligned structure, this comprising a group of twenty post-holes forming a rough square measuring 4.00m by 4.00m. If these indeed represented structures, perhaps they were some kind of small outbuilding.

Groupings of post-holes and gullies within Enclosure III may have represented a structure, although they are not dated and could be assigned to either the earlier or later phase of Roman activity. This possible structure was only partially exposed, and consisted of a line of three post-holes and a right-angled drip gully (F1155, F1158, F1160 and F1168). The east side of the building had been truncated by later features, while its northern extent lay beyond the edge of excavation. The post-holes and eaves-gully suggested a north-west–south-east alignment, although the true extent of the putative structure remains unknown. To the south of this possible building, further groups of post-holes and angled gullies might represent other small structures, although no coherent structural pattern could be seen. The south-eastern corner of another possible structure was seen in an evaluation trench. This consisted of two right-angled horizontal beam slots, measuring 3.50m by 4.00m, suggesting a building aligned north–south.

Twenty-eight fragments of quernstone were recovered from Roman contexts, all but one of lava stone. A whetstone and a possible polishing stone were also recovered from features assigned to this phase. Forty-one fragments of Roman building material were recovered, of which twenty were residual. Of these, four were incised box-flue tiles and another four were tegula pieces. This material occurred in insufficient quantities to suggest that it formed a major component of these buildings. The presence of the tile is more likely to reflect secondary usage, for example in hearth or oven bases, and possibly as post-pads or supports. Stone, other than flint nodules, was found in the form of small limestone slabs and ?locally quarried greensand, and in similar contexts to the tiles. The lack of surviving building materials suggested that all structures were of more perishable materials.

Other Roman small finds recovered *in situ* and from later contexts included a whetstone, two non-lava quernstone fragments, three stone spindle whorls, two cannel-coated beads, a small number of fragments of early Roman glass vessels, a Langton Down-type brooch, a possible strap-end and strap-fitting, an iron staple, a possible iron tool, a triangular loomweight fragment and a late Roman double-sided composite bone comb; the ear-ring found in a Phase 8 context is also possibly Roman.

When considered alongside the artefacts and building material, the pottery assemblage (Chapter 4, p.61) — dominated by local wares and with relatively little fine material or amphorae — suggests that this was rural occupation of low to medium status. This is supported by the paucity of coin evidence, and by the environmental remains. Just under 3000 animal bones were assigned to Roman contexts, of which 713 could be identified to species. Of these, 45% (by NISP) are sheep/goat (and similarly sized) and 40% cattle. Otherwise pig bones account for 7% of the assemblage, and horse 4%; as well as ten dog (1.4%), five cat (0.7%) and two deer bones (0.3%), there were eleven bird bones, with individual finds of Brent goose, mallard and crow, four chicken and eight goose bones. A partly digested pike vertebrae was also recovered from a Roman context.

The plant remains are similar to those of the Iron Age occupation. The only real developments are seen in an increased importance of spelt wheat, the occurrence of Celtic bean, and the presence of stinking chamomile amongst the weeds. The latter is associated with the cultivation of heavy soil and may support the pollen evidence (Chapter 5, p.114) for an increase in arable farming.

Discussion

It is difficult to characterise activity at West Fen Road in the 1st century AD, and this is not helped by the fact that Conquest-period sites on the Isle of Ely are poor in metalwork — including coinage and brooches, the key 'type-markers' of the period's chronology (Evans 2003b). Against this, the recovery of pre-Flavian Romanised wares (butt beaker) certainly indicate a Conquest-period presence, and thereby some kind of Iron Age–Roman continuity. As discussed above, the Iron Age occupation on the northern side of West Fen Road continued into the 1st century AD, and the evidence reported on here was probably marginal to this activity.

One possibility is that the Iron Age Enclosure I was given over to a cemetery; it is difficult otherwise to account for the evidence of the inhumations within this area (Fig. 2.8). While this would appear inconsistent with well-known and characteristic Late Iron Age burial rites, which generally involve cremation, generalisations of this kind rest largely on comparison with mortuary practices known from the Gaulish-influenced Aylesford-Swarling 'core area' of south-eastern England. No formal Late Iron Age cremation cemeteries are known from the Isle of Ely, which lay at the northern fringes of this zone (Hill *et al.* 1999), and it must be conceded that we do not know what local contemporary burial rites involved. (Further south, in the northern part of the Aylesford-Swarling core area, inhumations occur side-by-side or immediately post-date late Iron Age cremations — the latter being striking, since early Roman funerary practice was also dominated by cremation.) On the basis of the areas of high pottery density, and also given the layout of the (sub-)rectangular small compounds and the sheer density of ditches and other features, it is clear that the focus of the Roman activity lay in the central-northern third of Area B (Fig. 2.9). This corresponds with the area of Enclosures III, IV, V and IX; within the boundaries of the CAU excavations, it extends over an area of almost a hectare. This probably represents the southern half of a sub-rectangular settlement core, as it is known that very few Roman

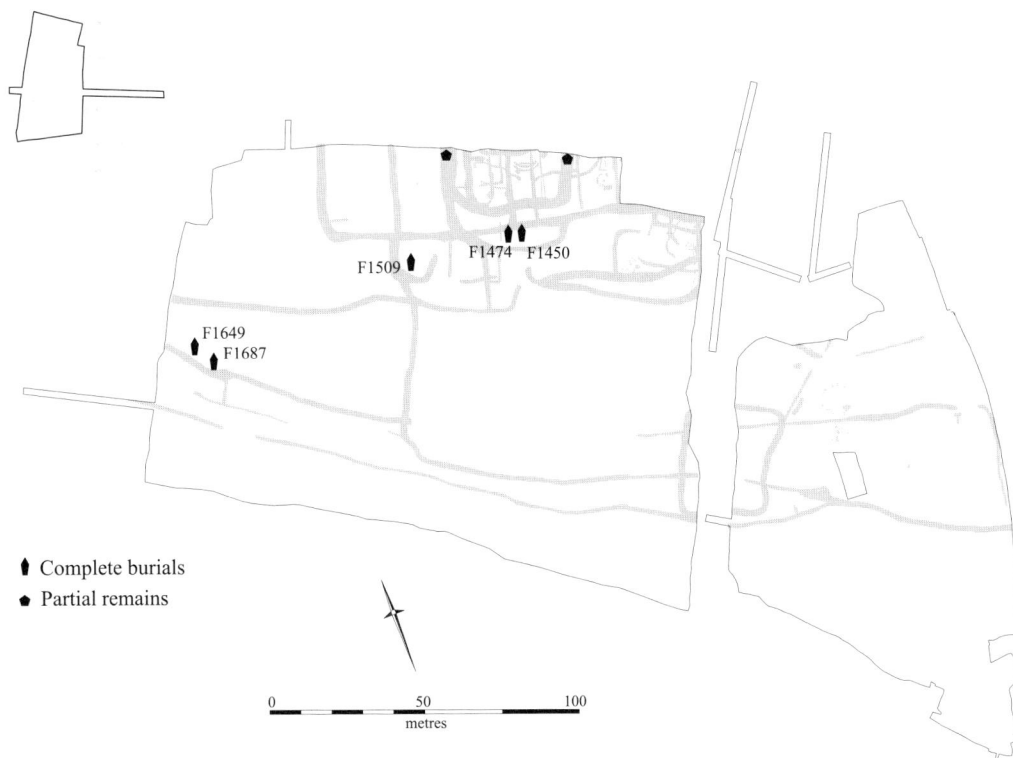

Figure 2.8 Location plan of Iron Age and Roman human remains/burials, against Iron Age and Roman features

F1474 F1450
F1509
F1649
F1687

♦ Complete burials
⬟ Partial remains

0   50   100
metres

Number of sherds
100+
51-100
21-50
10-20

0   50   100
metres

Figure 2.9 Distribution plot of Roman pottery, shown against Roman features

23

features were found by the excavations north of West Fen Road. It is probably sensible to characterise the site as a modest farmstead, with no pretensions to any kind of special function. The *floruit* of its usage — from the mid-2nd to the mid–later 4th centuries AD — corresponds with that of the main Roman centres known in the fenland such as Stonea (Jackson and Potter 1996) and Chatteris (Evans 2003b).

3. The Saxon and Medieval Settlement (Periods II and III): Site Narrative

I. Introduction

This chapter describes the features — the ditches, pits, post-holes, wells *etc.* — associated with the Saxon and medieval occupation of the site. Descriptions are in phase order; within each phase the evidence is presented with reference to the enclosures with which the features were associated. Discussion of the buildings, pits, wells and enclosure ditches in Chapter 6 will pay special attention to the variety displayed by the evidence, and any indications of changes over time. Attempts have been made here to distinguish domestic buildings from non-domestic structures. These have rested heavily on the presence of substantial contemporary finds assemblages from surrounding features, which have been taken to indicate occupation as opposed to purely agricultural use. Wherever possible, an interpretation has been offered for each of the major linear features. Pairs of relatively slight ditches a distance apart, sharing a common direction, have been regarded as trackways; parallel larger ditches lying closer together (or situations where a single ditch appeared partly filled with material that had slumped from an associated bank) as hedgebanks.

II. Phase 5: Mid Saxon (early 8th–mid 9th century)
(Figs 3.1 and 3.2)

Summary
There is plausible evidence for domestic buildings occupying Enclosures 1, 4 and, 6, along with a probable non-domestic structure in Enclosure 3 and further possible structures in Enclosures 2 and 5. There are a few small pits around the buildings in Enclosures 1 and 5 and a well lies along the southern boundary of Enclosure 8. The relationship of these remains with those excavated to the north of the road will be explored in Chapter 7.

The establishment of the settlement
The post-Roman occupation of the site begins in the Mid Saxon period, at Phase 5, with what appears to have been the deliberate laying-out of an extensive settlement. Parts of this initial settlement layout, to the south of West Fen Road at least, were shaped to some extent by the surviving Iron Age and Romano-British earthworks. Due to the insubstantial nature of much of the evidence, and to severe disturbance by later archaeological features, little remained of the evidence for widespread, and relatively intensive, settlement activity in this phase. However, a basic plan of the settlement's layout could be recorded and sufficient artefacts — principally pottery — were recovered to allow some understanding of the settlement's internal dynamics. Evidence of occupation including structures was seen along the northern and eastern edges of Area B, to the south of the road, with the southern and western excavation areas

unoccupied, as they had been in the Roman period. The southern Roman boundary ditch also appeared to mark the boundary of the Mid Saxon settlement.

The absence of even moderate quantities of hand-made Saxon pottery implies that the settlement cannot have been established until after the introduction of the wheelmade Ipswich wares, which dominate the pottery assemblage from this phase. (Occasional sherds of contemporary Maxey ware were found too.) Recent work suggests that Ipswich wares were introduced no earlier than *c.* 725 (P. Blinkhorn, *pers. comm.*), and they probably remained current until around 850. A silver *sceatta* dating to *c.* 730–760 (Series L, type 18) was recovered from a gully adjacent to Structure 4 (Enclosure 3). It is suggested that the settlement was established in the second quarter of the 8th century. Like those of the Roman settlement, the Mid Saxon enclosures were strung along the southern side of West Fen Road (although those excavated north of the road followed a north–south layout — see Chapter 7). The Roman trackway seen in the southern part of the site also marked the southern limit of the Mid Saxon settlement. The settlement was represented by shallow-ditched paddocks or enclosures, most of which contained structures, either domestic or agricultural. Within the enclosures and around the buildings, smaller lengths of gullies indicate further subdivision or localised drainage schemes. The enclosure ditches were generally narrow and shallow, filled by natural clay accumulation and show no evidence of recutting or cleaning (although the large Roman boundary ditch to the south of Enclosure 1 had been redefined). Perhaps enclosures had been defined by upcast banks, maybe turfed, which could have supported hedges or fences in situations where ingress or egress needed to be restricted. Such banks would have continued to mark the house-plot and paddock boundaries once the ditches had become infilled. Four structures were identified, while sites for two others were suggested; each lay within its own enclosed compound. Five of these (Enclosures 2–6) were extended along the axis of West Fen Road, while another lay to the south-east (Enclosure 1). These six areas, with two larger, unoccupied enclosures behind them, formed the core around which the enclosure systems developed through subsequent phases of occupation, after the abandonment of the settled area to the north of West Fen Road. Along the back of the enclosures fronting West Fen Road, a possible access track connected them to each other and to the larger compounds, Enclosures 7 and 8.

Enclosure 1
The enclosure occupied the south-eastern corner of the Romano-British field system and was set within the main southern Roman boundary ditch at the eastern end of the southern Roman trackway. The southern boundary ditch, F530, may initially have been a re-cutting or re-use of the Roman ditch, though it has been further truncated by later features. A subsequent parallel ditch cut to the north, F598, was up to 1.40m wide and 0.40m deep. The western boundary was formed by a series of short,

Figure 3.1 Phase 5 overall plan, with Phase 3 features as background and interpretation below

shallow ditch cuts, F2334, F2338, F604 and F624, up to 0.85m wide and 0.30m deep. To the north there was a confused shared boundary with Enclosure 2, the principal ditches being F291 and F337, which were both just 0.20m deep.

A post-hole building, Structure 3, was set parallel to the southern boundary ditch of this enclosure (Fig. 3.2a). It was aligned north-west–south-east, and represented by a short north-west wall composed of four post-holes and a longer south-west wall of seven post-holes, its north and east sides having been removed or obscured by later features. It would have measured at least 11–12m by 5m. Only one post-hole produced an artefact: a single, large, fresh sherd of Ipswich ware. Other circumstantial dating evidence for the building is provided by its probable contemporaneity with the parallel ditch to the south, F598 (which contained Ipswich ware alongside some later Thetford and St Neots wares in its upper fills) and its location at the centre of the densest concentration of this pottery from the site.

Five or six pits were scattered across the southern half of the area. The only well-preserved example, F385, lay *c.* 30m to the north-west of Structure 3. It measured 1.96m x 1.26m and was 0.56m deep, with one steep and one shallower end, and contained a small but comprehensive domestic waste assemblage (including pottery, bone, burnt clay, fishbone, eggshell and hammerscale), although it was not thought primarily to have been a rubbish pit (see Chapter 6 for discussion).

Enclosure 2
A right-angled gully 1.15m wide and 0.10m deep along the east edge of the excavation, F2302, might represent the western end of a structure which was concealed almost entirely beyond the limits of excavation. No estimation of the structure's size is possible. The lack of adjacent pitting or of significant quantities of finds within the enclosure would suggest that any building was not a domestic one; this was reinforced by the absence of finds from excavated sections across the gully. The gully was

A

B

Sceat

C

D

0   10
              metres

E

F

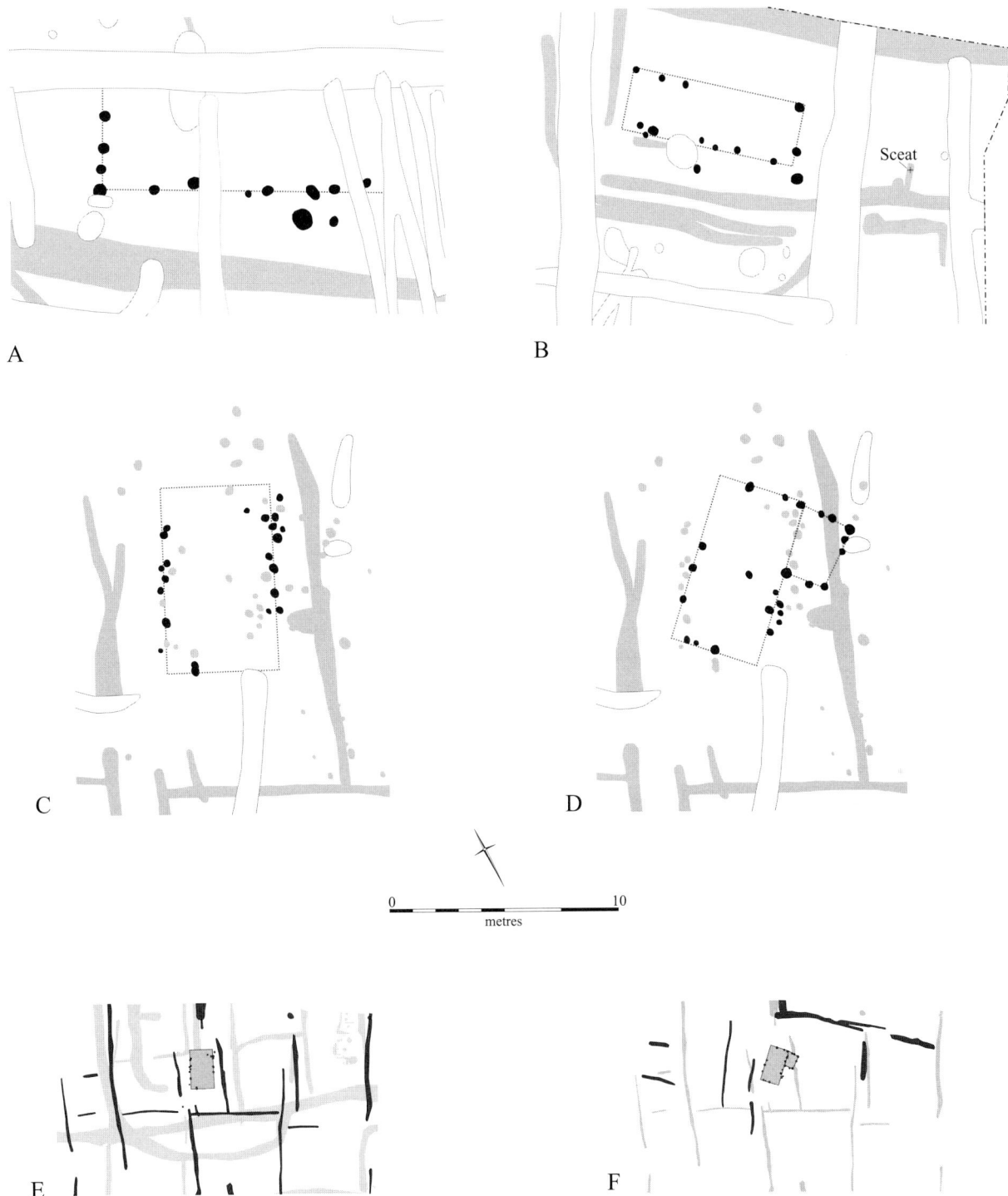

Figure 3.2 (a) Structure 3 (b) Structure 4 (c) Structure 5 (d) Structure 6, with (e) and (f) representing the respective enclosure systems of Structures 5 and 6

dated by surface finds of two sherds of Ipswich ware. It is possible that Enclosures 1 and 2 formed part of one property with Enclosure 2 containing a non-domestic building, perhaps a barn. The trackway along the backs of the properties to the west, and the larger Enclosures 7 and 8, could have been accessed by a narrow, and possibly gated, pathway. (Although no post-holes were observed, there was a gap of just under 2m between the two ditches.)

Enclosure 3

Most of this enclosure lay outside the excavation area to the north and east. Within the trenches between the two main excavated areas, it proved nearly impossible to recognise all but the most obvious features. The remains of a small and heavily truncated post-hole building, Structure 4, lay along the southern boundary of the enclosure and was aligned

north-west–south-east (Fig. 3.2b). Parts of both the long sides survive, the north wall being represented by four post-holes and the south by seven, with a further element — possibly a repair — at the west end. The building was small, measuring 8m by 3m; part of a second structure or fence-line to the south-west, ran off parallel with Structure 4's long axis in a westerly direction. A long gully was recorded behind the building to the south and a short gully at the west; these features (F1081: up to 0.60m wide and 0.20m deep) were probably integral to each other, but their junction is cut away by later features. A narrow northward extension of the gully a little to the east of the structure — possible beam slot or fence element F1024, which was 0.25m wide and 0.25m deep with vertical sides — produced the *sceatta* of *c.* 730–760.

There was no pitting around the building, and it appears to continue in use through into Phase 6. No concentration of finds of Phase 5 or Phase

27

6 was recorded in the vicinity, and Structure 4 was probably non-domestic. The area that it occupied was dense with Romano-British artefacts and features, which the building stratigraphically overlay, and a few (mostly residual) sherds of Ipswich ware came from the area. The structure is assigned to the Mid Saxon phase principally due to the *sceatta* recovered from ?related feature F1024, the excavated pottery assemblage from gully F1081, which includes four sherds of Ipswich ware, and on the basis of its spatial and stratigraphic relationships with Late Saxon features.

Enclosure 4

This enclosure, at the centre of the settlement, broadly corresponded to the core of the Romano-British settlement. This was the area of densest Iron Age and Romano-British occupation; when the Saxon settlement was first established, it may have been crowded with earthwork features, possibly abandoned buildings, midden heaps, trees and scrub. Within Phase 5, two possible phases of activity were recorded. From amongst a mass of post-holes, two distinct overlapping structures (Structures 5 and 6) have been discerned. These followed slightly different orientations which appeared to correspond with the layout of a series of successive surrounding ditches (Fig. 3.2c, d). A total of 48 post-holes were recognised, although many others were almost certainly present originally. Of these, 25 were excavated, although in many cases only the bases survived: those of Structure 5 were up to 0.05m deep, and those of Structure 6, up to 0.13m deep. Structure 5 is suggested to have been a rectangular post-hole building without clearly identifiable end walls, oriented north–south and measuring 5m wide by *c.* 8m long. Structure 6 is also reconstructed as a post-hole building, aligned north–east–south–west and measuring 7m by 4m, with a possible porch or extension at the north-east measuring 3m by 2m. These reconstructions, however, are both tentative.

The presence of two consecutive buildings whose alignments were at variance might account for the two distinct alignments that could be seen in the ditches and gullies that surrounded them. The earlier of these two proposed alignments clearly conforms with that of the underlying Romano-British features, to some extent re-using and echoing the surviving earthworks (Fig. 3.2e). The 'north–south' elements of the later alignment were aligned further towards to north-east–south-west; some of the earlier features had been infilled and built-over, and it is possible that parts of the Romano-British earthworks had been levelled (Fig. 3.2f).

In the earlier of these phases there were shallow gullies (F1532 and F1498, up to 1.00m wide and 0.35m deep) along either side of the length of Structure 5, and what may have been post-trench at right-angles to these behind the building; the latter feature, F1482/1540, was vertical-sided, 0.40m wide, 0.21m deep. A narrow (possibly gated?) entrance through this gave access to the rear trackway and the west part of Enclosure 8. There were other similar, shallow sub-enclosure gullies in the remainder of the area. Structure 6 was set within a more open enclosure, with narrow gullies F1552 and F1563 (widths up to 0.55m, depths to 0.35m) to the north-west and a wider ditch, F1489 (1.05m wide, 0.37m deep), to the north-east.

The datable finds assemblage was dominated by residual Romano-British material but included a single sherd of Ipswich ware from Structure 6. A second sherd was recovered from gully F1532 to the west of this building, and a fragment of a Mid Saxon bone comb came from a post-hole within the middle of the structure. The dating of the buildings rests upon these items, and on a handful of stratigraphic relationships with Romano-British features.

The quantities of Iron Age and Romano-British material from this part of the site far outweigh the small amounts of material attributable to the Mid Saxon occupation, and it was difficult to assign many features to the Saxon period with certainty. Ditch F1489 was extensively excavated specifically because it was thought likely to date to the Mid Saxon phase; however, nearly 90% of the pottery assemblage recovered from it was residual Iron Age and Roman material (78 Iron Age and Roman sherds *vs.* six of Ipswich ware).

Enclosure 5

The presence of a building within this enclosure was suggested by a number of (ultimately unexcavated) post-holes at the northern limit of the site, set within rectangular gullies F1617, F1618 and F1647, which were up to 0.65m wide and 0.30m deep. The size and alignment of any structure here is not known. There were further small gullied compounds directly south of this, and also occasional pitting within these areas: pit F1618 produced a single sherd of Ipswish ware and also one Roman sherd. The whole group of features was confined closely within the remnant Romano-British earthworks. Very few finds of any date were recovered from the enclosure, suggesting that activity here was never intensive in either Phase 3 or Phase 5. The dating of any putative structure to the Mid Saxon period rests upon a single sherd of Ipswich ware from

one of the surrounding gullies. Pit F1589 (sub-circular with gradually sloping sides, 1.50m x 1.20m x 0.30m deep), which truncated the two main internal ditches in the south of the enclosure, F966 and F1602 (these features up to 0.50m wide and 0.14m deep), contained a small, mixed assemblage of domestic waste including three sherds of Ipswich ware. Other finds were sparse, although a single Iron Age sherd was found on the stripped surface of F1602.

Enclosure 6

The remains of a building, Structure 7, aligned north-east–south-west and of post-hole construction, lay at the eastern edge of the westernmost part of Enclosure 6. Only parts of the western, and possibly the northern, wall survived, the southern half and most of the eastern side being cut away by later features. The dimensions of the structure were not clear, although it may have been *c.* 8m long and between 3m and 5m wide. No datable finds were recovered from the excavated post-holes. A Mid Saxon date is suggested by the concentration of (mostly residual) Ipswich ware from the immediate vicinity and by the manner in which component features had been truncated by two Late Saxon features to the south. The almost total lack of Roman pottery within the area would seem to preclude a pre-Saxon date. There were many other, undated, post-holes within this area, some of which may have represented further small structures belonging within this phase. To the south-west, the enclosure was bounded by intermittent ditches F2642 and F2648. This alignment was probably continued south-eastwards in the main part of Area B by gully F930, which had been heavily truncated by later features along its line. All of these ditches/gullies were up to 0.60m wide and 0.10m deep.

Enclosures 7 and 8 and the central trackway

The largely unoccupied Roman enclosures at the centre of the site remained so. There was some remodelling of the existing sub-enclosures along the north side of Enclosure 8. Five of these were clearly visible, partially defined by ditches (from the west) F959, F1458, F1592, F938, F1212, F1422 and F1077 (Fig. 3.1). These ditches were all quite slight (0.30–1.00m wide and 0.10–0.40m deep) with the exception of the deeper, curving ditch F938 (1.10m wide x 0.62m deep), which may have partially enclosed a structure or a particular activity area of some kind. The area within it was re-enclosed repeatedly throughout the occupation of the site (Phases 6 to 9, below). Other than this possible indication of a structure, there was no direct evidence for occupation within these sub-enclosures. In this, as in other respects, the Mid Saxon re-use of the Roman landscape reflects the earlier patterns of use quite well, with the sub-enclosures ranging off the southern sides of, and possibly 'belonging to', Enclosures 3 and 4.

A central trackway, or back access route, is indicated, running north-west–south-east through Enclosures 7 and 8, broadly parallel to the northern route along West Fen Road. While it is to be assumed that the principal access/communication route lay along West Fen Road, the question of intra-site access must also be considered. Gaps, or possible gaps, may be identified all the way along the southern boundaries of Enclosures 3, 4, 5 and 6, and in one of the north–south divisions within Enclosure 8. In Enclosure 2 to the east, and in Enclosure 4, possible narrow, controlled entranceways may have given access to this trackway. South of the trackway there is some evidence for the subdivision of Enclosure 8 into three or four large, rectangular paddocks, running off the back of the smaller sub-enclosures in the north. These are principally marked by narrow ditches early in Phase 6, and might possibly have represented outfield divisions.

While it is possible that contemporary occupation within these enclosures went unrecorded, perhaps due to masking or obliteration by later activity, the relative paucity of residual Ipswich ware recovered from later features hereabouts would argue against this. Enclosure 8 also saw little intensive use in later phases. A well along the boundary at the south of the compound, F1219, had been infilled in the Later Saxon period; while assigned to Phase 6, its location might indicate that it originated in Phase 5. The presence of a well in an otherwise 'empty' enclosure could indicate the watering of animals, possibly kept within the larger paddock or stock enclosures.

III. Phase 6: Late Saxon I (mid 9th–10th/11th century)
(Figs 3.3–3.6)

Summary

Five domestic buildings occupied Enclosures 1, 6, 7 and 12, and four probably non-domestic buildings were seen in Enclosures 1, 3, 7, and 9. Three other conjectured buildings lay in Enclosures 2, 4 and 10, as well as a few small pits around the buildings in Enclosures 1 and 3 and a well alongside the structure in Enclosure 12. While many of the enclosures retained their Mid Saxon (Phase 5) boundaries others were created anew, either through subdivision of earlier, larger enclosures or by expansion into previously unoccupied areas. In the northern half of the excavated area, the east part of Enclosure 3 became Enclosure 9, and the east part of Enclosure 6, Enclosure 10. In the southern half of the site Enclosures 11, 12, 13 and 14 were created by the breaking up of the previously unoccupied Enclosure 8, reflecting settlement expansion southwards. This re-organisation may have been due, at least in part, to the

abandonment of the settled area to the north of West Fen Road around this time (Chapter 7, p.150).

Enclosure 1

As is to be expected within a developing and active settlement, changes in enclosure configuration were apparent from one phase to the next. Enclosure 1 saw contraction along its western boundary. A series of substantial ditches (F351, F374, F315, and F655, up to 1.40m wide and 0.60m deep) saw excavation and subsequently recutting, marking this as a major boundary extending the enclosed area to the north, probably incorporating Enclosure 2 from the previous phase.

The southern boundary of this larger compound was defined by recutting the line of the original Roman ditch (and possible Phase 5 boundary) F530, with an entranceway into Enclosure 14 to the south. Again, the character of this boundary — marked by ditches F687, F688 and F528 — indicated multiple episodes of cutting and recutting; F528

Figure 3.3 Phase 6 overall plan, with Phase 5 features as background and interpretation below

29

had been re-defined at least twice. These were substantially bigger ditches than in the previous phase, with widths to 1.90m and depths to 0.75m. There was now no significant boundary between the former Enclosures 1 and 2, and it seems clear that they form part of a single unit, with the major boundary being that to the west. The fills of the southern boundary ditches were dated by fairly large assemblages of Thetford and St Neots wares, although residual prehistoric, Roman and Ipswich ware sherds were also found. Within the area of Enclosure 1, a number of square or sub-square divisions could be discerned within clearly separated northern and southern halves, both of which contained buildings.

Structure 8, probably a domestic building, lay a few metres to the north-west of the area occupied by Structure 3 in the previous phase, and was perhaps its replacement; it was of similar alignment and dimensions, measuring 10.50m x 5.00m (Fig. 3.4a). Parts of all four sides of the building survived, principally represented by post-holes (maximum depth 0.17m) but with one section of narrow beam-slot (0.30m wide x 0.05m deep) within the north-west wall. Another narrow beam-slot (0.15m wide x 0.05m deep) and post-holes subdivided the interior into two unequal halves, 6.00m and 4.50m in length; part of a possible porch/entrance was indicated by post-holes to the north-east. Nearly all the post-holes were shallow, probably as a result of heavy truncation. On the central axis of the building was a possible hearth, F577: this was the base of a sub-circular pit 0.50m in diameter, filled with burnt material (charcoal in red/orange silty clay).

The building was enclosed by gully F431 along its northern and eastern sides, this being broken by an entranceway at the south-east. The southern side of this entranceway was marked by a large elongated pit (F523, 5.00m x 2.00m x 0.92m deep), which produced almost no finds. Its interpretation as a catchwater or well was supported by its fill, which was of waterlain, weathered silty clay. Many other pits were seen within the building's sub-enclosure, principally to the south and east, and also within the immediate area of the structure itself, along with a number of post-holes. Most of the pits were very shallow and contained few finds. They ranged in size from 0.70m x 0.60m to 1.60m x 1.25m in plan, with depths of between 0.06m and 0.14m; each contained just a few fragments of bone and pottery. Six others were deeper and of varying profile, yet still with small artefactual assemblages. At least two of these, F578 (1.80m x 1.10m x 0.45m deep) and F541 (1.30m x 1.00m x 0.35m deep) were like Phase 5 pit F385, a few metres to the north, with one steep and one shallow end. Though four pits had been dug in the area of the building itself, none had a clear relationship with the structure's post-holes or beam-slots and their date relative to the structure is unknown.

Structure 9, a possible subsidiary building to Structure 8, was surrounded by a gully (F305) and set within its own enclosure (Fig. 3.4b). The building lay c. 15m to the north of Structure 8 and was aligned at 90° to it. The group of fifteen surviving post-holes and the beam-slot was heavily truncated and only parts of the south and west sides survived; it would have measured c. 7m x 4m. Three further post-holes (two of them substantial) c. 1m to the south might have formed part of the structure, or of an extension to it. A group of short, intercutting beam-slots to the south-east of the Enclosure 1 buildings (F423, F424, F426, F427 and F428; 1.50–3.00m long) truncated an earlier ditch, F425. Similar slots continued to be cut in this area throughout Phases 8 and 9. While they did not represent recognisable buildings they were probably structural remains of some kind. There was further small-scale pitting to the south and east of Structure 9. These pits were sub-circular to oval in shape, ranging from 0.80m x 0.60m to 1.50m x 0.70m in plan, and were mostly shallow (0.15–0.40m deep). Like the majority of those around Structure 8, they produced few finds.

Enclosure 2
The possible structure in the northern part of the area (or a successor) may have continued in use from Phase 5, the curving gully being recut as F282. The enclosure's western boundary, F261, was now more clearly defined, and aligned with that of Enclosure 1 to the south. The boundary with Enclosure 1 was formed by narrow ditch F270 (up to 0.70m wide and 0.45m deep). A broad ditch, F340, up to 1.80m wide and 0.50m deep, divided the south part of the enclosure into east and west halves.

Enclosure 9
This enclosure represented southward expansion south into area of the earlier unoccupied Enclosure 8. Its eastern boundary was marked by a sequence of large ditches, F334 and F345 (up to 1.60m wide and 0.50m deep). To the south lay shallow ditches and fence lines F634, F679 and F603 (0.30–0.63m wide and up to 0.15m deep), around an entrance to the stock enclosures of Enclosure 13. The western boundary was marked by the first in a long sequence of ditches, F2430, 1m wide and 0.45m deep. Structure 10 (Fig. 3.4c) lay in the southern part of the enclosure. Aligned

broadly north–south, it was represented by substantial post-holes, 0.40–0.60m in diameter and 0.05–0.30m deep; those of the south wall were deeper, which might reflect the sloping terrain. The structure was only 3.50m wide. Its length is unknown but the western side appeared to stop short of the edge of excavation. It may have formed a small square structure, similar to Structure 18 established here later in Phase 8. Short, shallow gullies (both 0.40m wide and 0.11m deep) ran along the west (F699) and south (F2333) sides of the building. Other linear features, some of them possibly fence-lines, ran east-to-west behind these: F587 and F642 were 0.35–0.80m wide and 0.10–0.45m deep, with the deeper, narrower lengths having vertical sides and flat bases. There was small-scale pitting to the south of the structure, principally around gully F642 (F645, F703 and F2424). Two of these pits were shallow, oval and flat-based, but the third, F703, was rectangular, with steep north and south sides but more shallowly sloping edges to the east and west (1.10m x 0.50m x 0.38m deep).

Enclosure 3
The Phase 5 enclosure saw some remodelling; the western boundary was extended further, being marked by ditch F1175, and there was also slight expansion southwards. At the centre of the enclosure, the Phase 5 Structure 4 may have remained in use; the gully along the southern side was recut twice as F1082. If so, the building now occupied a sub-rectangular compound with entranceways along the south-western side. The features' fills were dated by finds of Thetford and Ipswich ware. There was still little evidence of domestic occupation activity from the surrounding gullies, however, and the building (if still in existence) probably remained non-domestic.

Enclosure 4
The lack of contemporary pottery (Thetford and St Neots wares) from the north part of Enclosure 4 suggested that it was now unoccupied, the putative Mid Saxon buildings, Structures 5 and 6, having been abandoned. The southern part of the enclosure was divided into three small east–west blocks, the easternmost of which may have contained a sequence of conjectured structures. This is suggested partly by the way in which surrounding features, across four phases, appear to have respected a central (and therefore perhaps occupied) area, and partly by the quantities of finds material recovered from the surrounding ditches, which included fairly large assemblages of Thetford, St Neots and residual pottery. There were two possible beam-slots, F1470 (0.60m wide, 0.09m deep) forming the western side of a putative building; F1462 (0.52m wide, 0.05m deep) may have been a central division. A few unexcavated post-holes were scattered to the east while there was also a central line of three post-holes, only one of which was excavated. These traces are not considered sufficient to warrant assigning any structure numbers here, although the constant redigging of the enclosure gullies and the quantity of finds material from the area's surroundings are not otherwise easily explained.

The ditched enclosure measured c. 25m by 20m. The eastern boundary was shared with Enclosure 3 while the south and west boundary was formed by curving ditch F931 (up to 1.50m wide and 0.50m deep). Although not extensively excavated, this produced a substantial finds assemblage, mainly of pottery but including some metal strips and scraps.

The western boundary of the larger enclosure was marked by ditch F1577, the smaller sub-enclosure divisions by ditches F960, F976 and F931 (above). All four ditches were of similar proportion and form, with widths of 1.30–1.85m, depths of 0.50–0.60m, steep sides and rounded bases. There would have been access to the trackway at the south of the enclosure from both its south-east and south-west corners.

Enclosure 5
There was little change to the boundaries of Enclosure 5. The earlier Structure 10 and its small enclosure were abandoned, and there was a possible division of the enclosure into west and east parts by a ditch (unexcavated); both parts would have had access to the trackway to the south. The east boundary was shared with Enclosure 4; the south-east was formed by a 2.00m-wide unexcavated ditch, the south-west by ditch F921 and its recuts (1.10m wide and 0.25m deep), and the west by curving ditch F907 (up to 2.00m wide and over 0.60m deep). Whether or not there were further buildings to the north along West Fen Road is not known, but there was little sign of any domestic occupation in this or subsequent phases. It seems likely that this enclosure was now unoccupied and remained so hereafter.

Enclosure 10
With a north–south division recorded towards the west, and structures possibly lying in both its north-western and south-eastern parts, Enclosure 6 is considered in two parts with regard to the Phase 6

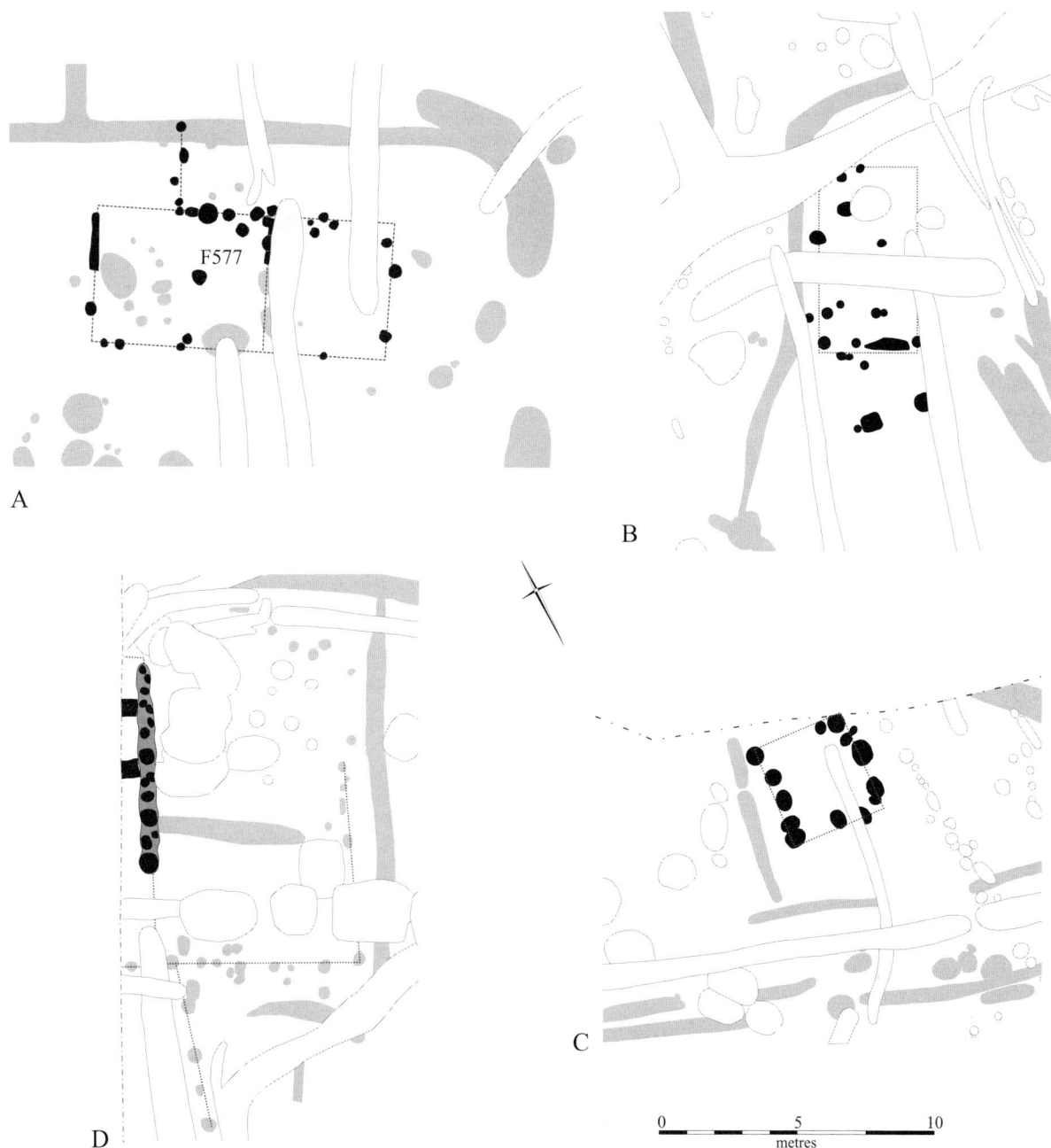

Figure 3.4 (a) Structure 8, (b) Structure 9, (c) Structure 10, (d) Structure 11

evidence, with the south-east half now designated Enclosure 10. A building may have stood here: a single row of five posts (F901–F904), some containing sherds of Thetford ware, aligned north-west–south-east and lying close to the edge of excavation, may have represented its southern end wall. The post alignment measured *c.* 5.5m across — the presumed width of the building — and all five post-holes were excavated. A gully, F916 (0.50m wide and 0.20m deep) ran along the presumed west side of the building; the whole would have lain within the south-east corner of a ditched enclosure, marked by the same feature that marks the western boundary of Enclosure 5, F907.

Enclosure 6
Within the now-reduced Enclosure 6, the earlier Structure 7 was replaced by the much more substantial Structure 11, although this was only partly exposed by excavation (Fig. 3.4d). This was of post-in-trench construction and north-east–south-west aligned, with a partially fenced yard attached to its eastern side. Only the eastern wall of the building lay within the area of excavation, along with parts of two beam-slots marking possible internal divisions. The east wall post-trench, F2614, was 7.50m long, 0.40–0.60m wide and 0.22–0.30m deep. At the base of the vertically-sided cut fifteen

post-impressions were recorded, these being up to 0.05m deep and 0.15–0.60m in diameter. A gap of 3.00m separated the main surviving part of the building from the fence-line/south wall. If this gap represented a doorway into the yard, the length of the building would have been 10.50m. Its width is unknown. Further post-holes to the south may have represented a fence-line or lean-to structure. Both the structure and yard were bounded by similar, shallow ditches, F2593 on the east and F2588 on the north (0.70m and 0.80m wide and 0.25m and 0.40m deep, respectively).

Enclosure 7
Enclosure 7 maintained its Phase 5 boundaries, but activity within it expanded somewhat to the south; with this expansion came a transition from non-domestic use to domestic occupation. The enclosure was divided into two main compounds, the south-west area containing two domestic buildings, Structures 12 and 13, and the south-east part a probably non-domestic building, Structure 14. There would have been access to both the south and central trackways.

Structures 12 and 13 were aligned north-east–south-west and set end-to-end. Both were of similar post-in-trench construction and were *c.* 13m long and 5m wide, with a gap between them of 2m (Fig. 3.5a). The

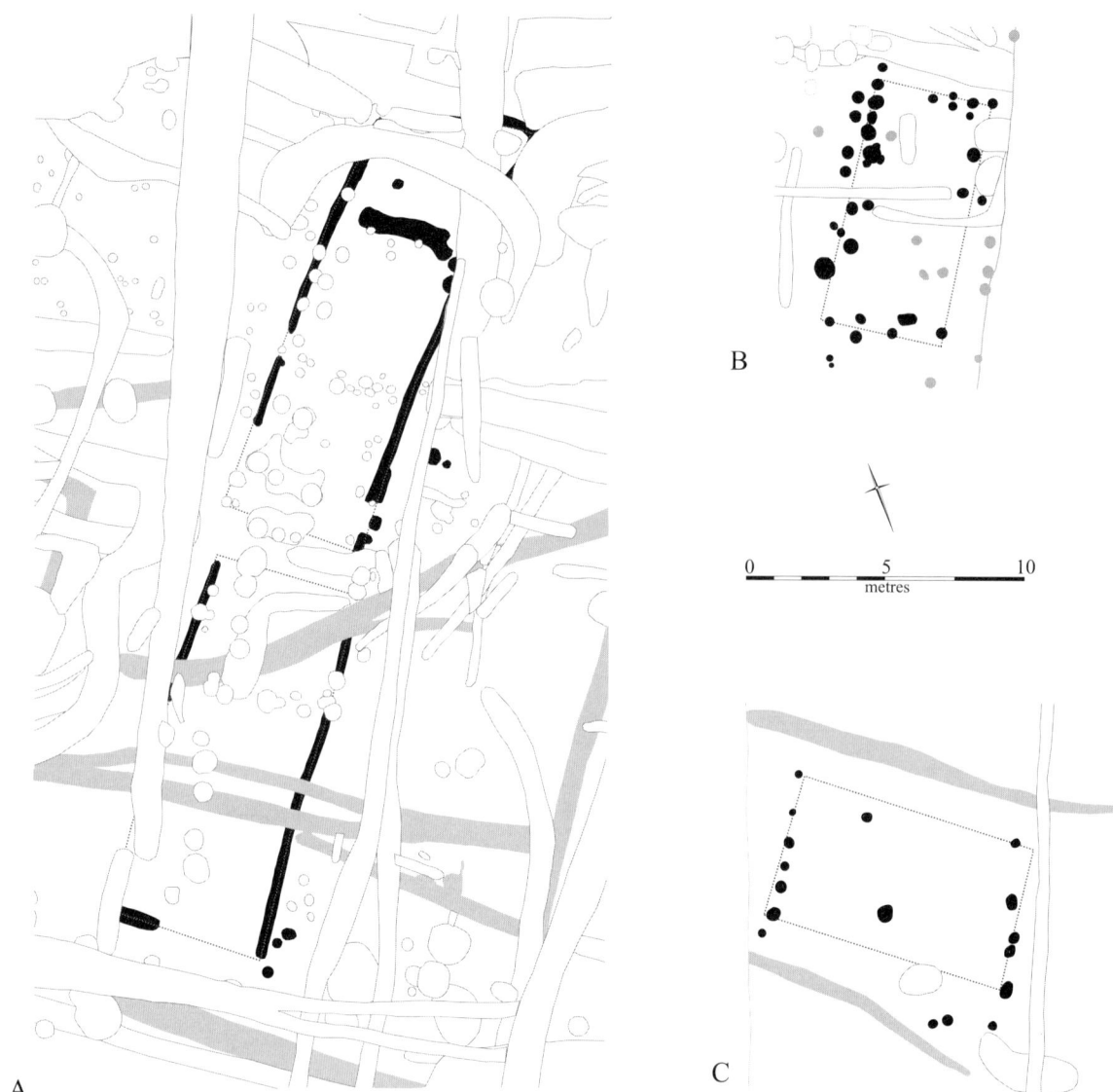

Figure 3.5 (a) Structures 12 and 13, (b) Structure 14, (c) Structure 15

northern Structure 12 was constructed first, with all four walls of post-in-trench construction: the wall trenches were a maximum of 0.45m wide and 0.30m deep (though truncated in their southern part to a minimum depth of 0.03m). Post-pipes and the bases of shallow post-holes were visible. A possible repair or addition was identified at the southern butt end of the eastern wall, and beyond this were two square-cut post-holes with identical profiles. There was also a possible internal division towards the northern end, represented by a deep post-trench, *c.* 3.25m long, 0.60m wide and 0.70m deep. The structure was set within ditched boundaries to the south and east (F1835, F1821 and F1840, 1.00–1.10m wide and 0.33–0.40m deep), and with a right-angled fence line parallel to its north end, F1621 (0.40m wide and 0.35m deep).

Structure 13 was subsequently constructed across the line of these southern ditches, either as a separate building or as an extension to Structure 12. Its north-western wall consisted of a post-trench 4.00m long but with an original length of *c.* 12.00m, which had been truncated to the south; this was up to 0.10m deep, with vertical sides and a flat base. The south-eastern wall also consisted of a post-trench, here in two sections separated by a small gap part way along, and somewhat truncated; it was of similar width to the north-west feature but up to 0.70m deep. The south-west wall consisted of a short length (1.50m long x 0.50m wide) of unexcavated post-trench. A major post-trench fence-line, F1922, had been constructed to butt against its eastern side. If Structure 12 is seen as an extension of its neighbour, perhaps for non-domestic purposes, the 2m gap between the two may represent a covered entrance/passageway. This interpretation might be supported by

the lack of any clear wall lines either side of the possible passageway. Structure 13 was up to 5.50m wide; Structure 12 measured 5.00m across at its widest point (being slightly bow-sided). Structure 12 displayed the more complex design, with a narrow division apparent at the north-eastern end.

Structure 14 (Fig. 3.5b) lay to the east of Structures 12/13. It appears to have lain within a rectangular subdivision of Enclosure 7, defined on its south side by fence-line F1922 (see above), to the west by ditch F1840 (see above) and to the north by ditch F1777 (1.50m wide, 0.47m deep). The structure measured 8.50m by 4.50m. It was aligned approximately north-east–south-west and parts of all four walls survived, with the western wall showing as a double row of posts (sixteen post-holes, with diameters of 0.20–0.60m and 0.05–0.25m deep). The south, east and north walls consisted of six, two and six post-holes respectively, of similar size and depth.

In the northern part of the enclosure a long, angled fence-line, F43, defined a pathway leading from the central trackway to the domestic buildings. The entranceway leading to it from the trackway was *c.* 5m wide; a large oval pit, F31 (2.90m long, 1.90m wide and 0.50m deep — possibly a shallow well, with slump-infilled vertical sides), was located there at the butt end of the southern trackway ditch F1.

Enclosure 11

Enclosure 11, in the centre of the site, was separated into three blocks: a thin northern strip and two equal sub-square enclosures in the south. There were no buildings, no pitting, and very little contemporary pottery or other finds to suggest this saw residential occupation. There was access both from the central trackway to the north and from the south, but seemingly no direct access west or east. To the north the trackway was bounded by ditch F942 (1.70m wide, 0.75m deep); around the south and west of the enclosure were ditches F2094 (1.40m wide, 0.54m deep) and F2096 (0.55m wide, 0.40m deep); ditch F906 to the east was a shared boundary with Enclosure 12 and is dealt with there (below). The internal enclosure divisions were narrow segmented ditches F946 (east–west) and F2102 (north–south); these were up to 0.60m wide and 0.30m deep. Only the trackside ditch and that on the eastern side contained significant quantities of finds, these consisting mainly of bone, burnt clay and lava quern; a small quantity of pottery was mainly residual, but included two sherds of St Neots ware.

Enclosure 12

Enclosure 12 was split into two north–south strips with a possible further small enclosure to the east. It is possible that during this phase the holding incorporated some of the curving enclosures currently attributed to Enclosure 13 to the east, the interface between these land units remaining unexcavated. Alternatively, the eastern boundary of the enclosure may have been north–south ditch F1217, a substantial feature with a similar profile to that of the west boundary F906. These ditches were 2.00m+ and 3.40m wide, and 0.71m and 0.95m deep, respectively; both were bowl-profiled with a drainage channel cut in the base. The north trackside boundary was a continuation of ditch F942 (see above). The central north–south division was formed by shallow bowl-shaped ditches F894/895, up to 1.80m wide and 0.48m deep, whose large finds assemblage produced two of the perforated bones (Fig. 4.13, no. 192).

The southern butt ends of ditches F894/895 were subsequently overlain by Structure 15 (Fig. 3.5c). This was a small timber-framed structure, perhaps trapezoidal in plan and approximately 9m by 5m, aligned north-west–south-east and with run-off gullies along its two long sides, F1428 and F1431. The former was 0.38m wide and 0.15m deep, the latter 0.90m wide and 0.30m deep, this discrepancy presumably reflecting the slope locally. The east and west end walls were clearly defined, with five and six post-holes respectively, these being up to 0.46m in diameter and 0.33m deep. At the southern ends of both walls,

and slightly offset to the west, were two post-holes of identical size (0.24m diameter and 0.06m deep); further post-holes were seen in the interior of the structure. Although no long walls could be seen, these may have been laid within shallow beam slots.

To the east of the building lay well F1219, which was probably first dug in the previous phase but continued in use into Phase 6, its fill containing 38 sherds of St Neots and Thetford ware. This was ovoid, 4.00m by 2.50m at the surface, with a bowl-like upper profile above a vertical well shaft c. 0.60m in diameter. Excavation ceased at a depth of 1.50m due to the danger of collapse and the presence of rising water. There were drainage gullies cut tight to each side of it (F1214 and F1216, 0.50m and 0.84m wide, respectively, and up to 0.21m deep), and a short ditch further to the north, F1228, formed the other side of an entranceway opposite the butt ends of these features. All the pottery (which included 32 sherds of Thetford and St Neots ware), and most of the other material, was recovered from the dumped material within the upper 0.50m of the well, the same sealing dump that infilled gully F1216.

Enclosures 13 and 14

The establishment of Enclosures 13 and 14 represented the first major expansion of the settlement southwards beyond the old Romano-British and Mid Saxon settlement boundary, starting a process that was to continue in subsequent phases. Yet the old boundaries were not completely disregarded, and much of the former southern limit became incorporated in the new system. Both areas show a tangle of ditched enclosures and sub-enclosures, with frequent recuts and remodelling (Fig. 3.6). There were no structures, and the whole appears to have represented a series of ditched and banked paddocks or stock enclosures (Paddocks A–H). Individually, none of these were very large, varying in extent between 250 and 550 square metres, and they were possibly attached to the surrounding properties. There were access points from Enclosures 1 and 9 in the north, and from Enclosure 12 in the west, as well as directly from both the south and central trackways. There were also a few small pits and post-holes in the east corner of Enclosure 14. The majority of these were sample-excavated, producing small

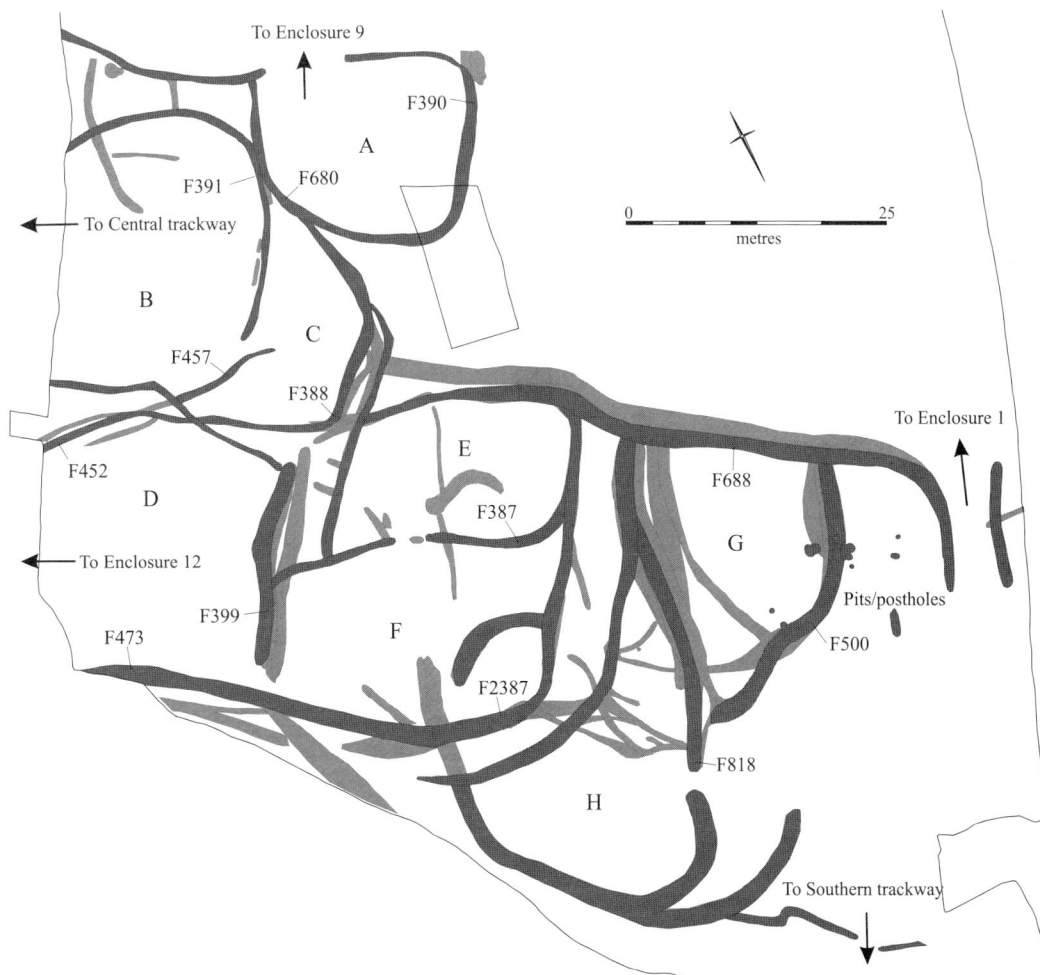

Figure 3.6 Phase 6 paddocks, Enclosure 13/14

contemporary assemblages of Thetford and St Neots wares, bone and burnt clay.

In Paddock A, the south-western boundary feature, F680, was a palisade trench, up to 0.80m wide at the surface but narrowing rapidly with depth to a deep slot 0.25m wide and up to 0.60m deep. The western and eastern arms (F390) were shallow rounded ditches up to 0.80m wide and 0.20m deep. Most of the ditches of Paddock B (F391) were narrow and shallow with bowl-shaped profiles, 0.50–0.75m wide and 0.10–0.35m deep. F457 to the south, which formed one side of an entranceway, was a truncated but square-profiled fence-line trench, 0.35m wide and 0.25m deep. The shallow bowl-profiled ditches of Paddock C, F388, were 0.50–1.00m wide and 0.15–0.40m deep. The eastern side of Paddock D was marked by successive recuts of ditch F399. These were more substantial than the other ditches in the area, being up to 1.90m wide and 0.25–0.45m deep. To the south lay a large boundary ditch, F473, up to 2.50m wide. The ditches at the north of the enclosure (F452) were further shallow bowl-profiled features, 0.40–0.90m wide and 0.15–0.30m deep. The ditches of Paddock E, F387, were 0.50–1.30m wide and 0.12–0.45m deep, and generally had shallow bowl profiles. Only the south-eastern section of boundary of Paddock F was not shared with those described above; these ditches (F2387) were bowl-profiled, 1.00m wide and 0.30–0.45m deep. The back of Paddock G was formed by the main Enclosure 1 ditch F688 (Phase 6, see p.29); the eastern and western sides were both formed by large, recut ditches with steep sides and flat bases (F500), 0.80–1.95m wide and 0.30–0.55m deep. The northern and south-western ditches of Paddock H (F818) were again substantial, though with much rounder profiles, and were 0.80–2.40m wide and 0.30–0.70m deep. Compared with ditches in other enclosures during this period, they tended to produce larger finds assemblages, especially of pottery (up to 125 sherds of St Neots and Thetford ware, in the case of Paddock 9), bone and lava quern.

Roads and access

The east-to-west trackway through the centre of the site continued in use into the Late Saxon period, although with minor alterations. It would have continued to serve its main intra-site function, providing access between the various enclosures. It is assumed that West Fen Road was still the principal east–west communication route serving these. The northern boundary of the settlement was now established along the line of the road in this period with the contraction of the Mid Saxon settlement to the north of the road (Mudd 2000). However, with this expansion to the south, and the construction here of both domestic and non-domestic structures and of large stock enclosures, it must be assumed that by this time there was a secondary east–west access route along the southern boundary of the site. At this stage it is unlikely to have lain as far south as the later Green Field trackway and it may have run within the southern limit of excavation, where it was subsequently covered over as the settlement expanded further south.

IV. Phase 8: Late Saxon II (10th/11th–mid 12th century)
(Figs 3.7–3.10)

Summary

Possibly domestic buildings lay within Enclosures 7 and 9 while non-domestic buildings were tentatively identified in Enclosures 1 and 9, with another possible structure in Enclosure 4. Structures from the previous phase appear to have remained in use in Enclosures 6, 12 and 15.

Enclosure 1

Enclosure 1 was reduced in area, both to the west and south, these boundaries further defined by broad, deep ditches F406/663 and F617 respectively (both up to 1.50m and 0.60m deep). An outer enclosure was created to the south by the cutting of F617, with shallower ditch F520 (1.04m wide, 0.40m deep) redefining the earlier southern boundary immediately inside its line. The north boundary ditch was recut as F269 (with similar dimensions to F520) slightly further to the north and a major east–west internal ditch F304 divided the area into two. Here F304, an earlier near-vertical sided ditch 0.70m wide by 0.50m deep, was recut as a larger U-profiled ditch 1.80m wide and 0.65m deep. There was still access to Enclosures 2 and 14 to the north and south respectively. All of these boundary ditches contained more substantial finds assemblages than those of the previous phase, with greater quantities of Thetford, St Neots and Ely wares, animal bone and lava quern, although the Phase 6

domestic building Structure 8 appears to have gone out of use at some point during this phase.

The north area was further sub-divided into two unequal compounds, connected to each other and to Enclosure 2 by narrow ?gated entrances. The larger, eastern, area contained a probably non-domestic building, Structure 16 (Fig. 3.8a). This was aligned east–west, was of beam-slot construction (these features being 0.30–0.40m wide and 0.10m deep with vertical sides and flat bases) and *c*. 5.5m wide. It extended beyond the edge of excavation but was at least 4m long.

Two narrow parallel north–south ditches, F316 and F435, further subdivided the south part of the enclosure; the earlier buildings hereabouts had gone out of use, with Structure 8 possibly truncated by the new southern boundary and Structure 9 by these internal divisions. In the area to the east of these divisions were a number of narrow beam slots and gullies. They were 0.25–0.60m wide, were aligned both north–south and east–west, and ran broadly, but not exactly, parallel to each other: occasionally they intercut. Whatever activity they represented — and they appear to have had some structural significance — was an ongoing process rather than a single construction episode; they appear to have continued in use, and to have been cut, through into the next phase. They may have been related to the series of short gullies immediately to the west (F423–428) assigned to the previous phase.

The ditched passageway between Enclosures 1 and 14, established in Phase 6, continued in use. The entrance measured 3.5–4m wide and extended *c*. 10m southward into Enclosure 14. Between the entrance ditches lay a whole series of broad, shallow gullies, collectively termed F600, occasionally intercutting or running into each other. Of variable size (0.45–1.10m wide and 0.05–0.30m deep), these had bowl-shaped profiles and uneven bases. Their fills — which were quite different from feature fills seen elsewhere on the site — were heavily mixed and characterised by chalky marl and gravel inclusions, as well as occasional chunks of redeposited natural clay, stones and brick/tile fragments. They are interpreted as wheel ruts, channelling through the ditched entrance, with the chalk, gravel and other material lain as hardcore to firm up the wet clay surface. They could not be traced northward beyond ditch F616, though this may reflect relatively heavy truncation further to the north.

Enclosure 2

There was little change in either the layout or activities in Enclosure 2 although ditches F257, F268 and F309 represented recuttings of the western boundary. These features were of variable dimensions, being 0.80–1.42m wide and 0.40–0.48m deep, with varied finds assemblages. The conjectured Phase 6 building to the east (Fig. 3.3) may have remained in use — the possible building-enclosure gully was recut for a third time (F2301: 0.50m wide and 0.20m deep but producing no finds).

Enclosure 9

A large north–south aligned domestic building, Structure 17 measured *c*. 11m by 4.5m (Fig. 3.8c). The west wall consisted of 26 post-holes (seventeen single, three double and one triple), the south wall of five post-holes, the east wall of three post-trenches (these 0.80m, 4.60m and 1.70m long, with widths of up to 0.37m and depths to 0.38m) and two post-holes. There was no evidence for the north wall, which may have been founded upon a shallow beam-slot, or else have lain beyond the edge of excavation. The building occupied the south-eastern part of the enclosure compound, and was perhaps a replacement for Structure 10 from the previous phase. Just over a third of the way from the north end of the building (at the point where there is a suggestion of opposing doorways), and in exactly the same location as that in Structure 8 in Phase 6, was the base of a possible hearth, *1734*. This was sub-circular, 0.45m in diameter and 0.16m deep, containing a substantial amount of burnt clay and charcoal.

To the south of the larger structure lay a small post-hole building, Structure 18 (Fig. 3.8c). Measuring *c*. 4m by 3m, it may have represented a privy or cookhouse to Structure 17. The fifteen post-holes which made up the exterior walls were 0.15–0.35m in diameter and 0.05–0.15m deep. Three further post-holes, one of them substantial, were excavated in the interior. It is possible that a doorway in the north side of this structure allowed access through another possible doorway in the south wall of Structure 17, with a narrow covered passage in between.

Further ditches were cut along the shared boundary with Enclosure 2, F301 (1.30m wide, 0.46m deep), perhaps simplifying and straightening the boundary (Fig. 3.9). An offshoot from this series of features, F322 (1.65m wide and 0.40m deep), divided the area east of Structure 17. A curving enclosure to the west of the structures, marked by ditched features F643, F644 and F618 (0.35–0.80m wide and 0.09–0.35m deep), contained a relatively high concentration of pits, mostly large, shallow and flat-bottomed. At the eastern butt end of F618 was a short recut length, F622. Though all apparently heavily truncated,

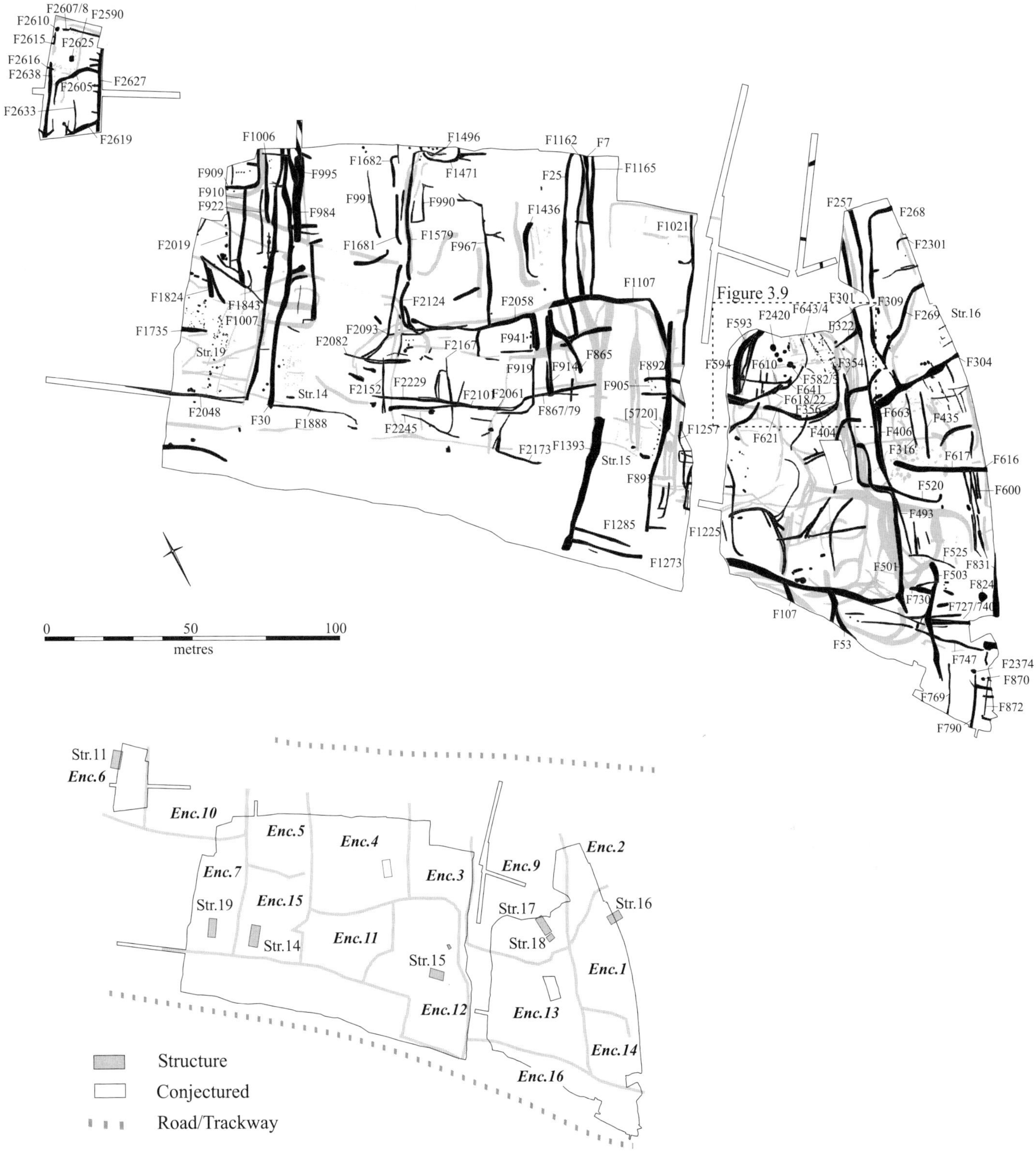

Figure 3.7 Phase 8 overall plan, with Phase 6 features as background and interpretation below

some of the larger pits within the group (F582, F583, F641 and F2420, with lengths of 1.80–2.30m, widths of 0.80–2.00m and depths of 0.12–0.37m) contained relatively small mixed domestic assemblages including Thetford and St Neots pottery, animal bone and lava quern fragments, suggesting they may have been contemporary with the buildings. There were shallow traces of a rectilinear gully or slot system within the south-west part of this area, F610 (0.70m wide and 0.30m deep, with a mixed assemblage including a dog skull).

The southern curve of the main enclosure boundary, echoing that of the inner enclosure, was formed by a series of ditches and fence-lines: a 2m-wide entrance lay between F621 and F404 (1.40m and 0.60m wide,

0.50m and 0.5m deep, respectively), which at some point was blocked by the larger ditch F356 (1.40m wide and 0.35m deep) but was apparently respected subsequently by the north-west terminus of later ?fence-line F595 (represented by a linear feature 0.25m wide and 0.10m deep, with vertical sides and a flat base, which might have held a timber sill or base-plate). To the east, a funnel entrance between ditches F356 and F354 appeared to lead southward from the two structures to Enclosure 13. The western boundary of the enclosure was formed by a series of frequently recut, curving ditches, F593 and F594 (of U-shaped profile, 0.80m and 1.70m wide, 0.48m and 0.55m deep, respectively).

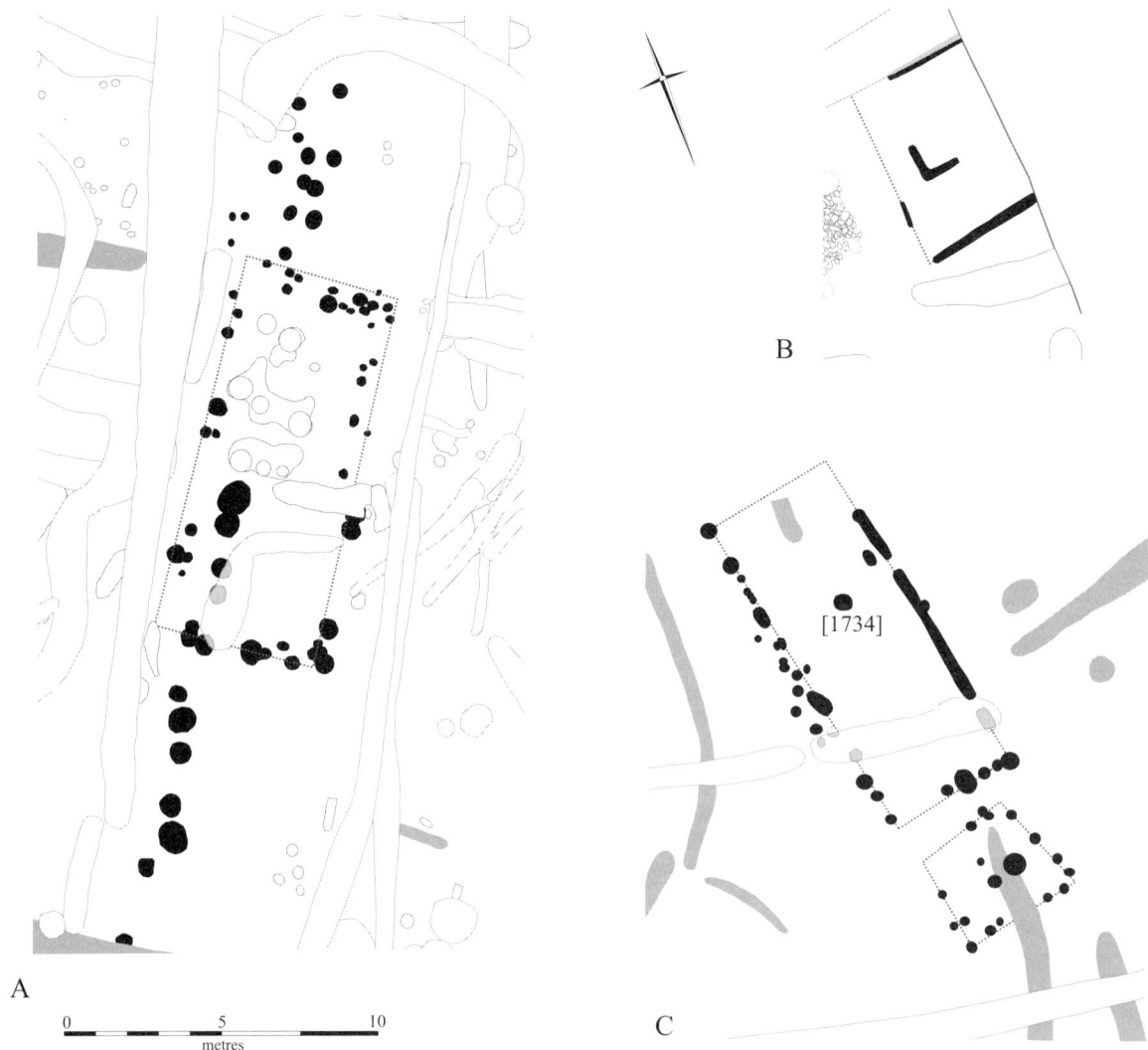

Figure 3.8 (a) Structure 16, (b) Structure 19, (c) Structures 17 and 18

Enclosure 3

Enclosure 3 seems to have been unoccupied in this period, the earlier Structure 4 having gone out of use; its boundaries, while recut, remained unchanged. The east and west boundaries were marked by ditches F1021 and F7/F1165 respectively, the south boundary by ditch F1107. These features were of similar profile and size, being 1.10–1.50m wide and 0.45–0.66m deep, with a varied finds assemblage including Thetford and St Neots pottery. There appears to have been very little change in the layouts of Enclosures 3, 4, 5, 6 and 10, or activities within them, across the entire northern part of the site. Their boundaries shifted only slightly as ditches were recut along broadly the same lines as those already extant. The major difference was seen along their southern sides where the central trackway became redundant, cut across by north–south ditches.

Enclosure 4

Here, too, the enclosure boundaries were recut along pre-existing lines, being represented by F25 and F1162 to the east, F1579 and F2124 to the west and F2058 to the south (these ditches ranging in size from 0.45–1.70m wide and 0.28–0.64m deep), and the enclosure area only expanded southward to take in the trackway area. The south part of the enclosure was divided into equal east and west halves by ditch F967 (0.90m wide and 0.12m deep); in the north-west corner a small ditched pen, F990 (0.60m wide, 0.15m deep), was recorded.

The conjectured building in the south-eastern area of the enclosure may have been modified or re-built, and a new enclosing gully, F1436 (1.90m wide, 0.13m deep), was cut around its west side. In the north-western part, just inside the excavation area, was the rear limit of a small sub-enclosure, F1471 (0.40m wide, 0.20m deep, containing redeposited human bone and a dog burial), within which lay possibly

building-related gullies (F1496; 0.40m wide, 0.20m deep) and post-holes (unexcavated).

Enclosure 5

There was still no clear evidence of residential occupation within Enclosure 5, though again the boundary ditches were recut on broadly the same lines as before. Along the east boundary, shared with Enclosure 4, were narrow recuts F1681 and F1682; to the west were the far larger ditches F995 and F984. The latter was part of a major ditched feature, possibly a hedgebank, that now crossed the site from south to north. A thin north–south ditch, F991, defined a narrow sub-enclosure, 8m wide, parallel to the eastern boundary.

Enclosure 10

Little was seen of Enclosure 10 except its south-east corner, and here again the boundary ditch was recut (F909, 1.20m wide and 0.45m deep).

Enclosure 6

Structure 11 and its adjacent yard appear to have continued in use into this phase. There were indications of alteration or repair to the interior of the building, with two beam-slots, F2615 and F2616 (up to 0.45m and 0.15m deep), running westwards beyond the edge of excavation. Two large and shallow pits, F2610 and F2625 (the former 1.60m in diameter, the latter 2.00m by 1.50m), representing the beginnings of a sequence that was to extend through the succeeding two phases, were cut along the edges of the fenced yard. The enclosure's northern boundary ditch was recut as ditch F2590 (0.65m wide and 0.45m deep). The entrance created at the west was then cut across by gullies F2607 and F2608 (up to 0.40m wide and 0.10m deep).

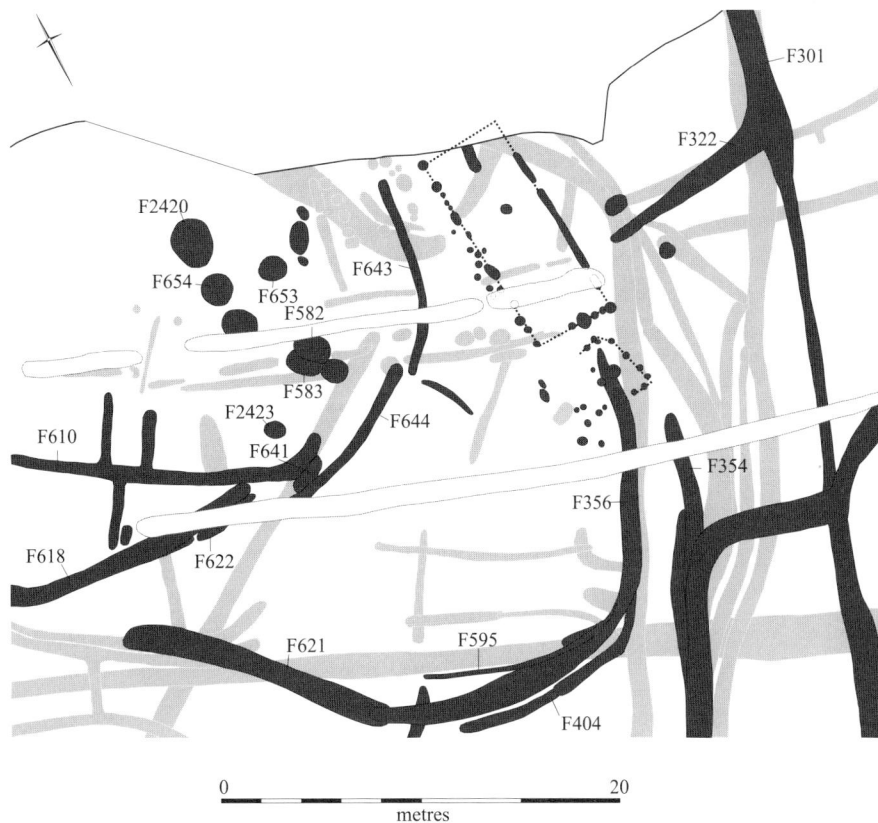

Figure 3.9 Detailed plan of Phase 8 features within Enclosure 9

The main eastern boundary ditch was recut as F2627 (2.00m wide and 0.55m deep); a parallel, broad but very shallow ditch, F2638 (0.90m and 0.06m deep), was excavated very close to the back of the structure, while the rear of the yard was further defined by curving ditch F2605 (1.35m and 0.50m deep). The area enclosed to the south of this ditch was bounded by F2619 (1.35m and 0.41m deep) at the south and a small north–south ditch F2633 (0.50m and 0.27m deep) divided this area into two.

Enclosure 7

Enclosure 7 was divided into two by a major north–south double ditch, probably representing a hedge-line, creating the smaller Enclosure 15 to the east. The two earlier post-trench buildings were replaced by a single building of post-hole construction, Structure 19 (Fig. 3.8a), measuring c. 12m by 5m. The building had been superimposed upon both its predecessors and straddled the gap between them. It was aligned north-east–south-west and appeared to have been composed of two cells, slightly offset from each other; each of these consisted of 26 circular post-holes and measured 6m long. The southern cell was represented by much larger post-holes than that to the north (up to 0.80m in diameter and 0.60m deep) and contained considerably more finds (27 sherds of mainly Later Saxon pottery, predominantly Thetford ware, as against the single Thetford and St Neots sherds and single fragment of burnt clay from the northern cell). The pottery assemblage is consistent with the building's disuse in the early 12th century. Later truncation made it hard to discern the possible locations of any doorways. There were further groups of post-holes both to the north-west and south-west of the building; the former group may have represented part of a subsidiary structure or structures (there were also many unexcavated post-holes immediately to the west), the latter perhaps a fence-line.

The building lay square in the south-east corner of the enclosure, adjacent to the major double hedge-line ditch F1007 (1.40m wide, 0.50m deep) to the east, and with narrower ditch F2048 (0.70m wide and 0.25m deep) lying to the south. An east–west ditch immediately to the west corresponding with the northern end of the building (F1735; 0.90m wide and 0.15m deep) might have demarcated a second structure or structures to the north; other adjacent post-holes might have represented traces of its eastern end. This area, however, was too badly truncated by later features for any certainty about this.

The enclosure was divided into roughly equal halves by angled ditches F1843 (0.45m wide and 0.17m deep) and F1824 (consisting of three recuts, each 0.85–1.00m wide and up to 0.38m deep); the building(s) in the south and the northern part were further separated by parallel north–south ditches F910/F1006 (up to 1.75m wide and 0.45m deep) and F922/F2019 (up to 0.70m wide and 0.15m deep). The two ditch pairs contrasted in both form and alignment and almost certainly represent separate phases of development within the span of Phase 8, with the former, larger, ditches being the earlier.

Enclosure 15

The eastern part of the Phase 6 Enclosure 7 was cut off by the large north–south hedge-line (at this point F30, but continuing northwards as the west boundary of Enclosure 5 as F984) and is renumbered here as Enclosure 15. It is thought that the non-domestic Structure 14 may have continued in use, given the absence of any features cutting across the centre of the enclosure, but there was little other evidence of activity. The south boundary was a continuation of that of Enclosure 7, F1888, and may have marked the northern side of an east–west trackway. The east boundary appeared more confused and was formed by a series of narrow ditches, F2093, F2082 and F2152. A rectangular sub-enclosure was formed by a large unexcavated ditch, up to 2.00m wide, to the north of the building.

Enclosure 11

Enclosure 11 was reduced to the east by the expansion of Enclosure 12 and remained unoccupied, although further internal alterations to the paddock layout confirmed that it remained in use. The west and north boundaries were shared with Enclosures 15 and 4, while the east boundary was another substantial, although shorter, double-ditched hedgebank; the ditch fill displayed evidence for slumping from the bank. This latter feature was represented by ditches F941(1.50m wide and 0.40m deep) and F919 (0.60m wide and 0.20m deep). The south boundary was more complex, with two phases of ditching. The first of these saw ditches F2245 and F2167 (up to 0.50m wide and 0.25m deep) forming shallow-ditched paddocks; these were then cut across by slightly larger ditches F2101, 2229 and 2061 (up to 0.78m wide and 0.35m deep), clearly representing a straightening of this southern boundary. These ditches contained noticeably fewer finds than those surrounding the enclosures featuring domestic occupation. A small sub-enclosure in the north-east was formed by three short, unexcavated ditches.

Enclosure 12

Enclosure 12 expanded both west and south, while the north and east boundaries (as far as could be seen, to the east) remained largely unchanged, though with alterations and some evidence of recutting. The main west boundary was the wide hedge-line separating it from Enclosure 11, F914 (1.00m wide and 0.70m deep); a new curvilinear enclosure was formed to the south of this by ditches F867/879 and F2173 (up to 0.80m wide and 0.21m deep). Two large north–south ditches, F1393 (with many recuts, 0.64–1.60m wide and 0.50–0.90m deep) and F891 (1.30–2.90m wide and 0.40–0.60m deep) divided the remainder of the enclosure into two narrow strips. The more westerly of these was fairly empty, though probably still containing Structure 15; the eastern displayed recuts of earlier gullies and ditches around the (by now defunct) well. Close to the edge of excavation further steep-sided ditches, F1225 (0.55m wide and 0.29m deep) and F1257 (1.00m wide and 0.50m deep) represented other, undefined, enclosures. The south limit of the main enclosure was marked by another double-ditched hedgebank, F1273/1285; this was up to 1.25m wide and 0.30m deep, with a later, larger recut.

In the north-west part of the enclosure a number of small 'paddocks' were divided by broad ditches, such as F865 (1.00m wide and 0.50m deep); to the north of Structure 15 a small possible four-post structure, F905, was set between a pair of parallel ditches F892. The conjectured structure produced no finds, and is assigned to this phase simply on account of its spatial relationship with the surrounding ditches, but might belong to any phase from the Iron Age onwards. The two parallel ditches each contained a handful of Thetford ware sherds. A line of seven post-holes *5720* lay immediately to the east of Structure 15 and curved slightly to follow the line of ditch F891; they produced a total of fourteen Thetford and St Neots ware sherds. Five of these post-holes were large (*c.*

0.30m in diameter); there were smaller examples (*c.* 0.15m diameter) at either end.

Enclosure 13

The paddock system within Enclosure 13 saw further additions, recuts and realignments (labelled here I to P), and it is hard to discern where access points to the individual paddocks may have lain (Fig. 3.10). The boundary between Enclosures 13 and 14 had been straightened and become part of the main north–south boundary defining the western edge of Enclosures 1 and 2. Enclosure 14 was no longer a part of the paddock system. Clearly many of the earlier ditches, or their banks and hedges/fences, would have been retained.

Paddock I (F682/361) shared its north-eastern boundary with Enclosure 9, its eastern with Paddock M (F685) and its north-western with Paddock J. Ditches F682/361 to the south had been recut to maximum dimensions of 1.00m wide and 0.40m deep, and had U-shaped profiles. The central core of Paddock J was retained, and extensions to the south and east were defined by ditches F446 (up to 0.60m wide and 0.20m deep, with bowl-shaped profile) and F613 (a possible fence-line post-trench, up to 0.80m wide and 0.30m deep, with a vertical east side, stepped west side and flat base). The northern boundary was recut as F662 (1.10m wide and 0.45m deep, with steep sides and a stepped base) and the western as F470 (0.76m wide and 0.27m deep, with near-vertical sides and a flat base). The northern and eastern sides of Paddock K had been recut (at least three times) as one continuous boundary, F447; the ditches were 0.45–1.00m wide and 0.15–0.28m deep, with bowl-shaped profiles. At the western boundary, ditch F465 (a continuation of F470 from Paddock J) was up to 1.00m wide and 0.24m deep. The south boundary was retained. Paddock L shared its western boundaries with Paddocks J and K, while its southern boundary was rectilinear ditch F395 (width 0.70m and depth 0.35m). The eastern boundary of Paddock M recut curving ditches F648 (up to 1.45m and 0.65m deep); the northern was shared with Paddock I and recut as F678 (up to 0.70m and 0.42m

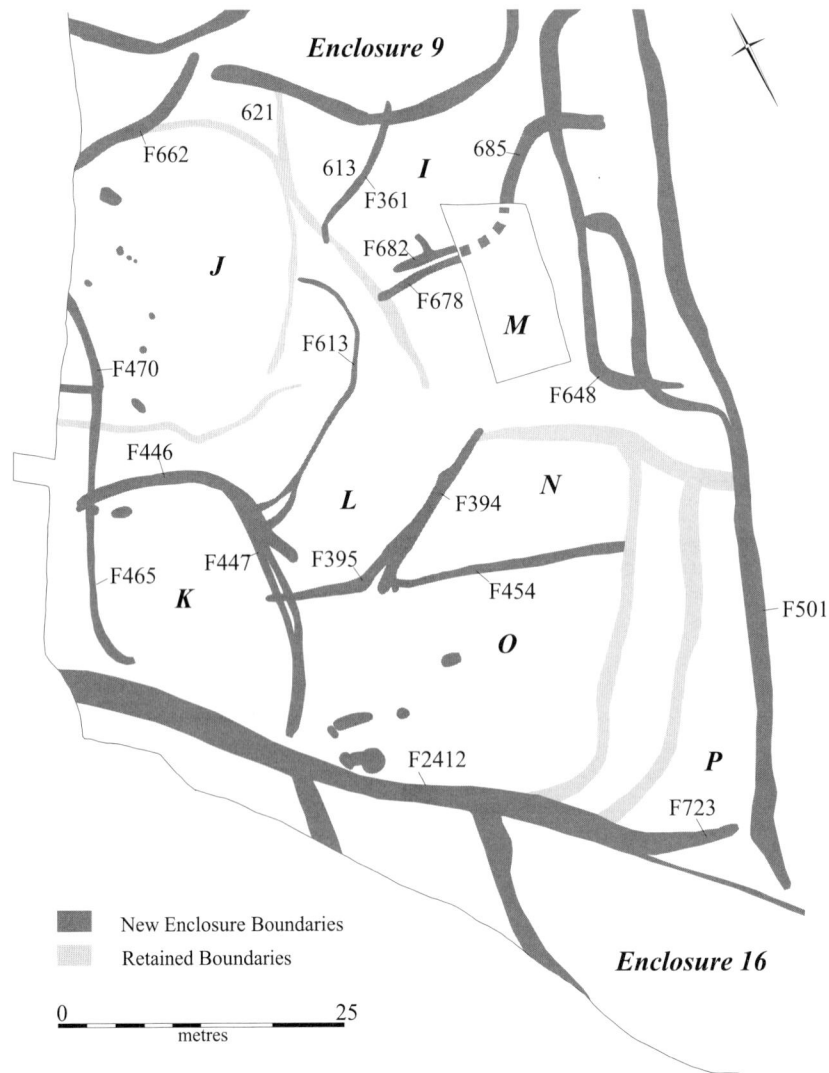

Figure 3.10 Phase 8 paddocks, Enclosure 13/14

deep, U-shaped profile). The western boundary of Paddock N was shared with Paddock L and recut as F394 (width 0.80m and depth 0.30m, U-shaped profile). The eastern boundary of Paddock O was retained, the western boundary shared with Paddock K, and the northern partly shared with Paddock L and partly recut as F454 (0.60m wide and 0.30m deep, U-shaped profile). The south boundary was retained and recut as F2412 (1.20m wide and 0.40m deep, V-shaped profile with narrow rounded base). Paddock P was defined to south and west by ditches F501 and 723, the latter (up to 1.40m wide and 0.40m deep, with a steep eastern side and a more gradual western one) representing a new, roughly straight eastern boundary. Short ditch length F723 (up to 0.93m and 0.40m deep) formed a part of the southern perimeter.

The narrow Paddock P, all that remains of the larger Paddock H in Phase 6, was apparently still used for middening. The finds assemblage — particularly that of the pottery — from the uppermost ditch fills was very large. Altogether 50% of the sherds from the paddocks in this phase (108 of Thetford ware, 106 St Neots ware and 5 Ely ware, with some residual material) derived from the two ditches of Paddock P. A few pits and post-holes were recorded in Enclosure 13, along the west sides of Paddocks J and K and in the south part of Paddock O. Only those in Paddock O produced a (collective) finds assemblage of any significance, and this reflected only their relative size — it seems unlikely that any of the pits had been dug primarily for rubbish disposal.

It seems clear that domestic waste was not being disposed of within pits but on middens during this phase, with the remains of one such midden evidenced in the southern corner of Enclosure 13. The dumped material collected was mostly pottery (234 sherds, mainly Thetford and St Neots wares) and animal bone; the assemblage was very similar in make-up to the general debris which lay within the areas of the domestic structures, except, noticeably, for a complete lack of lava quern or other worked stone within the midden.

Enclosure 14
Enclosure 14, removed from the paddock system, contracted correspondingly to the west with the expansion of Enclosure 13. It appeared now to be 'dead ground' that saw little activity. A large boundary ditch to the east, F831 (2.30m wide and 0.38m deep), ran parallel to the west boundary, F501, which was shared with Enclosure 13. The south boundary of the enclosure appeared to follow the line of flat-based ditches F727/740 (up to 0.80m wide and 0.35m deep), which ran at 90° to them. A third large ditch, F503 (1.95m wide and 0.42m deep), again roughly parallel to F501, extended southwards into Enclosure 16 and formed the east side of two small, square enclosures that were separated from each other by ditch F730 (up to 0.70m wide and 0.20m deep). A larger, rectangular enclosure further to the north was formed by ditches F493 and F525 (up to 0.85m wide and 0.45m deep).

In the south-east corner of the enclosure was a well c. 3m in diameter and 1.2m deep (F824 — see Phase 9). The infilling of the well may date to Phase 10, but its first use might have occurred in the latter part of Phase 8. Two pits, F2355 and F2366, lay to the west of the well. They were both 4.00m long and 1.00m wide, and up to 0.20m deep; few finds were recovered, although there were three Thetford ware sherds and one of St Neots ware.

Enclosure 16
Enclosure 16 represented further southward expansion of the Anglo-Saxon settlement. A right-angled gully, F872 (1.10m wide and 0.50m deep), aligned north-east–south-west, may have represented a building enclosure or drip gully, although no structural elements were seen and there were very few finds. Two parallel ditches, F790 and F769, ran to the west of this feature. The northern boundary of the enclosure lay along ditch F747 (0.60m wide by 0.25m deep), with the west limit perhaps marked by ditch F53 or F107. Two small pits, F870 (circular, 0.60m diameter and 0.20m deep) and F2374 (oval, 1.60m by 0.90m, 0.25m deep) lay just outside the possible building gully.

V. Phase 9: 12th century
(Figs 3.11–3.15)

Summary
Four domestic or possibly domestic buildings lay within Enclosures 11, 12, 16 and 18, along with three probably non-domestic buildings in Enclosures 1, 5 and 11. Other structures are conjectured in Enclosures 4 and 7. The areas that saw direct occupation, be it domestic or 'industrial', were now fewer and better defined than they had been in the Saxo-Norman period. The intensity of occupation began to wane, and this process accelerated in Phases 10 and 11. In the east, only Enclosures 1 and 16 now showed any domestic occupation. While in Enclosure 1 the occupation was in decline, in Enclosure 16 it was expanding and becoming increasingly well defined.

Enclosure 1
The enclosure had contracted from its dimensions in the previous phase, and now sat within tight and deeply ditched boundaries, which produced relatively large finds assemblages (like some of the boundary ditches of Phase 8). The south boundary was formed by F416, a series of recut straight ditches up to 1.36m wide and 0.47m deep, while the north and west boundaries, F296 and F376 (up to 2.00m wide and 0.57m deep) broadly mirrored the earlier limits of the enclosure, with F296 cut slightly to the north. Internally, the broad but shallower ditch F2322 separated a small northern and larger compound, while an entrance at the west provided access into both parts of the enclosure.

The enclosure contained Structure 20, a building lying in the northern part of the compound opposite the gap in the ditched division (Fig. 3.12a). This was aligned north–south and was of post-hole and beam-slot construction, measuring 5.50m by 3.5m. The west wall consisted of nine post-holes and a beam-slot (up to 0.60m wide and 0.80m deep); the east wall was represented by just a single post-hole and by two narrower and shallower beam-slots, while the north and south walls were represented by a single beam-slot and post-hole respectively. The southern part of the building, an area of c. 3.50m by 3.50m, was roughly cobbled, these cobbles running up to, and in parts over, the post-trenches at the sides. The northern edge of the building coincided exactly with the edge of ditch F296. A further post alignment ran roughly parallel to the building to the west, possibly indicating a fence-line or lean-to extension. While relatively large quantities of pottery were recovered from surrounding contemporary features, the building may have been too small to represent a domestic structure.

Around this structure, small-scale pitting continued. Several of the pits contained relatively large domestic assemblages. A small but deep pit (less than 0.85m across but 0.50m deep) immediately to the west of Structure 20 (F2328) — with distinctive vertical sides, and clearly not excavated as a rubbish pit — contained a transitional pottery assemblage consisting of 89 sherds of Thetford ware, 23 of Ely ware and two of St Neots ware, and a single Stamford sherd. To the east and south-east respectively were two large, elongated pits (F324, F344). Both were aligned north–south, lay parallel to each other 12m apart, and measured 3.50m long by 1.00m wide with near-vertical sides. Both contained relatively large finds assemblages, principally pottery (altogether 174 sherds of Thetford, St Neots and Ely wares), and both had been cut into an earlier, infilled ditch. It is possible that these were cess pits. For such a feature to function efficiently, liquid cess has to be able to filter into the surrounding subsoil, leaving a relatively dry material that can break down and be reused. The positioning of these pits over earlier ditches may thus represent an attempt to utilise the relative free-draining quality of the ditch fills compared with the surrounding natural clay.

The system of narrow gullies in the southern part of the area persisted from previous phases although it is possible that, as with many features in Phase 9, they had simply gone out of use and were being backfilled at this time. Thetford ware was the earliest pottery from them, and there was no residual material. An entire articulated cow skeleton had been forced into one of these narrow gullies, F563 (0.35m wide, 0.14m deep), at the southern limit of the area. While this could have been a deliberate 'closing' deposit (see above, pit F578 in Phase 6), more straightforwardly it could represent waste disposal in the context of the area's abandonment.

Enclosure 2
Only the much reduced south-west corner of this enclosure remained extant, with east–west ditches F258/259 and north–south ditch F260 cut in this period. These were up to 1.40m wide and 0.70m deep. The rest of the area to the south and west, like that immediately south and east of Enclosure 1, was given over to open fields and/or ridge and furrow cultivation (Enclosure 17).

While it is suggested that this major contraction indicates a northward shift of occupation towards the frontage of West Fen Road, there was little evidence from most areas along this northern edge of the site to indicate the duration of any direct occupation, or what other activities may have taken place. That said, a small Phase 10 pit group cut into the corner of the enclosure does suggest occupation at least until this later period.

Figure 3.11 Phase 9 overall plan, with Phase 8 features as background and interpretation below

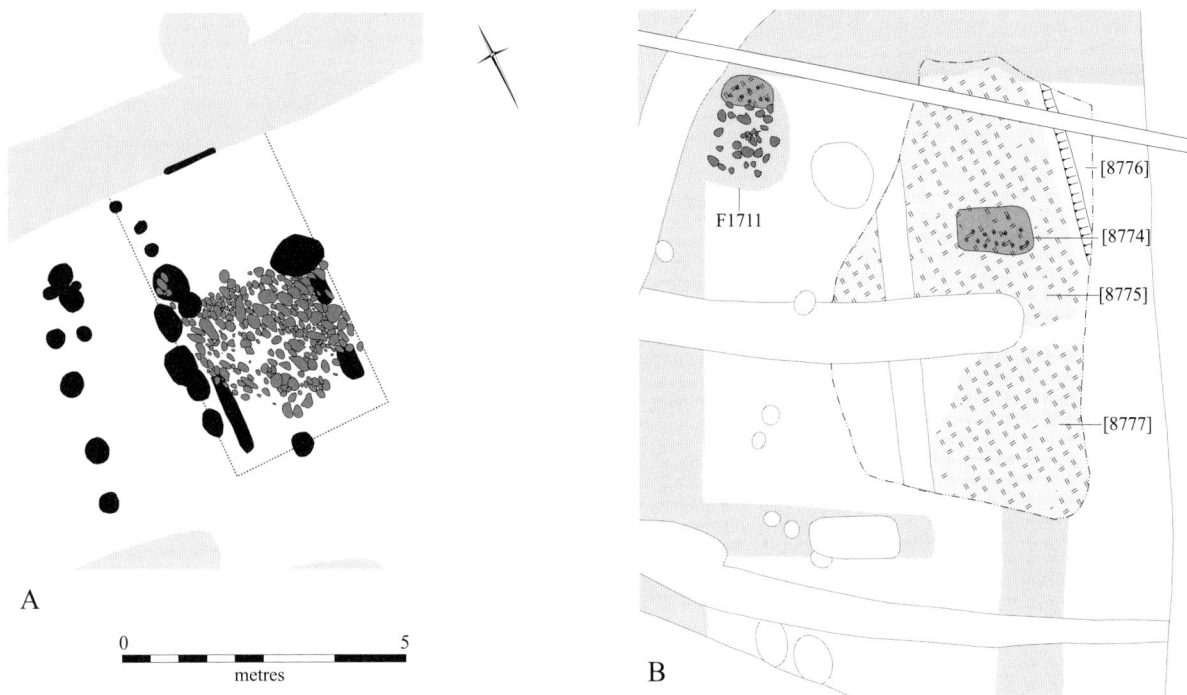

A

0   5

metres

[8776]

F1711

[8774]

[8775]

[8777]

B

Figure 3.12 (a) Structure 20, (b) Structure 22

Enclosure 9

Enclosure 9 retained its approximate west and east boundaries. The west side was comprised of ditches F1180 (1.10m wide and 0.56m deep, with an assemblage of 78 sherds of pottery dominated by Ely ware) and F1220 (0.50m wide and 0.14m deep), with the east boundary represented by ditch F1041 (1.45m wide and 0.50m deep). The enclosed area, however, expanded to the south and was now maked by ditch F1312 (0.60m wide and 0.58m deep), thereby absorbing much of the previous Enclosure 12. Between these boundaries a series of regular sub-square fields, some 20–25m square, were laid out (F1078, F1051, F1092–4, F2579 and F2281). Of varying widths up to 1.96m and up to 0.57m deep, these contained smaller finds assemblages, including Thetford and Ely wares, than the boundary ditches. These small fields or paddocks appear to have been linked by a broad trackway running up their western side, formed by ditches F1180/1220 and F1115 (see Enclosure 11).

Enclosure 4

There were minor alterations to the east boundary of this enclosure, which contracted westward, with F1119/F1124 forming the north-west end to the north–south trackway. The south boundary was 'squared up' by ditches F944 and F2049, these possibly superseded by ditch F912. All of these ditches were of comparable size, with widths of 0.50–1.10m and depths of 0.20–0.81m. Comparatively small finds assemblages support the argument that this area was not in domestic occupation. The west boundary probably now extended as far as the line of ditch F1012. This ditch obviously marked an important boundary, as it was constantly cleaned out along this line at least until the 16th century. This constant process of redefinition eventually generated an archaeological feature that resembled one large ditch, whereas in reality it represented a whole series of smaller ditched boundaries that shifted laterally over time. This constant reworking makes it difficult to date its initial establishment. While other ditches ran up to it from Phase 6 onwards, the small assemblages of Thetford and Ely wares suggested that it was probably not established as a continuous north–south division until Phase 9.

The north part of the enclosure appears to have been unoccupied during this period, although to the south the inferred non-domestic structure from Phase 8 may still have been extant, given that drains and ditches from this phase (F944 and F1478) still appeared to respect its space. Compounds were established in the south and west parts of Enclosure 4: ditches F26, F987/988 and F999 (all with widths to 1.60m and depths to 0.55m) and smaller features F1637 and F2510 (widths to 0.70m, depths to 0.30m) representing a series of internal subdivisions, possibly indicating animal paddocks.

Enclosure 5

This enclosure extended southwards as far as wide, shallow ditch F1970 (1.26m wide and 0.09m deep) with the west boundary demarcated by ditch F925 (0.75m wide and 0.10m deep). It is assumed that its east boundary lay along the line of F1012, while its north boundary remained unseen.

The enclosure was now occupied by a building situated within its south-west corner, Structure 21. The building was indicated by a series of metalled gravel surfaces covering a surface area of approximately 6.50m by 8m aligned north-west–south-east. No wall footings survived, although the presence of a roof was suggested by steep-sided drainage gullies along the south, west and north-east sides, F925, F1970 and F1785 (0.40m by 0.20m deep).

Immediately to the north of the structure a series of rectilinear gullies divided the enclosure into smaller compounds or paddocks (F1706, F1754, F1845 and F1873; widths to 0.58m, depths to 0.34m); these may indicate small horticultural plots lying around and close to the building. Two steep-sided pits lay at the junctions of these slight gullies (F1705 — oval, 1.10m wide, 0.48m deep — and F1900 — sub-circular, 2.00m diameter, 0.30m deep); their location suggested deliberate placement, possibly to act as small catch-waters. Further, shallower pits containing small finds assemblages were dug to the north; these possible quarry pits are discussed below.

Enclosure 10

The possible structure within this enclosure was abandoned prior to this phase; the east enclosure boundary was probably shared with Enclosure 5 along ditch F925. A large pond was seen in the assessment trench at the north-west of the enclosure but remained unexcavated.

Enclosure 6

Occupation of Enclosure 6 is surmised partly from the fact that a building was present within this enclosure through Phases 5–8 and partly because pitting occurred here throughout this and the subsequent phase, the pits forming a line along the western side of the fenced yard to the side of Structure 11 (F2696, F2601, F2602, F2612, F2623). These were mainly oval in shape and were substantial, ranging from 1.60m by 0.40m to 2.70m by 1.90m in plan. All were 0.20–0.53m deep, though generally they contained quite small finds assemblages (from five to twelve sherds of pottery, along with some bone, burnt clay and lava quern). Three further pits of similar dimensions (F2600, F2611, F2641) lay alongside this main group. Since pitting within the site is generally found in the immediate vicinity of a domestic building then a structural presence is assumed, probably somewhere to the north. From Phase 9 onward,

41

domestic structures appear to have shifted toward to the periphery of the settlement area, both southward (to lie along the trackway) and, presumably, northward towards West Fen Road.

Several small gullies (F2587, F2589, F2595, F2604; widths 0.40–1.00m, depths 0.18–0.50m) also attest to occupation of this enclosure, although a function other than localised drainage is difficult to ascertain.

Enclosure 7

A good deal of activity continued within Enclosure 7, indicating that this was still directly occupied. While little evidence for any structure was seen it is possible that a building occupied a similar area to Structures 12/13 and 19 from previous phases. This was suggested by the layout of ditches around an area that seemed generally 'blank' in this phase, and by the cutting of a semi-circular drainage gully that was infilled in the subsequent phase. If this was not the case then any domestic building must have shifted west, beyond the edge of excavation. Whatever the truth, the layout remains unclear. The area saw slight expansion to the south as far as ditch F1667 (1.50m wide, 0.75m deep), and some reorganisation of the east boundary around the new building in Enclosure 5. Ditch F1981 (2.30m wide, 0.46m deep) suggested that the enclosure was divided into north and south areas, the north area containing two large tank-like pits with steep sides and flat bases, F1611 and F1726 (the former 2.50m wide and 0.42m deep, the latter 5.00m wide and 0.15m deep), possibly suggesting a specialised working area away from the main domestic structure. While rather similar to the straight-sided, flat-bottomed pits mentioned above, these features were far larger. A smaller pit of vertical-sided/flat-based type, F1769 (2.20m wide, 0.15m deep), lay within this north compound, while an unexcavated pit to the east of this might have represented another. Other pits were scattered throughout the enclosure (F1632, F1714, F1818 and F1983). Although circular in shape with rounded profiles, and 1.00–2.20m wide by 0.28–0.45m deep, these probably had different functions, possibly as cess or rubbish pits. All of the above pits produced small finds assemblages (with three to seventeen sherds of pottery and between five and nineteen fragments of animal bone; three pits also contained burnt clay fragments, two had iron nails and one had a lead fragment).

Ditches F1850 and F1891 recut the south end of the large north–south hedgebank from the previous phase, most of which had been levelled and incorporated into Enclosure 5. This hedgebank had been a major new boundary during Phase 8 and was now completely superseded, the boundary being moved c. 15m to the east to ditch F1012. Curving ditches F1787 and F1938 may have been part of a paddock or stock enclosure system lying beyond the limit of excavation to the west, while other ditches within the compound were redefinitions of existing boundaries or interpreted as localised drainage features (F1659, F1699, F2018, F1985 and F1986). The majority of these were relatively narrow and shallow, less than 0.80m wide and 0.30m deep.

Enclosure 11

It is assumed that F1012 now formed the west boundary of this land unit, thus indicating that there had been some expansion on its west side. There was also further expansion to the east, which was now marked by ditch F1115 (up to 2.40m wide and 0.30m deep) and a straightening of the north and south boundaries of the enclosure.

Structure 22 (Fig. 3.12b) occupied the north-west corner of the enclosure, and probably owed its survival to two factors. First, the constant reworking of F1012 into the modern period would have created upcast, possibly burying the structure with a protective depth of soil; second, it lay under a ridge within the later ridge and furrow system. Despite this, it was still very truncated and therefore the dimensions of the building have to remain speculative. The surviving clay floor(s) *8775/8777* covered a maximum area of 8.00m x 4.50m; their yellow/brown clay was up to 0.15m thick. A truncated beam slot at the east of the floor suggested that the building was aligned approximately north-east–south-west; the east side of the slot impression *8776* had been cut away, while its surviving extent was vertically-sided, flat-based and 0.20m deep. The absence of post-holes around the floor indicated the building was founded on base beams and/or raised sills. Scorching over a slight ash filled depression within the floor *8774* suggested a hearth or brazier position, with some disturbed Ely (?hearth) tile lying in a make-up deposit to the south perhaps confirming this.

The remains of a clay floor and evidence for a hearth might suggest this was a domestic structure. The pottery from the associated enclosure indicated that the building and enclosure were in use by Phase 10, although the initial construction phase of the building more probably belongs to Phase 9. Associated with, or even originally part of, Structure 22, a small oval clay-and-cobble-based oven F1711 was located to the west of the building. All that survived of this oven/furnace structure was the burnt base and the remains of some roof/?sidewall collapse. The

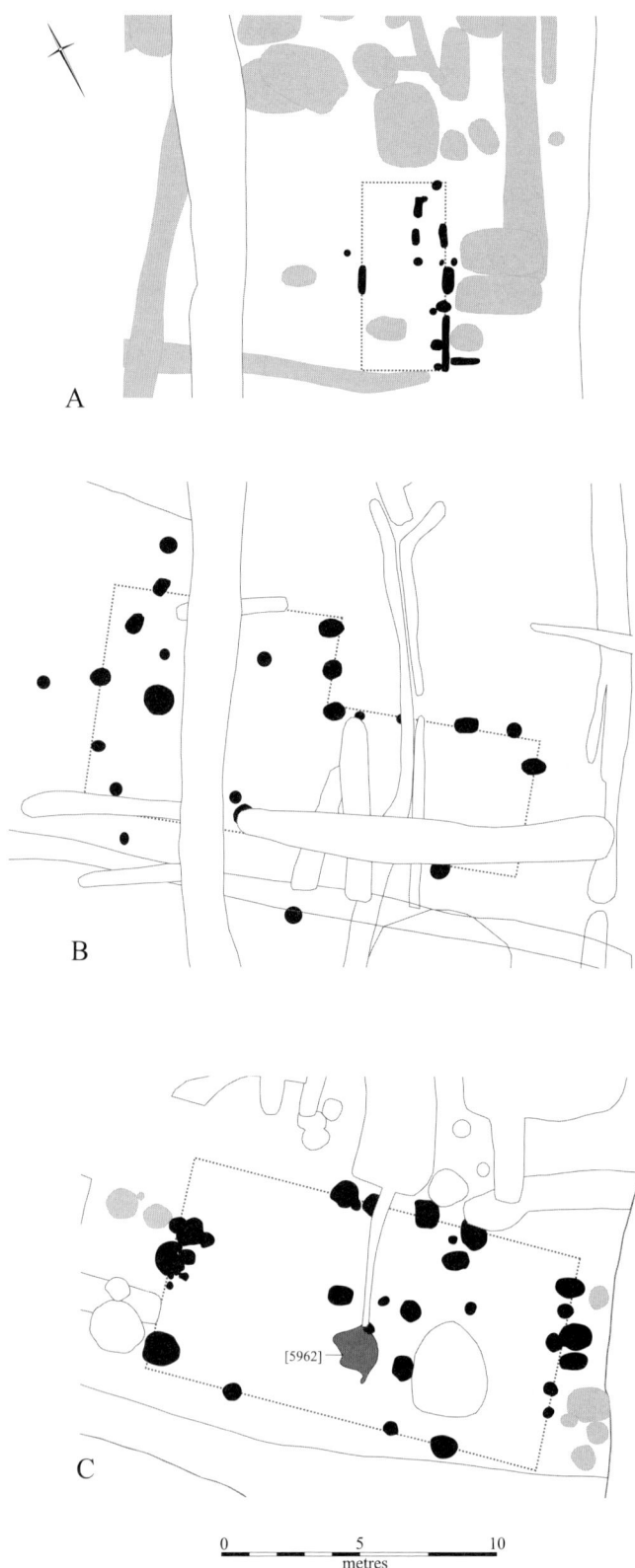

A

B

C

0		5		10

metres

Figure 3.13 (a) Structure 23, (b) Structure 24, (c) Structure 25

collapse deposit consisted of a mixed deposit of burnt orange/red clay, while the base was constructed of flint and sandstone nodules (maximum size 0.15m x 0.12m) set in yellow clay, this forming an oval measuring 2.00m x 1.50m.

The remains of a second small building, Structure 23 (Fig. 3.13a), were set in the southern corner of a small enclosure marked by ditches F2113, F2185 and F2252. Aligned north-east–south-west and measuring *c.* 6.50m by 3.00m in plan, its east side was formed by an alignment of eleven posts and four timber slots; another row of four posts lay to the west of this, while several other posts and slots lay within the immediate vicinity and may have been related. The post-holes were circular or oval and 0.20–0.35m wide, while the slots were 0.85–2.00m long and 0.25–0.35m wide. Given its small size and irregular post-hole alignment, it is possible that this represented some temporary structure, or perhaps racks of some kind. A large group of pits (F2114, F2115, F2142, F2145, F2230, F2236, F2265, 2268, F2272, F2549) were located around this structure and may have been associated with it. As seen with the groups in Enclosure 6 and in Enclosure 7 most of the pits were a distinctive oval or elongated shape with steep sides and generally flat bases, with dimensions ranging in plan from 1.20m by 1.10m to 4.00m by 1.15m. Depths ranged from 0.10–0.75m and finds generally consisted of small amounts of bone and pottery.

The eastern area of Enclosure 11 again appears to have been unoccupied, although not unused, in this phase. Ditches F2084, F2185, F2076, F2077 and F2117 (with widths of 0.45–1.20m and depths of 0.17–0.40m) outlined two similar-sized rectangular paddocks, with a larger space lying to the east. The right-angled form of ditch F294, mirroring that of the south enclosure boundary, forms a wide entrance with openings to north and west. It is possible that this area was used as some kind of shared or common space, with access both from the occupied compound to the west and from Enclosure 12 to the south.

Enclosure 18

The area encompassed by Enclosure 18 previously lay outside of the settled area, and represented the final expansion southwards from the settlement beyond the old Roman/Saxon boundary. The south boundary of the enclosure and the settlement was now demarcated by the trackway that runs along the south side of the settlement (*i.e.* 'Fieldside').

This metalled trackway F2558 lay immediately to the south of the present field boundary and stream. The trackway itself consisted of a rough gravel surface running the whole length of the field from east to west. The metalling and materials used (mostly coarse gravel and flint nodules) suggested that the surface was never substantial even in its original form, although severe rutting indicates it had been much used. In no excavated area was the coarse gravel that comprised the surface more than 0.24m thick, while the maximum exposed width was 1.80m. The surface may have originally been wider, its northern extent cut away by the periodic recutting of the present ditch or the scouring of the adjacent stream. No subsoil was noted under the gravel surface, which was lain directly onto natural clay; this indicated that any subsoil had been removed or excavated during construction, creating in effect a slightly sunken or hollow way. Within the bounds of the gravel surface a series of intercutting wheel rut impressions were seen in the natural clay, the ruts running the whole length of the surviving surface. The depth and frequency of the wheel ruts, some of them penetrating the natural clay by as much as 0.35m, suggested very heavy going for traffic at times when the soil was wet.

The course of the stream and its relationship to the trackway deserve a mention here. There was no reason to believe that the present course of the stream was not its original one, as there was no indication of a relic channel to the north or south. The flow of the stream was very gradual, and today it is no more than a trickle in summer. The creation of a low-lying or sunken trackway would have acted to channel the natural stream water and that of the surrounding higher ground, particularly in wet weather. It may then have been necessary to create a ditch immediately to the north of the track to drain excess water from its surface. This sequence of events, however, remains speculative given the modern recutting of the stream course.

To the north of the trackway, Enclosure 18 was occupied by Structure 24. At least 23 post-holes lay within an area some 16m by 8m. This had been cut away by later features, and badly rutted by contractors' machines prior to stripping, so it is likely that other post-holes had been lost, and the form of the building is thus unclear: the projected building shape shown on Figure 3.13b is only one possible interpretation. The lack of domestic material from the area of the building suggested that it was non-domestic, and perhaps a barn or cowshed. If the area is regarded as being related to livestock during this period, other features within the enclosure can possibly be explained. Pool or pond F2530 (7.00m wide and 4.50m deep, excavated to a depth of 0.40m), with overflow ditch F1644 (up to 2.50m wide and 0.48m deep), might be seen as a watering

hole, while rectangular enclosures created by ditches F2200 (2.30m wide and 0.21m deep), F2249 (0.85m wide and 0.37m) and F2549 (0.50m wide and 0.30m) could have been stock enclosures.

Enclosure 12

The area of Enclosure 12 had contracted southwards from its extent during the previous phase, and expanded slightly to the west to take up the whole of the trackway frontage.

Structure 25, situated along the trackway in the south part of Enclosure 12, is more clearly visible within this phase, although it was much disturbed by later activity, heavy rutting and truncation (Fig. 3.13c). Post-holes located around the area of the floors suggest that the structure was constructed at least in part with earthfast timbers, although timber beams and sills were probably also used as foundations. The structure was aligned north-west–south-east and measured 15m by 7.50m, making it similar in size to the building in Enclosure 18, and, like it, twice as long as it was broad. The dimensions of the building have been extrapolated from the locations of groups of post-holes and post-pits, not all of them immediately apparent on initial machining: only after secondary machining did some of the post positions emerge. The north-west corner of the building was never machined a second time during the excavations, so this area remained less clear. The primary dump/make-up layer for the building consisted of a layer of clay *6502*, into which the posts of the building were cut. The south-east wall of the structure consisted of an alignment of at least seven (and perhaps twelve) post-holes or post-pits (F1358, F1315, F1318, F1319, F1333, F1357 and F1365). The south-west wall consisted of a line of four or five posts, with F2508 at its eastern end. The north-west wall comprised between seven and twelve posts and pits including F1368, F1372–75 and F2503. The remains of a north-east wall with five posts, including *5887*, F2506 and *5966*, were seen. The primary floor of the building *5803* consisted of a trampled clay deposit which, towards the south centre of the building, contained an area of ash and scorching *5962* on its upper surface, probably indicating the presence of a hearth. Overlying this clay surface was a make-up layer *5883* for a flint gravel and cornbrash spread F1231, representing a phase of surface metalling. This gravel surface appears to be lain both within the building and outside it, where it might have indicated a path leading southwards from the building towards the trackway, and perhaps to a yard at the back. Only the gravel surface produced a substantial finds assemblage, 166 out of 247 sherds of pottery being of Ely ware.

Several zones of activity appear to have been laid out around the building. Within a small compound formed by ditches F1328 and F1345 (widths up to 0.70m, depths up to 0.30m) lay a small group of pits (F1281, F1287, F1291), situated away from the structure to the north-west. These were oval, with steep sides and flattish bases, ranging in size from 0.86m by 0.80m to 2.00m by 0.90m in plan, and 0.15–0.29m in depth. Other than a dog burial in F1281, they produced few finds. They were of similar type to the groups of pits seen in Enclosures 6 and 11, which, again, developed in this phase and continued into the next. Two large ponds or wells, F1377 and F1420 (the former 6.00m wide and over 1.40m deep, the latter measuring 9.00m by 2.50m in plan and of unknown depth), were cut to the north-east of the building. It is possible that while the deep, sub-circular well F1377 was a source of fresh water, the elongated ?pond F1420 acted as a soakaway for waste water; a narrow central drain within Structure 25 fed into it from the south.

Enclosure 16

Occupation within Area A was now limited to Enclosure 16, fronting onto the southern trackway, with much of the land behind now being ploughed.

Structure 26 was located in the south-east part of the enclosure (Fig. 3.14). It continued in use through Phase 10 (the 13th century) but by Phase 11 it was abandoned. A large part of the structure lay beyond the limits of excavation to the east and south, so a complete plan was never obtained. A horizontal stratified building sequence remained preserved within this area: while a clear sequence of floors was sample excavated, the structural elements of the building such as post-holes and beam-slots were less well understood. The published plan of the building includes all identified structural elements, and the exposed extent of floors from the latest phase of its construction.

Aligned north-east–south-west, the building fronted a cobbled path and gravel road over a length of at least 15m (and perhaps more than 20m), and was up to 7.00m wide. The gravel trackway F357 had been truncated to the south-west, but survived over a length of *c.* 18m and was up to 3.50m wide. To the east of the trackway was an area of flint and limestone hard-standing *1655*, possibly indicating a threshold into the building. Running between trackway and threshold was a linear gully, either a drain or the result of erosion by water run-off from a roof. The building itself appeared to have been divided into three rooms or bays

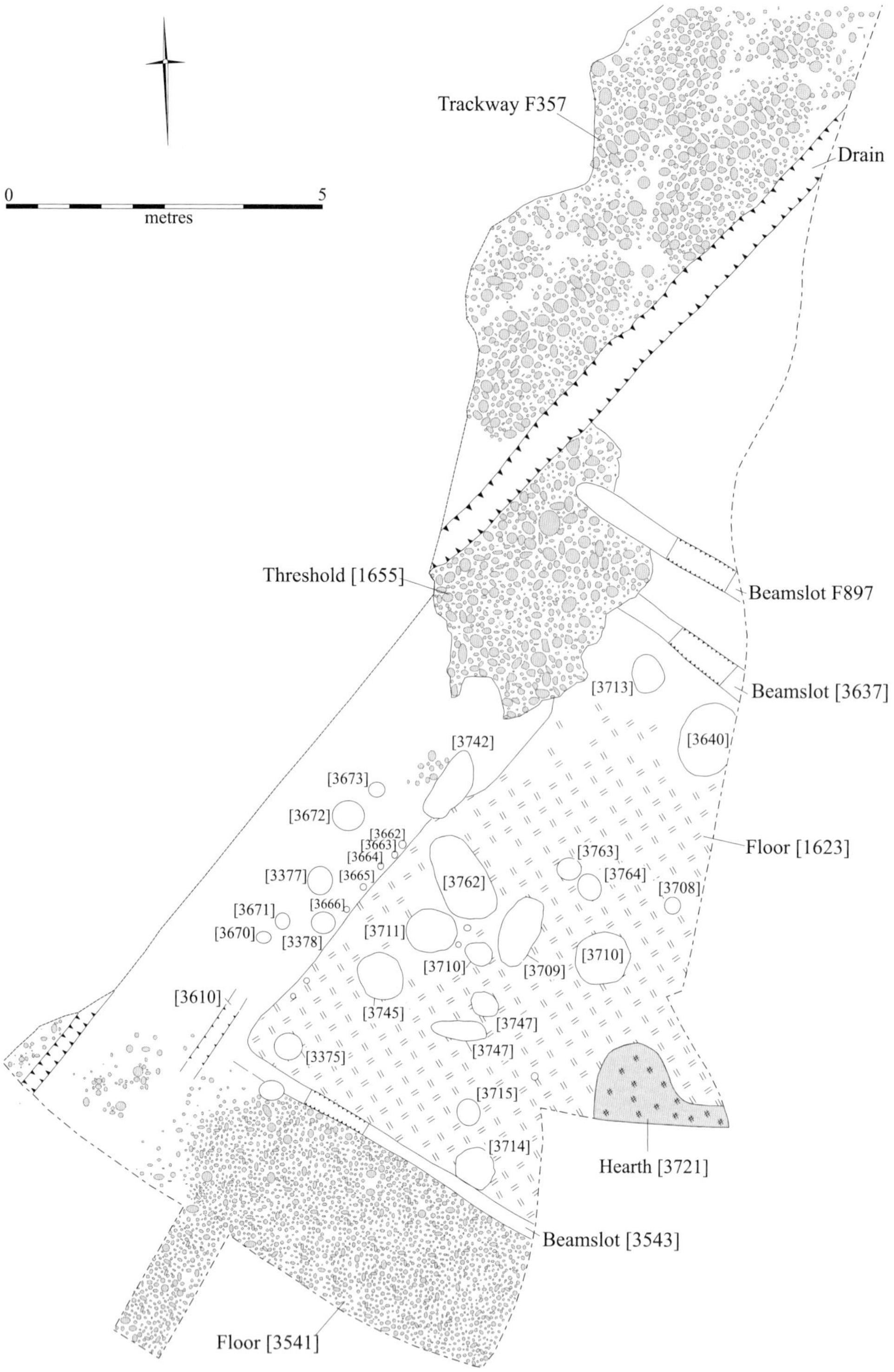

Trackway F357

Drain

Threshold [1655]

Beamslot F897

Beamslot [3637]

[3713]

[3640]

[3742]

[3673]

[3672]

[3662]
[3663]
[3664]

[3377] [3665]

[3671] [3666]

[3670] [3378]

[3763]

[3764]

[3708]

Floor [1623]

[3762]

[3711]

[3610]

[3745]

[3375]

[3710] [3709]

[3710]

[3747]

[3747]

[3715]

[3714]

Hearth [3721]

Beamslot [3543]

Floor [3541]

Figure 3.14 Structure 26

separated by wall lines indicated by timber slots and changes within floor make-up to either side of them. The floors of the building survived best within the two southern 'rooms' of the structure, and it is unclear whether or not the northernmost area, beyond beam-slot F897, was internal or external. The central 'room' was *c.* 10m long with the south wall defined by beam-slot *3543*, the west/external wall line indicated by alignments of post-holes (*3670–3, 3677, 3378* and *3742*) and stake-holes (*3662–6*), the latter perhaps indicating the use of wattling. A number of post-holes were located within the central 'room'. While some were undoubtedly structurally related to the building, several were only revealed after secondary machining and these may have related to earlier phases of the building. The three large central post-holes (*3709, 3710* and *3762*) may have represented internal structural supports.

The floor surfaces within this central 'room' were of clay or clay silt, some with a sandier content. All floors showed signs of disturbance or wear, and small dumps or levelling deposits within surfaces indicated constant repair. As seen with other medieval surface accumulations (for example at Ely Forehill: Alexander 2003), floors often appeared to have been deliberately disturbed or 'turned', possibly to level an internal area prior to the laying of new surfaces. Old surfaces become mixed with other deliberately dumped deposits during this process; while relatively large amounts of pottery can be found between floors and within make-up layers, this pottery probably derived not from occupation build-up over the floors (which were generally kept clean), but from these levelling dumps. Few large areas of floor surface survived this constant reworking undisturbed. Where they did, thin lenses of

44

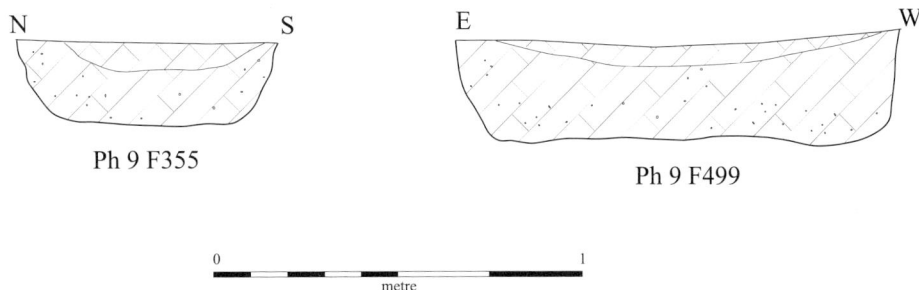

Figure 3.15 Sections across Phase 9 furrows

occupation accumulation could be discerned within and between floor episodes. This is particularly true around hearths or ovens, where they take the form of ash build-ups.

At least five distinct floor episodes were recorded within the central 'room', these being interspersed with discrete lenses and dumps (see below). Also located within the central room was a scorched/burnt clay surface *3721* associated with an ash deposit, *3146*, indicating the position of a hearth. The floors produced varying quantities of finds material, with the pottery assemblages determining their broad life spans: that associated with the first floor was mostly Ely ware, whereas that from the fifth included 12 sherds of Lyveden ware and five of Blackborough End ware along with 59 of Ely type. The southern 'room' of the building was excavated to the level of the first substantial floor surface, *3541*; this was a well-made compact gravel metalling. No west wall was apparent, only the faint trace of a beam-slot *3610*, although the good condition of the surface suggested that it had been an internal one. An excavated slot to the south could not be extended far enough to take in the building's south wall.

To the west and north, ditch F810 (up to 1.75m wide and 0.54m deep) defined the enclosure compound. Two wells appear to have been active in this phase: F775 (from Enclosure 14 in the previous phase) was 4.10m in diameter and 1.20m deep; further to the south-west lay the first in a series of large wells, F753. This was sub-oval and measured 7.00m by 5.50m and 1.21m deep, with steep sides and a rounded base. Whether both of these wells were active at the same time is unclear. South of the wells, a series of shallow gullies (F737, F776, F777, F804; widths 0.50–1.00m, depths 0.15–0.54m) formed rectilinear internal divisions within the compound, parallel to the structure and trackway.

Lying within these, and possibly contemporary with them, was a small group of circular pits (F755, F761, F762, F763 and F770; diameters ranging from 0.80–2.00m, depths to 0.30m and generally rounded bases). These may have represented the bases of rubbish pits, although a significant degree of truncation had taken place in this area. Few pits interpreted as being dug for waste disposal appear before this period; however, it is unclear why they may begin to appear in this phase (see Chapter 6). A further group of larger, straight-sided, flat-bottomed pits (F537, F539, F547, F548, F552, F579; possibly associated with a gully complex) lay to the north-west. These were oval and ranged in size from 2.20m by 1.05m to 3.00m by 2.25m in plan, with depths of 0.38–0.50m. These lay outside Enclosure 16 proper, and could have been associated with either Structure 25 or Structure 26. Whatever the case, the pits appear once again to have been deliberately placed away from the main domestic structures.

Along the north boundary of the enclosure around well F775 lay a group of large shallow pits (F794, F802, F803, F813, F824). These were of varying shapes, with sizes ranging from 1.50m by 1.25m to 4.00m to 3.25m in plan, and with depths of 0.18–0.22m; generally they contained few finds. The amorphous nature of the larger of these pits might suggest they were small localised clay quarries dug to win construction materials, such as for daub or cob walling.

Enclosure 17
The remainder of the east half of the site — previously occupied by Enclosures 3, 13 and most of 14 — now came under the plough within a new land unit, Enclosure 17. This represents the first area within the site to be given over to cultivation. Two alignments of ditches were seen, underlying the later ridge and furrow, an east–west alignment (F355, F588, F667) in the northern part of the area and a north–south alignment in its southern part (F499, F522, F556 and F718). The ditches were 0.60–1.40m wide and no more than 0.30m deep (Fig. 3.15), with small- to medium-sized mixed finds assemblages (up to 47 sherds from each, including Thetford, St Neots, Ely, Grimston, Blackborough End and Lyveden wares, occasional fragments of burnt clay, lava quern and

undated metalwork, and small amounts of animal bone — except F667 with over 2kg). The importance of these ditches is that they may have been early hand-dug strip-field divisions (the spoil being piled onto central ridges between the divisions); this would have developed into the ridge and furrow system that was eventually to cover much of the excavated area. The finds assemblages from the ditch fills, which are earlier than those recovered from the base of the extant ridge and furrow, suggest that these features are not traces of later cleaning of the furrow bases. These strip boundaries appear to have been excavated by hand, rather than developing as a result of ploughing: this is suggested by their flat bases and near-vertical sides, while the flat bases may also indicate that drainage was not their primary function.

VI. Phase 10: 13th century
(Figs 3.16–3.18)

Summary
The reorganisation of the settlement that began in Phase 9 is now seen far more clearly. Large areas of the site were now given over to agriculture, either arable (indicated by ridge and furrow) or pastoral. Domestic buildings in Enclosures 12 and 16 continued in use from the previous phase, as did non-domestic buildings in Enclosures 5 and 20; new domestic and other structures were raised in Enclosure 18.

Enclosure 1
Enclosure 1 was all but abandoned; the final building, Structure 20, was now derelict although the area remained in use, probably as a back plot belonging to a property lying to the east beyond the edge of excavation. That the area to the east was occupied is suggested by two large elongated oval pits, F382 and F383, the former (5.50m by 0.50m and 0.14m deep) apparently a recutting of the latter (6.50m by 1.27m and 0.33m deep). Their steep sides and rounded bases recalled the pits interpreted as cess pits from the previous phase. With the end of direct occupation the small-scale pitting seen in the previous phase all but stopped, the last of this activity represented by a small circular pit F307 (1.40m in diameter, 0.50m deep) cutting into the northern part of Structure 20. Some activity, however, was indicated by a heavily burnt feature F364 (1.30m in diameter and 0.15m deep) sunk into one of the earlier ditches at the centre of the area, which may have represented a fire pit. The area was now used as a dumping ground, with two waste deposits surviving over Structure 20 (F306) and within a hollow formed by an earlier pit group situated in the western part of the area, *1802* (Fig. 3.17). Almost 250 sherds of pottery (predominantly Ely ware) were recovered from F306, the layers above the surface cobbles of the building, while a contemporary assemblage was recovered from the deposit within the western dump. Two final sets of north–south gullies overlay what were the west limits of the enclosure (F289 and F310; both 0.40m wide, 0.25m and 0.37m deep, with steep sides and flat bases). These features appeared to have been structural and yet they cut right across the bank and ditch of the enclosure. While there is no finds evidence to support this suggestion, it is thought that these slots, or post-trenches, may belong to a significantly later phase of activity.

Enclosure 2
A small pit group, F263 (the largest feature 1.10m wide and 0.39m deep), in the corner of the enclosure was the only evidence of activity continuing within the vicinity; this was possibly a backyard area associated with buildings occupying the West Fen Road frontage.

Figure 3.16 Phase 10 overall plan, with Phase 9 features as background and interpretation below

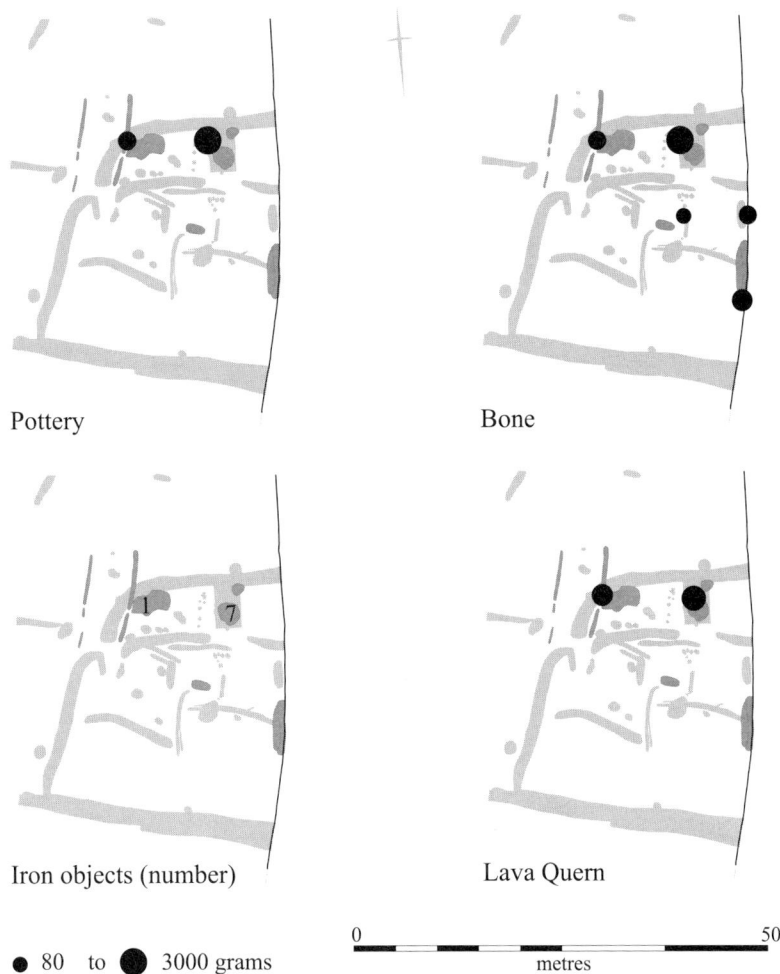

Figure 3.17 Enclosure 1, Phase 10 dumps

Enclosure 19
Enclosures 9 and 4 were combined to form Enclosure 19. There was no evidence to indicate whether (like Enclosure 17 to the east) the area was under plough, or was used as pasture.

Enclosure 5
Within Enclosure 5, substantial drainage gullies were cut around Structure 21 to the north and south, F1625 and F1969 (up to 1.90m wide and 0.56m deep); both produced sizeable finds assemblages, with pottery dominated by Ely ware, indicating continuity of domestic use from the previous phase. The floor of the building may also have been re-surfaced within this phase. A large sub-circular well, F1538 (7.00m in diameter and more than 1.20m deep) was cut to the north-east of the structure (continuing in use until Phase 12). Despite evidence of continuing occupation, however, there were other signs that activity within the enclosure was now on the decrease: only a few small pits (e.g. F1701) were cut to the north of the structure, and no further gullies were cut in this phase.

Enclosure 10
As in the previous phase, any Phase 10 activity within Enclosure 10 remained undetectable.

Enclosure 6
As in the previous phase, a number of substantial pits were cut, and these possibly indicated the back of the property fronting West Fen Road (F2592, F2603, F2613, F2621, F2622). These were oval, mostly with steep sides and flat bases, and ranged in plan dimensions from 2.00m by 1.80m to 4.00m by 2.00m, with depths of 0.16–0.45m. Their very small finds assemblages suggested they had a function other than as rubbish pits: their size and distinctive character again suggest a specific purpose, possibly as pig-fattening pens (see Chapter 6).

Enclosure 7
The boundaries of this enclosure remained relatively unchanged, although the south boundary ditch F1716 (up to 1.30m wide and 0.32m deep) shifted north and straightened, probably as a result of developments within Enclosure 18. Similar patterns of activity appeared to continue from the previous phase, with features at the centre of the area strongly suggesting the presence of a structure. Curving gully F1980 (1.20m wide, 0.39m deep), in particular, curved around the north limit of this 'blank' space, while other ditches and gullies (F1782, F1876, F1923, F1948; up to 0.85m wide and 0.35m deep) ran to and from this area. Several of these features produced large finds assemblages — including 168 sherds of Ely ware, again suggestive of domestic occupation. The curving ditches F1782 and F1876, along with F1636, indicate that the reshaping of the paddock system to the west, first seen in Phase 9, continued.

In the east part of the area a group of small pits (F1884, F1885, F1993, F1994) was cut within a rectangular compound defined by narrow gullies or fence-lines (F1882, F1883). The pits were circular or oval, with diameters of 0.50–0.95m and depths of 0.13–0.37m, and all but one produced few finds. A group of larger pits was located immediately to the north of the southern boundary of the enclosure (F1926, *8072, 8073, 8596, 8604*). Again these were circular or oval, with diameters of 1.00–2.00m and depths of 0.10–0.45m, and with gradually sloping sides, flat bases and small finds assemblages.

Trial trenching indicated that there was still abundant activity within the western area of the site, although much of this remained unseen since it lay beyond the edge of excavation.

Enclosure 18
Enclosure 18 was occupied by a domestic structure, perhaps for the first time. Its east boundary was now marked by ditch F1012, while the northern boundary had shifted slightly northward to incorporate part of the southern area of Enclosure 7.

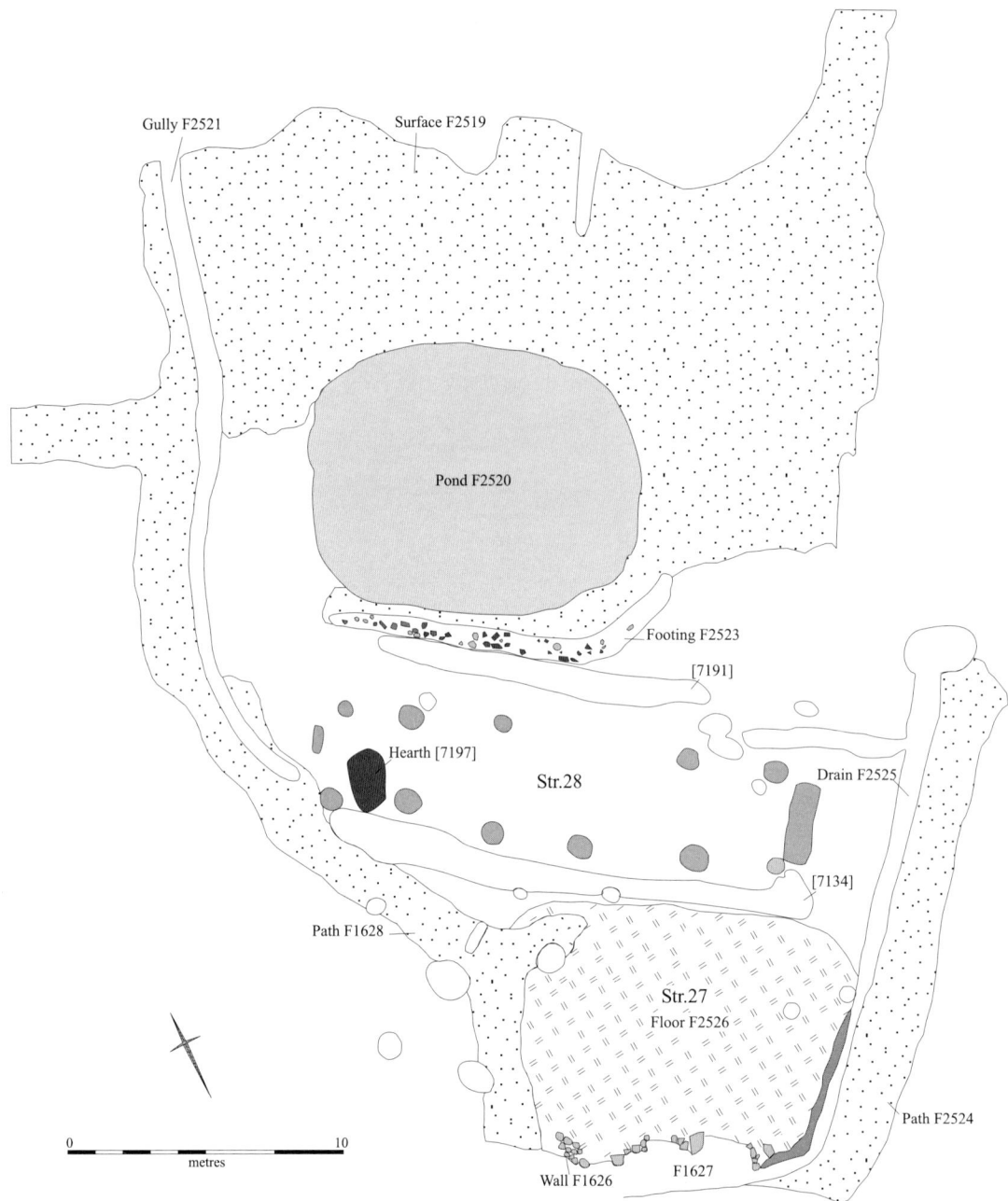

Figure 3.18 Structures 27 and 28

It is possible that Enclosure 7 and Enclosure 18 were both occupied at the same time. It is more likely, however, that this period saw the end of domestic occupation within Enclosure 7 (given that this area had become a yard by Phase 11) and a shift south to Enclosure 18 by the end of the phase, quite possibly by the same family or tenants. Two new buildings — domestic Structure 27 and non-domestic Structure 28 (Fig. 3.18) — were erected.

Structure 27 was built directly over the backfilled pond or well F2530. The well had been infilled with crushed sandstone 'hardcore' overlain by gravel (F1710, up to 0.10m thick), essentially a preparation make-up for a floor. The floor itself was a yellow-brown clay F2526 up to 0.08m thick, although this layer and the upper features of the structure were badly disturbed by machine disturbance down this south side of the site. The floor area of the building covered an area *c.* 12m long by 9m wide and was aligned north-west–south-east. A disturbed line of cornbrash and flint set in grey clay, F1626, had tumbled into a drainage ditch to the south of the structure, F1627 (0.60m wide, 0.25m deep). This may have represented the remains of a foundation sill, suggesting that the timber building rested partially on stone footings. A line of three post-holes, 0.30–0.50m in diameter, may have been the remains of a west

wall, while post-holes to the west of the floor — possibly the remains of lean-to structures — suggested some additions to this side of the building.

To the east of the building, a metalled trackway F2524 led off to the north. The path lay slightly lower than the floor surface of the building, and water would have drained from around the building into and along this partially sunken track. A narrow drain F2525 (0.45m wide and 0.25m deep) ran between the building and the path. The near-vertical edges of this drain suggested it may have been timber-lined, while the relatively clean silty humic fill implied that it was also covered.

A long, narrow building possibly representing an aisled barn or byre, Structure 28, was constructed to the north of Structure 27. The structure appears to have been clay-floored, with two parallel rows of paired posts forming the central supports. No traces of outer walls were seen, and these presumably rested on sills. Two parallel gullies (*7191* and *7313*, 0.90–1.00m wide) ran down the north and south sides of the building, the whole measuring 16m long by 4 or 5m wide. Two beam-slots at the west and east ends may have held base-plates. A patch of burnt floor surviving in the south-west part of the structure possibly indicated the position of an oven, hearth or small furnace (*7197*).

There was some pitting (F1670, F1743, F1910; with widths of 1.20–4.00m, depths of 0.26–0.33m and small- to medium-sized pottery assemblages dominated by Ely ware) within a small compound to the north-west of the enclosure defined by ditch F1697 (0.40m wide, 0.15m deep). To the east lay the remains of a small circular building, F1915, with a drainage gully (F1909). F1915 was a semi-circular arrangement of five circular post-holes, of 0.30–0.47m diameter and with depths of 0.06–0.10m, while F1909 was 0.40m wide and 0.08m deep. If agricultural in purpose, then the building may have represented a hay stand or a dovecote.

Enclosure 20
Initially the west boundary of the enclosure may have been formed by ditch F2121, prior to the major boundary change signified by the digging of ditch F1012. With this shift the enclosure took in parts of Enclosures 11 and 12. The east boundary was ditch F1384 (3.30m wide, 0.85m deep), a southward extension of the recut boundary to Enclosure 11, while the north boundary of the eastern arm of the enclosure was probably marked by ditch F2197, or possibly the parallel ditch F2217 to the south. The south boundary appears to have been redefined constantly during this phase, with a series of intercutting ditches between F1268 and F1363. The narrow western arm of the compound was occupied by Structure 22 (described above), situated between ditches F1012 and F2121, these features forming a narrow enclosure around the building. With the exception of F1012, the ditches described above had widths of up to 1.50m and depths to 0.55m. To the south of the building a series of gullies (F44, F45; widths to 0.80m, depths to 0.40m) were cut, probably to facilitate drainage. Two ponds lay on the south boundary of the enclosure: the smaller, F2575 (5.00m in diameter) was dug over the corner of an earlier building, Structure 24, with the larger, F2572 (12.00m by 5.00m), to the east overlying the south boundary ditches. A group of large pits clustered in the north-east part of the area. Generally oval or circular, with gradually sloping sides, these varied in size from 0.90m in diameter to 4.50m by 3.50m, and were up to 0.37m deep. Most contained few or no finds. The amorphous nature of the larger pits may indicate clay extraction.

Enclosure 11
This was reduced to a single, large square enclosure, defined by ditches F912, F2197 (both of them recut from the previous phase), F1443 and F2121. There was no evidence for ploughing at this stage, and the enclosure might have been a large stock compound.

Enclosure 12
In Enclosure 12 both the domestic building, Structure 25, and its pond/wells F1377 and F1420 continued in use. There were a large number of pits in the area immediately to the north and west of the building. The pits to the west of the structure appeared to occupy the edges of a rectangular compound formed by ditches F1270/F1337 (both 0.60m wide, 0.40m deep) to the north and F1266 to the south. The pits varied in type and possibly function, several being oval, steep-sided and flat-based. Also within this area were kiln/furnace F1248 and the disturbed remains of an oven (or fire-pit) F1341: this was an oval feature, 1.10m by 0.70m in plan and 0.18m deep. F1248 was oval, 1.70m by 1.10m in plan and 0.27m deep, and its edges had turned light yellow/red through burning. It contained 4kg of light grey green porous slag. While F1341 could have seen heating for numerous processes, the fly-ash/slag from F1248 suggests extremely high temperatures, probably up to 1200° C, which may have required the use of bellows. This may relate to an unidentified industrial process (J. Cowgill, *pers. comm.*) Traces of a metalled trackway were also evident, crossing the enclosure from the south before turning at right angles to the east. The track survived best at the south, close to the field edge, but even here it was only a rough scatter of pebbles. Elsewhere, evidence for the surface existed as patches of gravel within the tops of earlier features.

Enclosure 16
Enclosure 16, along the south trackway, remained the only part of Area A to show continuing, if not expanding, occupation. It broadly retained the same area as in the previous phase, although possibly with some contraction along its north boundary. The metalled track alongside domestic Structure 26 was resurfaced and a cobbled path added between it and the building. The first of the large wells, F753, to the north-west of the building was infilled and a second, F752, of similar size (4.60m in diameter and 1.20m deep with steep sides), was cut through it at its south-eastern edge. While the smaller well to the north-east, F775, was backfilled, a third, F796 (4.40m by 4.00m, sub-circular), was cut some 40m further out to the north-west. When excavated, both contained large finds assemblages: as well as 77 sherds of pottery (52 of Ely ware), F752 contained 33 tile fragments, while F796 produced a copper alloy ?badge

(no. 16, p.57) and a whetstone (no. 212, p.83), as well as a collection of 107 sherds dominated by Ely ware. A large group of oval and circular pits was cut into the western side of the trackway, with diameters up to 2.40m and often with rounded bases; some contained quite large assemblages. Another group immediately south of the backfilled well F775 (F821, F822, F823, F824, F2360) varied in plan from 1.70m by 0.80m to 2.40m by 2.10m, and were up to 0.20m deep; again, some contained large finds assemblages, with pottery dominated by Ely ware.

VII. Phase 11: 14th century
(Figs 3.19 and 3.20)

Summary
By the 14th century the settlement comprised three properties situated along the trackway to the south. The northern part of the site was almost exclusively agricultural land by this time. There were domestic buildings in Enclosures 16, 12 and 18 and a non-domestic building in Enclosure 18, with a second conjectured in Enclosure 16.

Enclosures 16 and 17
Enclosure 16 retained its overall size and shape, but appears to have been abandoned by the mid-14th century (see Chapter 1). Continuing activity prior to this was suggested by a group of pits (F771, F773, F791, F2375, F2407) that partially cut through the metalled trackway to the west of surviving building Structure 26. These are circular or oval with gradually sloping sides, ranging from 1.30m by 1.15m to 3.00m by 2.50m in plan and up to 0.85m deep; some contained significant pottery assemblages. Two further pits lay to the north-west beyond the well group. A series of rubble and clay dumps (*1578/3565/3567*) containing abundant pottery overlay the abandoned building. The presence of five Bourne ware sherds alongside Ely ware in the latest dumps allows reasonably tight dating.

A third example in the sequence of large wells was dug: F751 was sub-circular, measured 4.00m by 3.00m in plan and was 1.45m deep, with steep sides. This in turn was infilled and a smaller, deeper, circular stone-lined well, F729, dug in the centre of the backfill. This was 1.20m in diameter with a roughly-cut green sandstone lining. The well could only be safely excavated to a depth of 1.20m, but a sample of the waterlogged basal fill was obtained during subsequent construction work. The hollow area left by the earlier wells had been completely backfilled by this period and gravelled over to form a yard surface. There were slight remains of a small building, Structure 29, in the form of beam impressions and lines of foundation stones within this gravel surface, although this had been badly disturbed.

Enclosure/field 17 had now increased in area by absorbing both Enclosures 1 and 2 into the plough-land, leaving the remains of the single domestic structure, Structure 26, in Enclosure 16 at its south-east corner.

Enclosure 12 and Enclosure 19
A similar pattern of development was seen within the central part of the site. The area under plough or pasture increased, having absorbed Enclosure 11 and almost all of Enclosure 20, and formed one large field with a domestic compound (Enclosure 12) and building (Structure 25) at its south-east corner.

A decline in activity was seen within Enclosure 12 in this phase, and the domestic building Structure 25 came to an end early in this period or possibly even at the end of the previous phase. A good indication of the early demise of occupation within the enclosure was provided by the small number of pits assigned to this phase (F1242, F1252, F1271, F2221; these displayed a range of shapes and sizes, from the circular F1242, 1.65m in diameter, to the irregular F1271, measuring 4.50 by 4.50m in plan and 0.40m deep), while well F2572 became redundant and its site may have been ploughed over.

Enclosure 21 and Enclosure 18
The expansion of agricultural land was also noted in Enclosure 21: this took in the western part of Enclosure 18 and all the enclosures to the north (5, 6, 7 and 10) to form one large field, again with a domestic compound, Enclosure 18, in its south-east corner. This may have been the only occupied part of the excavated area by the end of the 14th century.

While Enclosure 18 contracted eastwards, it otherwise retained its shape. Both the domestic and non-domestic buildings, Structures 27 and 28, remained, although few changes to their layout were seen. One exception to this was the brick and rubble footing F2523, which may

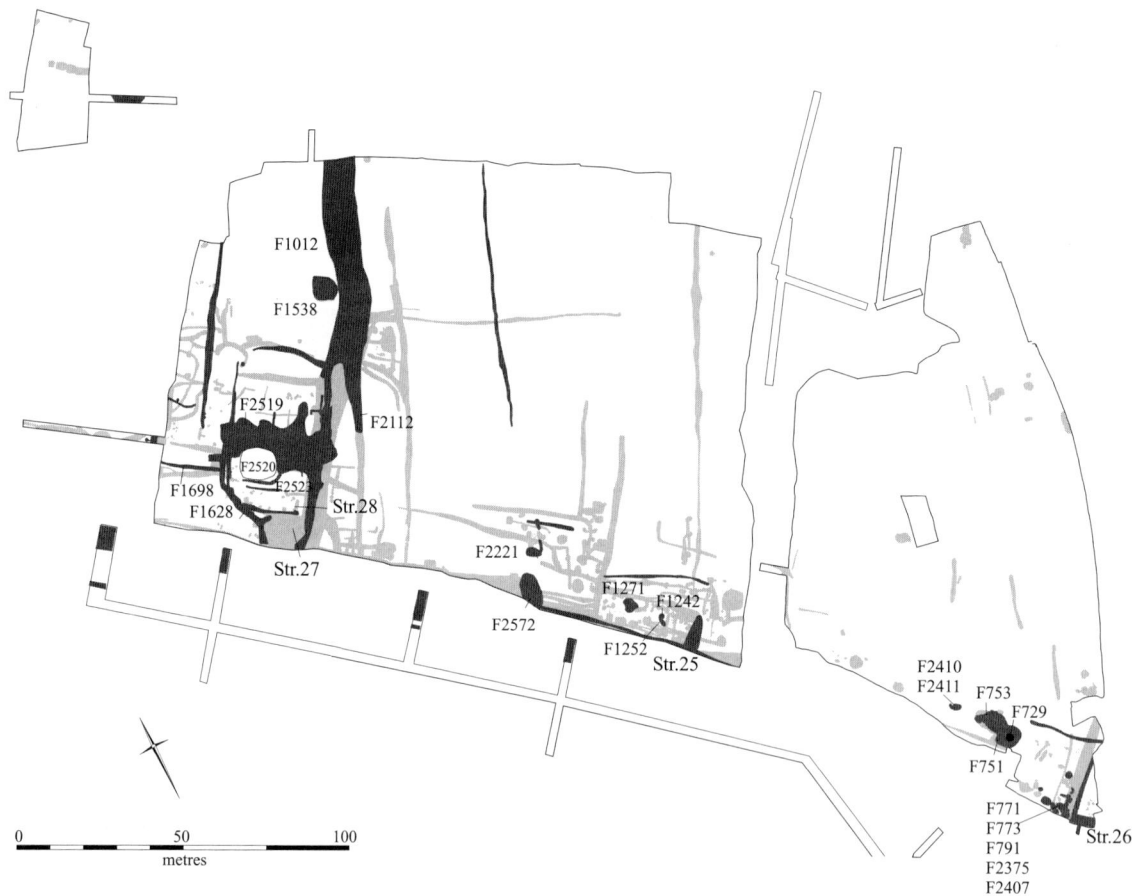

Figure 3.19 Phase 11 overall plan, with Phase 10 features as background and interpretation below

have formed an extension to Structure 28. This feature was hard to date as no complete brick dimensions survived, nor was any datable pottery retrieved from the footing: it is possible that this was actually part of a much later structure. A large sub-circular pond, F2520 (10.00m in diameter, over 0.70m deep), was dug behind the buildings to the north and an extensive gravelled yard (F2519) laid out around it, while sloping down into it to provide access. This surface consisted of small to medium-sized flint set in brown sandy clay and covered an area of 32m east-to-west by 17m north-to-south, with a maximum thickness of 0.20m. It produced a very large finds assemblage. In addition to animal bone, whetstones (nos 220–2), tile and a mixed collection of 170 sherds

of pottery, metal items included four horse-shoes (nos 287–90), a lead token (no. 271), a twisted wire object (no. 11), a lace tag (no. 22), a knife (no. 126), an iron punch (no. 188) and a thimble (no. 189). Gravel and cobble paths were laid out around the two buildings, F1628 (up to 1.70m wide) leading from the yard to the pond and the trackway at the south. Traces of timber slots and brick footings were seen within the yard around the pond to the north of Structure 28; these suggested that other farm outbuildings existed within this period, although few formed coherent structural patterns. There was a large well, F1538, at the east side of Enclosure 21. The date of its construction is not known but the

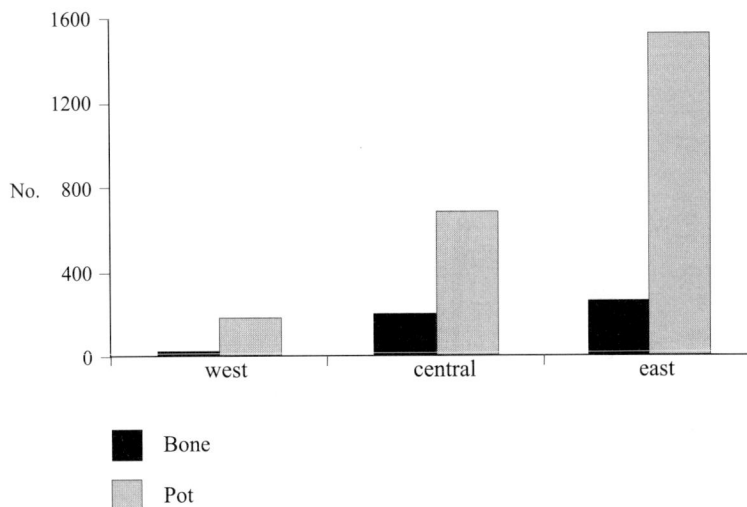

Figure 3.20 Phase 11 finds material by block

ditches of F1012 curved around it to accommodate it. It was probably abandoned during this phase or early in the next.

The level of activity within these three agricultural/domestic blocks, assessed on the basis of the contemporary finds assemblages recovered within them, appears to have decreased from east to west (Fig. 3.20), with the eastern block (Enclosures 16 and 17) producing approximately ten times the numbers of finds from the western block and twice as much as from the central. This may be taken as a rough guide to the relative length of time that these enclosures remained occupied through Phase 11. However, it was in the western block — in Enclosure 18 — that the most dramatic structural alterations occurred, with the excavation of the large pond and construction of the surrounding gravel surface. Despite these large-scale changes it is possible that this enclosure was the first to see the end of domestic occupation, but that the hard-standing, watering hole and dumping ground within it continued in use into the next phase and beyond. Other small buildings may have been erected within it at a later date. The pottery assemblage from the pond included a sherd of 16th-century German stoneware, that from the gravel surface included stonewares and earthenwares dating at least to the 17th century or later.

VIII. Phase 12: 15th century
(Fig. 3.21)

Enclosure 16/17
To the east, Enclosure 16 was now abandoned, although this area was never taken into the plough-land. The gravel surfaces of the trackway and those over the wells may have remained extant and been utilised as work areas or yards. The stone-lined well F729 was infilled and there was some dumping or demolition material, including brick and tile, from the far south-east of the area. It is possible that, on or soon after this abandonment, the whole of the developed ridge and furrow system to the north also came out of cultivation and was turned over to pasture.

Enclosure 12/19
Enclosure 12 was abandoned by this phase, and there is no evidence for any activity in the 15th century or subsequently. At the north edge of Enclosure 19, a separate evaluation trench between the main excavated area and West Fen Road provided evidence for a relatively short-lived gravel surface that was laid down at around this time. The surface overlay a build-up of 13th–14th-century soil, presumably ploughsoil, and was itself covered by further levels which included 16th-century material.

There does not appear to have been any domestic settlement activity associated with the surface, which may have represented a yard (Masser 2000).

Enclosure 18/21
The buildings in Enclosure 18 were abandoned in this period and the enclosed area shrunk to the point where it enclosed only the pond and gravel surface. Again, while occupation ended, the area was not turned over to the plough, and the yard remained as a hard surface which saw intermittent use, possibly along with some upstanding structures. F2529 was a brick rubble and sand foundation, 0.50m wide, 0.11m deep, which may have represented the south-east corner of a small building, while 7663 was a north–south aligned beam-slot 0.50m wide and 0.08m deep and 7326 a large oval post-hole. These footings were badly disturbed but possibly represented byres or animal sheds if the area, as suggested, was now pasture. Ditch F1012, possibly still indicating a property boundary, was re-cut during this phase. The large well F1538 at the edge of Enclosure 21 had been backfilled. A gravel surface, similar to that seen in Enclosure 19, was laid down in the north part of Enclosure 21: this probably represented a yard, again indicating a possible property fronting West Fen Road. No finds were associated with the surface so exact dating was impossible.

IX. Phase 13: 16th century and later
(Fig. 3.21)

A large pond, F2350 (4.00m wide and 0.70m deep), and a possible quarry, F2351 (11.00m wide and over 0.70m in depth), at the far eastern edge of the site in Enclosure 17 were the only features assigned to this phase. Both appear to have been backfilled by the 17th century and may have been associated with a property to the south-east lying beyond the edge of excavation.

In the western half of the site two large shallow pits, F41 and F42, were dug into the backfilled well in Enclosure 21; an articulated pig burial was also found.

F1012

F41-2

F1538

[7663]
[7326]

F2529

F2350

F2351

F729

0   100

metres

Structure

Road/Trackway

Enc.18/21   Enc.12/19

Enc.16/17

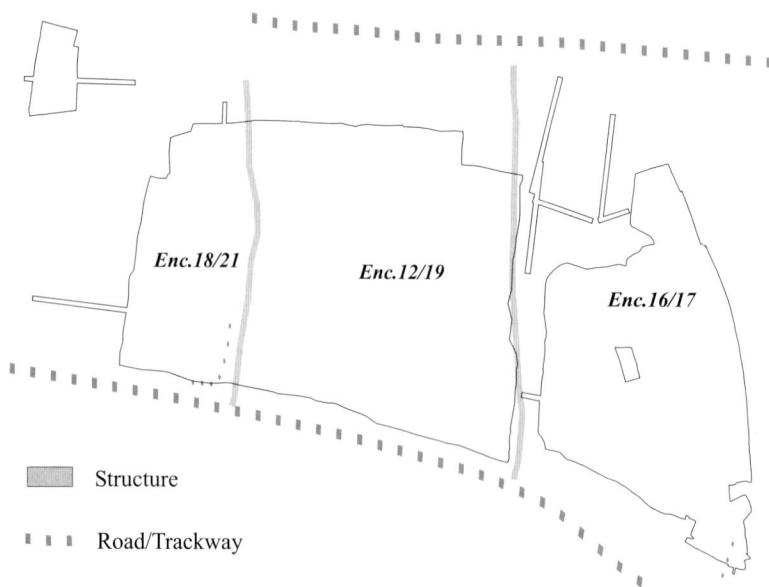

Figure 3.21 Phase 12 and 13 overall plan, with Phase 11 features as background and interpretation below

4. The Artefacts

by Paul Blinkhorn, David Hall, Sam Lucy, Gwladys Monteil, Richard Mortimer and Sarah Percival with Adrian Challands and Jane Cowgill

This chapter describes and discusses the artefacts from the site in terms of the functional categories of Margeson (1993). All small finds are individually described, with the exception of Neolithic and Bronze Age flint and pottery and the Iron Age awl (summarily reported in Chapter 2), post-medieval and modern finds from surface collection, and minor metal objects such as iron nails, strips, points, sheet fragments and lead scraps (see Table 4.1 for summary). Initial metalwork identifications were by Jane Cowgill, who also provided some of the object descriptions. Illustrated items are indicated with an asterisk in the catalogue sections. Each entry is followed by contextual information in the following order: Context number (Feature number where assigned)/Original catalogue number/Phase and further details of the context from which it derived. The significance of the artefactual assemblage is further discussed in Chapter 6.

All of the reports in this chapter are by Sam Lucy unless otherwise credited.

I. Dress and personal possessions
(Plates IV–VII; Figs 4.1 and 4.2)

Jewellery
The site produced a small range of jewellery items. There were probably just two finger rings: Fig. 4.1 No. 1 from a Late Saxon context (which might perhaps have been a redeposited Roman earring, to judge by its similarity to Crummy 1983, no. 1796 — it was found in one of the areas with dense Roman occupation) and No. 2 from an unphased context, though this might be too small unless it was a child's. The low numbers should occasion no surprise for such items are rare in archaeological contexts, the Norwich Survey excavations producing only four such items in total (Margeson 1993, 4–5). No medieval beads were recovered, again unsurprisingly, as necklaces of beads were not in fashion during this time (*ibid.*, 5). Two

probable Roman cannel coal beads, one cone-shaped and one barrel-shaped, were recovered (Nos 3–4). One was in phase, in the main area of Roman occupation, and the other residual, although in the vicinity of two truncated Roman burials. The blue glass bead with an applied white trail (Fig. 4.1 No. 5) was found in the post-hole of a Late Saxon structure, and is probably of Anglo-Saxon date (Guido 1999, type 6ix), although this is a long-lived type, found also in the Iron Age and Roman periods (Guido 1978, 63–4, fig. 21.1). The copper alloy bracelet (No. 6) found during surface collection could also be a Roman or an Anglo-Saxon type (*cf.* MacGregor and Bolick 1993, nos 26.1–3).

*1. Copper and ?silver alloy finger-ring or **earring**; incomplete open ring with one rounded terminal; trimmed flat face on one side; possibly Roman.
    4334 (F25)/*9082*/Phase 8 boundary ditch fill, Enclosure 4.

2. Complete white metal **ring**, possibly of tin or silver; thin fine tapering ring made from an irregular strip of sheet. D. 11–12m, T. 2mm.
    981/4424/Unphased.

*3. Fragment of a possible cannel coal **bead**, barrel-shaped; probably Roman.
    7000 (F2519)/*9020*/Phase 11 gravelled yard, Enclosure 18/21.

4. Fragment of a possible cannel coal perforated **bead**, truncated cone shape. D. 15mm, Ht. 4mm, central perforation D. 3mm. Probably Roman.
    7250 (F1499)/*9021*/Phase 3 gully, Enclosure 4.

*5. Fragment of a blue glass annular **bead**, with applied white trails; Iron Age to Anglo-Saxon type (Guido 1999, Type 6ix).
    2689/9017/Phase 6 post-hole, Enclosure 1.

6. Complete cast copper alloy **bracelet**, undecorated, D-section. D. 63mm, T. 4mm.
    MF1/4447/Unstratified.

Dress pins
(Plate IV)
Dress fittings were relatively common, with a small range of pins, brooches, fasteners and belt-fittings recovered. Altogether four were found, two of them Mid–Late Saxon and two late to post-medieval. One of the early pins (Fig.

Phase	Iron bars/rods	Iron strips	Iron points	Iron loops/rings	Iron sheet	Pb scraps	Unidentified
2				1			
3		2			1	6	1
4	2	2				2	
5	3	8	1	2	8	16	20
9	8	7	1	1	6	17	13
10	10	11	1	1	4	5	15
11	3	2	1	1	5		14
12	13	26		5			
13	1				1		
unphased		6	3	8	6	65	31

Table 4.1 Summary table showing amounts of non-described metalwork

4.1 No. 7) was found in a secure context, while the other (Fig. 4.1 No. 8) was a surface find; typologically they belong together (Biddle 1990, 553–4, Type A). The small size of the head distinguishes them from similar examples which date to the first half of the 14th century (Egan and Pritchard 1991, 302). No. 10, with a wire-wound head, is a medieval or post-medieval type (Margeson 1993, 11; Crummy 1988, Type 1). It was found here in a 15th-century context, according with the commonly-accepted date for their introduction from the Continent (although examples have been found in contexts three centuries earlier at Winchester: Biddle 1990, 560). Although often termed 'sewing pins', these seem in fact to have served as head-dress and dress-fastenings. Comparatively, West Fen Road produced low numbers of such pins (cf. 40 dress/hair pins and 72 'sewing pins' from Winchester, and ten and eighteen respectively from Norwich: Biddle 1990; Margeson 1993). The other pin, No. 9, consists of only the shaft, which makes it harder to date, but its gauge would accord with a 12th-century or later date (Egan and Pritchard 1991, 297). Two lengths of copper alloy wire were also recovered, both from later medieval contexts (Nos 11 and 12). At 1.5mm in diameter, these lie at the upper end of Biddle's range for sewing pins (1990, fig. 153), and perhaps had a different function: as a support for a head-dress, perhaps (J. Cowgill, *pers. comm.*), or for use as fasteners (*cf.* Margeson 1993, 19 for 15th–16th-century examples).

*7.   Copper alloy dress **pin** complete with polyhedral head with many diamond and triangular undecorated facets; cast; small collar; swelling at hip; 7th to 10th century. Plate IV.
      6446 (F1540)/*9092*/Phase 5 ?fence-post trench fill, Enclosure 4.
*8.   Copper alloy dress **pin** with polyhedral head with ring and dot on each facet; small collar; incomplete shaft broken at waist just above slight swelling at hip; 7th to 9th century.
      Surface/*9497*/Unstratified.
9.   Fine wire shaft of copper alloy dress **pin**. L. 36mm, D. 1mm; medieval to post-medieval.
      Tr12/*4446*/Unphased.
10.   Copper alloy dress **pin** with wire-wound head. L. 45mm, D. 1mm, head D. 2mm; medieval to post-medieval.
      7063 (F2529)/*9097*/Phase 12 building foundation, Enclosure 18.
11.   Twisted copper alloy **wire**. L. *c.* 190mm, D. 1.5mm; medieval.
      7000 (F2519)/*9094b*/Phase 11 gravelled yard, Enclosure 18/21.
12.   Copper alloy **wire**, possibly a head-dress fragment. L. *c.* 155mm, D. 1.5mm; medieval.
      7012 (F2528)/*9095*/Phase 13 ditch, Enclosure 7.

Brooches and a badge
(Pl. V)
Three brooches were recovered from the site, one of which appears to be Roman and two Late Saxon. The Langton Down brooch (Fig. 4.1 No. 13) was recovered from general surface collection, although is well-dated. Fig. 4.1 No. 14 clearly belongs to a recently identified class of Late Saxon *cloisonné* enamel brooches. Formally identified by Buckton (1986), these date to the late 10th and 11th centuries, though some have previously been assigned erroneously to the late 4th century (*cf.* Kendrick 1938, 67, fig. 13). While these usually have seven lobes set with enamel or other insets, one brooch from London has the same arrangement as seen here, with four principal lobes and eight subsidiary lobes arranged in pairs between them (*ibid.*, fig. 13 no. 2; Buckton 1986, no. 7), as does another from Quidenham, Norfolk (Gurney 1996, 395). This brooch is not a direct parallel, as the centrepiece design is different: a similar 'wavy equal-armed cross' design is, however, seen on two other (flanged, not lobed) brooches (Buckton 1986, nos 11 and 14), from ?Kent and from Billingsgate, London (the latter also employing blue and green enamel). These brooches have a distribution centred on the eastern counties, London and Kent (Backhouse *et al.* 1984, 101) and were perhaps intended to have an apotropaic function (Buckton 1986, 15). Buckton (*ibid.*, 16) also argues that the use of the double-stepped design, as here, is related to Byzantine or Ottonian enamel of the last third of the 10th century and the first half of the 11th.

Fig. 4.1 No. 15 only survives as a fragment, but is part of a Late Saxon disc brooch. A direct parallel in silver is known from Wetheringsett cum Brockford, Suffolk (West 1998, 104 fig. 134.8), and others in copper alloy from Norwich (Margeson and Williams 1985, 29 nos 1 and 2) and Sedgeford, Norfolk (Faulkner 1997). They are of 10th-century date and English manufacture (Wilson 1964, 48–9; Evison 1957, 1969), seemingly restricted to the area of the Danelaw, especially its urban centres such as York, Thetford and Norwich (Leahy and Paterson 2001, 197). A parallel for No. 16 has not yet been identified, though it appears to be a badge, rather than a brooch, perhaps suggesting a post-Conquest date, although the motif is seen on earlier pieces (J. Graham-Campbell, *pers. comm.*).

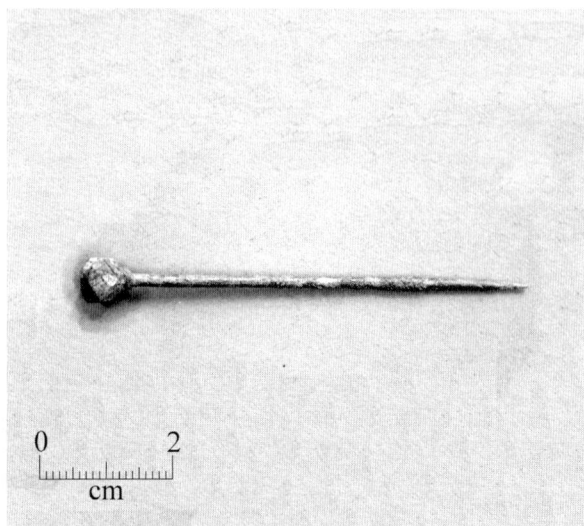

Plate IV Small find No. 7: copper alloy dress pin

Plate V Small find No. 15: copper alloy disc brooch

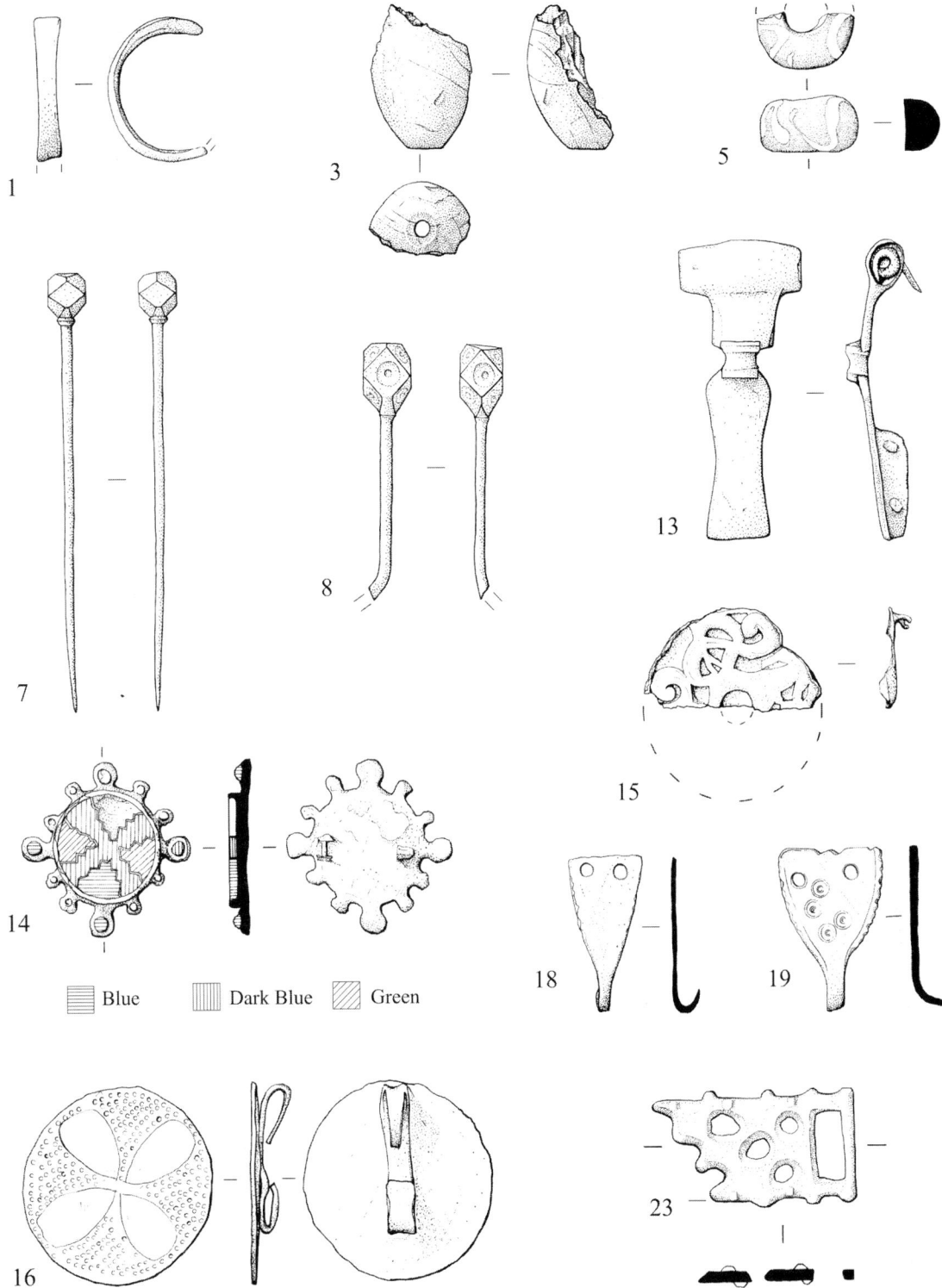

Blue   Dark Blue   Green

Figure 4.1 Small finds relating to dress and personal possessions I. All at 1:1

*13. Badly cast Langton Down Type copper alloy **brooch**; (not bowed or ribbed) with encased springs; T-shaped upper divided from the broad foot by a raised knob; Hawkes and Hull 1947 Type xii; 1st half of 1st century AD.
Surface/*9105b*/Unstratified.

*14. Copper alloy disc **brooch** with four principal and eight subsidiary lobes and *cloisonné* enamel centrepiece, in very good condition. The main lobes are inset with blue enamel, while the subsidiary lobes are set with spheres of copper. Traces of catch-plate and two lugs for spring on reverse, pin missing (but would not have corresponded with the axis of the cross design on the front). The copper gilt *cloisonné* enamel disc has four rather imprecise double step cells spread around the perimeter (two opposing are green, one is blue and the other missing), leaving a wavy equal-armed cross (also deep blue) in the centre; late 10th–11th century.
8948/9025/Unphased.

*15. Fragment of copper alloy disc **brooch**; around half survives; decorated with a concave-sided figure with corners extended to form interlaced double-contoured knots, with a circular sunken field in the centre; the whole sits within a plain narrow band for a border; damaged hinge on reverse. Decoration is debased Borre style; 10th century. Plate V.
Surface/*9106*/Unstratified.

*16. Copper alloy **disc** with incised lines outlining four petals, background in-filled with punched dots; unusual offset hooked attachment on reverse; possibly a badge.
3408 (F796)/*4436*/Phase 10 well fill, Enclosure 16.

Hooked tags and lace tags
(Pl. VI)

Of the four definite examples of hooked tags (Nos 17–20), two are triangular and two U-shaped. There may be a further example: No. 21 has only a single central perforation and no hook, so this must remain doubtful. The two examples found in archaeological deposits (Fig. 4.1 Nos 17 and 18) were at the east and west edges of the site, both in areas which saw intense occupation from Phase 6 onwards; these can be considered *in situ* finds. The four definite examples can all be dated to the Late Saxon period (Hinton in Biddle 1990, 548). While their definite function remains uncertain, there is evidence to support their use as clothes fasteners, garter hooks and purse fasteners (Margeson 1993, 16). No. 19 has ring and dot decoration similar to Biddle 1990 no. 1419, which, although found in a later context, was assumed to date to the 11th century or earlier. Crummy (1988, 12), however, suggests that their date range may stretch into the late 12th or 13th century (*contra* Biddle *ibid.*, who argues that no examples have been found from medieval Southampton).

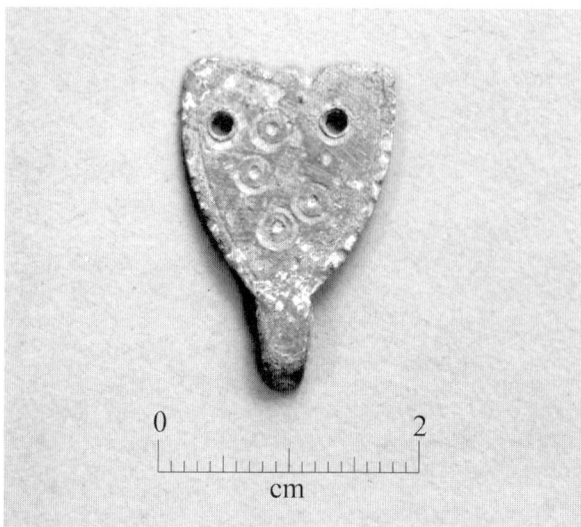

Plate VI Small find No. 19: copper alloy hooked tag

A single example of a lace tag (No. 22) was recovered, from a Phase 11 context. This would appear to be in phase, as these date to the 13th century at the earliest in London (Egan and Pritchard 1991, 281); the fashion for tighter, figure-hugging clothes in the 14th century created a greater demand for the use of laces (*ibid.*, 284), so several pairs of lace tags might be used on a single male or female costume (Margeson 1993, 22). In this light, the single example found here pales in comparison to the huge numbers usually found in medieval and post-medieval contexts (*ibid.*) — perhaps these new fashions were still only just filtering through to the site's inhabitants by the time occupation was in decline here.

17. Triangular copper alloy **hooked tag**; upper edge damaged and hook broken; no decoration; two perforations. L. 28mm, W. 13mm; 10th–11th century.
1531 (F315)/*4434*/Phase 6 boundary ditch fill, Enclosure 1.

*18. Complete copper alloy triangular **hooked tag** with two attachment holes, undecorated; probably 8th–11th century but long-lived type.
7813 (F1787)/*9099*/Phase 9 ditch, Enclosure 7.

*19. U-shaped copper alloy **hooked tag** with incomplete hook; notched upper edge and sides; two attachment holes; single incised line frames four faint ring and dot motifs; 10th–11th century. Plate VI.
Surface/*4429*/Unstratified.

20. Incomplete U-shaped copper alloy **hooked tag** with some detail around the edge, otherwise plain; only one perforation survives. L. 21mm, W. 14mm; 8th–11th century.
Surface/*4444a*/Unstratified.

21. Possible copper alloy **hooked tag**; small oval piece of sheet with small pointed extension in the same plane as the disc but unhooked; central perforation surrounded by six ring and dot motifs. L. (including projection) 18mm, W. 9mm; early medieval.
Surface/*4444b*/Unstratified.

22. Copper alloy **lace-tag**, with edges folded in (Margeson 1993 Type 2); L. 34mm; probably 15th–17th century but a long-lived type.
7000 (F2519)/*9094a*/Phase 11 gravelled yard, Enclosure 18/21.

Copper alloy buckles and belt-fittings
(Pl. VII)

Just three copper alloy buckles were found, all of them surface finds. Fig. 4.1 No. 23 may either be a rare example of a Mid Saxon openwork buckle, or may date to the 10th or 11th centuries. Openwork decoration is known from 7th- and 8th-century contexts, both on buckles and girdle-hangers (Evison 1956, 94), although Margeson (in Rogerson 1995, 65–6) has a very similar openwork hasp (no. 99) which she dates to the later period on the basis of its similarity with openwork strap-ends of that date. Otherwise the buckles are presumably medieval, although the tiny buckle Fig. 4.2 No. 24 is hard to parallel. The copper alloy wire ring No. 26 may also represent the remains of a medieval buckle. There are five copper alloy buckle plates. The bossed and stamped example Fig. 4.2 No. 27 came from a Late Saxon context. The undecorated No. 28 is hard to date, but probably belongs in its Phase 9 context, while the three surface finds all seem to be later. The zig-zag decoration on No. 29 is paralleled by a 14th-century London find (Egan and Pritchard 1991, no. 262), and No. 30 is also paralleled in medieval London (*ibid.*, no. 749).

Of the five copper alloy strap-ends, No. 31 was found in a Roman context and there is no reason to suspect that it is intrusive. No. 32, a split-end strap-end with an animal-head terminal, is clearly Mid–Late Saxon, although found through surface collection (*cf.* Hinton in Biddle 1990, 500–1 for parallels). The remainder are probably medieval: the punched triangular decoration on No. 33 suggests a broadly medieval date (*cf.* Egan and

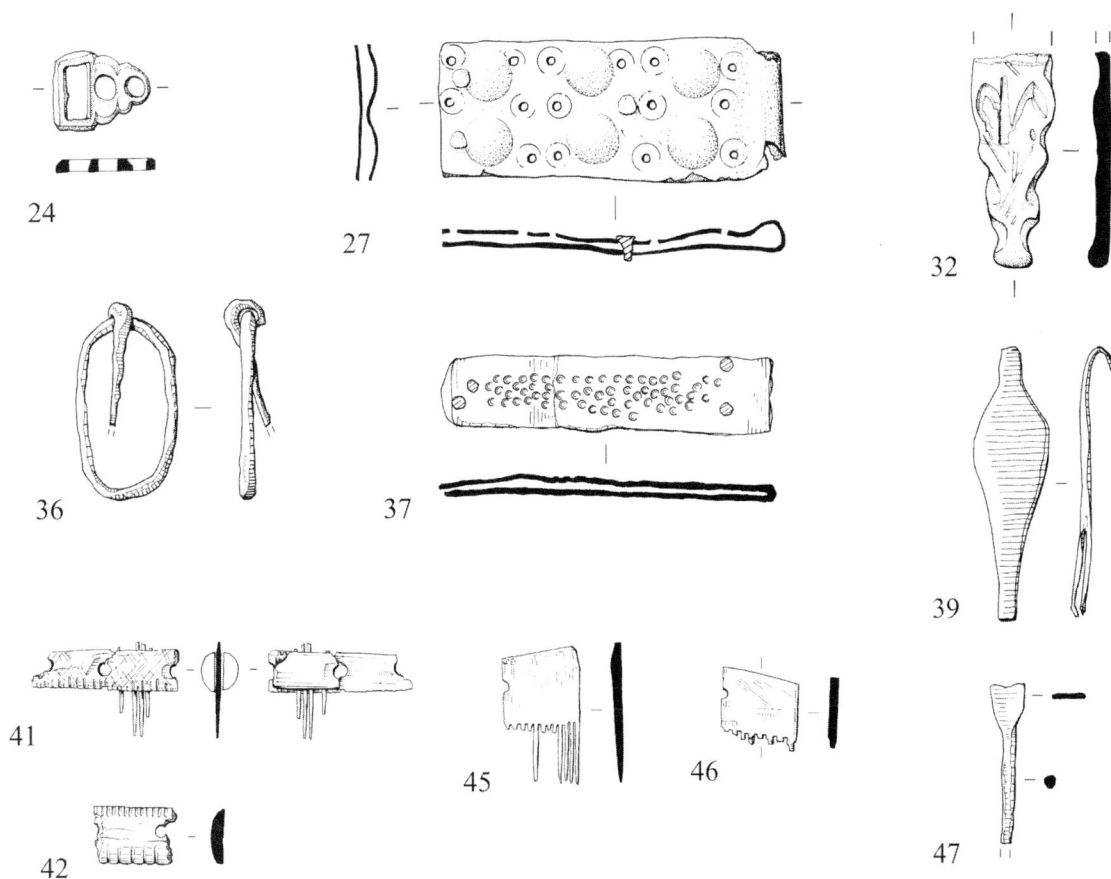

Figure 4.2 Small finds relating to dress and personal possessions II. All at 1:2 except Nos 24, 27 and 32 at 1:1

Plate VII Small find No. 32: copper alloy strap-end

Pritchard 1991, nos 303 and 514; Biddle 1990, no. 1092); No. 34 would have had a forked spacer, and indicates a 14th–15th century date (*ibid.*, 80), while the undecorated No. 35 was found in a Phase 9 context.

*23. Small copper alloy **buckle**, with openwork plate, broken; early medieval.
Surface/*4449*a/Unstratified.

*24. Tiny copper alloy **buckle**; rectangular frame with composite tiny triangular plate; circular hole for pin with another for rivet; too small for a spur buckle; medieval.
Surface/*4445*c/Unstratified.

25. Half a copper alloy **buckle** with cast oval plain frame of flattened oval section; W. 39mm, T. 4mm.
Surface/*4445*b/Unstratified.

26. Complete copper alloy **ring** made from wire, circular-section, distorted. D. *c*. 23mm, T. 2mm.
Surface/*4445*e/Unstratified.

*27. Rectangular copper alloy **buckle-plate**; made from sheet folded over and riveted together with three copper alloy rivets, recessed for buckle; decorated with six stamped raised domes, interspersed with fifteen incised ring and dot motifs; early medieval?
7055 (F1578)/*9096*/Phase 7 ditch, Enclosure 4.

28. Simple rectangular copper alloy **buckle-plate**, recessed for buckle. Folded and riveted sheet, with one broken domed rivet. L. 26mm, W. 28mm, T. 0.5mm.
3334 (F775)/*4435*/Phase 9 well fill, Enclosure 16.

29. Copper alloy **buckle-plate** fragment; thick sheet with single hole for rivet, bent towards the broken end; decorated with incised zig-zags along the sides. L. 32mm, W. 10mm, T. 1mm.
Surface/*4445*d/Unstratified.

30. Copper alloy **buckle-plate** consisting of a plain square sheet with five rivet holes, recessed for buckle. L. 27, W. 21mm.
Topsoil/*9114*b/Unstratified.

31. Possible **strap-end**. Copper alloy sheet fragment with the remains of a rivet? L. 12mm, W. 7mm.
7250 (F1499)/*9098*/Phase 3 gully, Enclosure 4.

*32. Copper alloy **strap-end** with crudely cast animal head terminal with a pronounced squarish snout in relief and extended rabbit-like ears behind; cut or broken across shaft; early medieval. Plate VII.
Surface/*9105*a/Unstratified.

33. Copper alloy **strap-end** made from thick rectangular sheet folded in half and joined by a single rivet; decorated with a double row of

punched triangles along both sides and the top. L. 26mm, W. 14mm, T. 4mm; medieval.
Surface/*4445a*/Unstratified.

34. Front plate from a composite copper alloy **strap-end** that would have had a forked spacer; round grooved aperture; two perforations, one containing a rivet. L. 43mm, W. 20mm; 14th–15th century.
Surface/*4448*/Unstratified.

35. Copper alloy **strap-end** made from sheet; undecorated; possible traces of leather strap; 37mm x 8mm x 2mm; probably late 13th–15th-century.
8 (F537)/*4430*/Phase 9 pit fill, Enclosure 16.

Iron buckles and belt-fittings

Just one iron buckle was found: Fig. 4.2 No. 36, with a simple oval frame, from a Late Saxon context. There is also a large iron strap-end (Fig. 4.2 No. 37), a Y-shaped fitting from a Roman feature (No. 38), and Fig. 4.2 No. 39 is an iron clip which may have fastened onto a strap or belt; it was found in a Late Saxon context and is paralleled at Coppergate, York.

*36. Iron **buckle**: complete simple oval frame with intact pin.
806 (F3108)/*4495*/Phase 7 pit, Enclosure 1.

*37. Large iron **strap-end**; made from folded sheet; possibly with rounded ends; four rivet holes, two at folded end with rivets *in situ*; punched circular indents (possibly hammering) form a basic decoration; plated.
4809 (F1090)/*9139*/Phase 7 ditch, Enclosure 12.

38. Iron **strap fitting**; Y-shaped object made from sheet metal. L. 33mm, W. 22mm, T. 4mm.
8028 (F1468)/*9242*/Phase 3 ditch, Enclosure 4.

*39. Iron **clip**; oval panel with a hooked terminal at one end; matching hook at other end probably broken off; plated; may have clipped onto a strap or belt; 9th to 11th centuries? (*cf.* Ottaway 1992, no. 3797).
3113 (F719)/*4559*/Phase 7 pit, Enclosure 13.

Combs
by Ian Riddler

Fragments of seven combs, mostly made from antler, were retrieved from separate contexts. Both single and double-sided composite combs are present. The earliest fragment (No. 40) comprises the central part of a tooth segment from a double-sided composite comb of late Roman date. The teeth on one side of the segment are heavily worn. In Roman Britain, these combs may date back to the 3rd century, but the majority belong to the 4th century (MacGregor 1985, 92; Riddler 1988, 374).

The comb fragments Fig. 4.2 No. 41 are undoubtedly of Mid Saxon date, although they came from a medieval context. They fit together and form part of a small, narrow double-sided composite comb, which is decorated on one connecting plate and blank on the other. This method of decorating just one of the connecting plates, and thereby producing a display side for the comb, is a Mid Saxon innovation (Tempel 1972, 57; Riddler 1997, 194). The comb is relatively narrow and may not have exceeded 35mm in width. Double-sided composite combs of similar dimensions are known from a number of Mid Saxon sites, including Canterbury, *Hamwic*, Ipswich, Maidenhead and *Sandtun* (Riddler 2001; Riddler *et al.* forthcoming). A comb fragment of a similar type, possibly of 7th-century date, came from Harston, Cambridgeshire (Malim 1993, fig. 20). The decoration of one connecting plate with a lattice pattern forms a design commonly seen in the earlier part of the Mid Saxon period and confirms the dating of this comb.

A connecting plate from a double-sided composite comb, Fig. 4.2 No. 42, came from a Late Saxon context. It includes broad teeth on one side and fine teeth on the other, and has a broad, undecorated connecting plate. Double-sided composite combs with both broad and fine teeth occur sporadically through most of the Anglo-Saxon period, although there are comparatively few from Late Saxon contexts — in part because of the 9th-century introduction of the horn and bone composite comb, which remained popular in England and northern France until the 12th century (Biddle 1990, 678–90; Pritchard 1991, 199–200). They have been found, however, at London, St Neots and York (Pritchard 1991, 199, fig. 3.79; Lethbridge and Tebbutt 1933, fig. 3.4; MacGregor *et al.* 1999, 1932–3, fig. 893 and 894). An unpublished Late Saxon double-sided composite comb from Canterbury (Longmarket) is undecorated and has teeth of different fineness on either side, in the manner of this comb.

The end segment and accompanying tooth segment No. 43 also come from a narrow comb, with a curved graduation of the teeth. It may be of Early or Mid Saxon date although it came from a Late Saxon context. Little can be said of the fragmentary tooth segment No. 44 from a Mid Saxon context, which includes teeth of similar fineness on each side. It is noticeable that some of the remnant tooth stubs are heavily worn, suggesting that the comb was only discarded following heavy use. The segment is riveted on one edge, utilising the most common system for the Anglo-Saxon period.

The two remaining tooth segments, Fig. 4.2 Nos 45 and 46, originally formed part of single-sided composite combs. At first sight, they have few characteristics that might serve to identify their comb types and relative dating. However, the former, from a Mid Saxon context, has a rising crest located above the line of the connecting plate. The rising line suggests that the segment lay towards one end of the comb and served as the first part of a winged terminal that extended across several tooth and end segments. Combs of this specific type, with 'extended' winged end segments, are confined to the Mid Saxon period and are known from elsewhere in East Anglia. They include combs from Barrington and West Stow, as well as several examples from Brandon and Ipswich (Malim and Hines 1998, fig. 3.63.105; West 1985, fig. 73.2; Riddler *et al.* forthcoming). No. 46 has a curved back and is made of bone or antler. It may derive from a single-sided composite comb but it is more likely to come from a handled comb. Similar handled combs with lightly curved backs are known from a variety of sites, including Barton Court Farm, Cottam, *Hamwic*, Ipswich and Pakenham (Miles 1984, fig. 33; Haldenby 1992, fig. 7.2; Holdsworth 1976, fig. 21.11; West 1963, fig. 55.1; 1998, fig. 119.1). Handled combs first occur in the later part of the 7th century and they continue in use during the Anglo-Saxon period (Riddler 1990a, b).

Few of the fragments can be dated with any accuracy but in general terms the Mid Saxon assemblage does correspond with the established pattern for the period, under which double-sided composite combs were used almost to the exclusion of single-sided composites in the south of England, but single-sided composites were more common to the north of the Thames. Handled combs were widely distributed in both areas (Riddler 2004, 146–7).

40. Fragmentary antler tooth segment from double-sided composite **comb**, teeth survive only as stubs. Originally six teeth per cm on either side; traces of wear on stubs, particularly on one side of comb; segment riveted along one edge. L. 14mm, T. 3mm.
8032 (F32)/*9023*/Phase 3 ditch, Enclosure 4.

*41. Fragment of double-sided composite **comb**, consisting of tooth segment and three sections of connecting plate, two of which fit together; six teeth per cm on either side, surviving teeth heavily worn. Two of connecting plate fragments decorated with lattice pattern of doubled crossing diagonal lines. Saw marks from cutting of teeth are prominently incised on one edge. Third connecting plate fragment is blank and does not include any saw marks; Mid Saxon.
2322 (F2354)/*9016*/Phase 10 ditch.

*42. Part of undecorated antler connecting plate for a double-sided composite **comb**. Saw marks indicate were originally three teeth per cm on one side and seven on other. Connecting plate fragment pierced by single rivet hole.
1926 (F426)/*2873*/Phase 6 beam-slot fill, Enclosure 1.

43. Fragmentary antler tooth segment and end segment from double-sided composite **comb**. End segment has straight back and curves towards teeth, more markedly on one side. Tooth segment originally included five teeth per cm on one side and six on other, riveted on one edge. End segment W. 36mm.
2362 (F388)/*3196*/Phase 6 boundary ditch fill, Paddock C, Enclosure 13.

44. Fragmentary antler tooth segment for double-sided composite **comb**, teeth survive only as stubs. Five teeth per cm on either side, although some cut to uneven widths. Stubs show traces of heavy wear. Tooth segment riveted on one edge. L.16mm.
753 (F598)/*9014*/Phase 5 boundary ditch fill, Enclosure 1.

*45. Incomplete antler tooth segment from single-sided composite **comb**, now lacking some teeth. Six teeth per cm, remaining show traces of wear. Tooth segment riveted on one edge and includes rounded top edge, which protruded originally above line of connecting plates.
6835 (F1524)/*9019*/Phase 5 post-hole fill, Structure 6, Enclosure 4.

*46. Fragmentary bone or antler tooth segment from single-sided composite **comb**, no teeth now surviving. Four teeth per cm originally, some stubs heavily worn. Segment riveted on one side and has lightly curved back.
Surface/*9026*/Unstratified.

Writing implement

A single possible iron stylus was found, broken at the shaft. Most Anglo-Saxon styli were made of copper alloy, although iron examples have been found in pre-Conquest contexts at York and Dorestad (Netherlands) (Biddle 1990, 730). Although Roman styli are usually of iron, these have narrow spatulate ends and slender moulded shafts (*ibid.*). This example more closely resembles Anglo-Saxon types, and was found in a Late Saxon context.

*47. Possible iron **stylus**; V-shaped head (W. 15mm); shaft incomplete.
2477 (F592)/*4541*/Phase 7 ditch, Enclosure 1.

II. Furnishings and household equipment
(Figs 4.3–4.5)

Furniture fittings

One copper alloy hinge fragment (No. 48) might once have belonged to a casket. Other possible medieval furniture fittings are an iron binding ('strap hinge', No. 49) from a Phase 9 context and some of the copper alloy strip fragments which have not been individually described. The cast copper alloy ring (No. 50), although on the large side, may have been used to suspend curtains or hangings (*cf.* Margeson 1993, 82), although it might easily have been a buckle frame, or used for vessel suspension (Egan 1998, 169). Aside from these, there is very little evidence for furniture, or other more homely items. No evidence was recovered of candlesticks or hearth equipment, for example, and just one copper alloy stud (No. 51, unphased) might have been used in some form of furniture (although it might also have belonged to a harness: *cf.* Margeson 1993, 83).

48. Copper alloy **hinge** fragment, with rectangular plate, four *in situ* domed rivets and one missing, two hinge attachments 8mm wide. L. 36mm, W. 30mm.
Surface/*4450*/Unstratified.

49. Iron **binding**; strap bent at right angle with a circular flat perforated plate at each end; both have remains of nails in situ; D-sectioned; mineral-preserved wood on reverse; grain runs transversely across strap; also known as box or strap hinges. L. 117mm, W. 20mm, T. 10mm.
3564/*4608*/Phase 9, fourth floor of Structure 26, Enclosure 16.

50. Cast copper alloy **ring**. D. 50mm.
Surface/*9105*c/Unstratified.

51. Copper alloy **stud**; quatrefoil around a domed centre stamped out from sheet; single thin shank on reverse. L. 12mm, W. 11mm, T. 3mm; probably medieval.
Topsoil/*4443*a/Unstratified.

Pottery

Iron Age pottery
by Sarah Percival

Introduction
Six hundred and fifty-five sherds of Iron Age pottery (7781g) were recovered from excavated contexts and surface collection. The earliest Iron Age pottery identified is a small quantity of flint-tempered sherds dating to the 5th–4th century BC. The second, more substantial, collection is of later Iron Age date, spanning the period *c.* 300BC to the 1st century BC, and is characterised by undecorated jars, predominantly in handmade sandy fabrics. A very small component of wheelmade later Iron Age/earliest Roman pottery was also present, including butt beakers, dating to the 1st century AD.

Fabrics
Sherds were assigned to fabric groups on the basis of the principal inclusion present. Five main groups were identified: with burnt flint, grog, shell, vegetable and quartz-sand (Table 4.2). Twenty-nine sherds of earlier Iron Age date were identified in burnt flint-rich fabric, F1. These included a flat-topped rim from a jar with a slightly everted neck (26g) and 28 undecorated body sherds. The sherds were relatively large (*c.* 16g each) and just under half showed signs of abrasion (thirteen sherds, 475g).

Thirteen fabrics were identified within the later Iron Age assemblage, from four main fabric groups: grog-, shell-, vegetable- and quartz sand-tempered.

Sandy fabrics
The assemblage was dominated by quartz sand-tempered fabrics, which represented 72.88% of the total assemblage by weight. The predominance of sandy fabrics shows strong parallels with other late Iron Age sites in and around the Isle of Ely, in particular Hurst Lane (76.39% of total weight), Watson's Lane, Little Thetford (73.77%), St Johns Road, Ely (82.3%) and Wardy Hill, Coveney (71.80%: see Hill in Evans 2003a for overview). The sandy fabrics were all very similar in appearance, being mostly red/orange brown to dark grey/black with a dense, hard-fired texture. The majority of the sandy sherds were of medium coarse fabric Q2, which contained visible rounded quartz grains but no other large inclusions. Fabrics Q3, Q4 and Q5 were similar to Q2 but contained additional inclusions of small quartz pebbles and red ?iron oxide fragments, sparse shell and sparse unburnt flint respectively. All these fabrics appear to represent durable, medium coarse wares for the production of utilitarian vessels. Fabric Q7 has a well-sorted sandy texture and burnished surface, and along with micaceous fabric Q1 represents the finer fabrics found at the site. The choice of sand-rich clay sources for pottery production, as opposed to fossil shell, seems deliberate and appears to be a cultural preference practised around the Ely area in the Mid–Late Iron Age, replacing an earlier propensity for flinty fabrics.

Only two wheelmade sherds were identified amongst the material examined (fabric Q6).

Grog-tempered fabrics
Two grog-tempered fabrics were identified, one containing quartz sand and sub-square grog while the other was a coarser more poorly mixed

Fabric type	quantity	weight (g)	% of total quantity	% of total weight
Flint	29	475	4.43%	6.10%
Grog	31	779	4.73%	10.01%
Quartz sand	506	5671	77.25%	72.88%
Shell	59	532	9.01%	6.84%
Vegetable	24	301	3.66%	3.87%
Undiagnostic	6	23	0.92%	0.30%
Total	655	7781	100.00%	100.00%

Table 4.2 Quantity and weight of Iron Age pottery by fabric group

fabric. The sherds do not appear to be wheelmade. Large pieces of grog are visible in several sherds of otherwise grog-free fabric, suggesting that they may sometimes represent accidental inclusions.

Shelly fabrics
Two shelly fabrics were identified. S1 contained a moderate quantity of shell with a mixed quartz sand, whilst fabric S2 contained an abundance of large shell pieces producing a light, vacuous texture to the sherds. Shelly fabrics represent only 6% of the assemblage and may have been chosen specifically for the production of large storage vessels; this is suggested by the unusual thickness of some of the sherds found.

Vegetable tempered fabrics
Six sherds (301g, 3.87%) contained voids indicative of vegetable tempering agents.

Flint-tempered fabrics
The lone diagnostic sherd in an earlier Iron Age flint-tempered fabric is from the upper part of a slack-shouldered jar, similar to those prevalent in the later Iron Age. This suggests that this form was very long lived and continued in use until the very latest Iron Age and the time of the transition to Roman ways.

Forms
The assemblage contains no whole vessels or complete profiles, though 132 rim sherds were found, the majority being flat-topped everted rims in sand-rich fabrics. Around 44 vessels are represented. Where larger sherds survive, their profiles suggest upright necks and rims with slack-shouldered bodies typical of the later Iron Age in the region (Hill in Evans 2003a). The vessels are medium sized, the smallest measurable rim being 120mm in diameter and the largest 240mm (one example). The majority of measurable vessels have a rim diameter of 140mm (75 sherds, 56.82%).

Other jar forms present include the partially complete remains of an open globular jar with no distinct neck from pit F1448, and a shallow, globular open bowl with incised curvilinear decoration similar to 'late pre-Belgic' material from Weekley, Northants (Jackson and Dix 1987; Elsdon 1993, E7a 55). Small quantities of similar La Tène-style decorated pottery have been found on several sites around Cambridgeshire, such as Greenhouse Farm, Fen Ditton, and are often associated with later Iron Age plain ware assemblages (Hill in Evans 2003a). A further substantial sherd from a vessel with an angular shoulder and upright rim in sandy burnished fabric Q7 represents one of the few finer vessels found on the site.

Burnishing occurs on 117 sherds (1485g, 19.08%) and is mostly combined with sandy fabrics. Small quantities of burnished shell-, grog- and vegetable-tempered sherds are also present. Less then 1% of the sherds have a smoothed finish. Ten sherds have a roughly scored surface but do not have the deeper, irregular striations that typify local scored ware assemblages. One sherd has a roughly wiped finish. Decoration is limited: apart from the La Tène-style bowl, only two other sherds are decorated, both with slashes or fingernail impressions to the rim top. This form of decoration is found on Early Iron Age sherds, mostly in combination with similar ornamentation to the shoulder, but becomes restricted to rim tops towards the later period.

Conclusion
Dating for the earlier material is based solely on the presence of burnt flint inclusions, which ceased to feature in pottery fabrics in Cambridgeshire from the end of the Early Iron Age (*c.* 300 BC). Close dating of the assemblage is not possible given the lack of diagnostic

sherds, but it appears that there was a limited presence at, or close to, the West Fen Road site during the early–mid 1st millennium BC.

The later Iron Age pottery is a plain ware assemblage typical of those of the period (300–100 BC) around the Isle of Ely. The assemblage is predominantly handmade, essentially domestic in character, and closely comparable to those recently excavated at nearby Hurst Lane (Evans *et al.* forthcoming) and St John's Road (Abrams 2000). All three are mainly comprised of a limited range of medium-sized slack-shouldered open jar forms in dense sandy fabrics, and feature little or no use of scored wares. It has been suggested that scored wares — distinguished by deep scoring in parallel lines or random cross-hatching — were imported into other Ely sites, suggesting that some trade or gift exchange was taking place. The lack of these wares at West Fen Road may indicate that this site was not taking part in such interaction, though further investigation of pottery from adjacent excavations is required to confirm this.

The La Tène-style sherd redeposited within a Late Saxon ditch F613 is of some interest, as small broken sherds of similar type appear to be a fairly regular component of later Iron Age assemblages from around Ely and within East Anglia as a whole (Hill in Evans 2003a). Dating to the 2nd and 1st centuries BC, the function of such vessels is believed to be distinct from normal domestic use and on other sites this is reflected in the deliberate way in which the broken sherds were disposed of. This does not appear to have been the case at West Fen Road, however. The small quantity of wheelmade sherds indicate that activity at the site continued into the late 1st century BC, when new pot-making technology and the associated lifestyle changes began to be adopted.

Roman pottery
by Gwladys Monteil
The assemblage of 1915 sherds is in poor condition, with most being small and extremely abraded. Much of the Roman pottery seems to have been redeposited in later features and many of the groups are very mixed (a high proportion was found residually in Saxon or medieval contexts). Long-lived coarse ware types are dominant and the evidence for a detailed phasing is scarce. The Roman pottery group will therefore be discussed as a whole. All the figures are based on the number of sherds and EVEs (Estimated Vessel Equivalent). The material provides a total EVE figure of 14.56 and an estimated number of vessels of 1513 (Tab. 4.3). When the number of sherds is compared to the Estimated Number of Vessels, the brokenness of the assemblage is even more apparent — 1.26.

Fabric	Total sherds	Total EVEs
Central Gaulish samian	9	0.08
Colchester colour-coated	2	–
Coarse sandy black-burnished	231	1.62
Coarse sandy buff ware	83	0.69
Coarse sandy grey ware	766	5.66
Coarse sandy red ware	408	1.97
Coarse sandy red slipped	5	0.10
Coarse sandy white slipped	4	0.08
Coarse sandy white ware	14	–
East Gaulish samian	1	–
Fine sandy black burnished	7	0.12
Fine sandy buff ware	3	–
Fine sandy grey ware	29	0.05
Fine sandy red ware	13	0.11
Hadham black slipped	3	0.04
Hadham grey ware	2	0.25
Hadham red ware	23	0.50
Harston colour coated	3	0.11
Italic amphora	1	–
'London ware'	2	–
Mica dusted	1	–
Nene Valley colour-coated	41	0.68
Nene Valley grey ware	1	–
Nene Valley white ware	34	0.60
Oxfordshire red ware	17	0.06
Shell-tempered ware	185	1.71
South Gaulish samian	5	–
Spanish amphora	1	–
Terra Nigra	1	–
Trier colour coated	4	0.06
Unidentified colour-coated	8	–
Unidentified samian	5	0.01
Verulamium white ware	3	0.006
Total	**1915**	**14.56**

Table 4.3 Proportion of fabrics present within the Roman pottery assemblage

Imports

A very small number of imports were identified. These include two types of amphorae: an Italic example and a Spanish Dressel 20. A little samian was also recorded (1.41% of the total assemblage), with most of it from Central Gaul (45% of the total samian sherds) followed by products from South Gaul (25%) and East Gaul. A very limited range of forms is present: four types of dishes (Dragendorff 35/36, 36, 31 and 31R) and one type of cup (Dragendorff 33). The last continental vessels come from Trier, with all the examples consisting of colour-coated beakers (0.20% of total assemblage).

Nene Valley wares

Surprisingly, a relatively small part of the assemblage (slightly less than 4% of the total number of sherds) is composed of products coming from the Nene Valley. Nene Valley grey wares account for less than 1% of the total number of Roman sherds, while Nene Valley Colour-Coated Wares constitute 2.14% and Nene Valley cream wares (including mortaria) represent 1.77%. The range of forms present is relatively limited but covers the chronological evolution of the industry itself up to the 4th century AD. The assemblage includes colour-coated beakers. Late colour-coated dishes with plain, triangular and flat-topped rims are in the majority. The colour-coated group also includes castor boxes, flanged bowls, imitations of the samian form Dragendorff 38, jars and jugs. Grey wares include a beaker; cream wares include mainly mortaria and several flagons, one of which has red-painted bands.

Colchester wares

A small number of vessels come from Colchester (0.10% of total number). A colour-coated beaker and a flagon are the only forms identified.

Hadham wares

The products from the little-known Hadham kilns are diverse and consist of grey, red and black-slipped wares (1.46% of total sherds). Plain-rimmed dishes are the only form identified for the black-slipped fabric, while the range of forms present for the Hadham red ware is difficult to assess; one flagon in a Hadham grey ware was recorded.

Oxfordshire wares

One mortarium in a red-slipped ware with multicoloured quartz grits was recorded, while bowls and dishes form the rest of this group (0.88% of total sherds). Few forms have been identified: beaded bowls and a possible C77 (Young 1977, fig. 62, 167).

Verulamium ware

Very few Verulamium examples were recognised, only one definite and two 'possibles'.

Local wares

The majority of the assemblage is made up of local coarse wares (73.4% of total sherds). Most forms represented were long-lived types of jars, beaded rim dishes and basic flanged bowls, most of them influenced by black-burnished ware and Nene Valley ware. Shell-tempered ware is also present in relatively large quantities (9.66% of total sherds). Although the main form is the cooking jar, plain-rimmed dishes are also present. As the assemblage lacks well-preserved vessels, some of these shell-tempered wares might belong to the medieval phase of occupation: St Neots ware is very similar to the Roman type and as it is difficult to distinguish them on fabric alone, the figures must be taken with caution. One mica-dusted beaker, two examples of local London wares and three examples of late Harston colour-coated ware were recorded, as was an unidentified colour-coated vessel with Romano-Saxon decoration. Also of some interest were a couple of cupped ring flagons in a fine unidentified buff ware, and butt beakers of the forms Cam 113 in a grog-tempered fabric.

Conclusion

In terms of pottery supply, this group is different from those at Stonea (Jackson and Potter 1996) and Wimpole (Horton *et al.* 1995) on account of its low fine ware percentages, especially of Nene Valley ware.

Although largely residual, the assemblage points to activity spanning the entire Roman period. A few groups could suggest a minor pre-Flavian phase of occupation, probably in continuity with the Iron Age. The Roman activity seemed to increase significantly in the Hadrianic and Antonine periods, with a clear intensification later in the 3rd century and the 4th century. Activity into the later 4th century is indicated by the small quantity of 'Romano-Saxon' pottery.

The general pattern of the site displays a clear dominance of jars (especially visible through EVE figures) and dishes/bowls as functional categories with, however, a surprisingly high level of drink-related vessels. When compared to Evans's study of ceramic consumption from different Romano-British sites (2001), the present jar-dominated pattern fits well with the basic rural sites model and the local pattern, as a similar proportion of jars were present at Wimpole (Horton *et al.* 1995, 60). The relatively high proportion of drink-related vessels can partly be explained by chronological factors, as several beakers are of the early form Cam 113 and some of the flagons are close to the early Cam form 155. These could belong to the later Iron Age phase, reflecting the manner in which pre-Conquest assemblages are typified by drinking vessels (*ibid.*, 32). The distribution of these early vessels clusters around the Roman structures and seems unlikely to be the result of manuring from another site.

This could point to pre-Flavian occupation/activity, as is also suggested by the Iron Age pottery discussed above.

By comparison, the pre-Flavian group reported on from an excavation on the St Neots/Duxford pipeline exhibits a similar functional pattern, mainly based on jars and bowls but with a high concentration of beakers (Lucas 1997). However, this relatively high proportion of beakers seems to persist in the later Roman period at West Fen Road as Nene Valley, Colchester and Trier colour-coated examples are also present. This functional trait could indicate a local tradition — this stability in beaker consumption was also noticed in the Wimpole assemblage (Horton *et al.* 1995, 60), but unfortunately comparative data are lacking from the St Neots/Duxford site.

The range of wares in use was remarkably homogenous, as the main supply seems to have been fairly local and most of the forms are long-lived. The limited use of non-local wares, especially for the supply of grey wares, is quite clear and can only be explained by a preference for locally produced domestic items. Nene Valley grey wares, for example, are fairly common on other East Anglian sites (Jackson and Potter 1996, 475). The small percentage of finewares (*i.e.* samian, Nene Valley and Colchester colour-coated ware) and amphorae emphasises the basic rural status of the site suggested by the high number of jars, and probably reflects a relatively low to medium status for the site; there is only a little evidence of glass vessels which might suggest otherwise.

Early to Mid Saxon pottery
by Paul Blinkhorn
(Figs 4.3 and 4.4)
The Early/Mid Saxon pottery assemblage comprised 234 sherds with a total weight of 5555g (approximately half the size of the corresponding assemblage recovered from the excavations to the north of West Fen Road). The Estimated Vessel Equivalent, by summation of surviving rim sherd circumference, was 4.31. The majority of the assemblage, which appears fairly typical of East Anglian groups of the time, comprised Mid Saxon Ipswich ware, although two sherds of Maxey-type ware and nine sherds of handmade pottery were also noted. While there is little doubt that there was extensive 8th–9th century occupation at the site, it is impossible to say with certainty that there was post-Roman activity before that time.

Early/Mid Saxon handmade wares
A total of nine such sherds (75g, EVE = 0.14) occurred, with fabrics as follows:

F1. Coarse quartz. Moderate, sub-angular clear quartz up to 2mm. Eight sherds, 67g, EVE = 0.14.
F2. Fine quartz. Moderate to dense sub-rounded quartz, most < 0.5mm. One sherd, 8g, EVE = 0.

The fabrics are fairly typical of handmade pottery in East Anglia, and can be paralleled at almost any site of the period in the region (*e.g.* Blinkhorn 1999) or, indeed, virtually anywhere in Early Saxon England. However, such wares are also known from Mid Saxon England, and assigning a more specific date to the material is extremely difficult. The presence of decorated pottery can be taken as a fairly reliable indicator of Early Saxon (5th–6th century) activity but, due to the fact that decorated pottery rarely accounts for more than 5% of any early Anglo-Saxon domestic assemblage, the absence of such wares cannot be used as evidence of a 7th-century or later date, despite the fact that the Anglo-Saxons generally stopped decorating pottery during the 7th century. In addition, Mid Saxon pottery assemblages in East Anglia tend to comprise mainly Ipswich ware, with a tiny proportion of handmade pottery sometimes also noted, so a small group such as this could equally well be of Early or Mid Saxon date. One sherd has a scar which may indicate where an applied boss has flaked away from the body. Such

decoration tends to be Early Saxon in date, but bossed Mid Saxon pottery is known from Kent (N. Macpherson-Grant, *pers. comm.*). The scar may also indicate that an applied lug has broken away from the pot: lugs, such as the rim-mounted example from this site, generally have no chronological significance.

Ipswich ware
Mid Saxon, slow wheelmade ware, manufactured exclusively in the eponymous Suffolk wic. The material probably had a currency from AD 725–40 to the mid-9th century in this region. There are two main fabric types, although individual vessels which do not conform to these groups also occur.

Group 1: Hard and slightly sandy to the touch, with visible small quartz grains and some shreds of mica. Frequent fairly well-sorted angular to sub-angular grains of quartz, generally measuring below 0.3mm in size but with some larger grains, including a number which are polycrystalline in appearance. Ninety-six sherds, 2342g, EVE = 1.84 (Jars 1.75, pitchers 0.09).

Group 2: Like the sherds in Group 1, these are hard, sandy and mostly dark grey in colour. Their most prominent feature is a scatter of large quartz grains (up to *c.* 2.5mm) which either bulge or protrude through the surfaces of the vessel, giving rise to the term 'pimply' Ipswich ware (*e.g.* Hurst 1976). This characteristic makes them quite rough to the touch. However, some sherds have the same groundmass but lack the larger quartz grains which are characteristic of this group, and chemical analysis suggests that they are made from the same clay. Total 124 sherds, 3407g, EVE = 2.10 (Jars = 1.83, pitchers = 0.10, Buttermarket-type bottles = 0.17).

The Ipswich ware assemblage overwhelmingly comprises small jars, with a small number of large jars and pitchers, and rare oddities in the form of Buttermarket-type bottles (Blinkhorn 1990). A single sherd was decorated with incised ?pendant triangles and stabbing. While such decoration is extremely rare, similar vessels have been noted in Ipswich. Sherds from two Buttermarket-type bottles were decorated with horizontal cordons, one of the standard techniques. Otherwise, decoration was entirely limited to finger-grooving on the shoulders and/or burnishing, both of which are well-known traits of the industry.

Maxey-type ware
Exact chronology uncertain, but generally dated *c.* AD 650–850 (*e.g.* Hurst 1976). Wet-hand finished, reddish-orange to black surfaces. Two main general sources, Northamptonshire and Lincolnshire. Both types are soft to fairly hard, with abundant fossil shell platelets up to 10mm. The Northants types contain Jurassic limestone, but the lack of visible brachiopod fragments in the sherds from this site indicates a non-Jurassic source, with Lincolnshire being the most likely. Vessels are usually straight-sided bowls with simple rims, and/or (in the case of the Lincolnshire types) upright triangular lugs, as were noted at the 'type-site' of Maxey (*e.g.* Addyman 1964, fig. 14, no. 44). Two sherds, 60g, EVE = 0.06.

The data show that the majority of the Ipswich ware assemblage occurred in Phase 7 — *i.e.* Late Saxon — contexts (Table 4.4). Whilst redeposition is almost certainly a factor, this suggests that at least some of the assemblage is of 9th-century date. The fragmentation data indicate that this may well be the case, as both the mean sherd weight and the mean rim completeness show little change from the Mid to Late Saxon periods (*i.e.* Phases 5 to 7). The situation is somewhat complicated by the fact that the mean sherd weight for each of the medieval contexts is actually greater than both the results for the Saxon contexts, although this is not without precedent. Ipswich ware, due to its unusual thickness, is exceptionally robust and body sherds appear highly resistant to redepositional fragmentation. This is not necessarily the case with rim sherds, however, and the rim fragmentation data does show what could be regarded as the expected pattern: the rim sherds from the non-Saxon contexts are considerably more fragmented than those from the Saxon groups. The number of Ipswich ware sherds from medieval contexts is also considerably lower than that from the Saxon assemblage, so the mean sherd weight may be distorted as a result.

Previous work (Blinkhorn in press a) has shown that there is a close relationship between the rim diameter and capacity of Ipswich ware jars. Consequently, a plot of the rim diameter occurrence of such vessels at a site gives a good idea of the range of vessels in use (Fig. 4.4). The jars can be broadly divided into two types, small and large, with the critical division between the two types appearing to be in the range of 161–180mm. The data indicate that the overwhelming majority of the jars from this site have rim diameters in the 'small' region. This is very typical of sites in the hinterland of Ipswich, and can be said to show that the pottery assemblage from this site is of a character that is typical of East Anglia. On sites outside the kingdom, large jars and pitchers tend to make up a much larger proportion of any Ipswich ware assemblage, with

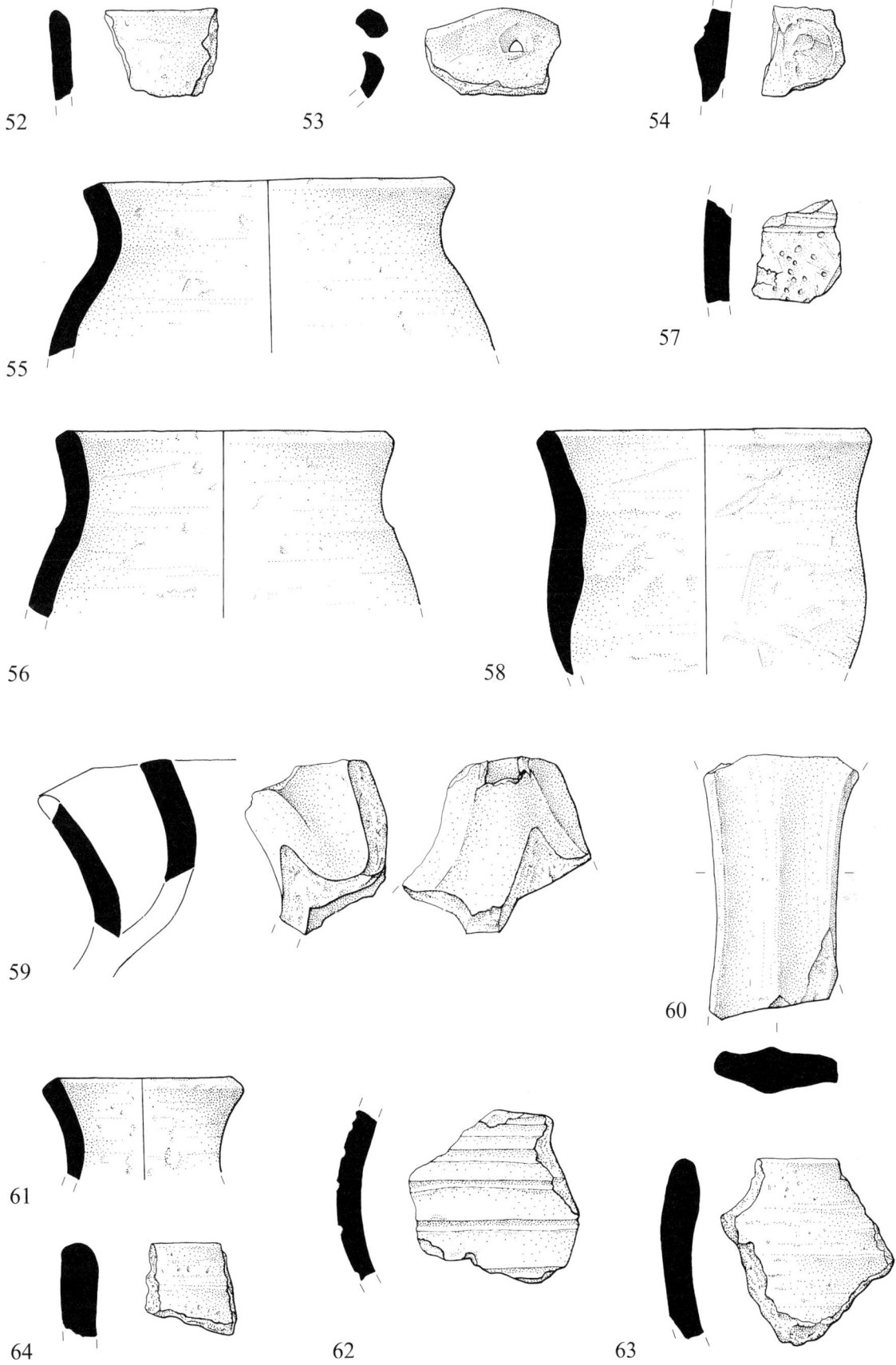

Figure 4.3 Illustrated Saxon pottery. All at 1:2

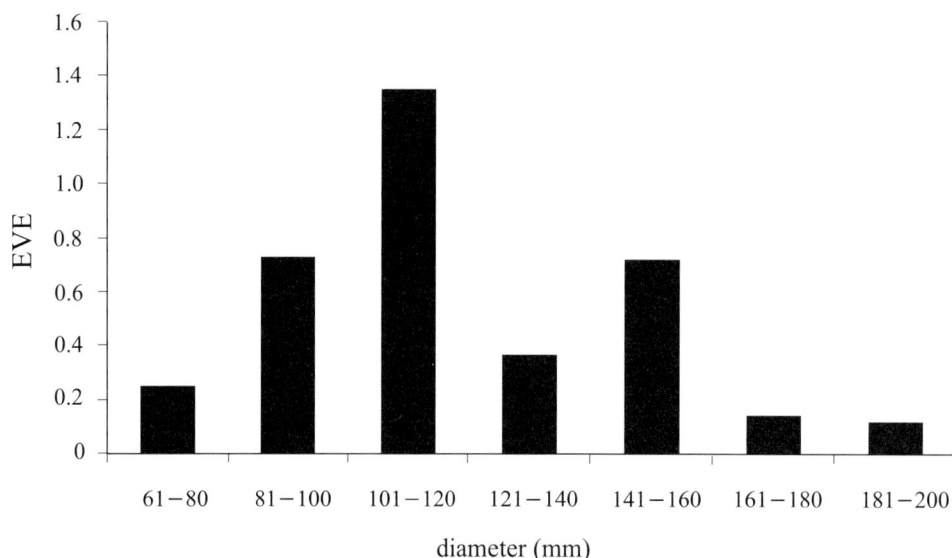

Figure 4.4 Ipswich ware: rim diameter occurrence by EVE

Phase	No	Wt	EVE	Mean Wt	Mean rim % complete
5	60	1445	1.40	24.1g	11.7%
7	109	2528	2.27	23.2g	10.3%
9	31	867	0.05	28.0g	5.0%
10	15	464	0.15	30.9g	7.5%
12	1	27	0.00	27.0g	0
Total	**216**	**5331**	**3.87**		

The pottery was initially bulk-sorted and recorded on a computer using DBase IV software. The material from each context was recorded by number and weight of sherds per fabric type, with featureless body sherds of the same fabric counted, weighed and recorded as one database entry. Feature sherds such as rims, bases and lugs were individually recorded, with individual codes used for the various types. Decorated sherds were similarly treated. In the case of the rim sherds, the form, diameter in mm and the percentage remaining of the original complete circumference was all recorded. This figure was summed for each fabric type to obtain the estimated vessel equivalent (EVE). The terminology used is that defined by the Medieval Pottery Research Group's Guide to the Classification of Medieval Ceramic Forms (MPRG 1998). All the statistical analyses were carried out to the minimum standards suggested by Orton (1998–9, 135–7) using a Dbase package written by the author.

Table 4.4 Ipswich ware occurrence by phase

the former presumed to have been used as containers for traded goods and the latter moving as pots in their own right, as Ipswich ware was the only indigenous industry of the period which produced such vessels.

A single cross-fit was achieved, between two body sherds from a Buttermarket-type bottle (No. 62). Two non-joining sherds from what is almost certainly the same jar were noted in F323, Phase 6 and F647, Phase 9.

Catalogue of illustrated sherds
(Fig. 4.3)

Fabric 1
*52. Rim from handmade jar. Coarse dark grey fabric.
 8181 (F1952)/*8003*/Phase 7 ditch, Enclosure 7.
*53. Upright, rim-mounted lug from jar. Dark grey fabric with black surfaces.
 6438 (F2511)/*6479*/Phase 3 ditch, Enclosure 4.
*54. Body sherd with scar from applied boss or lug. Uniform dark grey fabric.
 6838 (F1527)/*6859*/Phase 3 ditch, Enclosure 4.

Ipswich ware Group 1
*55. Jar rim, West type I.A. Uniform grey fabric.
 2221 (F542)/*1354*/Phase 5 ditch, Enclosure 1.
*56. Jar rim, West type I.A. Uniform grey fabric.
 4262 (F1489)*4915*//Phase 5 ditch fill, Enclosure 4.
*57. Decorated body sherd. Brick red fabric with smoothed grey surfaces.
 539 (F304)/*448*/Phase 8 dividing ditch fill, Enclosure 1.

Ipswich ware Group 2
*58. Jar rim, West type I.D. Pale grey fabric with slightly darker surfaces.
 780 (F345)/*638*/Phase 6 ditch, Enclosure 9.
*59. Pitcher rim and spout. Brick red fabric with grey surfaces.
 6489 (F1570)/*6526*/Phase 5 spread.
*60. Strap handle from pitcher. Uniform dark grey fabric with longitudinal burnishing strokes on outer face.
 1520 (F337)/*1005*/Phase 5 boundary ditch, Enclosure 1.
*61. Rim from Buttermarket-type bottle. Light greyish-brown fabric with darker surfaces.
 4991 (F1165)/*5387*/Phase 8 boundary ditch fill, Enclosure 3.
*62. Joining body sherds from Buttermarket-type bottle. Brick-red fabric with dark grey core and surfaces.
 5747 (F1214)/*5836*/Phase 6 gully, Enclosure 12 and *5750* (F1217)/*5842*/Phase 6 boundary ditch fill, Enclosure 12.

Maxey ware
*63. Rim sherd. Dark grey fabric with reddish-brown inner surface.
 2183 (F533)/*1327*/Phase 6 ditch, Enclosure 14.
*64. Rim sherd. Dark grey fabric with reddish-brown inner surface. Same vessel as No. 63?
 5754 (F1220)/*5855*/Phase 9 boundary ditch fill, Enclosure 9.

Discussion

The Mid Saxon assemblage from this site contains one of the largest groups of Ipswich ware excavated outside of the *wics* of London and Ipswich. When combined with the group from the area to the north of West Fen Road excavated by Northamptonshire Archaeology, the final count is over 600 sherds. From the data from both excavations, it seems that no great status can be attached to the site on the basis of the pottery alone.

The distribution network for Ipswich ware pottery, which all appears to have been manufactured in the eponymous Suffolk *wic*, was extremely efficient, to the extent that over 500 findspots of the ware are known from the county of Norfolk, and that the material was able to meet the domestic needs of the people of East Anglia to a level which meant that local, hand-made wares were rarely used. Thus the size of this assemblage alone cannot be taken as a sign of status, despite Ely's position as the site of one of the most important minster churches in Mid Saxon England. High-status inland sites of the period tend to produce imported pottery, usually material associated with the wine trade, such as Rhenish Relief-Band Amphorae or 'Frankish' Blackware jugs (Blinkhorn 1999). This is perhaps demonstrated by the fact that the excavations at the Lady Chapel in Ely produced three sherds of imported black wares from a Mid Saxon assemblage of around 100 sherds (Blinkhorn in press b), whereas the West Fen Road excavations did not produce a single sherd of imported material from a group six times larger. Assuming that these have not been mistaken for Roman wares, such material is absent from this site, perhaps showing it to be typical rather than exceptional.

Later Saxon and medieval pottery
by David Hall
(Figs 4.5–4.7)
The excavations produced 16,614 sherds of Late Saxon and medieval pottery, weighing 306kg and ranging in date mainly from the 9th century to the 14th century, with the bulk of material being St Neots, Thetford and medieval Ely wares (91%; Table 4.5). There were small quantities of medieval sherds from neighbouring counties but very few fine wares from further afield. Sherds later than the 15th century were not studied in detail.

Each context assemblage was examined during spot-dating to identify all the pottery fabrics as far as possible. Sherds were counted, and the numbers entered on an Excel spreadsheet that includes a free-text 'notes' section. In this, records of vessel forms, numbers of rims and bases, decoration, glazing, likely provenance, and any other relevant items were made, along with an estimate of the date range for each context. A copy of the table is deposited with the site archive.

In view of the very large number of sherds a full detailed analysis, involving the re-examination of every sherd, was not possible within the current resources of time and funding. During the spot-dating, notes were made of important sherds or larger collections that merited further study. These contexts were later examined, and from them samples selected for comparative studies and for illustration. The procedure was considered adequate for an assemblage that derived from sampling the contents of a large number of features as they were exposed: there was very little excavation of deeply stratified deposits to provide relative chronology. The dating depends, therefore, on that already established for each particular fabric, and on the presence of well-dated fineware fabrics.

Selected examples were drawn and compared to literature parallels. The terminology used for ceramic forms follows that recommended by the Medieval Pottery Research Group (MPRG 1998). The details of the fabrics identified were as listed below in relation to the site phasing. The forms are the standard types of medieval jugs, jars and bowls.

St Neots
This well-known Saxo-Norman material was fully described by Hurst (1956) in his primary study of material in the Cambridge region. Much more material has come to light since 1956. The ware is well-made on a wheel, in a fabric full of white shells, and often coloured dark purple with a soapy feel to the surface (2410 sherds, 14.3%).

Thetford
Primary sources for Thetford type wares are the Cambridge studies of Hurst (1957). Material has since been described from Norwich (Jennings 1981, 14–22) and many other places. It was made at places other than Thetford, although this is quite possibly the source of the Ely material. It is a wheel-made hard grey reduced ware, with thin sherds except in the case of large storage vessels. Jar rims tend to be smaller and more finely made than St Neots Ware, the hardness making it possible to craft smaller forms (4,519 sherds, 26.8%).

Stamford
The primary accounts for Stamford Ware are the Cambridge studies of Hurst (1958), with updated work by Kilmurry (1980). The early sherds have clear light green glaze, and 'Developed' Stamford Ware with dark green copper blotches, continues until the 13th century (130 sherds, 0.8%).

Medieval Ely ware
The largest fraction of the material recovered (8,365 sherds, 49.7%) was medieval ware produced at kilns in Ely located near or at Potters Lane (Robinson 1998). The fabric is hard, containing sand and white grits, and most of the forms were hand-made with limited wheel finishing. The industry lasted from the 12th to the 15th century. Ely wares were very conservative and changed little over the centuries, so that body sherds are difficult to date. Two principal sherd types occur: one 'oxidised' and the other 'reduced', the difference probably only reflecting the final oxygenation conditions in the kiln. Both fabrics are hard with a slight sand component, and characteristically contain white grits evenly distributed throughout the fabric and visible on the surface. The grits are usually small, but can be up to 1.5mm in diameter. Overall there is a wide variation in the sand, grit and oolite content. The oxidized sherds have surfaces coloured buff, pink and occasionally red. The core is usually dark. The reduced fabric has grey or nearly black surfaces.

It is often difficult to classify Ely ware into one type or the other, because sherds occur with, say, a buff or pink surface on one side and grey or black on the other. A few sherds are well made with few grits and reduced to a grey colour, very similar to Grimston material in appearance and probably deliberately imitating it. Many of the coarser wares, especially the bowls, are hand-made with limited wheel finishing. Some vessels have a patchy glaze that is almost always opaque, sometimes green, and often a muddy, opaque white colour with a rough pimply surface. The West Fen Road assemblage produced some fabric types not seen at Ely Forehill (with a rather sandy fabric and red finish), suggesting that there may have been other kilns in Ely.

Grimston fabrics
Sherds from the kilns at Grimston, Norfolk (Jennings 1981, 50–60; Leah 1994) occur at West Fen Road (171 sherds, 1.0%). Most of them are in the standard fine grey sandy fabric, with a highly translucent green glaze often containing flecks of brown. The fabric occurs less commonly in an oxidised buff or pink-red colour. Decoration consists of various arrangements of brown slip bands, some rouletted, as well as face jugs with very small handles ('arms') around the top. Glazed Grimston ware first occurred at Castle Acre in the late 12th century (Milligan in Coad and Streeten 1982, 225–6). At King's Lynn highly decorated Grimston wares were current mainly during the 14th and 15th centuries (Clarke and Carter 1977, 206–8), and late Grimston vessels have dense glazing. Jars were not glazed until later (*ibid.*, 233–5). The chronology is summarised by Little, showing the change in forms from 1100 to 1530 (Little in Leah 1994). Most of the Grimston sherds found at West Fen Road date from the *floruit* of production, in the 14th century.

Reduced sandy wares
Early reduced sandy wares are likely to have been a development of the Thetford ware tradition (359 sherds, 2.1%). Rim forms continue the Saxo-Norman tradition. The sandy fabrics are generally grey. Another type of reduced sandy ware occurs (222 sherds, 1.3%). The fabric is

Phase	5	7	9	10	11	12	13
approximate dating	8th–9th	9th–11th	12th	13th	14th	15th	16th plus
Ipswich	81	94	33	17	1	1	
Thetford	28	2422	1328	506	178	55	2
St Neots	17	1368	645	298	61	17	4
Stamford/Developed Stamford		16	47	56	11		
Crowland bowl type		1					
Ely	6	161	1671	3962	2015	539	11
Lyveden/Stanion		3	69	95	19	3	
12th/13th sandy wares		23	85	171	59	21	
Blackborough End type			27	109	76	10	
Grimston		4	8	25	104	29	
Essex Red		2	4	19	41	21	
Saintonge				1			
Scarborough				3	1	8	
Toynton			1	8		2	
Newcastle							1
Brill						1	
Herts. fineware					1		
London/Surrey			1	3			
Other glazed				5	1	2	2
Colne				1			
Bourne						16	30
Glazed Red Earthenware							41
Germ S/W						2	3
Delft							1
Babylon							20
Eng salt glz							2
Other 16th							1
17th–19th							5

Table 4.5 Main phases of use for Saxon and medieval pottery, indicating numbers of sherds recovered in each phase

different from Grimston, having mainly sand in the grog with very few or no white grits. The colour is frequently a reduced black, but sometimes brown or grey. It is very thin and hard, and always much thinner than Grimston. Sherds in this fabric were assigned a Grimston provenance in the 1977 King's Lynn report, being called 'unglazed Grimston' (Clarke and Carter 1977, 191–6). Excavations at Pott Row, Grimston, produced a similar material, described as 'Unglazed Grimston ware' (Little in Leah 1994, 80, 84). A Grimston provenance for much of the 1977 Lynn pottery was doubted by Little (ibid., 87, 89). The fabric is not very similar to the fine sandy (generally grey) fabric of glazed Grimston vessels, but more like the reduced sandy material known from Blackborough End, Middleton, Norfolk (Rogerson and Ashley 1985). This site is near to Grimston and a north-west Norfolk source is likely for the material, since coarse wares of this type are unlikely to have travelled very far. The forms at Ely are almost entirely jars, and are paralleled closely by material from King's Lynn, Norwich and sites excavated at Grimston.

Essex red wares
A few fine quality red wares (87 sherds, 0.5%) come from a variety of Essex sources, most probably Hedingham (Huggins 1972) and Colchester (Cunningham 1982). Sgraffito ware, commonly called 'Cambridge sgraffito' from the place of its first recognition (Bushnell and Hurst 1953), is included with these fabrics.

Lyveden ware
The deserted village site of Lyveden, Northants, produced a pink shelly fabric, often soapy with shells up to 2mm (Steane 1967; Bryant and Steane 1969). Sometimes the shells are leached out giving a 'corky' surface. A grey reduced form of the fabric is known. Glazed jugs are decorated with a yellow slip of stripes and grill-stamped blobs, probably made at nearby Stanion (Bellamy 1983). The fabric produced at Stanion

is similar to Lyveden, but with very fine oolitic grits. At West Fen Road, 189 Lyveden sherds were identified (1.1%).

Toynton fabrics
Toynton, on the Lincolnshire northern fen-edge, produced jugs in a grey fabric with pink surfaces, often decorated with brown applied strips (Healey 1975; McCarthy 1988, 261). Only eleven sherds were recovered.

Bourne wares
Kilns at Bourne, Lincolnshire, produced a pink-orange fabric with a very smooth finish and small white inclusions. Sherds sometimes have a light green to yellow and brown glaze (Healey 1969; 1975) and sometimes large thumb presses. The dates of this fabric at King's Lynn were 15th–16th century, where it occurs with stonewares (Clarke and Carter 1977, 237). At West End Road 46 sherds (0.3%) were identified.

Groups of several contexts were linked together by phase, as dictated by the excavation evidence and the spot dating. This process evens out errors and uncertainties that can occur in the dating of any given single context, and shows the *floruit* of each fabric type at Ely. The date range for most fabrics lie within the accepted limits, except for Scarborough Ware which appears to run into the 15th century. However only a few sherds are involved and these derive from disturbed contexts.

Relative to the mass of coarse medieval Ely fabric, the Essex, Grimston, and Lincolnshire fabrics are 'fine wares'. Additionally four sherds of London/Surrey ware

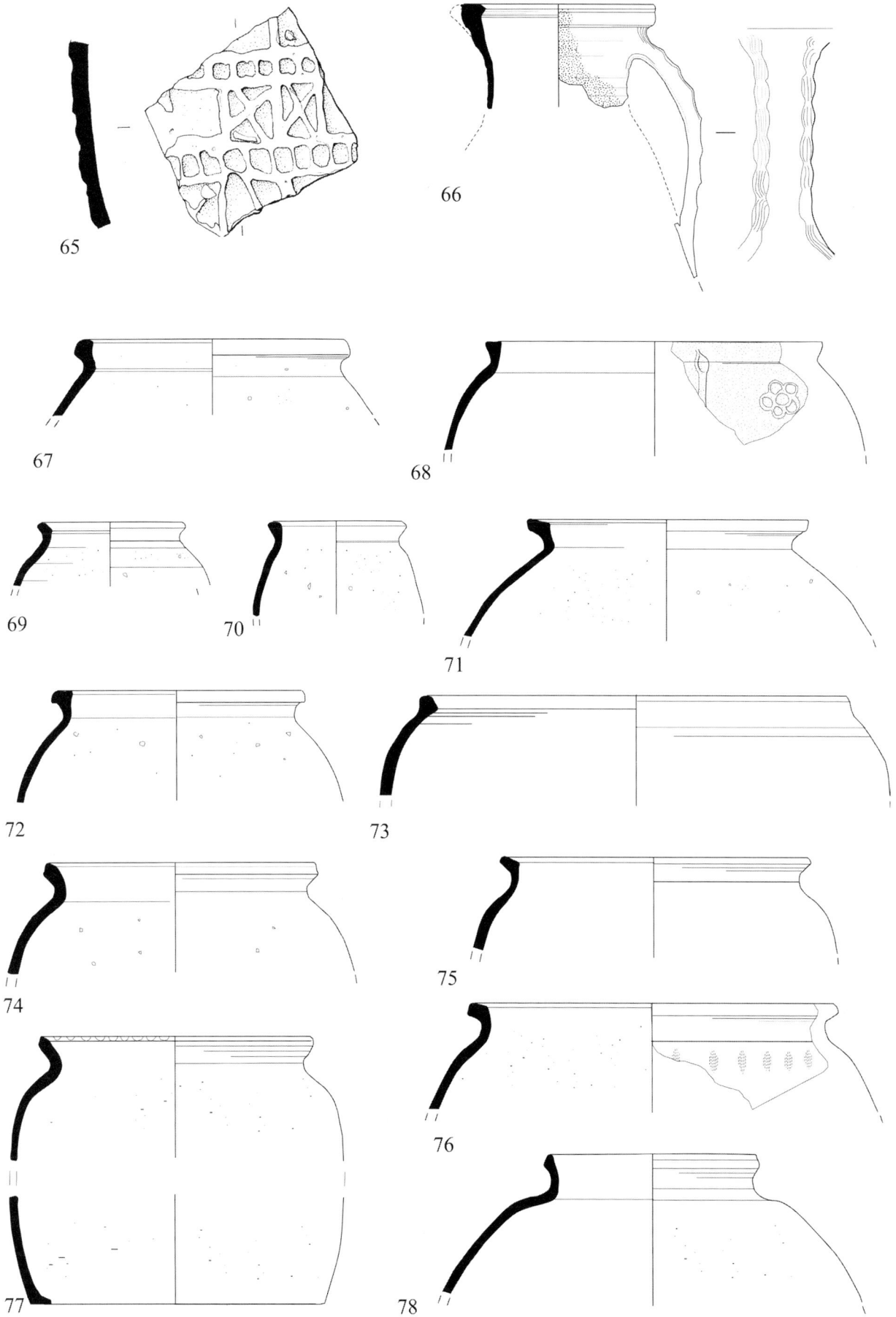

Figure 4.5 Illustrated medieval pottery I. All at 1:4 except No. 65 at 1:1

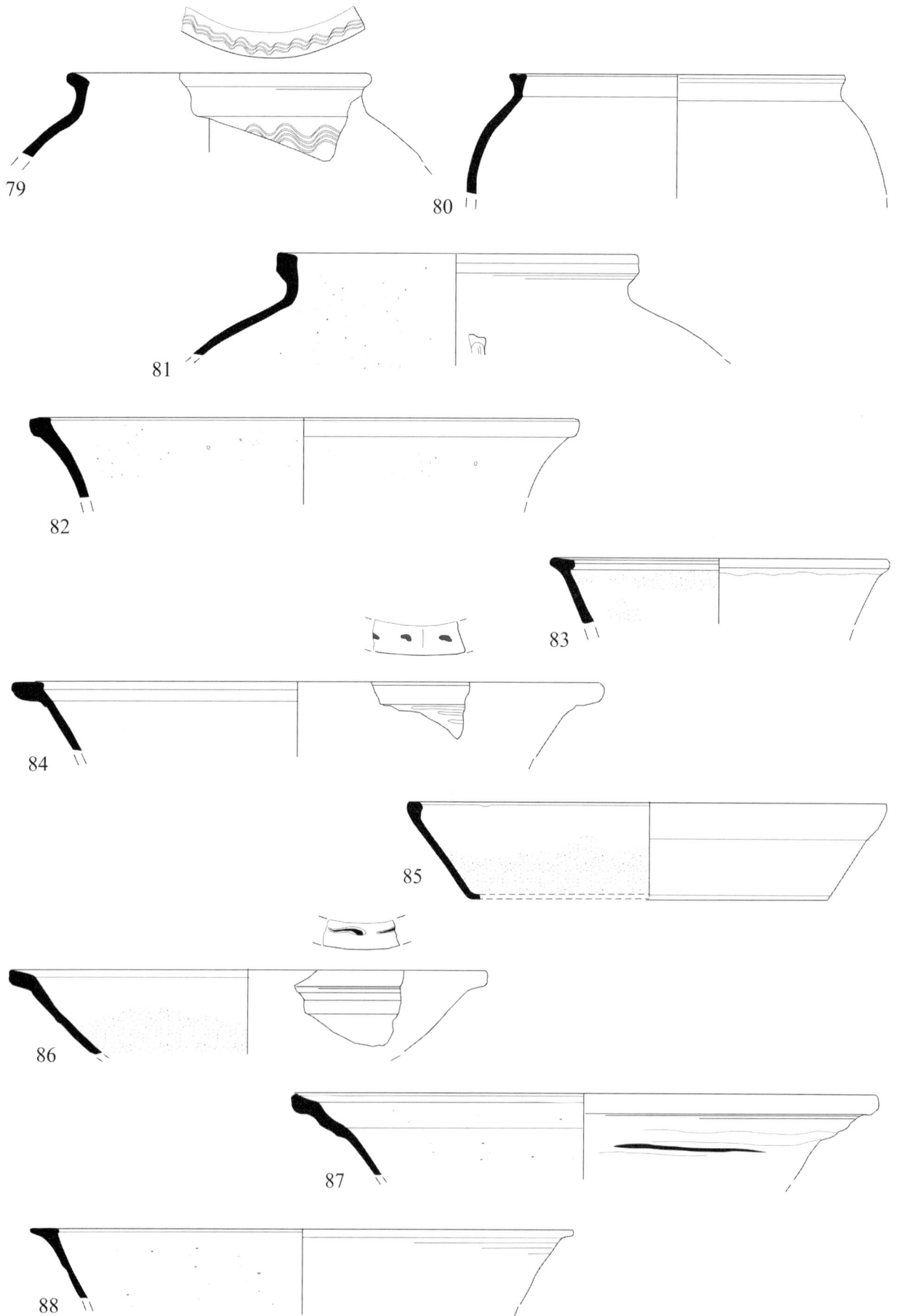

Figure 4.6 Illustrated medieval pottery II. All at 1:4

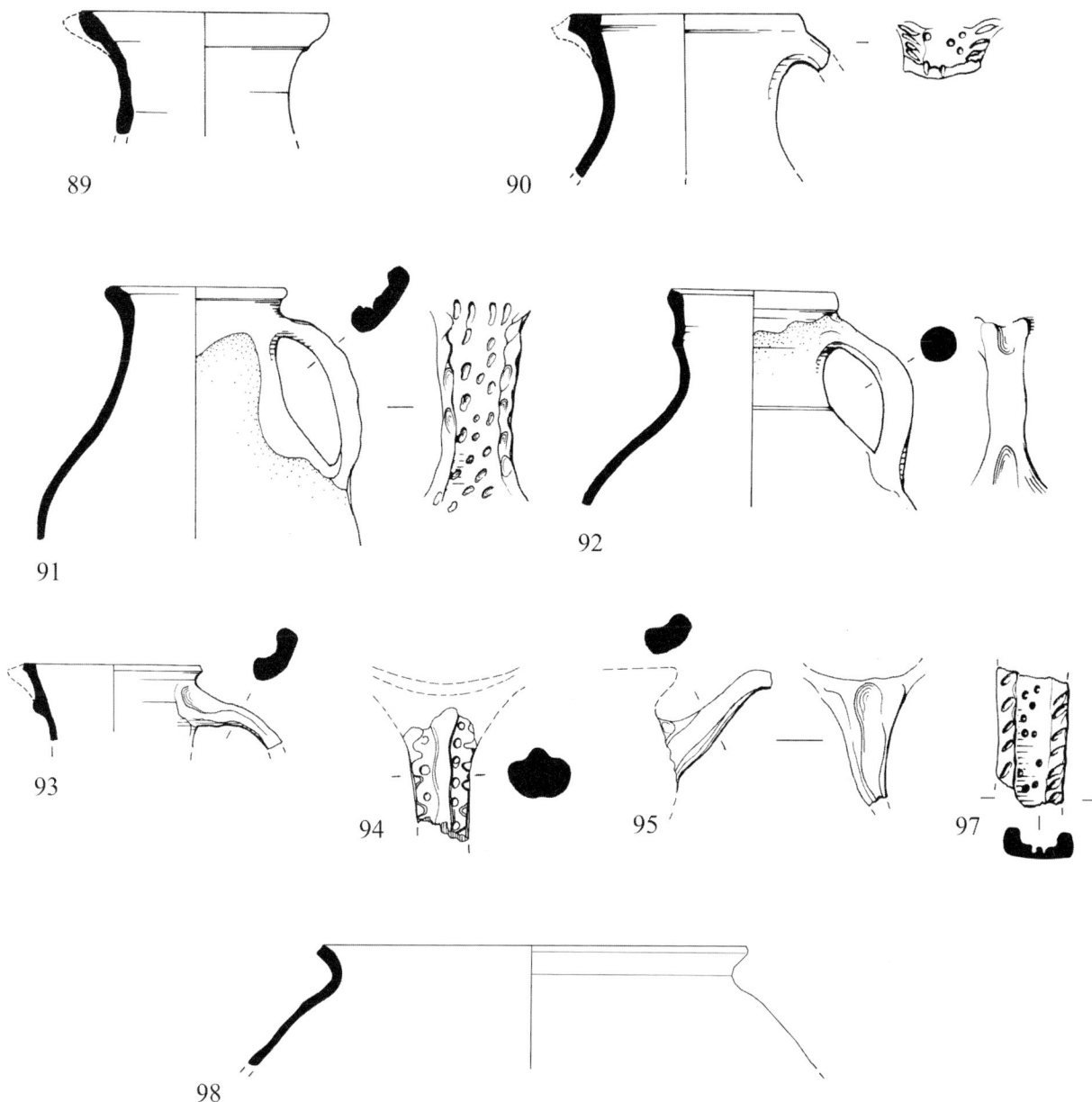

Figure 4.7 Illustrated medieval pottery III. All at 1:4

were found (McCarthy and Brooks 1988, 310–13) and a single sherd of a French Saintonge jug. There was also one sherd of Hertfordshire fine ware (Jenner and Vince 1983), and a single sherd of a Brill (Bucks) biconical jug. There was, however, one very unusual early fine ware — a piece of a decorated Saxo-Norman Crowland bowl, a very rare find (Cat. No. 65).

These fine wares represent only 0.2 percent of the assemblage (41 sherds). The collection suggests that it derives from a much poorer part of the Ely community than that living on the commercial front at Forehill. At Forehill, fine wares and imports were much more evident (Hall 2001). The West Fen Road site was mostly abandoned before the 16th century and imports of Dutch red ware and German salt glazes would not be expected here.

The St Neots and Thetford sherds were of standard type and none was drawn. Only the Crowland Bowl sherd

and one Stamford Ware jug are illustrated, along with a range of Ely wares.

Crowland
*65. A single sherd of a Crowland Bowl was discovered (kindly identified by J. G. Hurst). The fabric is similar to Stamford Ware, but pink, and with a brown glaze on both sides. Embossed on the outside are continuous rows of lattice-like panels separated by horizontal rows of 'rouletting'. Probably 12th century, though its context might place it slightly earlier. *cf.* Dallas 1993, fig. 138, no. 27, for an example from Thetford.
1137 (F322)/*922*/Phase 8 dividing ditch fill, Enclosure 9.

Stamford
*66. Jug in standard white fabric with pinkish outer surface; thumbed handle, blotchy green glaze of 'developed' form, 13th century.
8217 (F1998)/*8050*/Phase 10 ditch, Enclosure 7.

Ely medieval fabrics
The selected sherds add to the range already illustrated from Ely Forehill. All are in 'standard fabric' unless otherwise stated: this is hard with a slight sand component and characteristically contains white grits, evenly

distributed throughout and visible on the surface. The grits are usually small, but can be up to 1.5mm in diameter. There is a wide variation in the sand, grit and oolite content.

Jars
*67. Slightly pinkish, with internal hollow near rim, 13th century.
7015 (F1847)/*7045*/Phase 11 ditch, Enclosure 7.
*68. Glazed rosette decoration and vertical thumbed strip. Occurs with a Hedingham sherd. Similar decoration to Ely Forehill 43, 13th–14th century.
3302 (F771)/*1827*/Phase 11 pit fill, Enclosure 16.
*69. Small jar with rilled decoration, everted rim; standard fabric with visible grits, slight external blackening, 13th century.
7380/7335/Phase 10 ditch, Enclosure 7.
*70. Slightly grey on the outside, not many grits. Very small vessel, 12th–13th century.
8218 (F1998)/*8051*/Phase 10 ditch, Enclosure 7.
*71. Slight blackening on the outside, 13th century.
8115 (F1980)/*7932*/Phase 10 ditch, Enclosure 7.
*72. Standard fabric, 13th century.
3304 (F771)/*1829*/Phase 11 pit fill, Enclosure 16.
*73. Muddy internal glaze, 14th century.
6719 (F1420)/*6751*/Phase 9 well fill, Enclosure 12.
*74. Slight exterior darkening lower down, 13th century.
426 (F306)/*376*/Phase 10 spread over Structure 20, Enclosure 1.
*75. Thin vessel with a few incised lines below rim. Blackened outside, 13th century.
7957/7763/Phase 11 layer, Enclosure 18.
8612 (F1716)/*8269*/Phase 10 boundary ditch fill, Enclosure 7.
*76. Pink colour. Band of fingered decoration with faint striations within, 13th century.
8310/8151/Phase 10, Enclosure 19.
*77. Standard fabric but with coarse grits; fingertip decoration on rim top, 12th–13th century.
*78. Pinkish standard fabric; slightly hollowed rim with two fine incised lines on the rim top, 14th century.
7851/7671/Phase 10, Enclosure 7.
*79. Large jar with wavy decoration on upper surface of rim and at least one row of waves on body, 14th century.
7219 (F1629)/*7213*/Phase 10, Enclosure 7.

Sandy fabrics of Ely type
*80. Standard colours, but very few grits and contains fine sand.
3563/1951/Phase 11 floor, Structure 26, Enclosure 16.
*81. Standard fabric but hard and pinkish. Patchy internal glaze, one thumb impression, ?14th century.
5770 (F1384)/*5870*/Phase 10 boundary ditch fill, Enclosure 20.

Ely fabric

Bowls
*82. Standard fabric.
8124 (F1942)/*7939*/Phase 10 pit, Enclosure 7.
*83. Patchy internal green glaze. Hollowed rim with slight internal lip, 13th–14th century.
6719 (F1420)/*6751*/Phase 9 well fill, Enclosure 12.
*84. Stabbed hole decoration on rim top, 13th century.
7957/7764/Phase 11 layer, Enclosure 18.
*85. Pinkish fabric with one finger mark, 14th century?
5770 (F1384)/*5870*/Phase 10 boundary ditch fill, Enclosure 20.
*86. Rather sandy, pink buff surfaces, slashed decoration on rim, patchy green muddy glaze, 14th century.
3563/1951/Phase 11 floor, Structure 26.
*87. Hard sandy fabric with a few grits; pink buff surfaces, partly blackened.
3275 (F752)/*1821*/Phase 10 well fill, Enclosure 16.
*88. Slightly pink inside, flanged rim, 14th century.
6916/6928/Phase 10, Enclosure 7.

Jugs, without a collar below the rim
*89. Standard buff fabric.
7019 (F1847)/*7049*/Phase 11 ditch, Enclosure 18.
*90. Complete upper section with part of stabbed handle, 13th–14th century.
8105 (F2526)/*7921*/Phase 10, Structure 27 clay floor, Enclosure 18.
*91. Dark core, buff surfaces, patchy external green glaze; three rows of stabbing in the strap handle, 13th century.
7016 (F1970)/*7046*/Phase 9 ditch, Enclosure 7.

*92. Standard fabric with only a few grits. This example has a collar around the neck. Fair amount of external glaze, green but opaque, 14th century.
3563/1951/Phase 11 stake-hole, Structure 26, Enclosure 16.
*93. Standard fabric with only a few grits; external opaque green glaze, 13th–14th century.
3653/1951/Phase 11 stake-hole, Structure 26, Enclosure 16.

Handles
*94. Slightly pinkish. Probably pointed with stabbed decoration, 14th century.
7875 (F2530)/*7694*/Phase 9 boundary ditch fill, Enclosure 5.
*95. Standard fabric but pinkish with upper black surface; pointed type, 14th century?
3316 (F783)/*1835*/Phase 9 ditch, Enclosure 16.
96. Plain strap handle.
6702 (F1477)/*6729*/Phase 9 spread, Enclosure 4.
*97. Strap handle with stabbed decoration on the edges and holes in the centre, 13th century.
7957/7764/Phase 11 layer, Enclosure 18.

Blackborough End type
*98. Thin, grey-black sandy with a few white grits, coarse fabric and finish, 13th century.
3371 (F2375)/*1868*/Phase 11 pit, Enclosure 16.

Metal and glass vessels

Metal vessels
While no complete metal vessels were recovered, there are two possible and one definite fragments of copper alloy vessels. These are all probably late or post-medieval; cast vessels are presumed to date to the late 14th century or later (Egan 1998, 158–9), and a possible fragment from a lathe-turned vessel is probably also of this date (J. Cowgill, *pers. comm.*). The two intrusive finds were both from areas which were later covered by ridge and furrow, causing some redeposition of later finds into the upper fills of earlier features. There is also a complete copper alloy sheet rivet for repairing metal vessels, which was found in a Phase 9 context. There was no surviving evidence for wooden bowls or other vessels, although these would undoubtedly have been present during at least the medieval occupation phase (Morris in Margeson 1993, 95).

99. Cast irregular rim fragment of a copper alloy **vessel**; possibly miscast; large diameter, probably 500mm+. L. 65mm, W. 37mm, T. 4mm; late medieval–post-medieval.
793 (F356)/*4431*/Phase 8 ditch fill, Enclosure 9 (surface find over a Late Saxon context).
100. Possible rim fragment from a lathe turned copper alloy **vessel**, but appears straight. L. 48mm, W. 18mm, T. 1mm; late medieval–post-medieval.
Surface/*9104*a/unstratified.
101. Possible rim fragment of a cast copper alloy **vessel** but edge appears straight; L. 24mm; late medieval–post-medieval.
2642 (F629)/*4647*/Phase 5 post-hole, Structure 3, Enclosure 1 (intrusive in a Mid Saxon context).
102. Complete copper alloy **sheet rivet** for repairing sheet vessels; medieval (*cf.* Margeson 1993, no. 575).
983 (F499)/*4432*/Phase 9 ditch fill, Enclosure 17.

Glass vessels
Fragments of Roman glass vessels were recovered from contexts of Phases 3, 6, 8 and 9. These are all probably of the early to mid-Roman period (J. Price, *pers. comm.*). The majority come from areas which were in intensive use during that time, and can be considered chance incorporations in later features.

103. Rim fragment of a blue glass **jar** or flask; late 2nd and early 3rd century.
22 (F8)/*40*/Phase 3 ditch, Enclosure 3/4.
104. Rim fragment of a blue glass **jar** or flask; late 2nd or early 3rd century.

7125 (F1593)/*9292*/Phase 3 ditch, Enclosure 4.

105. Rim fragment of a blue glass **jar** or flask, with an applied trail; late 2nd or early 3rd century.
2620 (F610)/*3423*/Phase 8 gully fill, Enclosure 9.

106. Fragment from the side of a blue glass square **bottle**; late 1st to 2nd century AD.
1864 (F423)/*2849*/Phase 6 gully fill, Enclosure 1.

107. Fragment from the side of a blue glass square **bottle**; late 1st to 2nd century AD.
2011 (F565)/*2938*/Phase 9 ditch, Enclosure 13.

108. Fragment from the base of a blue glass square **bottle**, with a raised circle; late 1st to 2nd century AD.
1693 (F2317)/*2736*/Phase 8 beam-slot fill, Enclosure 1.

109. **Unidentified fragment** of blue glass, possibly Roman.
4696 (F1081)/*5451*/Phase 5 ditch fill, Enclosure 3.

Implements
(Fig. 4.8)

A total of seventeen complete or fragmentary knives were recovered, one of which was from a Mid Saxon context and four from Late Saxon contexts. Three of these were early medieval types (J. Cowgill, *pers. comm.*), but one, No. 115, has a 13th-century parallel (Biddle 1990). It was, however, found on the surface of the deposit from which it came, and may not necessarily be directly associated with it. The remainder derive from post-Conquest contexts: just one, No. 116, may perhaps be residual, as it is a possible early medieval type, but recovered from a Phase 9 context (although these types are quite long-lived). The scale-tang knives Nos 124–6 are all from Phase 10 or 11 contexts, in accordance with the proposed date for their introduction in the 13th or 14th century (Margeson 1993, 128). No. 126, however, also has a bolster, which dates it to the 16th century or later (*ibid.*, 130) — this may therefore be an intrusive item, perhaps dropped later onto the surface of the gravelled yard. While most of these appear to be utilitarian items, the possible knife No. 123 has a decorative inlay along the ?blade edge, while No. 125 has a number of decorative features. The only other utensil recovered, a fragmentary pair of shears, Fig. 4.8 No. 127, is a medieval type and was found in a Phase 10 context.

110. Iron **knife** with no tip or tang but definite triangular section; profile suggests worn and broken where blade meets tang; appears to have parallel grooves along length of blade; condition poor. L. 97mm, W. 22mm.
2222 (F598)/*4529*/Phase 5 boundary ditch fill, Enclosure 1.

111. Possible iron **knife**; long tang (L. 90mm) which appears to flare out slightly to form a narrow ?knife blade; blade possibly of triangular section but no real shoulder; possible mineral-preserved wood on handle; disintegrating. L. 113mm, 'blade' W. 15mm; if knife then possibly early medieval type.
884 (F603)/*4497*/Phase 6 ditch fill, Enclosure 9.

112. Iron **knife** with complete tang (L. 33mm); blade broken where worn near the sloping shoulder. L. 44mm, blade W. 12mm, T. 6mm; early medieval?
751 (F503)/*4492*/Phase 8 ditch, Enclosure 14/16.

*113. Complete iron **knife**; long tang (L. 102mm); sloping shoulder; straight back with angle near tip down to blade; blade worn to above level of tang; mineral-preserved wood handle on tang.
3678 (F501)/*4621*/Phase 8 boundary ditch fill, Paddock P, Enclosure 13.

114. Complete iron **knife** with whittle tang; angled back to slightly up-curving tip; evidence of wear. L. 128mm (from X-ray); early medieval?
5736 (F1225)/*9155*/Phase 8 boundary ditch, Enclosure 12.

115. Iron **knife** with complete whittle tang (L. 50mm); straight back; blade angles up steeply (50 degrees) to meet back, an unusual feature; traces of non-ferrous shoulder plate?; mineral-preserved ?wood handle on tang. L. 110mm, blade W. 18mm; mid to late 13th century.
119 (F663)/*4458*/Phase 8 boundary ditch, Enclosure 1 (but recovered from surface spread).

116. Iron **knife** with short tang (L. 23mm) and very worn incomplete blade; worn to above level of tang; sloping shoulder; straight back. L. 66mm, blade W. 17mm, T. 5mm; early medieval?
2126 (F522)/*4526*/Phase 9 ditch, Enclosure 14.

117. Iron **knife** blade and tip; straight back with slight angle near tip where blade curves up to back. L. 59mm, blade W. 19mm, T. *c.* 5mm.
6199 (F924)/*9170*/Phase 9 dividing ditch fill, Enclosure 11.

118. Iron **knife** with tapering tang with end bent at right angle to secure handle in place; broken near shoulder; back in line with tang; triangular section. L. 87mm, blade W. 15mm, T. 7mm.
8876 (F2076)/*9262*/Phase 9 ditch, Enclosure 7.

119. Possible iron **knife**; long tang (L. 92mm); 'blade' broken near shoulder; triangular section; mineral-preserved wood handle on tang. L. 103mm, blade W. 15mm.
597 (F2328)/*4477*/Phase 9 pit fill, Enclosure 1.

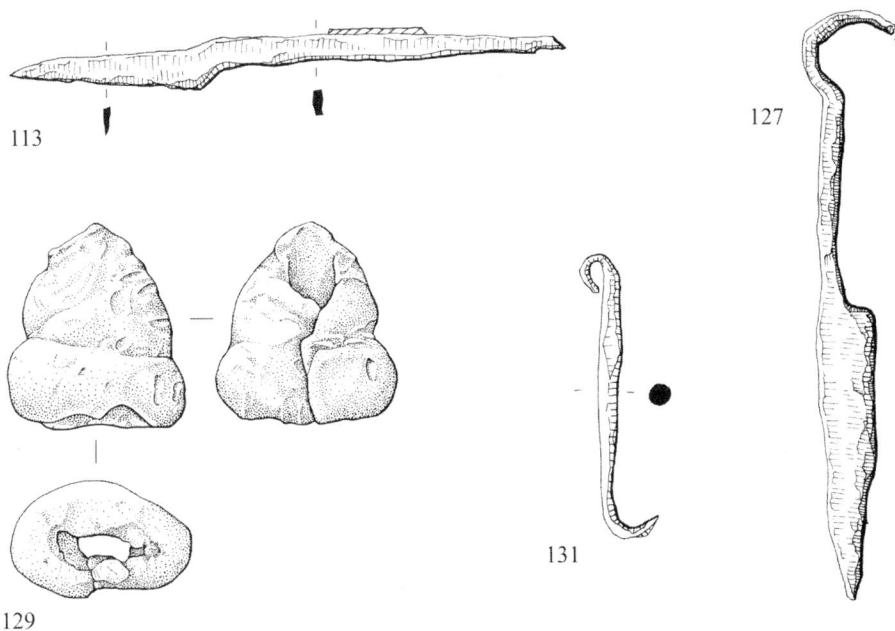

Figure 4.8 Small finds relating to furnishings and household equipment. All at 1:2

120. Possible iron **knife blade**; triangular section but no tang or tip; iron of strange appearance under x-ray; object cracking. L. 100mm, W. 18mm.
3334 (F775)/*4578*/Phase 9 well fill, Enclosure 16.

121. Possibly complete iron **knife** but whittle tang very short (L. 28mm); simple plain knife with straight back; does not show wear pattern common on many early medieval knives. L. 140mm, W. at shoulder 18mm.
7366 (F1636)/*9226*/Phase 10 curving ditch fill, Enclosure 7.

122. Possible iron **knife fragment**; triangular section; probably part of the whittle tang, blade and shoulder. L. 58mm, blade W. 16mm.
8292 (F1980)/*9248*/Phase 10 gully fill, Enclosure 7.

123. Possible iron **knife**; triangular section but upstanding rivet; inlaid with line of facing triangles along the ?blade edge plus two on the thicker back edge; mineral-preserved ?horn handle. L. 72mm, W. 25mm, T. 4mm; 11th–13th century?
5649 (F1272)/*9152*/Phase 10 boundary ditch fill, Enclosure 20.

124. Iron **knife** with scale tang handle broken at the shoulder; bone scales held in place by five tubular non-ferrous rivets; probable plain sheet end plate; shoulder plate ?disintegrating; 14th–15th century.
153/*4459*a/Phase 10, Enclosure 19.

125. Iron **knife** with scale tang; wooden scales attached by two solid non-ferrous rivets with small circular head plates; also two false tubular rivets; between rivets is an inlaid copper alloy trefoil with curved stem; solid cast 'horse hoof' end plate; broken at shoulder.
153/*4459*b/Phase 10, Enclosure 19.

126. Iron **knife** with scale tang with bolster; tang and blade broken; straight back with no shoulder. L. 82mm, blade W. 21mm, T. 4mm; 16th–17th century.
7000 (F2519)/*9209*b/Phase 11 gravelled yard, Enclosure 18/21.

*127. Pair of iron **shears**; simple plain single arm with blade and half spring remaining; arm section square?; medieval.
8000 (F1716)/*9240*/Phase 10 boundary ditch fill, Enclosure 7.

Miscellaneous equipment
(Fig. 4.8)
Two lead weights, No. 128 and Fig. 4.8 No. 129, may have been used for weighing down nets or hangings. The iron S-hook (Fig. 4.8 No. 131) from a Phase 9 context may have formed part of a chain, perhaps to suspend a vessel over a fire (Goodall in Margeson 1993, 140).

128. Lead **weight**, conical. D. 17mm, Ht. 12mm, weight 18g.
Surface/*4415*d/Unstratified.

*129. Probable lead **fishing weight**. Rough thick sheet of lead, wrapped around to form a cone, crudely worked, weight 35g.
574 (F260)/*4395*/Phase 9 boundary ditch fill, Enclosure 2.

130. **Tube** made from copper alloy sheet; squashed flat at one end. L. 27mm, max. D. 27mm.
4425/*9084*/Unphased.

*131. Iron **S-hook**; complete loop below which shaft widens before narrowing to form hook; rectangular section.
6756 (F1611)/*9178*/Phase 9 pit fill, Enclosure 7.

132. **Suspension ring**; U-shaped iron hinge strap with opposing pierced straps *c.* 16mm apart; plated heads on three *in situ* rivets; L. 80mm, W. 40mm, strap T. 8mm; large intact ring attached with rounded-rectangular section (13mm x 10mm); D. 90mm; medieval.
3487 (F791)/*4603*/Phase 11 pit fill, Enclosure 16.

133. Iron **hasp** of extended leaf-shape with loop at one end; other is broken; no staple.
4297 (F1180)/*9126*/Phase 9 boundary ditch fill, Enclosure 9.

134. Iron **rivet** with large slightly domed head (27mm x 23mm). L 28mm.
7576 (F1601)/*9234*/Phase 8 post-hole of Structure 19b, Enclosure 7.

III. Buildings
(Figs 4.9 and 4.10)

The buildings and other structures on the site appear to have been mainly constructed from materials such as wood, wattle and daub, and perhaps thatch. A small number of items, discussed below, form part either of the structure of such buildings, or of associated fixtures such as doors and shutters. Overall, the impression that remains is of a relatively poor site. Only one building, Structure 27, shows any evidence of (albeit crude) masonry construction; otherwise all were timber-framed in some way.

Structural ironwork
The three identified staples (Nos 135–7) come from a variety of contexts: one Roman, one Mid Saxon and one post-Conquest. Being U-shaped or looped, they could all have served to hold chains in place, or as supports for tethering rings (Goodall in Margeson 1993, 143), although the smaller Mid Saxon example could also have been a furniture fitting. Similarly, the two iron spikes (Nos 138–9) may have served a structural function, as undoubtedly the two wall-hooks (Nos 140–1) did. The clench bolt and rove (Nos 142–3), both from Phase 10 contexts, may have been parts of doors or covers, while the looped hook (Fig. 4.9 No. 144) from a Late Saxon context may have held a door or window shutter open (*cf.* Margeson 1993, no. 1225). Two rivets and 287 nails were also recovered from archaeological contexts, and were not reported on individually. Nails were recovered from contexts of all phases except the Mid Saxon Phase 5, with a noticeable peak in Phase 12 (Fig. 4.10), and are seen in a variety of forms, with round, oval and square heads, both flat and domed.

135. Iron **staple** with double-spiked loop. L. 53mm, W. 22mm, T. 8mm.
2533 (F596)/*4544*/Phase 3 boundary ditch fill, Enclosure 2.

136. Small iron **staple**; U-shaped. L. 29mm, W. 16mm, T. 2mm.
6315 (F1380)/*9171*/Phase 5 ditch, Enclosure 4.

137. Large U-shaped iron **staple**; pinched shoulders; disintegrating. L. 80mm, W. 62mm, T. 5mm.
1622/*4514*/Phase 9 floor level, Structure 26, Enclosure 16.

138. Iron **spike** of square section. L. 78mm, W. 8mm, T. 7mm.
2957 (F618)/*4552*/Phase 8 ditch fill, Enclosure 9.

139. Iron **spike**, disintegrating. L. 145mm, W. 15mm, T. 13mm.
2127 (F502)/*4527*/Phase 10 ditch, Enclosure 14.

140. U-shaped iron **wall-hook**; rounded square section. L. 55mm, W. 32mm, T. 9mm.
1035/*4505*/Phase 9, Enclosure 16.

141. Iron **hook**, possibly for a wall; rectangular section. L. 117mm, W. 17mm, T. 10mm.
153/*4459*c/Phase 10, Enclosure 19.

142. Complete iron **clench bolt**. Circular nail head, rectangular rove. L. 42mm, W. 30mm, T. 10mm; shank L. 55mm.
1802/4521/Phase 10 spread over Structure 34, Enclosure 1.

143. Iron **rove**; square and slightly domed. L. 43mm, W. 43mm, T. 7mm.
998 (F758)/*4502*/Phase 10 ditch, Enclosure 16.

*144. Iron **hook**; well forged strip with detailed hook at one end (L. 44mm); at other end at right angle to main plane the beginnings of a loop (W. 7mm); a possible fitting.
7512 (F1660)/*9231*/Phase 6 gully, Enclosure 5.

Iron door, window and furniture fittings
The possible small pintle ('hinge pivot', No. 145) from a Late Saxon context, together with the leaf-shaped iron fitting (No. 146) and the twisted iron fitting (No. 147), both from Phase 10 contexts, may be further evidence for ironworking pertaining to buildings.

145. Possible small iron **pintle**; disintegrating. Arms L. 43mm and 57mm.
8054 (F1844)/*9243*/Phase 7 ditch, Enclosure 7.

146. Iron leaf-shaped furniture or structural **fitting**; circular and square ?nail holes. L. 70mm, W. 37mm, T. 5mm.
7380/*9228*/Phase 10 ditch, Enclosure 7.

147. Spirally twisted iron **fitting** with a circular flattened and pierced terminal (D. 13mm); possibly used for suspension. L. 126mm; medieval.
7281 (F1923)/*9221*/Phase 10 gully fill, Enclosure 7.

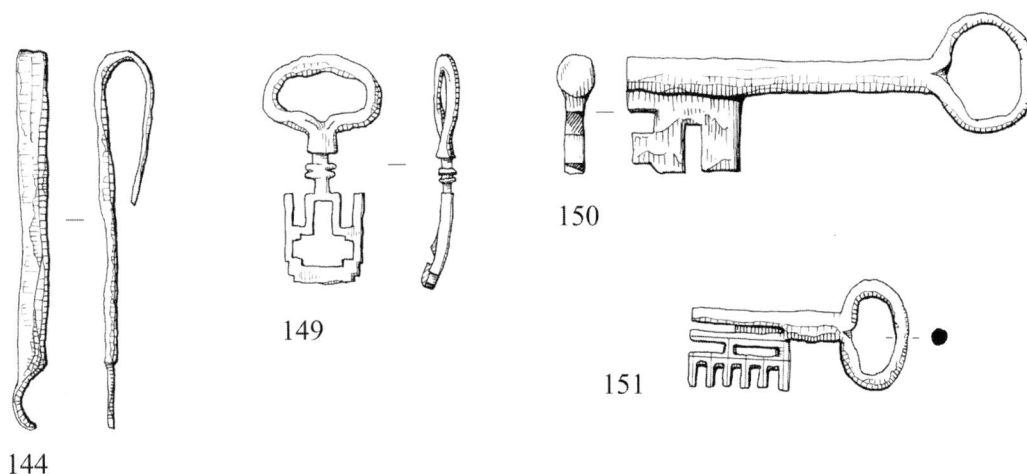

Figure 4.9 Small finds relating to buildings. All at 1:2

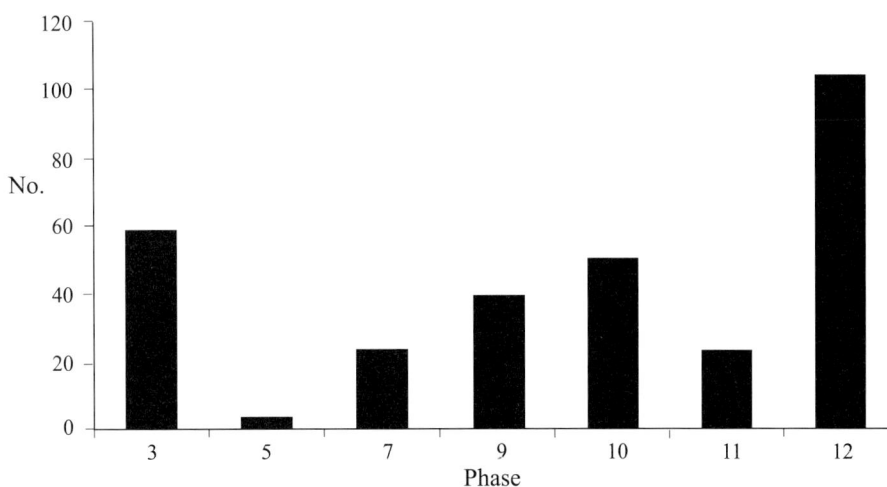

Figure 4.10 Chart showing quantity of nails by phase

Lock furniture, hasps and keys

This evidence includes an iron padlock (No. 148) from a Phase 10 context, an iron padlock key (Fig. 4.9 No. 149) from a Phase 11 context, and two rotary keys (Fig. 4.9 Nos 150–1) from post-Conquest contexts. One has a close parallel from London, apparently of the 14th century, although only the butt survives here (Egan 1998, no. 312). The iron loop hasp (No. 152), found in a Phase 12 context, may have been used in conjunction with a padlock to secure a door or shutter.

148. Cylindrical iron **padlock**; mechanism with slightly oval plate (24mm x 22mm) with a single complete spring (L. 70mm); a single reinforcing strip from the case appears to be attached; external parts appear brazed on x-ray; medieval.
3431 (F824)/*4595*/Phase 10 well fill, Enclosure 14.

*149. Complete iron **padlock key**; symmetrical elaborate key with oval bow and very short shank decorated with double knobs; complex shield-shaped bit with T-shaped aperture in bit; notably well-made key; London parallel 1350–1400 (Egan 1998, nos 269 and 270).
5649 (F1272)/*9152*/Phase 10 ditch fill, Enclosure 20.

*150. Complete iron **rotary key** with oval bow and two wards on the simple bit; shank appears hollow on the x-ray; probably 8th to 11th century (*cf.* Ottoway 1992, no. 3619).
9635 (F2596)/*9491*/Phase 9 pit fill, Enclosure 6.

*151. Elaborate iron **rotary key** with D-shaped bow; bit complex with asymmetrical clefts and a channel parallel to the shank; plated and possibly inlaid; late 14th century (*cf.* Egan 1998, no. 312).

3293 (F751)/*4573*/Phase 11 well fill, Enclosure 16/17.

152. Oval iron **loop hasp** with straight parallel sides; looped tab at one end; used with padlocks *etc.* to secure doors and shutters. L. 142mm, W. 30mm, T. 8mm.
7000 (F2519)/*9209*c/Phase 11 gravelled yard, Enclosure 18/21.

Ceramic building material

by Richard Mortimer

A relatively small sample totalling 588 fragments (28.98kg) of ceramic building material (CBM) was recovered from the excavation. Of this total 62 fragments (22.82% by weight) were identified as brick and 426 (73.72%) as tile, while 70 fragments (3.44%) were undiagnostic. The quantities of CBM attributed to each phase of the site indicate a peak during the 12th–13th century with a sharp decline thereafter.

The fabrics of the ceramic building materials were observed and described. In all six fabrics were identified (Table 4.6). Within these fabric groups there appear to be differences but when studied closely most are actually from the same source and are merely variants. The exceptions are fabrics 3 and 7. While both appear similar, fabric 3 occurs overwhelmingly in the Roman period while fabric 7 appears in brick manufacture in the medieval period. The majority of the fabrics (fabrics 1, 2,

4, 5 and 6) appear associated with plain roofing tile manufacture and appear mostly in the medieval Phases 10 to 13. Apart from Roman forms, almost all the floor tile (fabric 2) may be associated with the local Ely pottery or floor tile industries. The range of fabrics present suggests that tile used at West Fen Road, as at Forehill and Broad Street, was obtained from a variety of sources, with some possibly produced at Ely itself.

Roman tile

Forty-one fragments of Roman building material were recovered, of which twenty were recovered from later medieval deposits. This small assemblage contained 22 fragments of floor tile ranging in thickness from 16–45mm; two of the thickest fragments could be described as bricks but could equally represent fragments of large tiles. Four examples of box flue tiles were present, varying in thickness from 21–22mm. All examples were variously combed or scored with incised patterns of diagonal cross hatching, vertical lines and circular combing. Roof tile or *tegula* accounted for only four fragments, these varying in thickness from 22–47mm. The rest of the Roman material (eleven fragments) could represent fragments of any of the above, although they shared the distinctive Roman fabric (fabric 3). Little can be said about such a limited assemblage, beyond the fact that ceramic building material was not employed to any extent within buildings of the Roman period here. If not used in its primary function as part of a roof, floor or heating system, then brick or tile may have been used as hearth or oven bases, or employed as a levelling agent in mass wall coursing or perhaps as post-pads.

Post-Roman floor tile

The building material collection was dominated by locally made Ely ware tile, accounting for 256 fragments of the total assemblage or 40.59% by weight. The tiles varied in thickness from 12–27mm. Although no complete example was recovered, a square form with a length of eight inches could be extrapolated from the more complete fragments. Four of the fragments displayed evidence of nail punctures or holes that appear to have been applied prior to firing. The reason for these holes remains slightly enigmatic as the tiles would appear to have been manufactured for flooring, being for the most part small and thick and probably unsuitable for roofing. Many of the tiles were friable and appeared to have undergone heating or burning after manufacture. It is likely that one of the major uses of the tiles was as hearth tiles. Lucas (1993, 157) states that the brick and tile industry in Ely appears to date from the 15th century. Evidence from West Fen Road suggests a parallel production of tile and pottery from Ely kilns from the early 13th century, however, or possibly even as early as the late 12th century.

Post-Roman plain tile

115 fragments of plain tile were recovered, this representing the major medieval form of roof tile present although it accounts for only 14.65% of the entire CBM assemblage by weight. Produced from a flat slab of clay, the tile could be suspended from the roof structure either by peg-holes (pierced holes in the clay slab) or applied clay lumps (called nibs), or a combination of both. The only type found here was peg tile, with either two circular peg-holes placed at one end toward the corners, or one circular peg-hole again centrally at one end. Of those that displayed evidence of peg-holes the fragmentary nature of the assemblage (no complete examples were recovered) made it difficult to state clearly which of the two types, if either, was more abundant within the collection. Plain tiles occur as early as the 13th-century phases at West Fen Road (at Forehill it occurs in 14th-century deposits but may have been in use earlier).

Pantile

No definite examples of pantile were recovered although one possible fragment occurs within a 14th-century deposit.

Brick

Most of the bricks recorded can probably be assigned to between the 14th and early 16th centuries (Lloyd 1925, 89–100). Dating bricks by measurement alone is quite difficult as regional variations need to be taken into account, both in dimensions and manufacturing processes. However, generally speaking, medieval bricks are relatively long, broad and thin. Of the 62 brick fragments recovered, only four examples provided definite measurements. Such limited usage of brick on the site even within the later periods suggests, as with the Roman period, that other building materials were used, with brick coming onto the site through secondary sources. This is somewhat unexpected, given that bricks were certainly being used in Ely during the 14th century (Hall 1996, 37). The lack of brick may indicate that the buildings still standing after the 14th century were constructed prior to the wider introduction of brick as a building material, or that the site was not of sufficient status to warrant such investment.

Fired clay
by Richard Mortimer

There follows a summary of the non-ceramic fired clay material. Altogether 2528 discrete samples of fired clay were recovered, with a total weight of 12.41kg. All samples were examined individually, although they are described below as groups. A basic description of the material is provided by fabric type, and possible functions are suggested. Ascribing function to these fragments is problematic, as clay can be used in many contexts where it can be subject to the effects of fire. Burnt clay can be the result of deliberate usage, for example when employed as kiln or oven lining/furniture or in the creation of objects such as loomweights (these are discussed separately below). It can also be accidental, either where fires have been lit over a clay area, or where fire has destroyed a structure in which clay was employed. In the latter case clay used as daub over wattle is the most obvious class of find, and the fired clay may preserve impressions of the

Fabric No.	Form	Earliest date (from phasing)	Description
1	Plain roof	Phase 10 (to 12)	Hard, irregular fracture with dark grey core and orange margins and surface; moderate-frequent quartz and occasional angular flint inclusions.
2	Floor	Phase 9 (to 11)	Slightly soft, crumbly texture, orange red; moderate-frequent limestone and chalky flint inclusions with moderate quartz.
3	Roman floor, roof and box flue tile	Phase 3 (to 13)	Hard, smooth fracture, orange with redder (sometimes reduced grey) core; very occasional mica, flint (<10mm) and limestone (<5mm).
4	Plain roof	Phase 10 (to 13)	Hard, smooth fracture, grey core with buff-yellow to orange surface; moderate-frequent limestone/shell inclusions (streaky) and occasional flint and quartz some with vesicular texture due to leaching out of shell.
5	Plain roof	N/A	Hard, laminated fracture, orange; occasional quartz, limestone and red grog (<5mm).
6	Plain roof and brick	Phase 12 (to 13)	Slightly soft, irregular fracture, buff-white; very sparse limestone, flint (<5mm) and red grog (<10mm).
7	Brick	Phase 10 (to 13)	Similar to 3 but occurring in Medieval brick.

Table 4.6 Ceramic building material fabric descriptions

rods and sails of the wattle structure. It may also be explained by demolition: when an old wattle structure has reached the end of its useful life it may be burned down in order to reduce risk of vermin infestation, thus partially firing the clay daub.

Three main fabric types were noted, although variations within these broad groups were present.

Fabric 1   Hard, buff-pink to orange fine fabric with occasional inclusions of limestone and quartz grains; some fragments contained shell although this may derive from fossils within the limestone.

Fabric 2   Hard, orange-red, very sandy/gritty fabric with occasional rounded grains, angular flint and limestone inclusions.

Fabric 3   Soft, orange-red, fine fabric with sparse inclusions of mica, sub-rounded quartz and angular flint.

By weight, 39.2% of fired clay was assigned to fabric 1, 31.0% to fabric 2 and 28.9% to fabric 3. Within the overall assemblage 8% of the samples displayed evidence of smoothed surfaces, while 5.5% showed evidence of organic impressions within their fabric. The organic impressions fall into two categories: (a) that caused by the rods and sails of wattle structures, usually the partial impression of wood (of the sample only 1.6% had identifiable wattle impressions), and (b) grass/straw and occasionally seed impressions. The inclusion of straw/grass within the clay mixture (later burnt, hence the impressions) no doubt added body and cohesion to the material used within the structures although some may have been included through accident. Given that the average weight for each fragment is 4.9g, this gives an indication of the generally small size of the individual fragments. All three types of fabric contain both wattle and straw grass impressions and the overwhelming majority of the assemblage probably represents the remains of wattle and daub structures.

Most of the material was recovered from secondary contexts, the original structure or feature having been destroyed. The fragments were either then dumped as midden waste or found their way into later features such as pits, ditches or gullies. This leaves very fragmented remains, but they do point to the continuing cycle of destruction and reconstruction of domestic structures and features on the site.

Fabric 1, while occurring within later phases, was particularly prevalent within the Late Iron Age and Roman periods (Phases 2 and 3) and much of this material found within later periods is likely to be residual. The distinct nature of this fabric as opposed to fabrics 2 and 3 might suggest either an alternative source of clay from that used within the later medieval periods, or that the clay was prepared for use in the structures in a different way.

IV. Occupations, industry and crafts
(Plates VIII–IX; Figs 4.11–4.15)

Metalworking
Aside from a number of iron bars and rods, fragments of iron and copper alloy sheet (some of which seem to be waste fragments) and scraps of lead, the only evidence of metalworking on the site consists of slag and a single associated tool. The slag is not reported on individually, but Figure 4.14 shows the amount by weight from each phase, with the peaks corresponding to the phases in which the site saw intensive occupation — the dramatic peak in Phase 10 is due to one kiln/furnace (F1248) which produced 4kg of slag, the result of an unidentified industrial process. In general, the slag was mostly the result of ironworking, with a variety of hearth-bottom forms in evidence. The iron chisel (No. 153) from a Phase 11 context would probably have been used to cut smaller pieces of iron (*cf.* Goodall in Margeson 1993, 176).

153.   Complete iron **chisel**; splayed head, small, rectangular section. L. 61mm, W. 17mm.
       8938 (F2221)/*9265*/Phase 11 pit fill, Enclosure 12.

Woodworking
The iron spoon auger (Fig. 4.12 No. 154) from a Late Saxon context would have been used to bore holes in wood (Goodall in Margeson 1993, 179); otherwise the only other woodworking tool in evidence is a possible wedge (No. 155), although three other possible tools are listed here also.

*154.   Iron **spoon auger**, almost pointed with slightly bent tip set centrally and in same plane as shaft; shaft of rectangular cross-section, with no distinct tang; small complete example; common on 9th–11th century sites but form remains unchanged since Roman period (Ottaway 1992, 532–5).
       683 (F600)/*4489*/Phase 8 gully fill, Enclosure 1.

155.   Possible iron **tool**; incomplete bar with one thin rounded end; swelling in the middle to 13mm; then flaring out and thinning towards broken end. L. 60mm, W. 15mm, expanding to 18mm. Possibly a woodworking wedge (*cf.* Ottaway 1992, no. 2557).
       3615 (F2383)/*4618*/Phase 9 pit, Enclosure 16.

156.   Possible iron **tool**; short tang (L. *c.* 20mm) which flares out to form an oval-sectioned tool? L. 64mm; W. 17mm; T. 13mm.
       4867 (F1203)/*9140*/Phase 3 ditch, Enclosure 4.

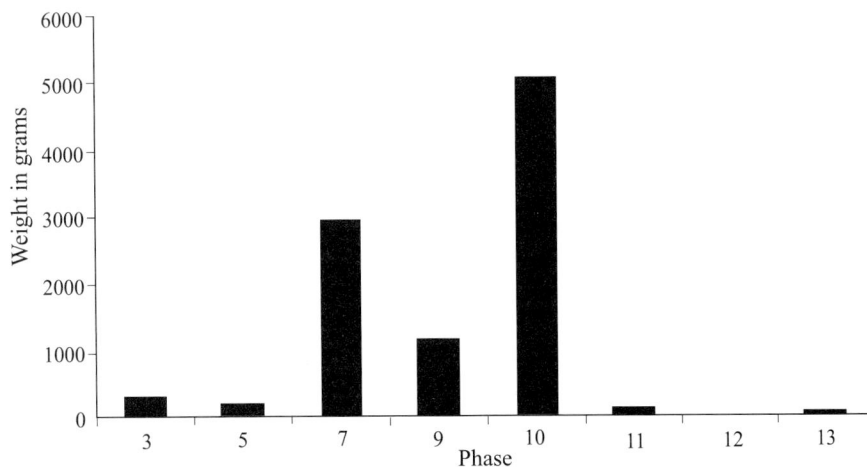

Figure 4.11 Chart showing slag by phase

154

160

163

164

165

166

168

171

173

174

175

180

178

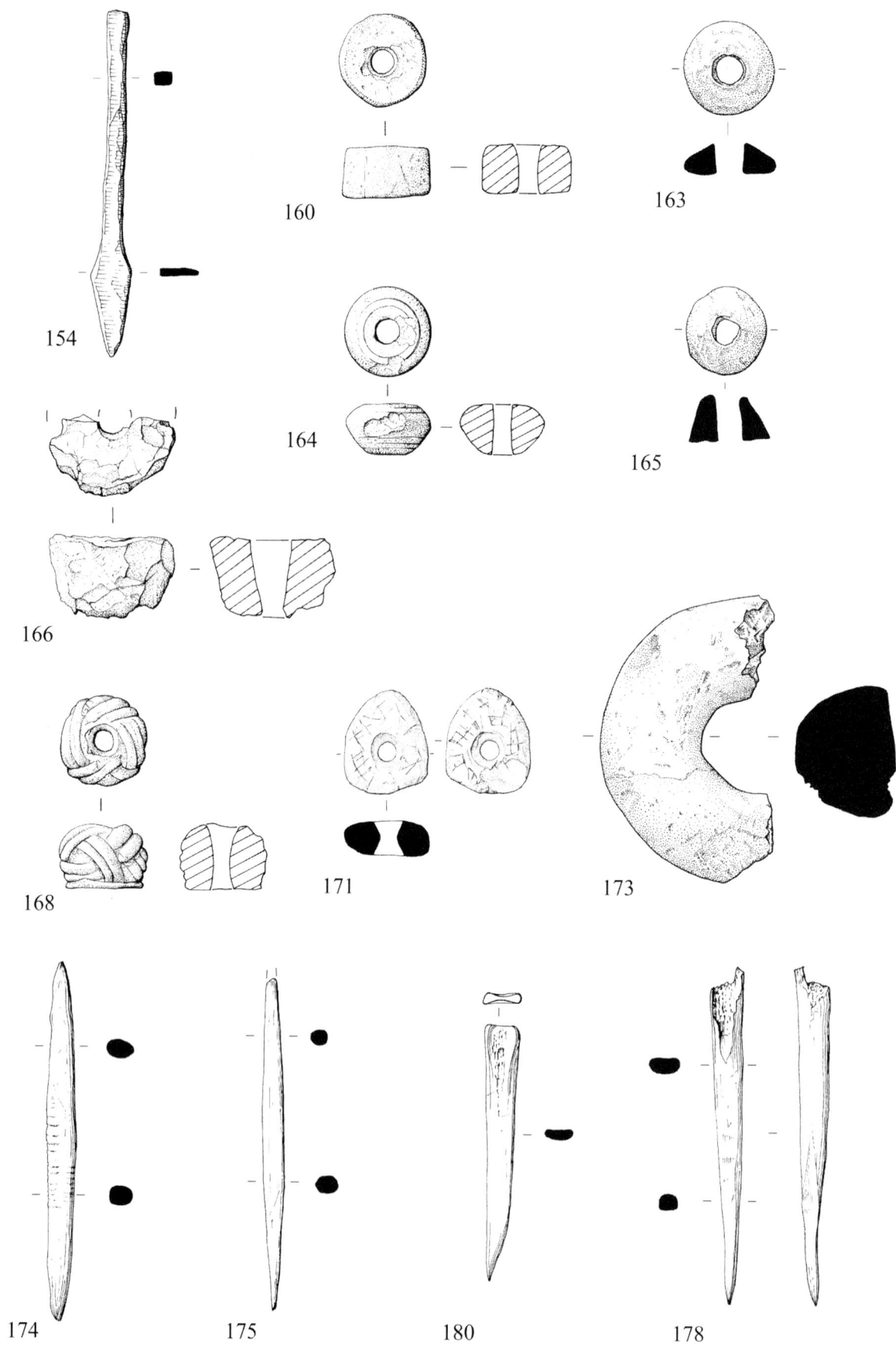

Figure 4.12 Small finds relating to occupations I. All at 1:2

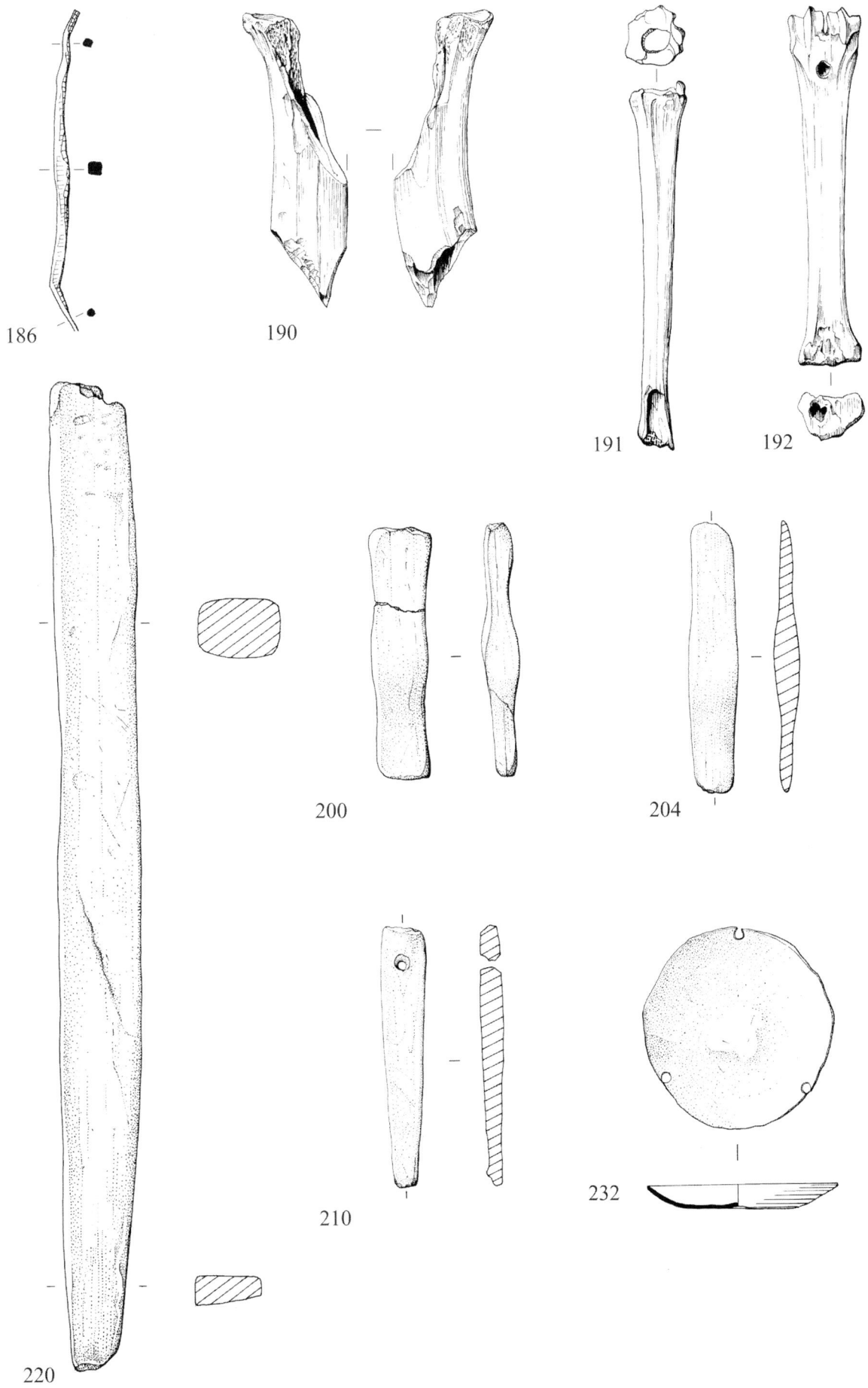

Figure 4.13 Small finds relating to occupations II. All at 1:2 except No. 232 at 1:1

157. Possible iron **tool**; triangular object (axe-shaped) with rounded corners; forged not cut from sheet; no blade edge or obvious method of attachment. L. 65mm, W. 65mm, T. 4mm.
549 (F337)/*4473*/Phase 5 boundary ditch fill, Enclosure 1.

158. Possible iron **tool**; rectangular bar with square-section tang (L. 40mm); unclear if complete object is represented. L. 140mm, W. 25mm, T. 8mm.
5002 (F2519)/*9145*/Phase 11 gravelled yard, Enclosure 18/21.

Textile manufacture

The site produced a range of evidence for the production of textiles, spanning all aspects of the process, from carding and spinning to finishing. Associated implements were distributed widely across the site, perhaps suggesting a domestic context for textile production. The preparation stage is attested to by an iron flax- or woolcomb spike from a Phase 9 context, which would originally have been mounted in a wooden block with a handle (Goodall in Biddle 1990, 214). Several spindle whorls were also recovered: five lead ones from Phases 8, 9 and 10 (plus one unstratified) and six stone examples (one apparently a fossil vertebra) from Phases 3, 9 and 10. The perforated, incised chalk or clunch object Fig. 4.12 No. 171, although unphased, could be a further example: white 'chalk' whorls were common in Winchester until the 13th century (Woodland in Biddle 1990, 216–25). The range of weights of these spindle whorls suggest that a variety of textile types were being produced. The stone examples weighed between 16g and 37g (though the latter was probably unfinished).

Although Walton Rogers (1997, 1731) argues that Roman spindle whorls have central holes with a diameter of 6–8mm, and Late Saxon and medieval examples have central holes of 9–11mm, this is not borne out by the contextual associations here. The examples (all stone) found securely in Roman contexts here have central perforations wider than this, while two of the lead examples (found in late medieval contexts) have perforations which would place them into Walton Rogers' 'Roman' range. Rather than see these as intrusive or residual, it is better to see the chronological variation in these whorls as more flexible. Likewise the heaviest whorl, at 80g, falls outside Walton Rogers' weight range (up to 55g) (*ibid.*). However, the range of whorls published from Winchester includes even heavier examples, as Woodland (in Biddle 1990, 218) argues that such heavier whorls are needed for doubling or plying the yarn — a need met by the small number of relatively heavy lead whorls found at Winchester and other sites. A whorl of similar weight from a 12th-century context at Townwall Street, Dover, may have been used to produce heavy yarn for cordage, rather than textile (I. Riddler, *pers. comm.*)

Evidence for textile production also comes in the form of two fragmentary loomweights: one triangular example from a Roman context, and an annular example from a Mid Saxon context. Both are evidence for the use of an upright warp-weighted loom. Other loom tools are discussed by Ian Riddler below.

159. Iron **flax- or wool-comb spike**. L. 84mm; possibly dates to before end 12th century.
619 (F2321)/*4478*/Phase 9, Enclosure 1.

****160.** **Spindle whorl** of fine calcareous sandstone, probably local Greensand, with flat base and upper surface and vertical sides. Some incised markings, one of which is an 'X', one a vertical line and one a possible rune, weight 25g.
4876 (F25)/*5326*/Phase 3 slot, Enclosure 3.

161. Limestone disc, possibly a fossil vertebra employed as **spindle whorl**. Oval disc, concave upper and base with central perforation D. 11mm; overall D. 49mm, Ht. 12mm, weight 33g.
8580 (F2039)/*8250*/Phase 3 ditch, Enclosure 7.

162. **Spindle whorl** of fine local Greensand with flat base and domed profile, turning lines on upper surface and base. D. 32mm, central perforation D. 9mm, Ht. 13mm, weight 19g.
6746 (F1505)/*9018*/Phase 3 ditch, Enclosure 8.

****163.** Lead **spindle whorl**, undecorated, roughly cast, weight 53g.
4188 (F1021)/*9041*/Phase 8 boundary ditch fill, Enclosure 3.

****164.** Half a rough **spindle whorl** of local Greensand, with flat base. Roughly hemispherical, possibly broken during working. and unfinished, weight 37g.
2423 (F484)/*3248*/Phase 9 ditch.

****165.** **Spindle whorl** of very fine, probably local, Greensand, with turning circles on upper and base, weight 16g.
3316 (F783)/*3924*/Phase 9 ditch, Enclosure 16.

****166.** Lead **spindle whorl**, undecorated, roughly cast and knife-trimmed, weight 52g.
6999 (F1706)/*9063*/Phase 9 ?paddock gully fill, Enclosure 5.

167. Lead **spindle whorl**, undecorated, crudely cast. Ht. 9mm, D. 27mm, central perforation D. 8mm, weight 30g.
1579 (F357)/*4398*/Phase 9 gravel trackway, Enclosure 16.

****168.** Hemispherical **spindle whorl** of fine local Greensand, with flat base and knotted decoration, weight 29g.
8267/*9024*/Phase 10, Enclosure 7.

169. Lead **spindle whorl**, undecorated, cone-shaped of oval section 19mm x 15mm, Ht. 10mm, central perforation D. 6–8mm, weight 13g.
8717 (F1012)/*9068*/Phase 10 boundary ditch fill, Enclosure 18.

170. Lead **spindle whorl**, undecorated, rod-shaped. Ht. 15mm, D. 30mm, central perforation D. 13mm, weight 80g.
Surface/*4415*b/Unstratified.

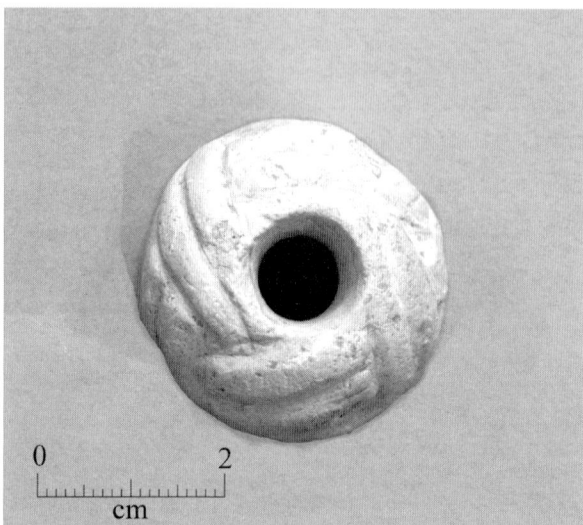

Plate VIII Small find No. 168: Greensand spindle whorl

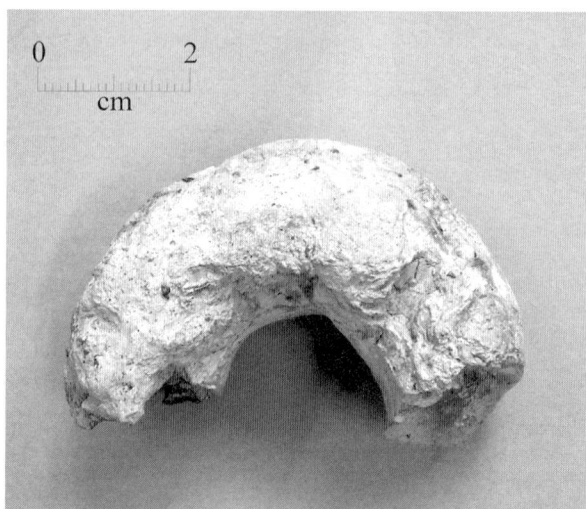

Plate IX Small find No. 173: fired clay loomweight

*171. Perforated chalk/clunch object, possibly a **spindle whorl** or weight. Sub-rectangular, decorated with incised (rune-like) markings and large central perforation, weight 16g.
Subsoil/*9027*/Unstratified.

172. Fired clay fragment, from a sub-triangular **loomweight** of Iron Age or Roman date, with two perforations visible. Rough fabric, with large stone inclusions, buff-red exterior, black interior. L. 128mm, W. 70mm, T. 34mm.
4232 (F1045)/*4892*/Phase 3 boundary ditch fill, Enclosure 8/9.

*173. Large fragment of an intermediate fired clay **loomweight**, tempered with medium flint and stone inclusions.
6488 (F1490)/*8827*/Phase 5, Enclosure 4.

Bone and antler textile implements
by Ian Riddler

The two principal forms of bone and antler pin-beater known from the Anglo-Saxon period are both present in this assemblage. Three pin-beaters are double-pointed and a further fragment is probably also of this type. In addition, there are two single-pointed pin-beaters and one fragment that cannot be identified to type.

The double-pointed pin-beaters include one complete example and a second object which is almost complete, and whose original length can be reconstructed. The complete example (Fig. 4.12 No. 174) is highly polished (a prerequisite of pin-beaters, allowing them to pass easily through and across textile) and retains knife or rasp marks along its central section. Similar marks can be seen on examples from Pennyland and Shakenoak, as well as on several unpublished double-pointed pin-beaters from Brandon, Suffolk (Riddler 1993, 117 and fig. 61.69; Brodribb *et al*. 1972, fig. 63.94).

The incomplete double-pointed pin-beater (Fig. 4.12 No. 175) is also made of antler and has a slender profile and near-circular cross section. It is similar to several examples from West Stow, and the same characteristics are shared also by a number of pin-beaters of Mid Saxon date, from a variety of sites (West 1985, figs 207.10 and 210.13; Brodribb *et al*. 1972, fig. 62.86; Riddler *et al*. forthcoming). A third pin-beater (No. 176) is oval in section and highly polished. It includes long smoothing marks on its surface, which were probably produced by a draw-knife. A fourth fragment (No. 177), although flatter in section, probably also stems from a double-pointed pin-beater.

Double-pointed pin-beaters were used with the warp-weighted loom throughout the Anglo-Saxon period (Brown in Biddle 1990, 226). They show little variation in formal characteristics over time. It has been suggested that they may have been maintained — and possibly used — in pairs (Riddler 1993, 117–19). They are common implements and examples are known from several Anglo-Saxon sites in Cambridgeshire, including Barrington, Hinxton and Maxey (Malim and Hines 1998; Addyman 1964, fig. 16.21–2; Riddler 2004). Two of the four examples in this assemblage come from 12th-century contexts and are presumably residual, as few pin-beaters (of either type) can be dated later than the 11th century, this being the time at which the horizontal loom came to prominence (Walton 1991, 328).

The single-pointed pin-beater (Fig. 4.12 No. 178) is complete and had been repointed during the period of its use. The recut end has been shaped to a crude point to one side of the object. The blunt end is indented on both broad faces, producing a 'thumb groove' (Brown in Biddle 1990, 227). A second example (No. 179), although fragmentary, clearly belongs to this implement type. It is polished and tapers to a crude point, with a noticeably flat section. An

incomplete, tapering implement of bone (Fig. 4.12 No. 180) is highly polished and is related to this series. It differs from the others, however, on account of its curved profile and the choice of raw material. Nonetheless, it would have served equally well as a pin-beater. It can be compared with several bone pin-beaters from Ipswich (Riddler *et al*. forthcoming).

Single-pointed pin-beaters largely occur in 9th–11th century contexts, and are associated with the vertical two-beam loom (Walton Rogers 1997, 1755–7). The latest known examples come from 12th-century contexts at Beverley, Dover and London (Foreman 1992, nos 481–4; Riddler and Walton Rogers forthcoming; Pritchard 1991, nos 232–3). They are generally shorter than the double-pointed series, and flatter in profile. One end served to pick out threads on the loom, whilst the broader end could be used to push them into place. Over 70 examples have come from excavations in Ipswich and they are also plentiful at Thetford, as well as other sites of Late Saxon date (Riddler *et al*. forthcoming; Rogerson and Dallas 1984, figs 191–3; Dallas 1993, fig. 160.7–8; Andrews 1995, fig. 87.8 and 10).

The broad and relatively crude shape of a fragmentary needle (No. 182) is a defining characteristic of the object type. Needles made from pig fibulae occur in considerable numbers throughout the Anglo-Saxon period and they cannot be closely dated (Riddler 1991, 47; 1993, 114). This particular example came from a Late Saxon context. They served a number of purposes in the production, repair and maintenance of both textiles and netting (Riddler *et al*. forthcoming). They could be produced quickly and simply from pig fibulae and no particular skill was required in their manufacture.

*174. Complete double pointed antler **pin-beater** of oval section. Highly polished, includes series of transverse marks about middle section, produced with aid of knife or file. Profile a little irregular towards one end.
1155/*9015*/Phase 7, Enclosure 9.

*175. Incomplete antler **pin-beater** of double-pointed type; oval section, tapers to rounded points at either end, one of which now missing. Original L. 120mm.
9558 (F2604)/*9328*/Phase 9 gully fill, Enclosure 6.

176. Fragment of central part of double-pointed bone or antler **pin-beater**, highly polished. L. 81mm, D. 6mm.
1526/*2622*/Phase 9 pit fill, Enclosure 1.

177. Fragment of antler **pin-beater**, probably of double-pointed type. Traces of polish from use. L. 58mm, D. 8mm.
2842 (F667)/*3559*/Phase 9 ditch fill, Enclosure 17.

*178. Complete single-pointed antler **pin-beater**, with flat, rounded rectangular section narrowing at broad end to provide thumb groove. Pointed end recut in antiquity.
7461 (F1651)/9022/Phase 5 ditch, Enclosure 4.

179. Fragment of single-pointed bone or antler **pin-beater**, rounded rectangular section, tapers to a rounded point, with traces of wear. L. 51mm, W. 10mm.
Surface/*8998*/Unstratified.

*180. Tapering bone **implement**, with cortile tissue present at fragmentary broad end, highly polished and tapers to rounded point; lightly curved in profile.
3063 (F701)/*3757*/Phase 6 post-hole fill, Structure 10, Enclosure 9.

181. Point of bone or antler **pin-beater**, which cannot be assigned to type; burnt. L. 24mm.
3841 (F918)/*4293*/Phase 7 ditch, Enclosure 12.

182. Point and part of the shaft of a bone **needle**, produced from pig fibula; L. 60mm, W. 7mm.
3682/*4213*/Phase 7 gully, Enclosure 13.

Other textile implements

The only other finds associated with textile production were a needle from an Iron Age context (No. 184), an unphased copper alloy pin shank (No. 185), and a glass slick stone (No. 185). This was probably a small example (now in five fragments), these usually being 80–90mm in diameter and 23–41mm thick; while they were used in the Roman period they reappear only at the end of the 9th century, becoming more common in the 10th (Walton Rogers 1997, 1775–9).

183. Incomplete copper alloy **needle**; beginning of slot cut into shaft leading to eye. L. 58mm; D. 2mm.
4337 (F1573)/*9083*/Phase 2 boundary ditch fill, Enclosure 1.

184. Possible copper alloy **pin** shank; cast tapering rod with oval section, bent in two places. L. 70mm; max W. 5mm.
8716/*9100*/Unphased.

185. Glass **slick stone** ('linen smoother'), glass black to the eye, in five fragments. Appears of be of usual 10th–12th century type, circular and slightly domed. D. *c*. 64mm, Ht. 21mm.
3275 (F752)/*3910*/Phase 11 well fill, Enclosure 16.

Leatherworking

Two iron awls (Fig. 4.13 No 186, No. 187), both from Late Saxon contexts, suggest leatherworking on the site, as these were used to pierce holes in leather in preparation for thread (Goodall in Biddle 1990, 249). Likewise, a horn-handled punch (No. 188) from a Phase 11 context suggests similar activity later on. The thimble (No. 189) is of the ring type used for specialist purposes, including leatherworking, in late and post-medieval times (Margeson 1993, 187). That both the punch and the thimble came from the same feature may indicate the location of leatherworking in the later medieval period on the site.

*186. Iron **awl**; rod pointed at both ends; square section in centre and one end; awl point round section.
3662 (F501)/*4620*/Phase 8 boundary ditch fill, Paddock P, Enclosure 13.

187. Possible iron **awl**; tang? of oval section; condition poor. L. 60mm, W. 12mm, T. 8mm.
3437 (F503)/*4597*/Phase 8 ditch fill, Enclosure 14/16.

188. Complete iron **punch**; punch head 12mm x 13mm; horn handle. L. 111mm.
7000 (F2519)/*9209a*/Phase 11 gravelled yard, Enclosure 18/21.

189. Copper alloy **thimble** of ring type with large triangular holes; used for coarse work by tailor or leatherworker (Holmes 1988). L. 29mm, W. 10mm, T. 6mm; late 15th to 16th century.
7000 (F2519)/*9094c*/Phase 11 gravelled yard, Enclosure 18/21.

Miscellaneous tools

Bone tools
by Ian Riddler
Aside from those bone tools and implements discussed above and below, a number of other pieces from Enclosures 1 and 12 represent tools of some sort. The single example of a socketed point (Fig. 4.13 No. 190) has been produced from the proximal end of a cattle metatarsus. The articular surface has been perforated axially (and largely removed) and the midshaft has been tapered to a crude point. Socketed points are commonly seen on sites of 10th–12th century date, both in England and in northern Europe; appropriately, this example came from a Late Saxon context (Roes 1963, 47; van Vilsteren 1987, 28 no. 15; Foreman 1991, 187 and fig. 130.1144; MacGregor *et al.* 1999, 1989–90; Lauwerier and van Heeringen 1998, 124–5; Riddler *et al.* forthcoming). The majority are made from the proximal ends of cattle metatarsals, although other species and bone types were used on occasion.

The function of these objects has yet to be determined. At the turn of the last century Nina Layard argued that they served as the ferrules for poles used by skaters to travel over ice (Layard 1908, 74) and this interpretation has been repeated recently (Lauwerier and van Heeringen 1998, 125). There is no real evidence to support this suggestion, however, and it is much more likely that those ferrules were made of iron (MacGregor 1976, 66; 1982, 97; 1985, 174). In his 12th-century description of skaters at Moorfields, William Fitz Stephen noted that they were 'holding poles shod with iron in their hands' (MacGregor 1976, 62). Roes made a distinction between shorter and longer bone socketed points, the former series seemingly more carefully finished than the latter (Roes 1963, 47). The twofold division was retained for the analysis of the Lincoln assemblage, alongside Roes' suggestion that the shorter examples served as tallow holders (Mann 1982, 27, 31 and figs 26 and 32). MacGregor has argued that the longer examples were used in leatherworking, whilst Foreman and O'Connor have suggested that the objects in general formed a part of implements used to stun cattle, prior to butchery (Foreman 1991, 187).

Although they were not used as ferrules, it is clear that they could have acted as socketed implements. A related object from Castricum, made from a cattle humerus, retains a part of the wooden pole to which it was attached (Lauwerier and van Heeringen 1998, fig. 5). Although some examples are carefully finished, the object type is essentially a simple one, utilising a large, crude point cut from the midshaft of the bone.

A range of perforated bones were also retrieved, most of which came from Late Saxon contexts. Two groups can be identified on the basis of the animal species. The first consists of ovicaprid metapodia, most of which probably derive from sheep, and the second includes several examples of perforated cattle bones.

The ovicaprid metapodia have been perforated axially through the proximal articulation, either centrally or a little to one side of the mid-point. The perforations are usually irregular in shape and 6–9mm in width. The objects are otherwise unmodified. Laterally perforated ovicaprid metapodia occur in Iron Age and Roman contexts, and they may have been used as textile implements (Wild 1970, 63; Sellwood 1984, 389–92). A number of examples were discovered at West Stow, where they are not necessarily of Anglo-Saxon date (West 1985, fig. 155.7–9).

Axially-perforated metapodia would not necessarily have all been used for the same purpose, and their function is unclear. In some cases, and with one example in particular (Fig. 4.13 No. 191), it appears that an iron rod of square or rectangular section may have been driven into the bone. A small number of similarly perforated sheep bones of Roman date came from Grandford, Cambridgeshire, and Stallibrass noted that some of the perforations could have been of natural origin (Stallibrass 1982, 106 and pl. IVa). Subsequently, however, axially-perforated sheep metapodia have been encountered in reasonable numbers from other sites; although some holes had been fashioned more carefully than others, with many examples there does appear to have been a deliberate intention to perforate the bone.

Axially-perforated sheep metapodial bones formed Types 4–7 of the metapodial tools from Dragonby in Lincolnshire (Taylor and May 1996, 355 and fig. 14.5). Two of the West Fen Road examples are fragmentary and, in the absence of the distal ends, they can only be equated with Types 4–7 from Dragonby. The complete example

(Fig. 4.13 No. 192) has an axial perforation through the proximal end and a lateral perforation close to the condyles on the posterior side of the bone; it does not correspond precisely with any of the Dragonby types. The latter were largely recovered from Iron Age contexts, although they may have continued in use into the early part of the Roman period. All of the metapodial tools from Dragonby were related to textile manufacture (Taylor and May 1996, 357).

Few comparable examples from later contexts have been published, but a series of perforated ovicaprid bones have been recorded from *Hamwic*, and their details are summarised here (Table 4.7). The three examples recorded here accord well with the *Hamwic* sample. Although it is not clear why these bones were perforated, at least it can be noted that they do occur in post-Roman contexts. The West Fen Road examples come from Late Saxon contexts and they could therefore be of Late Saxon date. Equally, they may be residual objects of Iron Age origin.

The remaining modified bones include an axially perforated cattle humerus (No. 194) from a Late Saxon context, while a cattle radius (No. 195) from a medieval context had been perforated in a similar manner.

*190. Incomplete **socketed point**, produced from cattle metatarsus. Proximal end perforated axially and midshaft tapered to point on posterior face.
3037/3727/Phase 7 spread, Enclosure 1.

*191. **Perforated bone**. Ovicaprid metatarsus, perforated axially through proximal articular surface, perforation rectangular.
93 (F87)/*126*/Phase 7, Enclosure 1.

*192. **Perforated bone**. Ovicaprid metatarsus, perforated axially through proximal articular surface.
6398 (F895)/*6439a*/Phase 6 ditch, Enclosure 12.

193. **Perforated bone**. Ovicaprid metacarpus, perforated axially through proximal articular surface, sub-circular perforation D. 6mm.
6398 (F895)/*6439b*/Phase 6 ditch, Enclosure 12.

Site	Code	Bone type	End	Quantity
Clifford Street	SOU32	Metacarpus	Proximal	4
Clifford Street	SOU32	Metatarsus	Proximal	6
Clifford Street	SOU32	Metatarsus	Distal	1
Clifford Street	SOU32	Tibia	Distal	1
Downham Baker	SOU177	Tibia	Distal	1
Six Dials	SOU23	Metatarsus	Proximal	3
Six Dials	SOU24	Metacarpus	Proximal	3
Six Dials	SOU24	Metacarpus	Distal	1
Six Dials	SOU26	Metacarpus	Proximal	11
Six Dials	SOU26	Metatarsus	Proximal	9
Chapel Road	SOU7	Metatarsus	Proximal	2

Table 4.7 Axially-perforated ovicaprid bones from Mid Saxon contexts at Hamwic

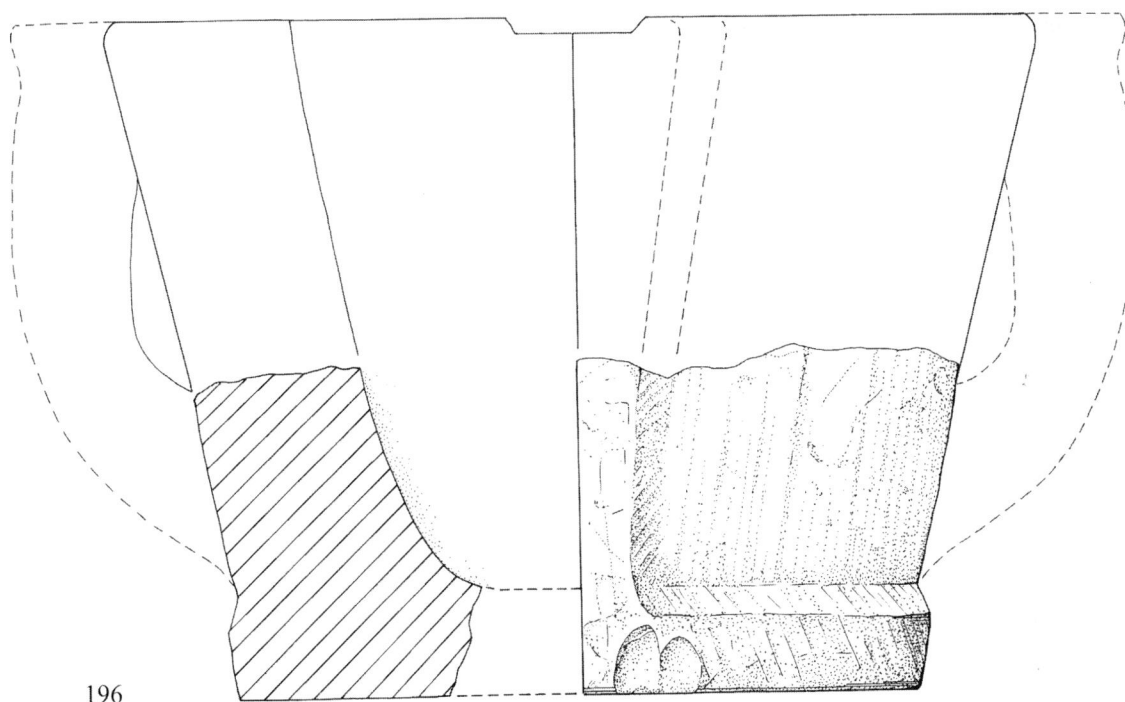

196

Figure 4.14 Mortar No. 196 (1:1)

194. Perforated bone. Axially perforated cattle humerus. Perforation
D. 11mm.
5750 (F1217)/*5843*/Phase 6 boundary ditch fill, Enclosure 12.

195. Perforated bone. Fragment of proximal end of cattle radius,
perforated axially. Perforation D. 7mm.
9128 (F2196)/*8634*/Phase 11 pit, Enclosure 12.

Mortars

The two mortar fragments, one of Purbeck marble and one
of limestone, indicate grinding or mixing of pastes on the
site. Purbeck marble was used for mortars in the Roman
period; the former could, therefore, be residual. However,
given its location to the south of the excavated area, far
removed from areas of Roman occupation, it seems more
likely that it belongs to the period which saw the
production of domestic stone mortars in quantity, from the
13th century onwards (Dunning 1961, 283).

*196. Fragment of base and part of wall of a steep straight-sided Purbeck
Marble **mortar**. Narrow band at base of wall chisel-dressed,
interior smooth, underside and one wall are pecked.
9128 (F2196)/*8637*/Phase 11 pit, Enclosure 12.

197. Mortar fragment of Jurassic Limestone (Barnack or Northants).
L. 155mm, W. 150mm, T. 50mm.
Topsoil/*8993*/Unphased.

Whetstones

The site produced evidence for a relatively large number
of whetstones, in a variety of stones: local Greensand, fine
siltstone, mica schist, shale, Kentish ragstone,
metamorphic chlorite schist and sandstone examples are
all seen. The assemblage here, certainly in the Mid to Late
Saxon period, seems to be an *ad hoc* (perhaps
predominantly local) accumulation of such items. It is
notable here that the majority of Greensand examples
derive mainly from Mid and Late Saxon contexts, with
those of Kentish ragstone and schist coming from later
medieval contexts; this may represent a widening of the
trade networks available to the inhabitants from the 11th
and 12th centuries on. This corresponds broadly with the
chronological patterning noted by Ellis (1969). Fig. 4.13
No. 210 was presumably for personal use, as may have
been some of the other small fine examples, while larger
ones may have been used for sharpening agricultural and
other larger tools (*cf*. Ellis and Moore in Biddle 1990,
869).

198. Fragment of large fine siltstone **whetstone**, with deep sharpening
groove towards edge of one side, broken at one end. L. 78mm, W.
56mm, T. 35mm.
7125(F1593)/*7165*/Phase 3 ditch, Enclosure 8.

199. Whetstone of local Greensand, sub-rectangular section, broken at
one end and pointed at other. L. 53mm, W. 41mm, T. 23mm.
10(F4)/*133*/Phase 5 ditch, Enclosure 4.

*200. Small **whetstone** of local Greensand, roughly rectangular with
central swelling.
286(F268)/*2306*/Phase 8 boundary ditch fill, Enclosure 2.

201. Probable **whetstone** of local Greensand, rectangular section, all
four sides worked. L. 46mm, W. 35mm.
613 (F304)/*2435*/Phase 8 boundary ditch fill, Enclosure 1.

202. Probable **whetstone**, possibly of mica schist, with many worn, flat
surfaces, irregular section. L. 39mm, W. 26mm, T. 10mm.
1241/*2596*/Phase 7, Enclosure 13.

203. Very fine shale **whetstone** of rectangular section, broken both
ends. L. 55mm, W. 6mm, T. 4mm.
2405(F600)/*3233*/Phase 8 passageway gully fill, Enclosure 1.

*204. Small **whetstone** of metamorphic fine-grained phyllite, well-
worn, especially at ends. Rectangular section with central
swelling.
8010(F1838)/*7828*/Phase 7 gully, Enclosure 7.

205. Well-worn **whetstone** of fine-grained local Greensand.
Sub-square section, but tapering, sharpening grooves on one face,
broken both ends. L. 58mm, W. 32mm, T. 29mm.
8025(F1865)/*7848*/Phase 7 ditch, Enclosure 7.

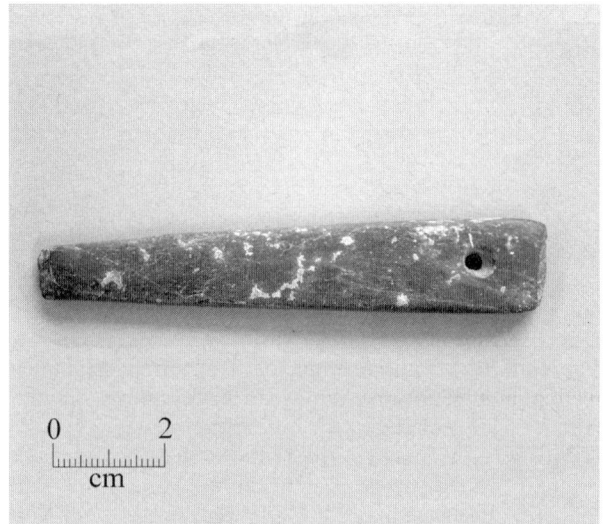

Plate X Small find No. 210: metamorphic schist
whetstone

206. Whetstone of banded local Greensand, flat base, irregular section,
broken both ends. L. 99mm, W. 40mm, T. 30mm.
9769(F2633)/*9447*/Phase 8 dividing ditch fill, Enclosure 6.

207. Whetstone. Local Greensand.
3790(F790)/*4258*/Phase 8 boundary ditch fill, Enclosure 16.

208. Whetstone fragment of Kentish ragstone, sub-rectangular section,
worn one end, broken at other. L. 53mm, W. 20mm, T. 11mm.
8689 (F2050)/*8307*/Phase 9 ditch, Enclosure 4.

209. Possible **whetstone** of metamorphic chlorite schist, irregular
section, very worn, tapering at both ends and broken at one. L.
151mm, W. 47mm, T. 8mm.
1622(F3142)/*2677*/Phase 9 floor level in Structure 39, Enclosure 16.

*210. Largely complete tapering **whetstone** of metamorphic schist,
probably as inclusion in the Greensand. Sub-rectangular section,
broken at tip, suspension hole at one end.
3143/*3814*/Phase 9 floor, structure 26, Enclosure 16.

211. Whetstone of chlorite schist, sub-rectangular section with
rounded edges, broken both ends but little worn. L. 77mm, W.
21mm, T. 12mm.
3144/*3816*/Phase 9 floor, Structure 26, Enclosure 16.

212. Whetstone of metamorphic chlorite schist, flat faces, rounded
sides, worn and partly broken down one side and at both ends. L.
98mm, W. 44mm, T. 11mm.
1998(F796)/*2924*/Phase 10 well fill, Enclosure 16.

213. Whetstone fragment of Kentish ragstone, slightly banded. Oval
section, broken both ends. L. 30mm, W. 27mm, T. 10mm.
3285(F768)/*3915*/Phase 10 ditch, Enclosure 16.

214. Whetstone of chlorite schist, sub-rectangular section, broken on
one side and at both ends. L. 52mm, W. 25mm, T. 20mm.
3323(F774)/*3931*/Phase 10 pit fill, Enclosure 16.

215. Whetstone fragment, possibly a hard sandstone. Almost square
section, rounded corners, broken at one end. L. 53mm, W. 32mm,
T. 28mm.
6000(F1301)/*6118*/Phase 10 ditch, Enclosure 12.

216. Whetstone of metamorphic chlorite schist, oval section, broken
both ends. L. 79mm, W. 23mm, T. 10mm.
7202(F2526)/*7192*/Phase 10 floor, Structure 27, Enclosure 18.

217. Whetstone fragment of fine-grained metamorphic rock,
sub-rectangular section, slightly worn, broken both ends. L.
98mm, W. 25mm, T. 21mm.
5681(F1272)/*5781*/Phase 10 boundary ditch fill, Enclosure 20.

218. Whetstone fragment of local Greensand, sub-rectangular section,
worn and broken both ends. L. 53mm, W. 16mm, T. 10mm.
3553(F2410)/*4109*/Phase 11 pit fill, Enclosure 16/17.

219. Whetstone of banded siltstone. Sub-rectangular section,
sharpening grooves on two faces, broken at middle, complete at
top. L. 55mm, W. 30mm, T. 17mm.
3302(F771)/*3918*/Phase 11 pit fill, Enclosure 16.

*220. **Whetstone**, nearly complete, possibly of Kentish ragstone.
Roughly rectangular in section, tapering both ends (one end
broken near tip), worn.
7000(F2519)/*7023a*/Phase 11 gravelled yard, Enclosure 18/21.

221. **Whetstone** fragment, possibly Kentish ragstone, of rectangular section, largely unworn but with some sharpening grooves, broken both ends. L. 211mm, W. 27mm, T. 16mm.
7000(F2519)/*7023*b/Phase 11 gravelled yard, Enclosure 18/21.

222. **Whetstone** fragment, possibly Kentish ragstone, of sub-rectangular section, worn and broken both ends. L. 116mm, W. 29mm, T. 18mm.
7000(F2519)/*7023*c/Phase 11 gravelled yard, Enclosure 18/21.

223. **Whetstone** fragment of metamorphic chlorite schist, sub-rectangular section, very worn, broken at one end. L. 124mm, W. 35mm, T. 13mm.
7078/*7122*/Unphased.

Querns

The majority of quern fragments from the excavations were of grey vesicular lava; these are only commented on here, and not reported on individually. Like the collection from Norwich, it is probable that all were of Rhenish origin (also known as Mayen or Niedermendig) (*cf.* Margeson 1993, 202). A total of 1478 fragments of lava quern were recovered from the site, weighing 63.80kg (Table 4.8). The material has been examined and measurements taken where applicable. Eighty-two per cent of the assemblage, by number, are undiagnostic fragments, having no unambiguous surfaces and no measurable thickness. However the remainder make up 72% of the assemblage by weight. The querns vary in thickness from *c.* 11–75mm and in diameter from *c.* 400–800mm (Fig. 4.15). A raised shoulder around the central hole is present on five fragments. The degree of wear on the inner, working surfaces varies greatly, and no attempt has been made here to classify it. Tool marks are present on many of the outer surfaces of the querns. By weight and by number, there is a dramatic peak in the Late Saxon period, which tails off dramatically in the later medieval period; this may reflect the increasing legislation governing milling during this period.

Aside from the lava querns, quern fragments are also seen in sandstone, local Greenstone, another conglomerate stone, Millstone Grit and granite. There is also a basalt rubstone from a Late Saxon context. All of these querns may have been used for grinding flour, or possibly malt (Margeson 1993, 202), and to judge from their site-wide distribution, would have been used in domestic contexts.

224. Possible **quern** fragment. Conglomerate grading to coarse sandstone, possibly Devonian sandstone, Forest of Dean or Culham Greensand. L. 70mm, W. 70mm, T. 40mm.
8952/F1055/Phase 3 ditch, Enclosure 3.

225. Possible **quern** fragment, of hard, fine, local Greensand, one smooth surface. L. 76mm, W. 67mm, T. 35mm.
2509(F602)/*3317*/Phase 3 ditch, Enclosure 8.

226. Millstone grit **quern**, 52mm thick, good inner and outer surfaces.
232(F257)/*2403*/Phase 8 boundary ditch fill, Enclosure 2.

227. Probable **quern** fragment, of conglomerate stone, in two fragments (a) L. 65mm, W. 32mm, T. 32mm (b) L. 67mm, W. 56mm, T. 28mm.
8151(F1933)/*7964*/Phase 9 post-trench, Enclosure 7.

228. Granite **quern** fragment of igneous metamorphic, probably an erratic. Flat base and top, sloping sides, rounded edges. L. 100mm, W. 90mm, T. 40mm.

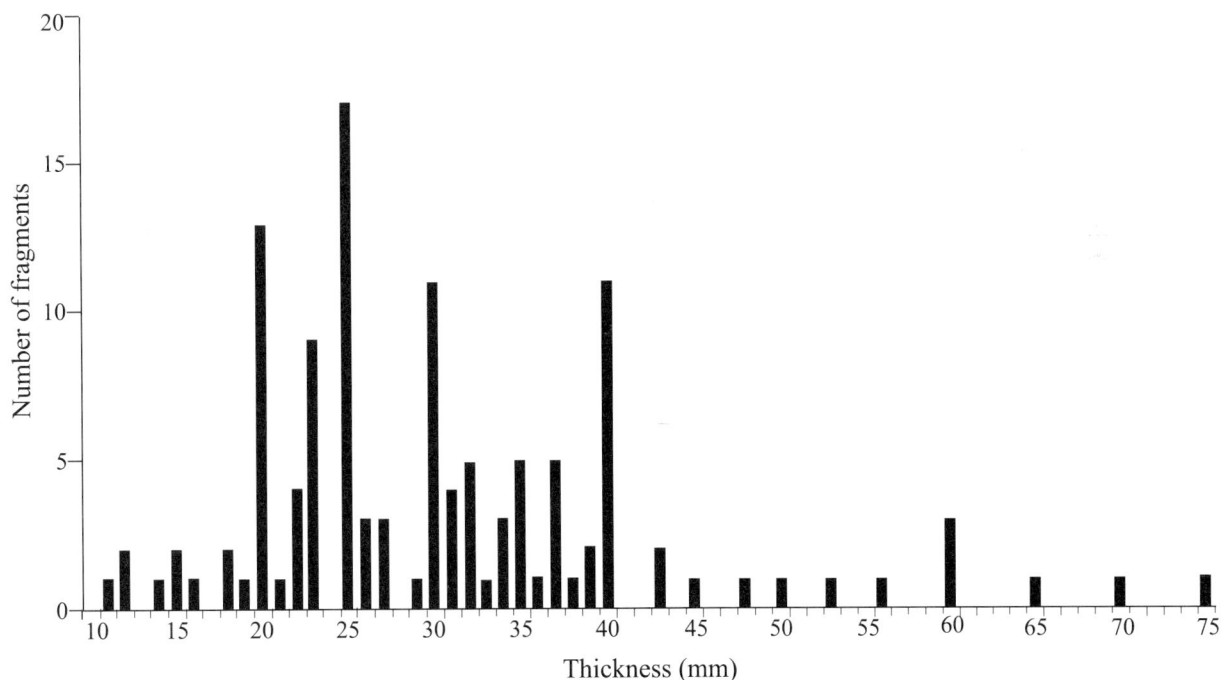

Figure 4.15 Chart showing lava quern by thickness

	Number	Weight (kg)	Average wt. (g)
Undiagnostic	1204	17.907	14.8
Diagnostic	274	45.888	167.5

Table 4.8 Table showing breakdown of lava quern fragments

1521(F2304)/*2620*/Phase 9 ditch, Enclosure 1.

229. **Quern** fragment of fine-grained millstone grit, South Pennines or Derbyshire. Burnt. L. 57mm, W. 41mm, T. 31mm.
7273/*7253*/Phase 10 pit, Enclosure 7.

230. Basalt **rubstone**, one good surface. D. 290mm, T. 62mm.
2690(F644)/*3450*/Phase 8 boundary ditch fill, Enclosure 9.

Briquetage

A single fragment of briquetage was tentatively identified; this may have been a prop for a tray associated with salt production.

231. Possible **briquetage** fragment of roughly triangular section, possibly salt-affected; may have been a prop for tray or pedestal. Deep pink coarse fabric, medium to large flint and stone inclusions. L. 62mm, Ht. 38mm, T. 29mm.
6445(F1489)/*6486*/Phase 5 boundary ditch fill, Enclosure 4.

Commercial activity

by Sam Lucy with Adrian Challands

Evidence for continuous commercial activity on the site consists mainly of stray losses of coins, jetons and tokens. A scale pan from a Late Saxon context suggests that someone here engaged in this commercial activity. There are also two fragmentary lead weights, which fall within the weight range for the lead discs reported from London (Egan 1998, 307). Both are possibly stylistically of 14th-century date, although since both derive from Phase 9 contexts this identification is somewhat doubtful. The coins and tokens are generally unstratified surface finds, but those that did derive from archaeological features are generally in accordance with the phasing. Of particular note is the silver *sceatta* (No. 250) from a Phase 5 context. This type currently has a distribution spanning northern Kent and the Thames Valley, Essex, Hertfordshire and Cambridgeshire, with outliers in Lincolnshire, North Yorkshire and Gloucestershire (http://www-cm. fitzmuseum.cam.ac.uk/Coins). It belongs to the late Secondary phase of *sceatta* production, and Series L is notably base (Grierson and Blackburn 1986, 172). Fifteen Roman coins were also recovered, though only two occurred in context (Nos 236–7); the remainder are generic metal-detector finds. These are listed below. Eight of these are 3rd-century (there are no earlier issues), with the remainder of 4th-century attribution. Coin loss seems to have ceased before the end of the 4th century, the latest issue, No. 247, dating to AD 367–375.

*****232.** Circular copper alloy **scale pan** with three perforations very close to pan edge; type used mainly for weighing coins.
4446(F891)/*9086*/Phase 8 dividing ditch fill, Enclosure 12.

233. Fragmentary **lead weight**, probably of circular form; on face: seeded fleur-de-lis. D. *c.* 35–40mm, Wt. 6g; 14th-century?
8941(F2211)/*9073*/Phase 9 ditch, Enclosure 11.

234. Fragmentary **lead ?weight**, of rectangular form, decorated on face with four radiating lines from central knob with pellets in between (*cf.* Egan 1998, no. 1008 for a circular parallel), possibly broken in half along the raised bar. Surviving dimensions: L. 17mm, W. 20mm, Wt. 7g; 14th-century?
6781(F1629)/*9061*/Phase 9 ditch, Enclosure 7.

235. Postumus AD 259–267; Obv. [IMP]CPO[STVMVSP]PAVG Radiate crowned and draped bust, right; Rev. MON[ETA AVG] Moneta, left. Minted AD 259–267.
Surface/*4444*/Unstratified.

236. Minimissimi; Obv. Head, right; Rev. Copy of soldier spearing fallen horseman; Minted *c.* AD 357–367.
4701(F1056)/*9088*/Phase 3 ditch, Enclosure 4.

237. Radiate; Obv. Legend illegible. Radiate bust, right; Rev. Legend illegible. Traces of altar and standing figure; Minted third quarter of the 3rd century AD.
6616(F1461)/*9093*/Phase 3 pit fill, Enclosure 4.

238. Constantine I AD 308–337; Obv. CONSTAN[TIN]VS AVG Helmeted and cuirassed bust, right; Rev. BEA[T

TRANQUILITAS] Altar inscribed VOTIS XX surmounted by a globe and three stars; Mint Mark PTR Trier. Minted AD 320–324.
Surface/*9102*/Unstratified.

239. Radiate (Official issue); Obv. Legend illegible. Radiate bust, right; Rev. Illegible; Minted last third of 3rd century AD.
Surface/*9103*/Unstratified.

240. Fragment of radiate (official issue); Obv. Legend illegible. Traces of radiate bust, right; Rev. Legend illegible. Traces of standing figure, right arm outstretched; Minted last third of the 3rd century AD.
Surface/*9106*/Unstratified.

241. Barbarous radiate; Obv. Traces of crude radiate crown; Rev. Traces of crude design; Minted third quarter of the 3rd century AD.
Surface/*9107a*/Unstratified.

242. Half coin of Theodora (2nd wife of Constantius I); Obv. [FLMAXTH]DORAEAVG Laureate and draped bust, right; Rev. [PIETAS RO]MANA Empress standing facing, head right, holding two children; Mint mark TRP Trier. Minted AD 337–341.
Surface/*9107b*/Unstratified.

243. Minim (unofficial copy of fel temp reparatio type); Obv. —NS— Well executed head, right; Rev. FEL— Well executed copy of soldier spearing fallen horseman; Minted *c.* AD 346–361.
Surface/*9112a*/Unstratified.

244. Cu Dupondius, probably Severus Alexander AD 222–235; Obv. Legend illegible. Laureate and draped bust, right; Rev. – OS – design illegible; The coin may be dated to the first half of the 3rd century AD.
Surface/*9112b*/Unstratified.

245. Radiate; Obv. - - - ? AV[G] traces of radiate bust, right; Rev. Illegible; Minted *c.* third quarter of the 3rd century AD.
Surface/9114/Unstratified.

246. Constantinian commemorative; Obv. CONSTAN[TINOPOLIS] Helmeted bust of Constantinopolis, left; Rev. No legend. Victory on prow; Mint mark TR•P Trier. Minted AD 330–335.
2695/*9297*/Phase 7 post-hole fill, Enclosure 1.

247. Hourglass perforation above bust; Valentinianic; Obv. Legend illegible. Draped and pearl diademmed bust, right; Rev. [FELICITAS ROMANOR]VM Victory to left, holding wreath and palm; Mint mark illegible. Minted AD 367–375.
Surface/*9298*/Unstratified.

248. Constantinian; Obv. illegible; Rev. legend illegible. Two soldiers one standard; Mint mark illegible. Minted AD 335–341.
Surface/*9299*/Unstratified.

249. Tetricus I; Obv. IMPT[ETRICVS PF AVG] Radiate bust, right; Rev. illegible; Minted *c.* AD 270–273.
Surface/*9300*/Unstratified.

250. Silver **sceatta**, Series L (Type 18) (N72). Obv. diademed bust right, cross. Rev. figure with cross and bird; broken, with piece missing. Weight: 0.70g; *c.* 730–760 AD (EMC No. 2001.0671).
4636(F1024)/*9087*/Phase 5 fence-line slot fill, Enclosure 3.

251. Henry II silver **penny**. Type N957 (Cross and crosslets (Tealby): C2). Obv. Legend: HENRI:REX A; crowned bust facing wearing

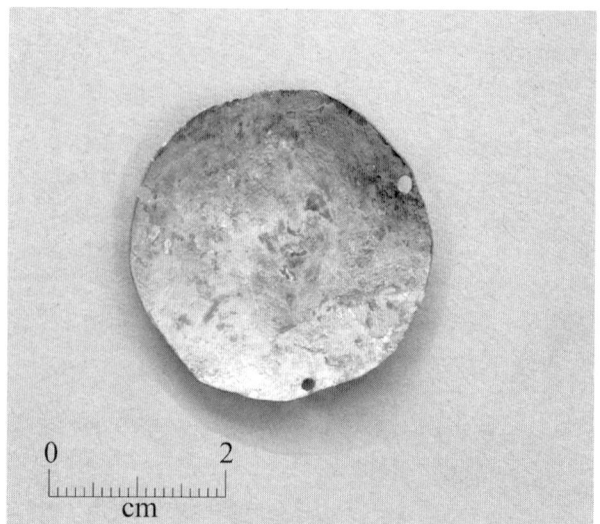

Plate XI Small find No. 232: copper alloy scale pan

armour and mantle with sceptre in right hand. Bust *C*. Rev. large cross potent with small potent in each angle; in centre a small cross in saltire. Weight: 0.61g; *c.* 1161–1165 AD (EMC No. 1999.0074).
1579(F357)/*4425*/Phase 9 gravel trackway, Enclosure 16.

252. Silver **coin**, Short Cross penny, Class VIa1. Issued post-1207, pre-1214.
786(F296)/*4423*/Phase 9 boundary ditch, Enclosure 1.

253. Silver **coin**, Edward I or II, *c.* 1306–7.
4077/*9081*/Unphased.

254. Silver **coin**, Edward III penny in two fragments, 1344–51, lack of wear probably suggests 14th-century loss.
Topsoil/*9111*/Unstratified.

255. Silver **coin**, Venetian solidino, 1400–13.
6439/*9091*/Unphased.

256. Henry VIII, posthumous coinage (1547–51), **groat**, Tower mint, bust 5. Fragment, corroded, cracked and buckled. Weight 0.78g.
Surface/*9077*d/Unstratified.

257. Lead alloy **token**, *c.* 20mm diameter, illegible, corroded and buckled. Weight 2.73g; medieval or early modern.
990/*4397*/Unphased.

258. Lead alloy **token**, *c.* 23mm diameter. Cross-hatched pattern of lines, uniface. Light corrosion. Weight 8.13g; medieval or early modern.
Surface/*4412*/Unstratified.

259. Lead alloy **token**, *c.* 21mm diameter. Obv. MT(?). Reverse: cross-hatched pattern of lines? Light corrosion. Weight 4.08g; medieval or early modern.
Topsoil/*4413*/Unstratified.

260. Lead alloy **token**, *c.* 18mm diameter, illegible, corroded. Weight 5.61g; medieval or early modern.
Topsoil/*4414*/Unstratified.

261. Lead alloy **token**, *c.* 33mm diameter. Pattern of lines/cross on circle. Light corrosion, chipped. Weight 11.31g; medieval or early modern.
Topsoil/*4415*a/Unstratified.

262. Lead alloy **token**, *c.* 24mm diameter, illegible, corroded. Weight 8.48g; medieval or early modern.
Topsoil/*4415*b/Unstratified.

263. Lead alloy **token**, ovoid, 15–18mm diameter, illegible, corroded. Weight 3.10g; medieval or early modern.
Topsoil/*4415*c/Unstratified.

264. Lead alloy 'Boy Bishop' **token**, Rigold series VII, Bury St Edmunds, late 15th to mid 16th century, *c.* 22mm diameter. Obv. Mitre, legend of strokes. Rev. Cross and pellets, single circle of inscription []NOBIS[], *cf.* Rigold (1978, pl. X.i). Corroded and buckled. Weight 4.04g.
8594(F2034)/*9067*/Phase 13 pit.

265. Lead alloy 'Boy Bishop' **token** ('groat'), Rigold series I, Bury St Edmunds, 1st half of 16th century, *c.* 26mm diameter. Obv. Facing mitred bust of St Nicholas, inscription around. Rev. Arms of Bury St Edmunds on cross, inscription around. Corroded, broken and buckled. Weight 5.50g.
Topsoil/*9077*a/Unstratified.

266. Lead alloy **token**, *c.* 27mm diameter. Obv. EA(?). Rev. Star pattern of eight lines. Corroded and chipped. Weight 8.35g; medieval or early modern.
Topsoil/*9077*b/Unstratified.

267. Lead alloy **token**, *c.* 20mm diameter. Illegible, corroded and buckled. Weight 5.24g; medieval or early modern(?).
Topsoil/*9077*c/Unstratified.

268. Copper alloy Nuremberg **jeton**, anonymous(?) Rose/Orb type, *c.* 1550s–1580s, 24mm diameter, corroded and bent. Weight 0.97g.
Topsoil/*4443*b/Unstratified.

269. Copper alloy Nuremberg **jeton**, anonymous Rose/Orb type, *c.* 1550s–1580s, 24mm diameter, corroded. Weight 1.34g.
Topsoil/*4444*c/Unstratified.

270. Copper alloy Nuremberg **jeton**, anonymous Rose/Orb type, *c.* 1550s–1580s, 21mm diameter, chipped. Weight 1.34g.
Surface/*4445*g/Unstratified.

271. Copper alloy Nuremberg **jeton**, anonymous(?) Rose/Orb type, 2nd half of 16th century, *c.* 20mm diameter, corroded and chipped. Weight 0.90g.
7000(F2519)/*9094*d/Phase 11 gravelled yard, Enclosure 18/21.

272. Copper alloy Tournai **jeton**, 15th century, 25mm diameter. Obv. Crown +AVE MARIA GRACIA.PL. Rev. Triple-stranded cross fleuretty in four-arched tressure. Large central piercing. Weight 2.08g.
Surface/*9112*d/Unstratified.

V. Diversions
(Plate XII; Fig. 4.16)

Bone skates and a sledge-runner
by Ian Riddler

The four skates are all made from horse bones and they show some variety in their physical characteristics. Two examples have been made from horse metatarsals, one from a metacarpus and the other from a radius. They conform with the customary selection of species and bone type for this class of object. Most skates were produced from horse or cattle bones, with metapodia the dominant bone type, although the radius was also utilised (MacGregor 1976, 58). A complete example (No. 276, Fig. 4.16) has a tapered and upswept distal end, which would have been used as the front of the skate, as well as an axial perforation through the proximal epiphysis. These are familiar features of bone skates, the proximal perforation being intended to retain a peg or nail that held leather heel straps in place. In contrast, the other complete example (No. 275, Fig. 4.16) has an upswept distal end that has not been tapered, and its proximal end has not been perforated. Whilst some skates used securing holes for straps, others are entirely devoid of any such fixtures (MacGregor 1975, 387). The two fragmentary skates (Nos 273 and 274) include an upswept distal end and a proximal radius from which the articular surface has been removed. All of these modifications represent slight changes to the natural form of the bone, and little else was required in the manufacture of skates (Ulbricht 1984, 39; Becker 1990, 20). MacGregor has argued that the posterior face of the bone, the side usually chosen to lie directly below the foot, could also be roughened to improve adhesion (MacGregor 1976, 59). No evidence for that process can be seen within this assemblage, however. With the three metapodial skates (No. 274, Fig. 4.16 Nos 275–6) the anterior face of the bone was in contact with the ice, and this is also the case also for the horse radius (No. 273). In most assemblages of a similar type which utilised horse bones, the anterior face lay on the ice (MacGregor 1985, 142). The two complete horse metapodial skates can be compared with those from elsewhere in England in terms of their lengths. In comparison with complete horse bone skates from Ipswich, London, York, one of the West Fen skates (No. 276) is fairly short, whilst the other example (No. 275) lies towards the other end of the scale.

Within England, no examples of bone skates have come as yet from Early Anglo-Saxon contexts but they are relatively common by the 8th century (MacGregor 1976, 65). Large collections have been recovered from Late Saxon and medieval contexts at London and York, in particular, with smaller assemblages from a range of other sites (Radley 1971, 55–7; MacGregor 1982, 97 and fig. 52; MacGregor 1995, 422 and fig. 159; Rogers 1993, 1406–8 and fig. 688; MacGregor *et al.* 1999, 1985–9; West 1983; Pritchard 1991, 208; Egan 1998, 294–5). Three of the West Fen Road examples come from contexts of Late Saxon date, whilst the fourth skate (No. 276) was retrieved from a 13th-century deposit. Skates occur in large quantities on a number of Continental sites, although throughout Europe there are settlements in temperate areas (including Bergen, Canterbury, Dublin and Southampton) where they have only been found in small numbers (Grieg 1933, 265; MacGregor 1976, 66; Becker 1990, 19).

In Anglo-Saxon England, a preference for cattle metapodial skates may be seen in the Mid Saxon period, with increased numbers of horse metapodia and radii used thereafter (Riddler *et al.* forthcoming). This circumstance is echoed also at Berlin-Spandau (Becker 1990, 272 and abb. 8). During the Late Saxon period, skates made from horse bones became more common.

Some of MacGregor's work was intended to counteract earlier scepticism concerning the use of these objects as skates (Semenov 1964, 191–3; Barthel 1969). Becker has recently re-opened the debate by focusing again on wear patterns (Becker 1990). MacGregor showed that wear patterns aligned predominantly along the main axis of the smoothed surface of the object are characteristic of bone skates (MacGregor 1975; 1985, 141–4; Becker 1990, 20). Equally, Barthel has suggested that wear patterns aligned mainly across the long axis signify that the object was used for another purpose, possibly as a net-spacer, smoothing bone or leather-working tool (Barthel 1969, 209–14; Becker 1990, 21–2). Becker has also argued that objects with these wear patterns were used as smoothers in leather-working (Becker 1990, 26).

In one case (Fig. 4.16 No. 275) the smooth surface does not survive well enough to enable wear patterns to be established. With a second object (Fig. 4.16 No. 276) there is little wear visible on the surface, which is just lightly smoothed, and little used. The surfaces of the two other examples (Fig. 4.16 Nos 273–4), however, are smooth and highly polished, and the wear patterns are visible along the length of the bone, with smaller groups set diagonally across the bone. Under the definitions provided above, therefore, both objects can be regarded as skates. Amidst the sequence of English skates, very few of those examined in any detail for wear patterns diverge from an alignment along the main axis of the bone.

A fragment of a horse radius (Fig. 4.16 No. 277) is similar to the bone skates described above, although there is no surviving worn flat surface. It differs, however, in the presence of a large circular perforation towards the proximal end, which passes through the anterior and posterior faces. This perforation allows the object to be identified as a sledge-runner of the most commonly known type, which utilises either the metapodia or radii of horse and cattle (MacGregor 1985, 144). The perforations allowed the bone to be secured either to a wooden frame or directly to a flat base board.

Few examples of sledge-runners have been identified from English archaeological contexts and their dating is largely dependent on Continental examples, which are more abundant (MacGregor 1985, 145). Their dating echoes that of bone skates closely. The earliest examples may go back to the Iron Age and they are well established by the Viking period (Stenberger 1961, 20 and abb. 51; Becker 1990, 20 and abb. 1–2). Medieval examples are known from a range of sites in the former Slavic territories and Scandinavia, as well as Holland (Rulewicz 1958; 1994, 215–6; Herrmann 1962, 43 and taf. 4e; Stenberg-Tyrefors and Johansson 1993; van Wijngaarden-Bakker 1981). Like bone skates, they continued in use until modern times (Hofland 1969; Lauwerier and van Heeringen 1998, 122). English examples have come from London, Lincolnshire, Huntingdonshire and Suffolk. Unfortunately, virtually all of them are 19th-century discoveries, devoid of detailed archaeological contexts. Two sledge-runners from Stonea, Cambridgeshire represent almost the only other examples to have come from stratified English contexts (Smithson in Jackson and Potter 1996, 668–70 and fig. 247). Both are made from horse radii, as is the case here, and they come from post-medieval contexts.

273. Bone **skate**. Fragment from proximal end of horse radius; epiphysis sliced away, leaving porous tissue surface, trimmed at one side. Anterior face of bone smoothed and highly polished; junction with ulna on anterior face cut away but bone otherwise unmodified. Wear patterns on smooth surface lie predominantly along main axis of bone, and also occur diagonally across it. L.156mm.
*273(F270)/2299/*Phase 6 boundary ditch fill, Enclosure 2.

274. Bone **skate**. Fragment of horse metatarsus, split along grain of the bone. Condyle at distal end trimmed diagonally on posterior face to provide upswept end; surviving portion of anterior face is smooth and polished, with abundant wear marks lying predominantly along main axis of the bone, and also seen diagonally across it. L. 155mm.
*1663(F304)/2710/*Phase 8 dividing ditch fill, Enclosure 1.

*275. Complete **skate**, produced from horse metatarsus; anterior face smoothed from wear, with distal end upswept but not tapered; centre of condyle trimmed on posterior face. Smoothed face not in good condition; no wear patterns can be recorded.
*3657(F501)/4198/*Phase 8 boundary ditch fill, Paddock P, Enclosure 13.

*276. Complete **skate**, produced from horse metacarpus, lightly trimmed (but not roughened) on posterior face, shaped to a tapering, upswept point at distal end. Proximal end perforated laterally; slight traces of wear on the anterior face, running along main axis of bone.
*6000(F1301)/6116/*Phase 10 ditch, Enclosure 12.

*277. Bone **sledge-runner**: fragmentary horse radius, proximal end tapered lightly on three sides. Object perforated laterally a little below proximal epiphysis.
*3553(F2410)/4106/*Phase 11 pit fill, Enclosure 16.

Horse equipment

The prick-spur (No. 278) is from a Phase 9 context, only slightly later than its suggested 10th–mid-11th century date. There is also a small iron pendant mount or harness/spur fitting (unphased, Fig. 4.16 No. 279) which is possibly 10th–12th century in date. Of greater interest are two circular mounts. One (Fig. 4.16 No. 280), from the surface of a Late Saxon context, appears medieval on the basis of its decoration, which is paralleled by a copper alloy belt fitting from Redcastle Furze, Thetford, dated to the 16th century (Andrews 1995, fig. 66, no. 8). While the other, Fig. 4.16 No. 281, was a surface find, it is a composite copper alloy gilded armorial mount closely paralleled by a group of three similar mounts from London (Egan and Pritchard 1991, no. 933) dated to the 15th century. These London examples were found in a foreshore deposit, possibly all wrapped in one cloth, which might indicate that they were abandoned covertly (*ibid.*, 184). Whatever the circumstances of their loss, they were certainly high-status items; another example was found at Rievaulx Abbey bearing the arms of Abbot John III (in office in 1449), with the suggestion that it might have adorned his travelling case (*ibid.*, 181). The present example has been interpreted as a harness mount, as it is assumed to have been a chance loss. Conservation revealed the coat of arms to be three crowns — the heraldic design of the diocese of Ely, representing the unity of the Holy Trinity. The mount interior was gilded on its raised areas (including the three crowns), with a copper-based paint applied to the recessed areas to give a red colour (B. Flackett, *pers. comm.*).

Other evidence for horse equipment comprises a medieval harness pendant (again, a surface find, No. 282), a swivel for such a pendant (No. 283) and several complete and fragmentary horseshoes, as well as horseshoe nails. One of the horseshoe fragments, No. 286, came from a Roman context (an escutcheon, No. 284, may also be Roman), while the others were all post-Conquest finds.

275

276

279

277

280

281

285

296

297

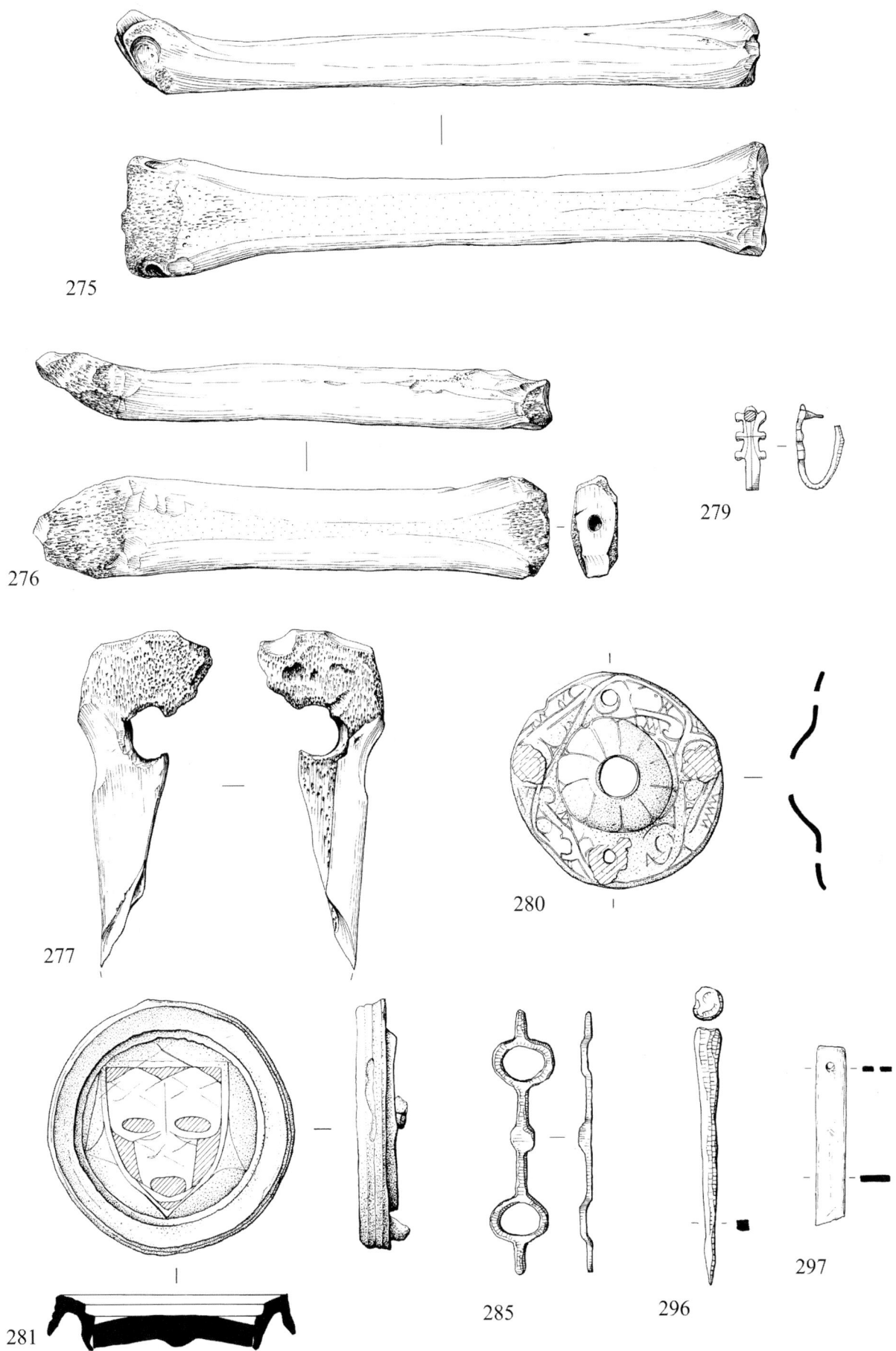

Figure 4.16 Small finds relating to diversions. All at 1:2 except Nos 280–1 at 1:1

Plate XII Small find No. 281: composite copper alloy gilded armorial mount

These are of a range of different dates, and both narrower and broader web types are represented (*cf.* Goodall in Margeson 1993, 225). The looped fitting (Fig. 4.16 No. 285) seems to be a side-link of a bridle-bit. Finally, the large copper alloy rumbler bell (No. 293) would probably have been attached to a domestic animal, and presumably represents an accidental loss.

278. Iron **prick spur** with short, possibly rounded goad; arms too distorted to discern shape; no decoration except plating; large rectangular buckle terminals (28mm x 16mm). L. arm and terminal *c.* 140mm; 10th–mid-11th century (Ottaway 1992 suggests type has east of England distribution).
   6469/9175/Phase 7 post-hole, Enclosure 5.

*279. Iron **pendant mount** or harness/spur fitting; U-shaped in section with rivet to attach the two ends; decorated with three projecting knobs along each side; slightly waisted; plated and incised decorative lines; 10th–12th century?
   Surface/*4453*/Unstratified.

*280. Cast domed copper alloy **mount** with four perforations for rivets (two *in situ*); 7mm hole in the centre; faint incised decoration resembling ten petals on raised boss surrounding central hole; outer band decorated with incised scroll ornament; 16th century?
   8745/9101/Phase 7.

*281. Composite copper alloy gilded **armorial mount**; thick disc set into turned frame; two square rivets, three missing; face decorated with armorial motif; 15th century (*cf.* Egan and Pritchard 1991, No. 933).
   Surface/*4449b*/Unstratified.

282. Incomplete copper alloy **harness pendant** of uncertain shape; gilded front face only; ring and dot decoration; possibly with a central perforation; cast in one piece with suspension loop. L. 27mm, W. 26mm, T. 6mm; medieval.
   Surface/*4426*/Unstratified.

283. Cast copper alloy **swivel** for pendant; probably for a harness mount. L. 20mm, W. 7mm, T. 10mm; medieval.
   Surface/*9114c*/Unstratified.

284. Copper alloy **escutcheon**; hollow cast drop pendant or handle with loop at the top; damaged or miscast. L. 20mm, W. 7mm, T. 9mm; Roman? (*cf.* Holbrook and Bidwell 1991, nos 163 and 164)
   Surface/*9114d*/Unstratified.

*285. Iron **bridle side-link** bar with central boss between two end loops; with decorated end projections; plated; 10th–11th century (*cf.* Margeson in Rogerson 1995, no. 109)
   1257/4509/Phase 7.

286. Iron **horseshoe** fragment with fairly broad web; slightly wavy profile; rectangular nail holes (three survive) with narrow countersunk slots; 13th–14th century (Clark 1995, Type 3).
   2791(F2444)/*4543*/Phase 3 ditch (surface find), Enclosure 8.

287. Very thin iron **horseshoe fragment** with angular profile; rectangular nail holes probably with countersunk area for nail heads; holes probably 3/3 arrangement; no nails; heels missing; 12th–early 13th century (Clark 1995, Type 2).
   7000(F2519)/*9209*/Phase 11 gravelled yard, Enclosure 18/21.

288. Iron **horseshoe** with broad web (W. 35mm); rectangular nail holes; 3/3 arrangement; one nail with square head; no evidence for clenching; very pointed feathered heel; post 1350 (Clark 1995, Type 4).
   6171(F2519)/*9168a*/Phase 11 gravelled yard, Enclosure 18/21.

289. Iron **horseshoe** with broad web; rectangular nail holes (four surviving) all containing nails that stand proud; square heads; modern style clenching; calkin at right angle; post-1350 (Clark 1995, Type 4).
   6171(F2519)/*9168b*/Phase 11 gravelled yard, Enclosure 18/21.

290. Iron **horseshoe** with broad web (W. 45mm); rectangular nail holes with 4/4 arrangement; three nails all standing proud with square heads, parts of four others; modern style clenching; calkin at right angles; post-1350 (Clark 1995, Type 4).
   6171(F2519)/*9168c*/Phase 11 gravelled yard, Enclosure 18/21.

291. Iron **horseshoe nail** of fiddle key type; late 11th–early 13th century.
   654(F2304)/*4482*/Phase 9 ditch.

292. Iron **horseshoe nail** of fiddle-key type; late 11th–13th century.
   1554(F306)/*4510*/Phase 10 sealing dump, Structure 20, Enclosure 1.

293. Large copper alloy **rumbler bell**; cast; incomplete. Ht. 40mm, D. 32mm; late medieval–post-medieval.
   Surface/*4428*/Unstratified.

Weapons and armour

The copper alloy scabbard chape was found on the surface of a Late Saxon context, but its decoration appears to place it in the 14th or 15th century (*cf.* Margeson 1993 no. 1856). Both the iron arrowheads appear to be of Late Saxon or later date by form, with Fig. 4.16 No. 296 appearing to fall into Jessop's 'M' class, designed to pierce armour (Jessop 1996); their archaeological context supports this.

294. Copper alloy **scabbard chape** made from sheet; trefoil/quatrefoil cut from the front; 14th–15th century.
   4445(F2578)/*9085*/Phase 7 ditch (but surface find), Enclosure 12.

295. Socketed iron **arrowhead**, but most of socket and arrow tip missing; leaf-shaped blade with probably quite a long socket; 11th–14th century?; L. 62mm, W. 15mm.
   5707(F1165)/*9154*/Phase 8 boundary ditch fill, Enclosure 3.

*296. Iron **arrowhead** with socketed point with ?closed socket; rectangular section. Possibly a long Type M6 (Jessop 1996), broadly dated to the 11th–14th century.
   350(F259)/*4468*/Phase 9 boundary ditch fill, Enclosure 2.

Bone mount
by Ian Riddler

A rectangular bone mount (Fig. 4.16 No. 297) came from a Late Saxon context. It is undecorated and includes a single, oval perforation at one end. Some bone undecorated mounts of Iron Age date are also distinguished by the presence of single perforations, but these are less substantial items, whose precise function remains unclear (Fell 1953, fig. 2.4). This mount has no saw-marks cut into its edges and it is relatively substantial, with polish on both sides. It is related to a small group of objects of Mid and Late Saxon date which have come from *Hamwic*, Maidenhead, North Elmham and York (Holdsworth 1980, fig. 15.1.6; Rogers 1993, fig. 686.5609; Wade-Martins 1980, fig. 259.6; Waterman 1959, pl. XX.2–3). A possible example has come from London (Cowie *et al.* 1988, fig. 38.12). They have been plausibly identified as wrist guards for archers.

*297. Fragmentary bone **mount** of rectangular section, perforated by single, oval hole at one end. Undecorated and highly polished from use.
   2807(F351)/*3534*/Phase 6 ditch fill, Enclosure 1.

5. Zoological and Environmental Evidence

I. Human bone
by Natasha Dodwell

Five inhumations were recovered from the site, along with a small quantity of disarticulated bone.

Most of the bone is in moderate to poor condition; very few of the epiphyseal ends of the long bones survive, the skulls and pelves are particularly fragmentary and there is evidence of insect/root damage on much of the cortical material. In the main, the disarticulated material recovered from the ditches is in better condition than the bones from the burials, which have been truncated by later features and damaged by ploughing.

The methods used in the osteological evaluation of all the skeletal material are those of Bass (1992), Buikstra and Ubelaker (1994) and Steel and Bramblett (1988). Due to the poor survival of the skulls, pelves and epiphyseal ends of long bones, an assessment of age was based on the stage of dental eruption, the degree of dental attrition (Brothwell 1981) and where possible the closure of cranial sutures (Meindl and Lovejoy 1985). These methods all have their limitations, and therefore the following broad age categories are used:

subadult	12–18 years
young adult	19–25 years
middle adult	26–44 years
mature adult	45 years +

The sex of each individual was ascertained, where possible, from dimorphic traits of the skull, metrical data and the general robusticity of the skeletons.

The small size and the generally poor condition of the bones preclude detailed comments on the assemblage, although the following points should be highlighted. With the exception of the inhumation interred with a pottery vessel and hobnail boots (F1509), the other burials and indeed the disarticulated material have been dated only tentatively by their proximity to, and relationships with, other features. (Note that disarticulated remains directly associated with Iron Age Enclosure 1 have already been discussed in Chapter 2 above, p.16–17, and are not included below.)

Possible Iron Age burials

Inhumation F1450 (6544) — Mature adult ?male
Moderately preserved but fragmentary skeleton lying approximately 5m to the east of burial F1474. The head was at the west end of the grave, the body was crouched and lay on its left side, the left arm was flexed so that the hand touched the shoulder, the right elbow was flexed at *c.* 90°. The individual had lost at least six teeth prior to death and all the surviving teeth were extremely worn. Increased porosity and small patches of eburnation, characteristic of osteoarthritis, were recorded on the articulating facets of the surviving lumbar vertebrae.

Inhumation F1474 (6643) — Adult ?male
Extremely poorly preserved and fragmentary skeleton: only scraps of the left arm and hand, skull, mandible, pelvis and vertebrae survived. The surviving bone was very disturbed and was found on the machined surface. The cranial fragments lay at the west of the scatter and the pelvis fragments at the east, probably indicating the orientation of the body. The individual had lost at least two teeth during life: the sockets for the 1st right mandibular molar and 2nd premolar had healed completely over

indicating that the teeth were not lost close to death. (The disarticulated bone *7104* — see below — may derive from this burial.)

Roman and possible Roman burials

Inhumation F1509 (6806) — Mature adult ?male
Moderately preserved, although fragmentary skeleton. The body was supine and extended with the left arm flexed at the elbow so that the hand rested on the right hip. The head apparently lay in the north-western end of the grave although no cut was visible. The torso was only represented by the cervical vertebrae, which exhibited changes characteristic of osteoarthritis: increased porosity and osteophytes on the bodies and articulating facets. The surviving teeth were extremely worn — many survived only as roots — and three large carious lesions were recorded. The skull faced west towards a small pot, which had been placed between it and the shoulder. Hobnails were recovered from around the feet, and large nails around the body suggested the presence of a coffin.

F1687 (7277) — Young/middle adult ?female
Poorly preserved, fragmentary and disturbed skeleton, its skull and legs had been truncated by two east–west ditches. The grave lay to the north of the Roman trackway, the head would have been in the north of the grave and the individual may have originally been buried on her left side, aligned approximately north–south and to the north of the Roman track/droveway. No cut was visible and no pathology was noted.

F1649 (7399) — Middle/mature adult ?male
Poorly preserved, fragmentary and very disturbed skeleton to the north of the Roman trackway. Some articulation was noted in the field (*e.g.* of the tibia and talus) and the surviving bones were very roughly in the correct anatomical position. No cut was visible and the burial must have been disturbed in the past, perhaps by earlier ploughing. Changes characteristic of osteoarthritis in the neck were recorded; an increase in porosity and polishing of the bone or eburnation were observed on the upper cervical vertebrae. The individual had lost at least two teeth prior to death and two large caries were recorded on the surviving, severely worn, dentition.

Disarticulated material

F1056 (4704)
A fragment of the posterior portions of the fused left and right parietals was recovered from a Roman ditch. The skull fragment derives from a middle/mature adult and the increased porosity on its outer surface is indicative of porotic hyperostosis, a condition associated with anaemia. The post-mortem breaks occurred in antiquity.

F1435 (6540)
The distal half of an adult phalange from a Late Saxon ditch; the ditch cut skeleton *6544* and so the bone may well derive from the crouched burial F1450.

F1583 (7104)
A right humerus shaft with pronounced muscle attachments, a right navicular and the distal end of a metatarsal/carpal were recovered whilst machining between burials *6544* and *6643*. The bones are adult-sized and they could derive from the ?Iron Age disturbed burial *6643*/F1474.

F1636 (7366)]
Two fragments of adult skull bone were recovered from a medieval ditch to the north of the Roman track/droveway. They do not refit and the post-mortem breaks had occurred in antiquity.

II. Large vertebrates
by Lorrain Higbee

Introduction
The total quantity of animal bone recovered from the site is 17,590 fragments or 231,887 grams (Table 5.1). For the

Phase/Date	Fragment count	% Fragment count	Weight in grams	% Weight in grams
Phase 2 Iron Age	550	3.12	6,795	2.93
Phase 3 Romano-British	2,967	16.86	35,697	15.39
Phase 5 Mid Saxon	435	2.47	5,009	2.15
Phase 7 Late Saxon	6,516	37.04	87,224	37.61
Phase 9 12th Century	4,178	23.75	54,366	23.44
Phase 10/11 Late 12th/14th Century	2,102	11.94	27,251	11.75
Phase 12/13 14th/16th Century	491	2.79	9,533	4.11
Phase 14 Unphased	341	1.93	6,012	2.59
Total	17,590	100.00	231,887	100.00

Table 5.1 Quality and provenance of faunal remains

purpose of this report, Phases 6 and 8 (*i.e.* Phase 7), Phases 10 (late 12th–13th century) and 11 (13th–14th century), and Phases 12 (14th–15th century) and 13 (16th century) have been combined, due to the smallness of the assemblage size. Bone recovered from unphased contexts has been quantified in some tables but will not be considered in the discussion.

The following published methods were used throughout the analysis: Dobney and Reilly 1988; Cohen and Serjeantson 1996; Silver 1969; Grant 1982; Payne 1973, 1985 and 1987; O'Connor 1989; Armitage and Clutton-Brock 1976; Boessneck 1969; Davis 1992a; Von den Driesch 1976; Von den Driesch and Boessneck, 1974; and Harcourt 1974. A full set of supporting tables are available in the archive; only those most relevant to the discussion are reproduced here.

Results

Condition and recovery
The assemblage is reasonably well preserved, and very few fragments were recorded with edge abrasion or surface exfoliation caused by rolling and trampling on the ground surface or sub-aerial weathering. Canid gnaw-marks were recorded on *c.* 15% of the total number of fragments, most typically at the ends of long bones (Table 5.2). The highest frequencies of gnaw marks were recorded on bones from Phase 10/11. In addition to gnaw-marks a small number of bone fragments were recorded as acid-etched as a result of having passed through the gut of a dog. The low frequency of canid gnaw-marks recorded for some phases may not necessarily reflect the true extent of destruction since canid gnawing can completely destroy and obliterate bones, particularly those from immature animals.

The vast majority of the assemblage was recovered by hand from excavated deposits and a relatively small quantity of material was retrieved from sample residues (*Plants and seeds*, p.102). Hand recovery is typically biased against the recovery of small bones and the bones of small species. This is reflected in the relative low frequency of these types of anatomical elements recorded from all phases.

Identification and species found
Approximately 21% of the total assemblage by fragment count could be identified to species; a further 19% could be assigned to a general size-category (*i.e.* 'cattle-sized'). Like most hand-recovered archaeological animal bone assemblages from England, approximately half of the specimens belong to cattle, sheep/goat and pig. Their frequencies and size variations are discussed below. Other mammalian species identified from the hand-recovered assemblage include horse, dog, cat, red and roe deer, hare and rabbit. Avian species identified include chicken, goose (both domestic and brent), mallard, teal, crow and woodcock.

Most, but not all, caprine (sheep and goat) bones are difficult to identify to species and are referred to as sheep/goat. Using the criteria of Boessneck (1969) and Payne (1985) it was possible to identify a selective suite of elements as diagnostic of either sheep or goat. Of the the caprine bones which could be identified to species, the majority were sheep. A small number of leporid bones were recovered from the site. In Britain hare is easily distinguished from rabbit by size. However, it was not possible to distinguish between brown hare, *Lepus europaeus*, and blue hare, *L. timidus*. Most *Lepus* bones are therefore merely recorded as hare. The most common bird species from the site is the Gallus/Numida/Phasianus group of closely-related galliformes. Most of the bones of these three species are difficult to distinguish (see MacDonald 1992); no guinea fowl or pheasant bones were positively identified, however, and it is therefore assumed that most fowl-like bones belong to chicken.

Butchery/cut marks
Approximately 10% of the total number of bone fragments had cut and/or chop marks on them (Table 5.2). Detailed description of the type, location and direction of butchery marks lies outside the scope of this report but this information was recorded consistently throughout the assemblage and is available in the archive. Chop and/or cut marks were recorded on 34% of cattle bones, 21% of sheep bones and 16% of pig bones. A small number of charred and/or calcined bone fragments were also recorded. All of this amounts to reasonable evidence that these animals were prepared for consumption. Butchery marks were also noted on the bones of other species, including 10% of horse bones, 6% of bird bones and a few red deer, rabbit and dog bones. Most butchery marks recorded on horse bones are consistent with dismemberment, and one metapodial from F1974 (Phase 9, Enclosure 11) was recorded with numerous fine cut marks along the length of the shaft. This evidence is consistent with skinning and may therefore represent waste from a fellmonger. The low frequency of butchery marks recorded on bird bones probably reflects the fact that the carcasses of birds require little dismemberment to provide manageable portions. One dog skull from F14 (Enclosure 4, Phase 3) was recorded with a ?sword cut across the occipital and a dog sacrum from F2519 (Enclosure 18, Phase 12) had been split along the medial axis (*i.e.* dorso-ventral).

In addition to chop and knife cuts, saw marks were recorded on a few bone fragments. These include a cattle axis vertebra from Phase 5, a cattle femur and sheep horn core from Phase 7, and a red deer radius and sheep horn core from Phase 9.

Frequency of species and parts of the skeleton represented

The hand-recovered assemblage is characterised by mammalian species, in particular domestic species, although some wild animals have also been identified. Avian species are also present but only account for a small fraction of identified fragments. The proportion of bird bones varies from one phase to another accounting for 0.64% to 3.31%.

The relative proportion of cattle, sheep/goat and pig bones for each phase have been calculated using the *number of identified specimens per species* (or NISP) and the *minimum number of individuals* (or MNI) (Tab. 5.3). Cattle and sheep/goat are the most common species in all phases and the pattern of relative frequency is complex. Cattle and sheep/goat are represented in almost equal proportions throughout the Iron Age and Mid Saxon periods (Phases 2 and 5). From the Late Saxon period to the late 12th to 14th centuries (Phases 7 to 10/11) cattle bones are more numerous than sheep/goat. This pattern is reversed in the final phase of occupation at the site (Phase 12/13) when sheep/goat bones are slightly more abundant than cattle. The proportion of pig is low in all phases but steadily increases in frequency over time from *c.* 8% in the Iron Age (Phase 2) to 21% in the 14th–16th centuries (Phase 12/13).

When MNI is considered, the pattern of relative frequency reveals a slightly different pattern (Fig. 5.1). Sheep/goat are the most common species in all phases with the exception of Phase 12/13, where the pattern is reversed. Sheep/goat account for 50% of the MNI in both the Iron Age (Phase 2) and Roman (Phase 3) periods but decline to *c.* 40% in the Mid Saxon period (Phase 5). The proportion of cattle increases slightly from 30% in the Roman period to 33% in Phase 5. However, the proportion of pig increases dramatically over these periods, from 12.5% in the Iron Age to 26.6% in the Mid Saxon period. Following this there is a rapid decline in the frequency of pigs culled at West Fen Road coupled with a steady increase in the frequency of the other two stock species through the 12th century to the late 12th–14th centuries. By the 14th–16th centuries the proportion of both cattle and pigs culled had increased, relative to a steep decline in sheep/goat.

MNI, by selected anatomical element for the three main domestic species, can be used to assess the survival and/or recovery of different anatomical elements by comparing the frequency of each element to the most common one. The MNI of cattle represented from all phases is 69 and the most common anatomical element is the radius. Anatomical elements with a high survival/recovery rate in all phases include major meat-bearing bones from the fore and hind limb, in particular the humerus. Teeth and small bones from the ankle and foot region are under-represented but this probably reflects recovery bias rather than survival. This general pattern is repeated for most of the larger bone collections (*i.e.* Phases 3, 7, 9 and 10/11).

The partial skeleton of a *c.* two-year old cow was recovered from gully F563 (Enclosure 1), assigned to the Late Saxon phase. Parts of the skeleton represented include the upper fore limbs, the hind limbs and the vertebral column from the lower thoracic to the caudal vertebrae. In addition a few articulating fore limbs were noted in the Phase 7 and 9 assemblages from F1962 (Enclosure 18), F2044 (Enclosure 11) and F1459 (Enclosure 4).

At least 100 sheep/goat are represented in the entire assemblage and the most common anatomical element in almost all phases is the tibia. Radii are also fairly common but other elements from the fore and hind limb are significantly under-represented. Tibiae and radii are relatively easy to identify in a fragmented state and this, together with survival/recovery biases, may account for the apparent under-representation of other meat-bearing elements. Teeth are relatively well represented, particularly in comparison to the recovery of cattle teeth which are significantly larger and therefore more likely to be collected by hand. However, the majority of sheep/goat teeth recorded were retained within mandibles as complete or partial tooth rows, unlike the majority of cattle teeth which were recovered as isolated elements.

At least 26 pigs are represented in the entire assemblage and the scapula is the most common anatomical element overall. Other meat-bearing bones that are common throughout the assemblage include the tibia, humerus and ulna. Teeth are also well represented overall, and again this is a reflection of the number of teeth retained in mandibles. Several complete or partial skeletons were also recovered. They include the complete skeleton of a four- to six-month old pig from Mid Saxon ditch F1249 (Enclosure 12); a *c.* two- to seven-week old pig from 12th-century ditch F594 (Enclosure 17) and the partial skeleton of a twelve- to sixteen-month old pig from 16th-century pit F42 (Enclosure 21). In addition, two articulating hind limbs were recovered from features F2245 (Enclosure 11, Phase 9) and F2042 (Enclosure 4, Phase 7).

With regard to the NISP by anatomical element for the less common mammalian species, goat bones have been positively identified from all phases, with horn cores by far the most common anatomical element. However, horn cores are also the easiest element of goat upon which to base definite species identification. Horse bones have also been

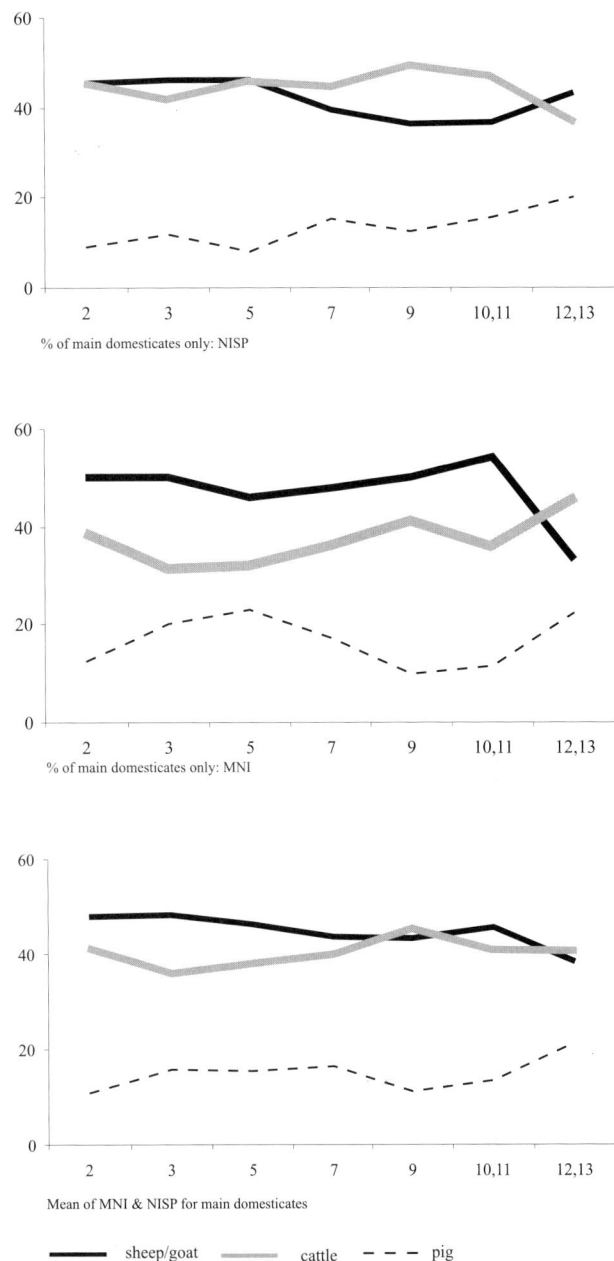

% of main domesticates only: NISP

% of main domesticates only: MNI

Mean of MNI & NISP for main domesticates

sheep/goat —— cattle —— pig - - -

Figure 5.1 Proportions of main domesticates by NISP and MNI

identified from all phases and range in frequency from less than 1% NISP to a maximum of *c.* 6% NISP in the 12th century. Loose teeth are the most common anatomical element of horse identified, and only 9% of these are deciduous teeth shed in life. The first phalanx is also fairly common, but in phases with significant numbers of horse bones there is generally a good representation of anatomical elements from different areas of the skeleton.

Dog bones have been identified from all phases except Phase 2 but only the larger stratified collections (*i.e.* Phases 7 and 9) yielded significant numbers. Complete/partial skeletons were recovered from two Phase 7 ditches F2412 (Enclosure 13) and F1473 (Enclosure 4), and from a gully F324 (Enclosure 1) and pit F1281 (Enclosure 12) assigned to Phase 9. In addition to these individual skeletons a further seven dogs are represented in the Phase 7 assemblage and a further three in the Phase 9 assemblage.

Cat bones were identified from all phases except Phase 2, although there does appear to be a strong recovery bias against small bones from limb extremities even where complete or partial skeletons were recovered. Complete or partial skeletons were recovered from several ditches. These include an adult cat and kitten from F1827 (Enclosure 7,

Phase	% canid gnaw marks	% butchery marks
Phase 2 Iron Age	12.9	13.6
Phase 3 Roman	17.5	12.1
Phase 5 Mid Saxon	10	15.4
Phase 7 Late Saxon	19.2	12.2
Phase 9 12th century	18.2	13.9
Phase 10/11 Late 12th/14th century	21.6	13.8
Phase 12/13 14th/16th century	10.9	14.6

Table 5.2 Frequency of gnaw and butchery marks on animal bones

Phase 7), a partial skeleton from F1825 (Enclosure 7, Phase 9) and a kitten from F1716 (Enclosure 18, Phase 10/11).

An insignificant quantity of deer bones have been identified from the assemblage and both red deer (*Cervus elaphus*) and roe deer (*Capreolus capreolus*) are represented. Red deer bones have been identified in the Phase 3, 7 and 9 assemblages and radii are the most common element indicating a preference for fore shank cuts of venison. Two roe deer bones were identified, one each from the Phase 3 and 10/11 assemblages. Fragmented deer bones can be difficult to distinguish from more common species of a similar size. Therefore, some red deer bones may have been incorporated into the 'cattle-sized' category and some roe deer into the 'sheep-sized' category. Rabbit and hare bones are also present in small numbers: rabbit has been identified from Phases 3 and 7 and hare from Phases 9 and 14.

Chicken (*Gallus*) and goose (*Anser*) are the most common avian species overall and have been identified from most phases. Of note is the partial skeleton of an immature goose from ditch F1380 (Enclosure 4, Phase 5). Duck (*Anas*), most probably mallard, has been identified from Phases 3, 5, 9 and 10/11; only bones from the wing are represented. Teal (*Anas crecca*) and crow (*Corvus corone*) have been identified from the Phase 5 and Phase 3 assemblages respectively, and woodcock (*Scolopax rusticola*) from the Phase 7 assemblage.

Overall the types of anatomical elements that are common in the assemblage are those which show a good survival and recovery rate on other sites, and which are easier to identify in a fragmented state.

Age at slaughter for common domestic species
The data for some phases is inadequate for the purposes of interpretation so only the main phases — i.e. Phases 3, 7, 9 and 10/11 — will be discussed unless otherwise stated. Further, the number of cattle and pig mandibles which could be assigned to one of O'Connor's (1989) categories were too few to allow interpretation, so both teeth in mandibles and isolated teeth are considered together for these species.

The epiphyseal fusion data for cattle (Table 5.4) shows that in all of the main phases the majority of cattle were culled at approximately three to four years of age. Almost all early-fusing anatomical elements are fused and the proportion of fused intermediate elements shows a slight degree of fluctuation over time. In the earliest phases the proportion of cattle culled aged *c.* two to two-and-a-half years (*i.e.* the intermediate category) is high but in the Late Saxon period and the 12th century (Phases 7 and 9) a small proportion were culled before these elements had fused. This kill-off pattern is repeated in the results obtained for tooth eruption and wear, which indicate that a large proportion of cattle were culled as beeves (cattle under three years) or early in their fourth year. In modern beef production cattle are culled at approximately 36 months of age.

The epiphyseal fusion data for sheep/goat shows that a wide range of ages were selected for slaughter (Table 5.5). The Roman (Phase 3) fusion data shows a fairly even distribution of ages which suggests that the flock was well managed, probably as part of a mixed economy. In later phases the proportion of sheep/goat culled between the ages of one to two years (*i.e.* the intermediate categories) increases significantly. Sheep/goat over three years are also represented, although the proportion is relatively low in all of the main phases. This general pattern is reflected in the data for tooth eruption and wear, which suggests that both lambs and prime mutton animals were slaughtered for local consumption. The general age pattern suggests that sheep/goat were exploited for their milk and wool as well as their meat.

Most of the pigs in all phases were slaughtered fairly young, which is the usual situation in most animal bone assemblages and is not surprising for an animal usually only reared for its meat and fat (Table 5.6).

Aberrant and pathological conditions
A small number of aberrant or pathological conditions were noted during the analysis, the majority on horse and dog bones. The low frequency of skeletal abnormalities recorded on the bones of domestic stock species is probably due to the relatively young age at which these animals were culled. Many pathological conditions leave little or no sign on bones, or only affect the skeleton in the advanced stages.

One cattle mandible from the F1725 (Enclosure 7/15, Phase 7) was recorded with misalignment of the premolar teeth. The p3 and p4 of this individual were skewed towards the buccal (outer) aspect of the mandible. A large lesion or abcess around the alveolus of these two teeth is the likely cause of the misalignment.

The ?sword trauma recorded on the dog skull from the Roman assemblage (Phase 3) and the butchery marks recorded on the sacrum from the 14th–16th century assemblage (Phase 12/13) have been described above. The possible sword cut may simply be explained as the method used to dispatch an old, ill or injured animal. The marks recorded on the 14th–16th century sacrum, however, are more difficult to interpret. The butchery evidence recorded on this specimen suggests that the carcass was processed for meat, as no cut marks suggestive of skinning were recorded on any of the dog bones from this or any of the other phases. The consumption of dog flesh by humans in western European historical contexts is usually related to extreme hardship generated by famine and warfare (Smith 1998; Simoons 1994; Murphy 2001). An alternative explanation might be the processing of dog carcasses for their fat, which may have found a use as a basic ingredient in cosmetic and medicinal salves and ointments (Gidney 1996).

In addition to the butchery evidence noted on the dog bones described above, signs of degenerative arthritis were noted on the lower lumbar vertebrae of an adult dog skeleton from 12th-century pit F1281 (Enclosure 12). The vertebral centra of this individual were recorded with peripheral osteophytosis caused by stress to the spinal column.

Joint disease was recorded on two horse bones, a distal radius and acetabulum, from Late Saxon Phase 7. Eburnation occurs when the cartilage is destroyed and the individual continues to use the joint. The underlying bone then becomes very hard (known as sclerosis) and polished. The underlying cause of this condition in horses is likely to be their use for traction. One incidence of dental pathology was also noted on horse teeth from the 12th-century assemblage, pitting being noted on the buccal and lingual surfaces of several teeth from one individual. It has been suggested that this aberration occurs as a result of changes in the pH of the saliva which might be linked to periodic variations in the diet, possibly relating to the provision of either high or low quality hard feed (Jaques and Dobney 1996).

Morphometry
Raw mensural data for all identified species is available in the archive. Descriptive statistics have only been calculated for measurements with a sample size of five of more. Interpretation of changes in the size/shape conformation of stock species over time is hindered by the low frequency of measurements from some phases. Scatter plots of related measurements (*e.g.* astragalus distal breadth against lateral depth) for phases with relatively large quantities of mensural data (*i.e.* Phases 7 and 9) failed to reveal any significant patterns that could otherwise be explained by sexual dimorphism. General observations and comparisons with other contemporary data-sets have, however, revealed the following.

Cattle
Measurements of metatarsal greatest length and distal breadth, astragalus greatest lateral length and humerus distal medio-lateral width show a large degree of sample variance. In most instances this variance is attributable to one phase (*i.e.* Phase 7) but the variance noted for

Number

Phase	2	3	5	7	9	10, 11	12, 13	14	Total
Cattle	40	180	76	574	343	228	47	57	1,545
Cattle sized	18	103	58	291	181	166	21	25	863
Sheep/Goat	39	192	73	473	235	170	50	22	1,254
Sheep	-	4	1	18	4	4	3	-	34
Goat	1	2	2	11	7	2	3	-	28
Sheep/Goat sized	20	120	58	332	145	107	33	13	828
Pig	8	50	13	193	85	75	26	14	464
Horse	8	29	9	87	66	45	18	4	266
Dog	-	10	1	108	14	5	7	4	149
Cat	-	5	1	9	5	3	2	-	25
Red deer	-	1	-	4	1	-	-	1	7
Roe Deer	-	1	-	-	-	1	-	-	2
Rabbit	-	-	-	1	-	-	-	3	4
Hare	-	-	-	-	1	-	-	2	3
Chicken	1	4	3	20	10	12	-	2	52
Brent goose	-	1	-	-	-	-	-	-	1
Goose	-	8	2	6	6	4	7	-	33
Mallard	-	1	1	-	1	1	-	-	4
Teal	-	-	1	-	-	-	-	-	1
Crow	-	1	-	-	-	-	-	-	1
Woodcock	-	-	-	1	-	-	-	-	1
Bird indet	1	1	-	2	1	-	-	-	7
Total	**136**	**713**	**300**	**2,130**	**1,105**	**824**	**217**	**147**	**5,572**

Percentage

Phase	2	3	5	7	9	10, 11	12, 13	14	Total
Cattle	29.4	25.2	25.34	26.9	31.1	27.7	21.6	38.8	27.7
Cattle sized	13.2	14.4	19.33	13.7	16.4	20.1	9.7	17	15.5
Sheep/Goat	29.4	27.8	25.34	23.6	22.3	21.4	25.81	15	23.62
Sheep									
Goat									
Sheep/Goat sized	14.7	16.8	19.33	15.6	13.1	13	15.21	8.8	14.89
Pig	5.9	7	4.4	9	7.7	9.1	12	9.5	8.33
Horse	5.9	4.1	3	4.1	6	5.46	8.3	2.72	4.77
Dog	-	1.4	0.33	5.1	1.25	0.61	3.23	2.72	2.67
Cat	-	0.7	0.33	0.4	0.45	0.36	0.92	-	0.45
Red deer	-	0.14	-	0.2	0.09	-	-	0.68	0.13
Roe Deer	-	0.14	-	-	-	0.12	-	-	0.03
Rabbit	-	-	-	0.04	-	-	-	2.04	0.07
Hare	-	-	-	-	0.09	-	-	1.36	0.05
Chicken	0.75	0.56	1	0.94	0.91	1.45	-	1.36	0.93
Brent goose	-	0.14	-	-	-	-	-	-	0.02
Goose	-	1.12	0.66	0.28	0.5	0.48	3.23	-	0.59
Mallard	-	0.14	0.33	-	0.09	0.12	-	-	0.07
Teal	-	-	0.33	-	-	-	-	-	0.02
Crow	-	0.14	-	0.04	-	-	-	-	0.02
Woodcock	-	-	-	-	-	-	-	-	0.02
Bird indet	0.75	0.14	0.33	0.09	0.09	0.12	-	-	0.13
Total	**100**	**100**	**100**	**100**	**100**	**100**	**100**	**100**	**100**

Table 5.3 Number of identified specimens per species

Table 5.4 Cattle: fused versus unfused epiphyses

Phase	2 Fused N	2 Fused %	2 Unfused N	2 Unfused %	3 Fused N	3 Fused %	3 Unfused N	3 Unfused %	5 Fused N	5 Fused %	5 Unfused N	5 Unfused %	7 Fused N	7 Fused %	7 Unfused N	7 Unfused %	9 Fused N	9 Fused %	9 Unfused N	9 Unfused %	10/11 Fused N	10/11 Fused %	10/11 Unfused N	10/11 Unfused %	12/13 Fused N	12/13 Fused %	12/13 Unfused N	12/13 Unfused %
Early	5	100	-	-	26	96.3	1	3.70	13	100	-	-	80	98.77	1	1.23	48	100	-	-	24	100	-	-	14	100	-	-
Intermediate	3	100	-	-	11	91.67	1	8.33	5	100	-	-	45	88.24	6	11.76	20	71.42	8	28.58	11	100	-	-	1	50	1	50
Late	2	100	-	-	7	50	7	50	4	80	1	20	28	54.91	23	45.09	14	38.88	22	61.12	3	23.07	10	76.93	1	100	-	-
Final	1	25	3	75	9	50	9	50	2	50	2	50	5	16.12	26	83.88	4	28.57	10	71.43	5	64.28	5	35.72	-	-	-	-

Table 5.5 Sheep/goat: fused versus unfused epiphyses

Phase	2 Fused N	2 Fused %	2 Unfused N	2 Unfused %	3 Fused N	3 Fused %	3 Unfused N	3 Unfused %	5 Fused N	5 Fused %	5 Unfused N	5 Unfused %	7 Fused N	7 Fused %	7 Unfused N	7 Unfused %	9 Fused N	9 Fused %	9 Unfused N	9 Unfused %	10/11 Fused N	10/11 Fused %	10/11 Unfused N	10/11 Unfused %	12/13 Fused N	12/13 Fused %	12/13 Unfused N	12/13 Unfused %
Early	7	87.5	1	12.5	11	68.75	5	31.25	6	85.72	1	14.28	39	90.7	4	9.30	17	100	-	-	9	81.81	2	18.19	3	100	-	-
Intermediate 1	-	-	1	100	2	50	2	50	-	-	-	-	7	63.63	4	36.37	3	60	2	40	2	100	-	-	1	75	1	25
Intermediate 2	1	100	-	-	6	50	6	50	3	37.5	5	62.5	25	67.56	12	32.44	10	83.33	2	16.67	5	55.55	4	44.45	2	66.66	1	33.33
Late	1	100	-	-	2	50	2	50	-	-	1	100	5	20	20	80	4	40	6	60	3	33.33	6	66.66	-	-	4	100
Final	1	33.33	2	66.66	6	60	4	40	2	50	2	50	13	40.62	19	59.38	4	23.53	13	76.47	4	57.14	3	42.86	1	25	3	75
Neonatal	-	-	1	100	-	-	3	-	-	-	-	-	-	-	6	-	-	-	2	-	-	-	2	-	-	-	-	-

Table 5.6 Pig: fused versus unfused epiphyses

Phase	2 Fused N	2 Fused %	2 Unfused N	2 Unfused %	3 Fused N	3 Fused %	3 Unfused N	3 Unfused %	5 Fused N	5 Fused %	5 Unfused N	5 Unfused %	7 Fused N	7 Fused %	7 Unfused N	7 Unfused %	9 Fused N	9 Fused %	9 Unfused N	9 Unfused %	10/11 Fused N	10/11 Fused %	10/11 Unfused N	10/11 Unfused %	12/13 Fused N	12/13 Fused %	12/13 Unfused N	12/13 Unfused %
Early	1	100	-	-	-	-	-	-	3	100	-	-	22	81.48	5	18.52	8	72.72	3	27.28	3	60	2	40	1	100	-	-
Intermediate 1	-	-	1	100	3	100	-	-	-	-	1	100	3	37.5	5	62.5	1	16.66	5	83.34	2	66.66	1	33.33	-	-	2	100
Intermediate 2	-	-	-	-	3	75	1	25	-	-	-	-	-	-	4	100	1	100	-	-	-	-	4	100	1	50	1	50
Late	-	-	-	-	3	60	2	40	-	-	1	100	-	-	11	100	-	-	-	-	-	-	3	100	-	-	1	100
Final	-	-	1	100	-	-	3	100	-	-	-	-	-	-	-	-	-	-	1	100	-	-	2	100	-	-	1	100
Neonatal	-	-	-	-	-	-	2	-	-	-	-	-	-	-	4	-	-	-	2	-	-	-	1	-	-	-	2	-

Context	Phase	Element	Greatest length (mm)	Est. shoulder height (cm)
5609	3	tibia	176	52.3
2552	7	humerus	140.57	45.5
3516	7	femur	155.16	47.4
3516	7	humerus	145.73	47.3
3516	7	radius	139.2	46.2
3516	7	tibia	160	47.6
6642	7	femur	193	59.3
6642	7	humerus	177	58
6642	7	radius	177	58.2
6642	7	tibia	190	56.4
477	9	femur	145.32	44.3
477	9	radius	132.19	56
477	9	tibia	143.39	42.8
5946	9	femur	185	56.7
5946	9	humerus	165	53.9
5946	9	radius	176	57.9
5946	9	tibia	191	56.7
5946	9	ulna	202	56.7
9617	10/11	ulna	234	65.6

Table 5.7 Dog: estimated shoulder heights

metatarsal distal breadth reflects a significant narrowing of the distal metatarsal from the Iron Age to the Late Saxon period. However, the sample size in all cases is small and such variation could easily be attributed to sexual dimorphism. In general terms cattle bones from West Fen Road resemble those from other sites of this period.

Sheep/Goat
Measurements of metacarpal and metatarsal Gl and the diameter of the humerus distal trochlea show the greatest variance. However, the sample size is small and once again this variance could be due to size differences between the sexes. Overall, the sheep bones from West Fen Road are rather small, and similar in size to the modern Soay.

Pig
Measurements show very little sample variance; furthermore, the greatest variance was recorded for measurements which are more affected by sexual dimorphism, such as post-cranial measurements and tooth-lengths (Payne and Bull 1988).

Means and ranges for a number of single measurements for these three species compare well with those from early Anglo-Saxon West Stow, Suffolk (Crabtree 1990); Mid Saxon Melbourne Street, Southampton (Bourdillon and Coy 1980); Late Saxon/medieval Eckweek, Avon (Davis 1991) and Saxon/medieval Burystead/Langham Road, Northampton (Davis 1992b).

Dog
Estimated shoulder heights have been calculated for various dog bones from Phases 3, 7, 9 and 10/11 (Table 5.7). These have been compared to the large corpus of published data on archaeological dog bones from various periods (Harcourt 1974). The Roman dog from F1203 (Enclosure 8) falls within the range for this period and is slightly larger than the mean height represented by Harcourt's data. All of the dogs from later phases fall within the range for the Anglo-Saxon period. Dogs from the Late Saxon period (Phase 7) range in size from 45.5cm to 59.3cm whilst the 12th-century dogs are slightly smaller, ranging in size from 44.4cm to 57.9cm. A large ulna from the late 12th–14th century assemblage (Phase 10/11) gave an estimated shoulder height of 65.6cm and is towards the upper size range for Anglo-Saxon dogs recorded by Harcourt.

Horse
Estimated withers heights have been calculated for various equid bones from Phases 2, 3, 7, 9 and 10/11. They range in size from 12.2 hh to 14 hh; therefore, both ponies and small horses are represented in the assemblage.

Summary
The largest stratified collections of animal bone from the site date to the Roman (Phase 3) and Late Saxon (Phase 7) phases, and to the 12th century (Phase 9). Domestic species dominate and cattle and sheep/goat are the most common species in all phases, with pig also important. The pattern of relative frequency between these three species and the age structure of the population reveals the following:

1. a steady increase in the frequency of cattle over time, declining relative to an increase in sheep/goat and pig during the late medieval period;
2. a peak in the number of sheep/goat in the Saxon and medieval phases of occupation determined from both NISP and MNI;
3. a peak in the number (MNI) of pigs culled during the Mid Saxon period and a steady increase in their frequency over time;
4. a consistent pattern of slaughtering cattle at the optimum age for prime beef and pigs at a relatively young age for pork and fat;
5. a decline over time in the number sheep/goat culled under two years of age.

Other domestic and wild species exploited for food are rare in the assemblage, indicating that venison, game and poultry formed only a small portion of the animal-based protein consumed at West Fen Road during the periods under consideration. Domestic fowl were probably kept for their eggs whilst capons may have been fattened for eating.

The presence of ponies and small horses coupled with the types of pathology recorded on some specimens indicates that this species was primarily used for traction. Butchery and skinning marks on some horse bones suggests that knackered horses may have been processed by a fellmonger to provide dog food and hides.

The presence of significant numbers of dogs from the main phases, coupled with the number of complete/partial skeletons recovered, suggests a close association between humans and dogs. Furthermore, the size range of animals present suggests working dogs which may have been valued for herding and hunting as well as companionship. Cats are also present in most phases although overall the numbers are low.

Discussion and conclusions

Analysis of the West Fen Road assemblage has revealed a remarkably consistent pattern of species exploitation and animal husbandry from the Iron Age through to the medieval period. This is particularly apparent if one considers the ratio between the three main stock species. Crabtree (1990), in her analysis of the large animal bone assemblage from West Stow, Suffolk, highlighted similar continuity between phases. She stressed that the animal husbandry and hunting practices apparent from analysis of the Early Saxon assemblage did not present a sharp break from those of the preceding Iron Age and Roman phases. Sheep/goat is only slightly more common than cattle in the earliest phases at West Fen Road (Iron Age–Mid Saxon). Depending upon which measure of relative frequency is considered (*i.e.* NISP or MNI) one becomes markedly more important than the other throughout subsequent phases (Mid Saxon to medieval). This is related to a steady increase in the proportion of pig. Cattle is the most abundant species by NISP, but if MNI is considered then sheep/goat is the most common species. Overall there is a general upward trend in the proportion of cattle over time but the trend for sheep/goat is less obvious due to the discrepancy between results obtained for NISP and MNI frequencies. A similar discrepancy was noted by Bourdillon and Coy (1980) in their analysis of the Mid Saxon assemblage from Melbourne Street, Southampton. At West Stow, Crabtree noted a general trend towards increasing numbers of sheep/goat and pigs, and a decreasing proportion of cattle over time. A similar trend was noted at the Late Saxon/medieval Burystead/ Langham Road sites in Northamptonshire (Davis 1992b). However, at other Saxon sites such as Carlton Colville, Suffolk (Higbee in prep.) and Cottenham, Cambridgeshire (Higbee 1998) cattle is the most common species. Furthermore, a significant increase in the frequency of pigs was noted between the Mid and Late Saxon phases at Cottenham. Aberrations from the general trend have been summarised above but require further explanation.

The peak frequency of sheep/goat (by MNI) in the medieval period (Phase 10/11 and 12/13) and the apparent decline in the frequency of young sheep/goat under the age of two years selected for slaughter reflects the growing importance of wool production in medieval England. The increase in frequency between these phases is slight but has been noted at other rural settlement sites that span these periods (*e.g.* Burystead/Langham Road, Northants). However, the increase is more marked in assemblages from urban samples, such as those from sites at Exeter (Maltby 1979) and Lincoln (O'Connor 1982; Dobney *et al.* 1996). Davis (1992b) suggests that the changes which occurred in rural areas are not as obvious, simply because increasingly large numbers of sheep — mainly older animals from which several fleeces had been shorn — were being sold into towns for the urban meat supply.

The dramatic peak in the number (MNI) of pigs during the Mid Saxon (Phase 5) period is significant and may reflect a slight change in strategy during this period. The proportion of pig recorded is higher than that from the earliest phases at West Stow. Here Crabtree (1990) suggests that pigs, due to their fecundity, would have allowed for the rapid establishment of animal husbandry, their numbers only declining once beef production increased. The subsequent decline in pigs established from MNI, and the increase in both cattle and sheep/goat, both support this interpretation.

III. Fish bone
by Phil Piper

Fish bones were recovered from 68 of the sorted bulk samples. The only three contexts of Iron Age date to produce any fish bones contained a digested vertebra of *Esocidae* (pike) and two indeterminate fish vertebrae (one digested). A further pike vertebra was recovered from a Roman context. The majority of fish bones were recovered from Saxon Phases 5 and 7, and the medieval Phases 9 to 12, and discussion will concentrate on these assemblages. Due to the small sample sizes this study will discuss the evidence within two broad chronological groups, Period II (Saxon) and Period III (medieval). Bones recovered from two undated post-holes (an eel and an indeterminate fish vertebra) will also be excluded from discussion.

The physical condition of most bones was moderate to poor. The predominance of the small, compact and robust vertebrae and the noticeable absence of other skeletal elements might indicate the loss through post-depostional destruction of less durable skeletal elements. Taphonomic studies of the microfaunal and palaeobotanical remains (*Small vertebrates*, p.99; *Plants and seeds*, p.102) both imply that there has been little post-depositional movement of biological materials caused by bioturbation and/or the effects of burrowing animals. A few of the bones were recorded as digested and/or masticated.

Period II: Saxon
By far the most common species of fish recorded in deposits of Saxon date was *Anguillidae* (eel: Table 5.8), which was present in 26 (52%) of the 50 samples of Saxon date. The most frequently and abundantly occurring marine fish was *clupea harengus* (herring), being recovered from six (12%) of the samples. In addition the bones of *Gadidae* (cod family: two records), *Pollachius virens* (saithe: one record), *Pollachius pollachius* (Pollock: one record) and *Sparidae* (bream family: one record) were identified in the Saxon zooarchaeological record. Almost all the samples contained no more than five bone fragments, suggesting that fish was recorded frequently but in no abundance. The exceptions were provided by *1834* (Phase 5 pit, F385) and *2218* (Phase 6 pit, F422), which both consisted of a mixture of eel and herring bones. All the bones within the *1834* assemblage were calcined.

Period III: medieval
Although the eel remains the dominant fish species recorded (29%), there is a reduction in its overall abundance. There appears to be an increase in the relative importance of marine fish from the Saxon to the medieval

Taxa	Saxon		Medieval	
	R.f.	R.a. (%)	R.f.	R.a. (%)
Anguillidae (Eel)	26	52	13	29
Clupea harengus (Herring)	6	12	10	22
Esocidae (Pike family)	5	10	4	9
Gadidae (Cod family)	2	4	3	7
Pollachius virens (Saithe)	1	2	2	4.5
Pollachius pollachius (Pollock)	1	2	1	2
Sparidae (Bream family)	1	2	0	0
Melanogrammus aeglefinus (Haddock)	0	0	1	2

Table 5.8 Fish bones in Saxon and medieval contexts

period; in particular herring (22%) appears to increase in frequency in the medieval period. Along with saithe, pollock and cod there is a single record of *Melanogrammus aeglfinus* (haddock). As is the case with the Saxon samples, the bones of fish occur relatively frequently in the medieval record, but are restricted to only a few bones per sample.

Discussion
In both the medieval and Saxon periods, the most predominant fish species is the eel. This was probably caught locally in the rivers using basket traps or fine mesh nets (T. O'Connor, *pers. comm.*). In addition a small number of pike were recorded in the assemblages. These were generally of a small size and probably incidental catches during netting for eels. The herring seems to be the most important marine resource available to the Saxon and medieval inhabitants of West Fen Road. These, along with small numbers of other marine fish, were imported through trade. Sites of equivalent Saxon date have produced fish assemblages of similar composition. The Mid Saxon site of Hay Green, Terrington St. Clement, Norfolk produced small numbers of herring and eel. The Mid–Late Saxon ditches at Chopdike Drove, Gosberton, Lincolnshire produced the remains of cod, haddock and eel (Baker 2002). At the Saxon site of Lake End Road, Buckinghamshire only eel and perch were present (Powell 2002).

There appears to be an increase in the relative importance and/or availability of marine fish in the medieval period. However, the small numbers of fish remains recovered from the archaeological samples imply that fish were not very important in the diet at West Fen Road (in contrast with the monastic community: Owen 2003, 66). It is possible that marine fish in particular were not readily available to buy, or that the local inhabitants were not able to obtain a diverse selection of marine resources, either as a result of social or economic constraints.

IV. Small vertebrates
by Phil Piper

In total, 1514 small vertebrate bone fragments were recovered from 75 archaeological deposits at West Fen Road. However, sediments of Iron Age and Romano-British date (Period I) only produced a total of seventy-four (4.6%) bones, too few to allow constructive comment on the taphonomic history of the small

vertebrate remains and/or an interpretation of the local environmental conditions during these phases of site occupation. Thus, analysis will concentrate on the remains recovered from the Saxon and medieval phases (Periods II and III, Tab. 5.9). The bones identified in two deposits from a stone-lined well of Phase 11 are discussed separately.

Interpretation of the small vertebrate bone taphonomy
The complete details of methods of analysis and quantification, and the identification of various taphonomic modifications observed in the individual bones recovered at West Fen Road may be found in Piper (forthcoming). The following discussion outlines some of the more interesting processes influencing the accumulation and preservation of the faunal assemblages.

The majority of the bones recovered from the various archaeological deposits appear to have similar physical characteristics at the microscopic level, pointing to their contemporaneity and genuine antiquity. An exception is the bone assemblage recovered from Phase 7 post-hole *2890*. The physical condition and appearance of these bones suggests that they are of a more recent date than the rest of the bone assemblage. Thus, the predominantly *Bufo bufo* (common toad) bones from this context are excluded from any further study.

The partial or complete skeletons recorded probably represent individuals that have fallen into features and died in them, or dead specimens incorporated in waste material discarded by the human occupants of the settlement. The presence of relatively complete skeletons, even in shallow features, suggests that bioturbation, subterranean invertebrates and burrowing vertebrates have not had a serious effect on the contents of features. This view is also tentatively supported by the presence of the house mouse in quite substantial numbers in the medieval period deposits, and its complete absence in the Saxon phases of occupation. Substantial amounts of bioturbation in the shallow intercutting features would probably have caused at least some relocation of house mouse bones into deposits stratigraphically below the medieval features. Thus, these sediments are unlikely to have been disturbed by humans after the bones had been buried.

In addition, a number of deposits contained concentrations of broken bones from numerous individuals which displayed evidence of abrasion. On the whole there is little evidence of weathering. However, the duration required to weather bone sufficiently so that it is observable in the archaeological record means that some pre-depositional modification cannot be discounted. On balance, it seems likely that much of the physical damage caused to the bones probably occurred once they had entered the burial environment, and/or during human re-working of archaeological deposits. For example, the re-alignment of ditches throughout the Saxon and medieval phases of occupation could have led to some re-working and re-deposition of small vertebrate remains into later features. Those bone fragments that are severely abraded and rounded have been excluded from the following palaeoecological reconstruction (see Piper forthcoming for discussion).

Evidence of digestion of bones was relatively common. The severity of the damage caused to the bones during ingestion, and the presence of the skeletal remains of cats and dogs in archaeological deposits on the site (*Large vertebrates*, p.91) suggest that domestic predators were the

Taxa	Common name	Saxon: Period II	Medieval: Period III	Well 4514/5 (Phase 11)	Total
Anura sp.	Frog/toad sp.	126	127	163	416
Bufo bufo	Common toad	8	3	2	13
Bufo sp.	Toad sp.	41	12	3	56
Rana lessonae	Pool frog	1	-	-	1
Rana sp. *phonomic*	Frog sp.	132	113	208	453
Rana temporaria	Common frog	20	19	28	67
Triturus cristatus	Great crested newt	2	4	6	12
Triturus vulgaris	Smooth newt	4	-	1	5
Triturus vulgaris/helveticus	Newt sp.	5	3	1	9
cf. *Vipera berus*	Viper or adder	1	-	-	1
Natrix natrix	Grass snake	4	5	35	44
Snake sp.	Snake sp.	2	-	5	7
Bird sp.	Bird sp.	3	4	-	7
Indeterminate	Indeterminate	14	27	4	45
Small mammal	Small mammal	3	14	4	21
Carduelis chloris	Greenfinch	-	1	-	1
Passerine	Song bird	2	-	-	2
Turdus sp.	Thrush sp.	1	-	-	1
Talpa europaea	Mole	-	-	1	1
Shrew sp.	Shrew sp.	2	2	-	4
Sorex araneus	Common shrew	4	-	-	4
Apodemus cf. *sylvaticus*	Wood mouse	1	-	-	1
Apodemus sp.	Wood/yellow-necked mouse	2	2	1	5
Arvicola terrestris	Water vole	-	1	1	2
Clethrionomys glareolus	Bank vole	1	-	-	1
Large rodent	Rodent sp.	1	4		5
Microtus agrestis	Field vole	8	4	1	13
Mouse sp.	Mouse sp.	1	10	1	12
Mus sp.	House mouse	-	20	1	21
Myomorph	Mouse/vole sp.	67	103	27	197
Rattus rattus/Arvicola terrestris	Black rat/water vole	1	1	-	2
Small rodent	Rodent sp.	1	-	-	1
Vole sp.	Vole sp.	8	2	-	10
Totals		**466**	**481**	**493**	**1440**

Table 5.9 Small vertebrates

cause of at least some of the small vertebrate mortality on the site. The charring noted on some of the skeletal elements was presumably caused by their inadvertent introduction, probably with fuel, into fires and ovens. The bones were then cleared with the ash and deposited in pits and other features.

Palaeoecological interpretation
In order to take sample size into consideration, the relative frequency of occurrence of each species of mammal, herpetile and bird has been calculated for the bulked Saxon and medieval phases of site occupation. The jackknife technique has then been applied to the resultant abundance lists to estimate a range of pseudovalues and mean for heterogeneity (Shannon Winer Indices), richness (Menhinicks Index) and evenness (calculated as the correlation of variation). The methodology follows that outlined by Kaufman (1998).

The mean diversity values of 2.8 and 2.32 for the Saxon and medieval periods respectively suggest moderately high species diversity in both phases of site occupation. The result of a t-Test (t=2.11, p=0.38) and ANOVA analyses (richness: f=0.52, p=0.48; evenness: f=0.09, p=0.77) calculated for the range of pseudo-values estimated for the three indices implies that no significant difference exists between the two microfaunal communities. However, the mean pseudo-values for diversity (Shannon-Wiener Index) and richness are markedly higher in the Saxon phase than those observed during the medieval phase of site occupation. This suggests that the diversity of the community, and the numbers of species present, was greater during the Saxon period. In addition, both the Saxon and medieval assemblages produced low pseudo-values for equitability (evenness). This suggests that both were dominated by a small number of species. Low equitability and low/moderate species richness are indicative of small vertebrate communities that inhabit disturbed and modified environments that contain a low floral diversity (Dickman and Doncaster 1987, 1989). However, values for diversity, richness and equitability describe nothing of community structure or composition observed in the small vertebrate communities recovered from the Saxon and medieval periods at Ely, which are of real interest.

Saxon: Period II
A total of eleven species of small vertebrate were represented in the Saxon assemblage. Amphibians and reptiles appear to dominate the zooarchaeological record, contributing seven of the eleven species: *Natrix natrix* (grass snake), *Vipera berus* (viper), *Bufo bufo* (common

toad), *Rana temporaria* (common frog), *Rana lessonae* (pool frog), *Triturus vulgaris* (smooth newt) and *Triturus cristatus* (great crested newt). (The native population of *Rana lessonae* has recently become extinct in the British Isles. Thus its ecology in the English fens is not well understood. The last stronghold was in ponds in the Norfolk Broads. For discussion see Gleed-Owen (2001).) The common frog was by far the most abundant species. It appears that the frog was well adapted to exploiting the disturbed habitats and resources available in and around the settlement.

The most abundant mammal species were *Microtus agrestis* (field vole) and *Sorex araneus* (common shrew). Both these species, as well as *Apodemus sylvaticus* (wood mouse), are most abundant in open ground with a dense vegetational cover. *Clethrionoyms glareolus* (bank vole) on the other hand is a shade-dependent species, preferring densely vegetated banks and hedgerows and rarely venturing beyond deep cover.

Medieval: Period III (excluding Phase 11, *4514/5*)
In all, only eight species of small mammal and amphibian were identified within the samples of medieval date. Thus, there is an overall reduction in species diversity and richness in relation to the preceding Saxon phase of activity on the site. In addition there are some noticeable changes in the structure of the community. The pool frog, smooth newt, viper, wood mouse, common shrew and bank vole are all absent. However, perhaps the most notable change to the composition of the community is the appearance of *Mus sp.* (house mouse). This species is completely absent from the Saxon record, but appears as the second most abundant and frequently occurring species in the later phases of activity. The house mouse is well adapted to humanly-modified environments in and around settlements, taking advantage of reduced inter-species competition and plentiful resources. There appears to be an increase in the frequency and abundance of the common frog and grass snake. This suggests that the common frog was also well adapted to take advantage of the ecological and environmental changes that occurred at the site during the medieval period. The frog may have benefited from a reduction in competition by other insectivorous and amphibian taxa as a result of the intensification of human activities on the site that ecologically excluded many taxa from the local environment. The grass snake feeds almost exclusively on amphibians, and its increase might reflect the greater abundance of frogs as a food resource (Beebee and Griffiths 2000, 163–4).

The frequencies of field vole and smooth newt remain approximately the same, and there is a single bone of water vole. This suggests that much of the local environment remained damp open grassland/pasture or farmland, with ponds and drainage ditches still available to accommodate breeding amphibians.

Well deposits *4514/5*, F729: Phase 11
Contexts *4514* and *4515* were recorded as the primary and secondary fills of the stone-lined well F729 (Enclosure 16) (Fig. 5.2). In all, 493 bone fragments were recovered from *4514*, of which nearly 84% were amphibian, with the common frog contributing by far the most bones to the assemblage. Thirty different anatomical elements of this species were present, including a number of small and fragile bones that are rarely recovered in the archaeological record. Inclusive of all taxa, 367 (75%) of the bones were complete, demonstrating little or no surface modification associated with weathering or post-depositional re-working of the assemblage.

Armitage and West (1987) analysed large numbers of microfaunal remains recovered from a series of deposits excavated from within a 15th-century stone-lined well at Greyfriars in London. Contemporary illustrations of wells (*ibid.*, 124) showed that most examples had a stone structure built above ground level that would have prevented access to the shaft by all but the most resourceful small vertebrates. Despite this, however, they concluded that the bone assemblage must be a result of pit fall trapping. Armitage and West argued that the well at Greyfriars had either been constructed without a solid structure extending above ground level, or the structure above ground had been dismantled towards the end of its use life. Both interpretations could explain the type of small vertebrate accumulations recorded in the well deposits. However, in the stone-lined well F729 the primary deposit *4515* consisted of dark black fine organic silt, and probably represents sediments accumulating during its use. Interestingly, the deposit contained only two amphibian bones. Context *4514*, stratigraphically above *4515*, consisted of a mixture of refuse and sediments accumulating at the base of the well during, or towards the end of its functional life. Thus, an above-ground structure that prohibited the entrance of small vertebrates into the well shaft early in its functional life must have been dismantled, or at least become permeable.

Much of the microfaunal assemblage probably represents a number of individuals that had fallen into the well and become trapped. Thus, the small mammals, reptiles and amphibians trapped within the well existed as part of a community that inhabited the environment close to the eventual point of deposition. However, in addition some bones were fragmented and demonstrated low or moderate incidences of surface abrasion and rounding, and two clearly showed the effects of predatory digestion. This implies that at least some of the bones had originated from other sources, possibly as a result of movement down through deposits above, or as isolated fragments of bone included as part of the deposition of sediments/refuse. Neither deposit contained a substantial amount of masonry which might have indicated that the well had been left to fall into disrepair. Assuming that the above-ground structure associated with the well was not constructed of wood, a certain amount of decay and reduction in maintenance of the well structure during or towards the end of its use-life is implied.

It is not possible to calculate from the faunal remains alone the length of time it took for this assemblage to accumulate. Thus, not all the vertebrate species identified may have occupied the immediate environment around the well at the same time. However, the single deposit *4514* within the well contained the remains of ten species of micro-fauna, five of them herpetile and five mammal. The number of species represented suggests a relative increase in the diversity and species richness of the small vertebrate community during the 14th century compared with the preceding medieval periods. The species richness probably reflects a reduction in the levels of human activity close to the well and a subsequent increase in the diversity of the local flora.

Conclusions
It is likely that the composition of the small vertebrate assemblage is representative of the small mammal, amphibian and reptile communities that inhabited the environment in and around the settlement at West Fen Road. The clear differences observed in the composition of the small vertebrate assemblages (reduction in the numbers of species and the introduction of the house mouse) between the Saxon and medieval periods of site occupation help to support this. However the re-working and re-deposition of some bone fragments of Saxon date into medieval contexts cannot be discounted.

During both phases of occupation the environment appears to have consisted of open, damp pasture and/or agricultural ground containing a series of drainage ditches, dykes and ponds. However, in the Saxon period prolonged, intensive human activity throughout the settlement was limited, allowing for a more diverse and richer ecological community to exist than during the medieval period. In addition there appear to have been more areas of dense vegetational cover, especially along the fringes of bodies of water. Field boundaries may have partitioned the field systems, providing cover for shade-demanding species.

In the medieval period there is a profound change in the structure of the microfaunal community. The house mouse appears for the first time, and there is a reduction in diversity and species richness. These factors combined suggest an intensification in human activity on the site. In addition there may have been an 'opening up' of the landscape and a corresponding reduction in the number of hedgerows, embankments and field boundaries that provided dense cover for those species that required it. The medieval period saw specialisation in cereal cultivation (*Plants and seeds*, below) and a more open landscape that saw increased crop production. As a result, the introduction of bulk storage and the establishment of increased trade perhaps facilitated the colonisation of the West Fen Road site by the house mouse for the first time.

If the fauna recovered from the shaft of the 14th-century (Phase 11) stone-lined well is representative of the species inhabiting the local environment, then this period saw an increase in the diversity and richness of the small mammal and herpetile community compared with earlier medieval periods. This seems to imply an encroachment by the local ecological community (floral and faunal) of the surrounding area into areas of the settlement that were becoming — or were already — abandoned by the human population.

V. Plants and seeds
by Rachel Ballantyne
(Figs 5.2–5.6)

A total of 89 bulk samples from West Fen Road were analysed for charred botanical remains. Aspects of their recovery, preservation and identification are outlined below. The majority of sampled contexts reflect the main emphases of archaeological interest, coming from Phases 7, 9 and 10 (mid 9th–13th centuries). Although good charred plant remains have been recovered from earlier and later phases, they derive from a limited range of contexts.

There is a significant shift in sample composition between the Iron Age and Roman phases, both of which were dominated by hulled wheat chaff, and the grain-rich medieval phases. The assemblage is outlined below chronologically, and this summary is followed by discussion of its key aspects.

Aims and methods

Sampling
The bulk sampling covered a selection of context types from all phases of the site. The intended sample volume was fifteen litres, but the overall average within the assemblage is nine litres, due both to the limitations of smaller contexts such as post-holes, and the practicalities of rescue excavation.

Processing
All samples, with the exception of those from two waterlogged contexts, were processed by hand using bucket-flotation. The heavy clay matrix required soaking overnight with detergent to facilitate disaggregation. Even after soaking, the recovery of charred plant remains by flotation met mixed success, with a small number of samples containing greater numbers of charred seeds within the heavy residue than flots. Flots were collected on 300μm sieves, and the heavy residue then washed over 1mm mesh. Both flots and heavy residues were subsequently dried. All heavy residue components greater than 4mm were sorted by eye for artefacts and ecofacts; fractions less than 4mm were sorted under a low-power binocular microscope (Leica MS5) for small bone and charred plants. The dried flots were sorted in full under the same low-power microscope. The two waterlogged contexts were soaked overnight without detergent, then washed through a stack of 2mm, 1mm, 0.5mm and 0.3mm sieves. The residues were scanned wet under a low-power binocular microscope.

Identifications and quantification
Seeds and vegetative plant remains were identified using the reference collections of the Pitt-Rivers Laboratory, Department of Archaeology, University of Cambridge. Manuals were also used where relevant (Berggren 1969, 1981; Anderberg 1994; Beijerinck 1947) and all plant nomenclature follows Stace (1997) for cereals and non-cereals. Plant items were quantified where possible by counting the minimum number within each sample. Grains were counted by embryo ends, chaff by glume bases, rachis internodes or culm nodes, and seeds by embryo or attachment point (whichever was more relevant). Legume cotyledons were counted and then halved to provide a minimum number of whole pulses. Other components which could not easily be quantified, such as stem and leaf fragments, were summarised qualitatively and have been listed in Table 5.20 and the appendix by the following system:

-	1 or 2 items
+	less than 10 items
++	10–50 items
+++	more than 50 items
m	mineralised items
u	uncharred items

Preservation

Plant remains
Charred plant macro-remains survived exceptionally well in the clay soil. The count density was high, and overall averaged 13.07 items (seeds, chaff, grain) counted per litre of sample processed (Table 5.10). The quality of preservation was also very good, with only limited fragmentation of remains. Many of the cereal grains were slightly distorted and puffed from charring, probably due to temperatures slightly higher than those ideal for preserving starchy seeds (cf. Boardman and Jones 1990). Due to charring distortion no attempt has been made to use measurement of oat seeds, for example, as a means of indicating relative proportions of wild or cultivated types. The poor preservation of starchy items is also reflected by the legume pulses, which rarely include identifiable hila (attachment points) or the surface texture of the testae (outer coats). In most cases pulses have survived with only gross morphology, and identification has been limited to a broad description of size.

Other more woody or siliceous plant components have been well preserved by charring. Seeds of many wild taxa are identifiable to species due to their well-preserved surface texture, shape, and lack of distortion. Seeds of the cabbage types *Brassica* and *Sinapis* have often survived showing details of the reticulum. Identification of coarse- and fine-patterned seed forms has therefore been possible. The two waterlogged contexts from well F729 (Phase 11, Enclosure 16) also contained very good preservation of both fruiting bodies and vegetative remains. Conditions

Phase	2	3	5	7	9	10	11/12	Overall
	Iron Age	*Roman*	*Mid Sax.*	*Late Sax.*	*12th C.*	*12/13th C*	*13–15th C.*	
Total samples	6	5	6	40	17	12	3	89
Total volume/ litres	37	46	45	352	161	135	29	805
Total cereal grain (with oat)	45	95	596	1622	769	672	61	3860
Total cereal chaff items	427	473	27	234	175	213	17	1566
Total non-cereal seeds	89	47	301	1089	774	2707	87	5094
Total count	561	615	924	2945	1718	3592	165	10520
Count density (items per litre)	15.16	13.37	20.53	8.37	10.67	26.61	5.69	13.07

Table 5.10 Summary of charred remains

suitable for waterlogging appear very limited at the site: for example, neither the base of well F752 nor pond F2275 produced any organic remains.

Only one sample contained mineralised remains: that from Phase 9 pit F774. The seeds are mid yellowish-brown in colour, and were probably preserved by phosphate salts. Other features identified as 'cessy' during excavation — pit F540, ditch F678 — did not contain any mineralised remains, and their interpretation cannot be supported or refuted.

Intrusive plant materials were apparent in low quantities within most samples. Fine rootlets were most common, but there were also untransformed seeds of Chenopodiaceae, *Picris echioides, Carduus/Cirsium*, and moss fragments. Many of these remains are fresh and can be linked to contamination during the excavation or storage of samples, rather than to the burial context itself. Aspects of the small faunal assemblage (*Small vertebrates*, p.99) also indicate stable burial conditions and a very low amount of intrusive material.

Other remains
Most samples include quantities of other artefactual and ecofactual remains, particularly within the heavy residues. Although some earlier contexts contain good mollusc remains, in most cases a mixture of glossy 'recent' (especially *Ceciliodes* sp., *Vallonia excelsior/ costata,* and *Trichia* sp.) and white mineralised 'archaeological' individuals (often of the same taxa) are present in low numbers. The shells have not been studied in detail since they do not provide an analytically viable assemblage. The two waterlogged contexts from well F729 (Phase 11) include entomological remains, which are summarised and discussed within this report.

Results

Period I: Iron Age and Romano-British
The six Iron Age samples come from four features (Table 5.11, in Appendix), and 84% of charred plant items are from the very rich gullies F1514 and F1491. Of the five Roman contexts sampled only one was botanically rich, that from pit F1461. The results for both phases are therefore highly context-specific.

In all rich contexts the charred remains are dominated by hulled wheat chaff. During the Iron Age a mixture of spelt (*Triticum spelta*) and emmer wheat (*Triticum dicoccum*) glume bases occurs, with spelt slightly predominant. Only spelt wheat chaff has been recovered from the Roman contexts. The wheat chaff always occurs in far greater ratio to grain than can be expected within intact ears of these cereals (1 grain:1 glume base), and it therefore appears that a late processing by-product is represented (*cf.* Hillman 1981). The burnt chaff may indicate the dehusking of grain by parching and pounding, a necessary stage for *hulled* wheats that do not release the grain during earlier threshing. There is good archaeological and historical evidence (M. Jones 1984a; White 1970) that during the Iron Age and Roman periods grain was stored with the straw removed, but still within the husks (in spikelets: grain encased by glumes). The chaff-rich contexts suggest their association with food preparation, where grain was removed from storage and dehusked prior to milling or direct consumption.

Other cereals are poorly represented, perhaps due to the specific association of charring events with the preparation of hulled wheat grain. Barley (*Hordeum vulgare sensu lato*) occurs as occasional grains and chaff fragments. One free-threshing wheat (*Triticum aestivum sensu lato*) rachis internode and a number of comparable grains have also been identified within both Iron Age and Roman contexts. Oat seeds (*Avena* sp.) are also present, but an absence of chaff has prevented their identification as cultivated or wild forms.

The few accompanying wild seeds are of arable/disturbed land types, probably weeds of the cereal crop. The range of taxa may be skewed towards those with morphologies that are difficult to remove during earlier stages of cereal processing (*cf.* G. Jones 1984). There are numerous goosefoots (Chenopodiaceae) — *Chenopodium polyspermum, C. ficifolium, C. album, Atriplex patula/prostrata* — all suggestive of nutrient-rich soil conditions. Other seeds include vetch/wild pea (*Vicia/Lathyrus* sp.), true sedges (*Carex* spp.) and brome grass (*Bromus* sp.). Only in Roman contexts does stinking chamomile (*Anthemis cotula*) occur, a weed associated with heavy clay soils (Hanf 1983). The appearance of this taxon may indicate the extension of arable farming onto such soils, which are common in the local area. The earliest evidence at the site for Celtic bean (*Vicia faba*), an archaic cultivated broad bean, occurs within Roman ditch F2039.

There is little change in the cereal crops represented, or the stage at which charring occurred during crop processing between the Iron Age and Roman phases. Spelt wheat became an increasingly important crop, and some extension of arable lands may have occurred. However the pattern of activities on-site appears to have remained largely unchanged, with charred dehusking waste predominant. Similar Iron Age charred assemblages exist in the Ely area at Hurst Lane where emmer wheat was common, and St. Johns Road (Abrams 2000) where spelt wheat predominated. Both sites also included barley, and free-threshing wheat was found at Hurst Lane. The weed assemblages were each dominated by Chenopodiaceae, with clovers (*Trifolium* spp.) and grasses, particularly brome and oats. The limited Roman cereals at West Fen Road compare well to Vicar's Farm, Cambridge (Lucas forthcoming), where there was rich spelt wheat chaff. It thus appears that on the southern fen-edge a relatively uniform cereal cultivation strategy was undertaken during the Iron Age and Roman periods. The constraints of limited sample size must, however, render such conclusions tentative.

Period II: Saxon

Phase 5: Mid Saxon
Mid Saxon contexts produced a small assemblage of six widely dispersed botanical assemblages, four of which were very rich (Tables 5.12 and 5.13, in Appendix; Table 5.14).

Cereals
Sample composition was markedly different to the earlier Iron Age and Roman phases (Fig. 5.3). The charred remains are mostly of free-threshing wheat grain, rather than hulled wheat chaff, and the shift in composition can be linked directly to the change in crop processing sequence (*cf.* Hillman 1981). Free-threshing cereals release the grain during threshing itself, without requiring further parching and pounding of the husks. The Mid Saxon grain-rich contexts, with few wild seeds, suggest that charring occurred once the grain had already been cleaned, and reflect 'domestic' food-preparation settings — not dehusking. Wheat is still the dominant charred cereal, but this is now a free-threshing type (*Triticum aestivum sensu lato*). Where chaff items (rachis internodes) survive they are poorly preserved, and hexaploid or tetraploid wheats cannot be identified. There are slightly greater quantities of barley grain and chaff relative to wheat than before; there are low numbers of rye (*Secale cereale*) grain and chaff, a cereal that occurred within Roman Britain but was not widely grown until the Saxon period.

Other plant remains
Possible cultivars include oats (*Avena* sp.), which are only represented by seeds and cannot be identified as wild or cultivated. A large number of well preserved Celtic beans (*Vicia faba*) in pit F1589 may have been charred in a similar food preparation setting to the cereal grain. Many of the wild taxa are characteristic of arable/disturbed soils, and may represent weeds collected with the cereal harvest. However, as the Celtic beans illustrate, not all the charred non-cereals within these contexts are necessarily arable weeds; an admixture of plant types is present. A number of seeds of great fen sedge (*Cladium mariscus*) within pit F385 and pit F1589 clearly represent a different source of plant material since this species requires wet soils, and has an extensive rhizome system that does not tolerate ploughing. Pit F1589 also includes a number of leaf fragments identifiable as sedge and, with the seeds, this suggests a collected resource.

There is an increase in wetland-associated plants, particularly true sedges (*Carex* spp.), which could be a mixture of weeds of the cereals and the collected sedge, or represent a resource themselves. Evidence for cultivation of damp soils is provided by the abundance of stinking chamomile (*Anthemis cotula*), a plant that characterises arable on heavy clay soils, and a low number of red bartsia (*Odontites vernus*). Legumes significantly increase in quantity compared to earlier phases and may indicate cultivation in less nutrient-rich soils, where such plants have an advantage as weeds due to the ability to fix nitrogen. Well preserved

Context	1834	2519	2642	2223	7162	7163	Phase 5
Feature	F385	F591	F629	F543	F1589	F1589	
Description	pit	pit	p/hole	ditch	pit	pit	
Volume/litres	8	12	4	8	8	5	45
Items counted	435	11	137	133	314	17	924
Count density	54.38	0.92	34.25	13.30	39.25	3.40	20.53

Table 5.14 Botanical samples from Phase 5

pulses within F385 are identifiable as common vetch (*Vicia sativa*), a plant commonly grown for fodder in rotation schemes in the past (Campbell 1994), although preservation quality has not been sufficient here to discern the cultivated or wild forms. Grass vetchling (*Lathyrus nissolia*), found on heavy clay or loams, also occurs.

Discussion

A diverse range of foods are represented despite the small number of samples. The lack of cereal chaff, and the range of grain and non-cereal foods, suggest this is charred material from 'domestic' food preparation. The remains thus contrast with those from the Iron Age and Roman phases, which specifically represent charred waste from hulled wheat dehusking. The increased diversity of taxa, for example rye and beans, in the Mid Saxon phase, may represent a real broadening of the subsistence strategy, or simply be a result of the shift in charring context.

Very few comparable Mid Saxon assemblages are known from local sites, the most relevant being Phase 1 (7th–9th century) at Cottenham, Cambs. (Mortimer 1998). Far lower amounts of charred plants were recovered but free-threshing wheat again dominated, although barley and rye occurred in slightly greater proportions. Low amounts of hulled wheat chaff were also present at Cottenham, but appear to be entirely absent from the Mid Saxon phase at West Fen Road. There is some debate about the continuing cultivation of hulled wheats in Saxon Britain (Pelling and Robinson 2000; Campbell 1994; Murphy 1994). The samples from West Fen Road indicate the absence of hulled wheats at the site during the Mid Saxon period, but again small sample size means this conclusion must remain tentative.

Phase 7: Late Saxon

The most comprehensive charred plant assemblage recovered spans the Late Saxon phase. Most of the identified plant taxa illustrate continuity with the Mid Saxon occupation although there is some increase in diversity, which could be due in part to the increased range of contexts examined.

Cereals

As in the Mid Saxon Phase 5, free-threshing wheat grain (*Triticum aestivum sensu lato*) is dominant. There are low amounts of wheat chaff, which is identifiable as a hexaploid type, possibly breadwheat (*Triticum aestivum*). Only one tetraploid wheat rachis internode has been recovered (ditch F1303, Enclosure 12) and this type does not appear to have been of importance. A moderate amount of barley grain and chaff is present (*Hordeum vulgare sensu lato*). Only in grain-rich pit F541 (Enclosure 1) is barley the major cereal (51% of all grain) — usually wheat is more frequent. The barley grains are often distorted from charring, but on some the faceted surface has been retained as evidence of a hulled type. A few grains are also twisted, providing some evidence of six-row barley; and of the chaff several rachis internodes are six-row forms (*Hordeum vulgare* L.). Most rachis internodes are single and fragmented, but six short articulated internodes in ditch F585 (Enclosure 1) illustrate that a dense-eared form was being cultivated.

Rye (*Secale cereale*) is consistently present in low quantities, usually as grain. However within ditch F528 (Enclosure 1) there is abundant chaff (39 rachis internodes to twelve grains) and this context also includes one large, probably cereal, straw joint (culm node). Two similar Late Saxon contexts were identified at Cottenham (Mortimer 1998), where rye rachis internodes outnumbered grain, and were accompanied by a number of culm nodes. Other charred components in these contexts, both at West Fen Road and Cottenham, appear 'normal': barley and wheat grain significantly outnumber their chaff, and there are few seeds of wild taxa. Stevens (in Mortimer 1998) interprets 'rye chaff' contexts as possibly indicating the storage of rye as sheaves, or the burning of whole sheaves. However, the phenomenon has a wider occurrence: 'rye chaff' contexts were present in later Saxon features at West Cotton, Northants (Campbell 1994) and in ovens at Stafford (Moffett 1994). There is good evidence that the straw/threshing waste of

rye was treated specially, perhaps due to its length, and some historical evidence supports this. Campbell (1994) quotes Markham (1681, 162) as specifying that rye straw should be used as bedding in grain-drying kilns. Whatever its precise use, rye is unique at West Fen Road as a cereal where chaff significantly outnumbers grain. In the few other cases where wheat and barley do occur in ratios of grain to chaff similar to those of ears, the contexts also include numerous indeterminate grains which if identified would lead grain to dominate.

There are continued low numbers of oat (*Avena* sp.) seeds. One oat floret base was recovered from pit F601 (Enclosure 13), but its condition was insufficient for speciation. At Cottenham (Mortimer 1998) there were Late Saxon cultivated oats, and these have been recovered within other southern British sites of this date (Greig 1991). The absence of hulled wheat continues into the Late Saxon contexts. Only one spikelet fork (*Triticum spelta/dicoccum*) has been recovered (ditch F447, Enclosure 13) and this could easily represent a weed cereal, or re-worked material.

Other plant resources

Only Phase 7 contains evidence of cultivated flax (*Linum usitatissimum*), with well-preserved charred seeds displaying traces of the distinctive pitted seed coat. The seeds occur singly or in pairs in widely dispersed locations: ditches F585 (Enclosure 1), F1914 (Enclosure 7/15), F2627 (Enclosure 6) and post-hole 9850 (Enclosure 6). Such limited remains cannot show whether flax was used for fibre, linseed, or both. Seeds of flax have been recovered charred from Saxon contexts at Cottenham (Mortimer 1998), Carlton Colville, Suffolk (Mortimer 2000a) and West Stow, Suffolk (Murphy 1985). Two sites — Mid Saxon Brandon, Suffolk (Murphy 1994) and Late Saxon West Cotton, Northants (Campbell 1994) — have produced waterlogged flax capsules, seeds and fibres suggestive of retting, showing that flax was used as a fibre crop. These two latter sites also had occasional charred flax seeds in settlement contexts, which could illustrate its presence as a weed within later cereal crops in the same fields.

There are further occasional finds of large, potentially cultivated legumes. As within Phase 5 some are identifiable as Celtic Bean (*Vicia faba*). Other large (>4mm), rounded pulses may be of pea (cf. *Pisum sativum*), but no well-preserved examples exist. The large pulses always occur in low amounts relative to grain, suggesting their incidental charring during food preparation. One context, ditch F1303, included numerous fragments of sedge (*Cladium mariscus*) leaves, although only one equivalent seed. The abundant charred vegetative remains suggest ash of sedge fuel, possibly from within a kiln or an oven.

Wild plant taxa

Despite the presence of a variety of sources of charred plants within sampled contexts (cereal products, legumes, sedge fuels) the majority of seeds characterise arable/disturbed soils and are probably associated with the cereal crops. Within contexts of 100 or more counted items there is variation in the amount of wild seeds present. In most cases seeds comprise 20–30% of the total count, but there are exceptions to this. Grain-rich pit F541 contained very few weed seeds, and the sample material appears to represent a fully cleaned grain product. Ditch F426 includes more seeds than grain (59% of total count), as does pit F601 (64%), and these are mostly arable weeds. The richer seed contexts suggest that waste from a final sieve cleaning of cereals may be present, or debris from other non-cereal plant resources.

The soils of cultivation appear to have been damp, clayey, and fairly nutrient poor, which is characteristic of the immediate area. The most frequent taxon, stinking chamomile, is regarded as an indicator of heavy clay (Hanf 1983). Of the major wetland types, common spikerush and great fen sedge (sedge), there is some difficulty of interpretation. As discussed within Phase 5, sedge is extremely unlikely to tolerate arable conditions, and probably represents other sources of charred material. Occasional contexts rich in sedge leaves support this interpretation. However, common spikerush frequently occurs in cereal-rich assemblages, and has been suggested (Jones 1981) as tolerant of shallow tilling. Whilst this might be true of earlier ard-based cultivation, it is less plausible during Saxon times, when good evidence exists for deep ploughing and the use of a mouldboard that turns the sod. Perhaps common spikerush grew on the damp margins of fields (*ibid.*).

Wild legumes (vetch/wild peas and clover) are far more frequent than in earlier phases, suggesting cultivation was upon increasingly nitrogen-poor soils. However Chenopodiaceae still occur, particularly fat-hen, and these favour nutrient rich soils and could perhaps denote manuring. A few of the legume pulses are identifiable, of which common vetch (*Vicia sativa*) may indicate its cultivation as a fallow crop, and then as a weed in subsequent cereal crops. Although not as frequent, there are consistent numbers of cabbage/mustard (*Brassica/Sinapis* spp.); both coarse and fine-patterned seed forms are present. Those with coarse patterning are small, and appear to represent black mustard (*Brassica* cf. *nigra*), rather than a cabbage type. The fine-patterned seeds correspond well to charlock (*Sinapis arvensis*) rather than other *Sinapis* spp. or cultivated *Brassica* spp. Although black mustard may be cultivated for seasoning, it is a wild plant that occurs on disturbed, especially damp, soils. Both black mustard and charlock appear to be weeds of the cereal crop. Further evidence of the admixture of charred plant sources is indicated by low numbers of charred hazelnuts (*Corylus avellana*) in ditch F528, ditch F678, ditch F2638 and post-hole *9847*, and seeds of elder (*Sambucus nigra*) in post-hole *2890*. Both species may represent collected foods, although elderberries may have been burnt with scrub-wood fuel.

Spatial patterning of remains
Although the majority of samples derive from Phase 7, spatial analysis is difficult due to their irregular distribution. However two comparable areas are represented by groups of samples:

Associated with Structure 8 (Enclosure 1)
The occasional very low sample volumes may have exaggerated some concentrations, but overall the post-holes are rich in charred grain (Table 5.15). One very rich context, from pit F541, is a cleaned grain product with a particularly high quantity of barley, which may have been placed as waste in this pit. Two nearby features to the north, pit F540 and ditch F523, are less rich. The high quantities in post-holes may reflect spreads of charred surface debris associated with the structure, which later slumped into the post-holes when the posts rotted or were removed.

Associated with Structure 11 (Enclosure 6)
The remains are much more specific than those for Structure 13. Not all post-holes had large amounts of charred plant remains, although *9727* showed signs of *in situ* burning (Table 5.16). The remains represent a cleaned cereal product, this time of free-threshing wheat. Other post-holes are less rich, and two ditches to the north of the structure included quantities of charred grain and seeds.

Other rich samples (with a count density over ten 'items per litre') are generally near to structures, probably directly linked to associated food-processing activities. Samples from ditches within the extensive enclosure system are often less rich, but not barren; charred plant remains are spread widely as surface debris across the Late Saxon site. Occasional contexts not associated with structures — for example pit F601 (Enclosure 13), and ditch F528 (Enclosure 1) — are rich, and appear to represent specific 'dumps' of charred material. Pit F601 produced a particularly high number of wild seeds, including a number of sedge and true sedge types. This may represent use of a wetland resource. Ditch F528 is rich in rye-chaff, and may again represent charred debris from a specific use. It is impossible to tell how displaced these charred tips are from their origin.

Period III: Medieval

Phases 9 and 10: 12th–13th centuries
Sufficient quantities of charred plant remains were recovered from Phases 9 and 10 to enable separation of their counts during calculations (Tables 5.17 and 5.18, in Appendix). Whilst the proportions of taxa vary between these two phases, the types are consistent. Both phases are thus discussed together.

Cereals
There is clear continuity from the Saxon phases and free-threshing wheat predominates both as grain and chaff. Where identifiable the chaff is always of a hexaploid variety (cf. *Triticum aestivum*). Barley (*Hordeum vulgare sensu lato*) continues to be present, but is consistently outnumbered by remains of wheat. Preservation of barley grains continues to be poor, but a number are clearly hulled (17% Phase 9, 11% Phase 10) and very occasionally twisted. Unfortunately no chaff (rachis internodes) of barley are identifiable to type, but the grain suggests that hulled six-row barley (*Hordeum vulgare*) may be represented. Rye (*Secale cereale*) occurs in low quantities as chaff and grain, and there are still seeds of wild/cultivated oats (*Avena* sp.). In contrast with Phases 5 and 7 there is a consistent, low presence of hulled wheat chaff (*Triticum spelta* and rarely *T. dicoccum*). The remains are from across the site and do not all overlie Iron Age or Roman-British activity. Perhaps these contexts represent the limited cultivation of hulled wheats and their associated presence as a weed in other cereal crops. The most significant remains are within pit F1684 (Enclosure 9, Phase 9) and F1368 (Enclosure 12, Phase 10).

Other plant resources
There are further low amounts of Celtic beans (*Vicia faba*) and large rounded pulses, which could be peas or beans. One mineralised context, cess-rich pit F774 (Enclosure 16) has two mineralised plum stones of a primitive type (*Prunus domestica*). The stones had probably been eaten with the fruit, as was common practice during the medieval period (Greig 1988). These later phases provide the first good evidence for use of sedge (*Cladium mariscus*) as a fuel, with increasing numbers of 'sedge-rich contexts'. The remains are characterised by high amounts of sedge leaf fragments, identifiable by distinctive surface texture, and occasionally with barbs on leaf margins surviving:

Feature/Context	F541	F567	2890	2441	F578	2981	F540	F523
Description	pit	ph	ph	ph	pit	ph	pit	ditch
Volume/litres	7	3	5	0.5	15	1	9	15
Grain	226	14	23	6	103	7	25	6
Chaff	0	3	10	0	3	0	1	0
Seeds	8	21	28	0	32	2	13	1
Items per litre	33.43	12.67	12.20	12.00	9.20	9.00	4.33	0.47

Table 5.15 Botanical evidence from Structure 8

Feature/Context	9727	F2590	F2588	9847	9850	F2618
Description	ph	ditch	ditch	ph	ph	ditch
Volume/litres	1	11	6	4	5	9
Grain	77	77	26	18	10	14
Chaff	3	8	4	1	0	1
Seeds	2	76	45	10	20	28
Items per litre	82.00	14.64	12.50	7.25	6.00	4.78

Table 5.16 Botanical evidence from Structure 11

Phase 9:   pit F467 (Enclosure 16), pit F2596 (Enclosure 6);
Phase 10:   post-hole *2461* (Enclosure 16), pit F1452 (Enclosure 12), pit F2601, pit F2622 (both Enclosure 6).

These sedge-rich contexts are widely distributed and usually within or associated with large, straight-sided pits, at the back of, or just outside enclosures. There are no characteristic associated taxa, but a varying admixture of other charred plants. The low amounts of other wetland plants include seeds of bog bean (*Menyanthes trifoliata*), black bog rush (*Schoenus nigricans*), true sedges (*Carex* spp.), common spikerush (*Eleocharis* cf. *palustris*), and *Cladium mariscus* itself. There are also large culm nodes of cereals, reeds (*Phragmites* sp.) or sedge. The association of sedge with cereal grain perhaps indicates that this was used as bread oven fuel, as documented in later periods (Rowell 1986).

Wild plant taxa
There is little change from the Saxon phases, although clover and red bartsia become more common; perhaps conditions were increasingly nutrient poor and damp. The cultivation of clay soils seems to have continued, with numerous seeds of stinking chamomile. One exceptional Phase 10 context (detailed below) shows good evidence for a rotation system in which common vetch was grown. The increase in legumes and docks could denote weed types which persisted from fallow periods into the cereal crops. High numbers of sedge and spikerush could be tied to the occurrence of sedge-fuel within some contexts. There is evidence for the greater influence of the fen, with a diverse range of wetland-associated taxa, though in low amounts. The seeds are not limited to sedge-rich contexts and include hairy buttercup (*Ranunculus sardous*), lesser spearwort (*R. flammula*), rushes *(Juncus* spp.) and water-plantain (*Alisma plantago-aquatica*). The rush seeds may represent use of the plant, perhaps as a light-source, in basketry, or for flooring (Mabey 1996). Two seeds of buckthorn (*Rhamnus cathartica*) in Phase 9 pit F1684 could indicate a specific use of this poisonous shrub, which is a source of dyes (Heywood 1978).

Notable feature assemblages
Pit F774 (Enclosure 16, Phase 10) produced a low number of mineralised seeds, probably preserved by phosphate salts indicating a high quantity of animal waste or rotting plants; this is the only sampled context identified as cess-rich during excavation that actually contained mineralised remains. The seeds are primarily of wild taxa: small-seeded docks (*Rumex conglomerates/obstutifolius/sanguineus*), and one possible forget-me-not (*Myosotis* sp.). Two stones of a primitive plum type (above, p.105) may represent human waste. A very low number of charred remains, mainly of seeds, are also present.

Pit F1368 (Enclosure 12, Phase 10), contains rich, well-preserved charred seeds that form a coherent assemblage, probably representing a single charring event (Table 5.17). There is a relatively low amount of grain, mostly of free-threshing wheat (79 grains), and an accompanying

amount of hexaploid wheat chaff (92 rachis internodes, of which 86 are hexaploid). Even when the 23 unidentified grains are included, the 'chaff to grain' ratio suggests that cereal chaff rather than ears were charred. A number of glume bases (chaff) of spelt wheat (*Triticum spelta*) are also well-preserved and appear specifically associated with this context.

The very high number of curled dock (*Rumex crispus*) seeds includes a small number of tepals (flower remains) which confirm the species identification. Several of the common vetch pulses exhibit minimal distortion from charring, and the testa and hilum remain intact; they compare well to cultivated types (*Vicia sativa* ssp. *sativa*). Knapweed seeds are identifiable here to greater knapweed (*Centaurea scabiosa*) and common knapweed (*Centaurea nigra*). Thistle seeds are identifiable to slender/welted thistle (*Carduus tenuiflorus/crispus*) and creeping thistle (*Cirsium arvense*). The range of wild taxa includes yellow-rattle (*Rhinanthus minor*) and contrasts markedly to all other samples; this may represent early cleaning of a threshed and winnowed wheat crop since:

a)   The cereal remains are dominated by free-threshing hexaploid wheat chaff (rachis internodes) with some grain. There is little straw (culm nodes) or light seeds which might be expected at winnowing. Some large sized culm nodes are present, and their good condition suggests that their absence in greater numbers is real and not a factor of preservation.

b)   Many of the seeds are large and heavy, and could be removed with coarse sieving (G. Jones 1984). Some smaller seeds, such as stinking chamomile, are held in seed heads and only break up once charred. Dock seeds are held within tepals and are 'large' until charred when the tepals break up. Despite many fragments of charlock pods there are very few seeds, which had perhaps remained within the grain product.

The wild seeds provide evidence of a rotation system that included a fodder crop of common vetch. The weeds of the fodder crop (dock, meadow-grass, yellow-rattle) and the vetch crop itself subsequently became weeds of cereal crops. Campbell (1994, 77) discusses the effects of crop rotation on wild flora, quoting Ellenburg (1988, 30), who suggested that the number of grasses and perennial weeds might be expected to increase in a field system including fallow, and Tusser (1557), who reported that docks and thistles were a particular problem on fallow land. Both these observations compare well to the flora outlined here.

Discussion
The cereal types show continuity with the preceding Saxon phases, with free-threshing wheat remaining significant. Cereal crops appear to have been treated in a similar manner at the site, with numerous grains and limited chaff exposed to charring during 'domestic' food preparation. The exceptional pit F1368 illustrates that common vetch was cultivated as a fodder crop, and that a crop rotation was undertaken. There is increasing evidence for the use of fen resources, most notably great fen sedge as a fuel. The sedge may well have had other uses, for example as thatching, but charred remains cannot demonstrate this. Low amounts of other fenland taxa, which could not be expected in arable contexts and are rarely charred, suggest that other fen resources were collected. The increased proportion of non-cereal taxa during Phases 9 and 10 seems tied to this increasingly diverse range of plants, most notably of collected sedge fuel.

Phases 11 and 12: 14th–15th centuries
Very few samples were collected from the later Phases 11 and 12 and three contexts, well F751 and layer *3565* (both Enclosure 16) and ditch F1012 (Enclosure 19/21), included sparse remains. Free-threshing wheat grain dominates, with lesser amounts of barley grain, and little chaff of either taxon. Wild plants are rare, but include vetch/wild pea, stinking chamomile, meadow-grass and great fen sedge. The pattern of charred remains thus mirrors the preceding Phases 9 and 10. Although well-base F751 (Phase 11) was not waterlogged it produced a number of mineralised duckweed seeds (*Lemna* sp.), showing that standing water had once been present.

The most important samples derive from basal fill *4515* and lower fill *4514* of the waterlogged well F729 (Phase 11: Fig. 5.2). The plant taxa present may be separated into those *in situ*, representing the local environment, and those introduced by human activities (Table 5.20). The insect remains from these two contexts have been identified by Dr. S. Clarke, University of Sheffield, and are discussed below (and detailed in the archive). Small faunal remains are discussed by Piper (above, p.99). Basal fill *4515* was relatively 'clean' despite its good organic preservation. The only abundant plant is black mustard (*Brassica nigra*), which is commonly found on disturbed and often damp ground. Other wild taxa associated with open disturbed ground are present, such as

Latin	English	Count
Rumex crispus	curled dock	1088
Anthemis cotula	stinking chamomile	558
Vicia sativa type	common vetch	13 & c.f. 249
Rhinanthus sp.	yellow-rattle	35
Vicia/Lathyrus sp. (2–4mm)	vetch/wild pea	29
Centaurea spp.	knapweed	27
Polygonaceae indet.	docks	24
Poa spp.	meadow grass	19
small *Trifolium* spp. (<2mm)	clover	13
Cladium mariscus	great fen sedge	10
Bromus sp.	brome grass	9
Carduus/Cirsium spp.	thistles	8
Convolvulus arvensis	field bindweed	2 & c.f. 1
Silene c.f. *vulgaris*	bladder campion	3
Silene nutans/latifolia	Nottingham/white catchfly	2
legume cotyledon fragments	pulses	50+ frags
Sinapis arvensis capsules	charlock seed-pods	10–50 frags

Table 5.19   Major, and selected lesser, wild taxa from F1368

Context	4514	4515	
Feature	F.729	F.729	
Description	lower well	base of well	
Sample volume/litres	12	0.5	
Fraction examined	1/4	1/4	Ecology
Waterlogged plant remains			
Ranunculus acris/bulbosus/repens	–	+	meadows
Ranunculus scleratus L.	–		marshy fields, ponds, ditches
Ranunculus flammula L.		–	all kinds of wet places
Thalictrum flavum L.	–		fens, streamsides, wet meadows
Cannabis sativa L.	–		cultivar/naturalised fibre/drug
Urtica dioica L.	++		disturbed & nitrogen rich
Urtica urens L.	++		disturbed
Myrica gale L.		+	bogs & fens, for flavouring
Chenopodium polyspermum L.		–	waste & cultivated ground
Chenopodium album L.	–		waste & cultivated ground
Atriplex patula/prostrata	++	–	waste & cultivated ground
Stellaria media (L.) Villars	++		cultivated & open ground
Stellaria sp.		–	-
Cerastium sp.	–		-
Agrostemma githago L.		–	cereal weed
Silene vulgaris/dioica/latifolia		–	-
Polygonum arviculare L.	+	+	open ground
Fallopia convolvulus (L.) Á. Löve	–		waste & arable ground
Rumex acetosella L.		–	open grassland or cultivated ground
Rumex hydropathalum Huds.	+		by lakes, rivers, canals,ditches
Rumex crispus L.		–	waste & rough ground, esp. damp
Rumex obstutifolius L.	+++		grassland, waste / cultv. ground
Rumex conglomeratus/obstutifolious/sanguineus	++	–	-
Malva sylvestris L.	++		waste & rough ground
Salix c.f. caprea scale	–		damp & rough ground
Brassica nigra (L.) W.D.J.Koch	+	+++	river banks, rough ground & waste
Sinapis arvensis L.	++	–	arable & waste land
Brassica indet. pod fragment		–	-
Anagallis arvensis L.	–		arable & waste land, open ground
Rubus subgen. RUBUS	–		-
Potentilla reptans L.		–	rough ground, hedgebanks, open
Epilobium sp.	–		-
Euphorbia peplus L.		–	cultivated & waste ground
Scandix pecten-veneris L.		–	arable & waste land
Pimpinella major (L.) Huds.		–	grassland, hedges, wood-borders
Conium maculatum L.	–		damp ground, roadsides, ditches
Bupleureum rotundifolium L.	–		cereal weed
Ballota nigra L.	++		hedgerows, waysides, rough ground
Galeopsis tetrahit L.	+		arable & rough ground, damp places
Plantago major L.	–	–	open & rough ground
Veronica hederifolia L.		–	cultivated and waste ground
Arctium sp.	+		variety of waste grounds
Carduus/Cirsium sp.	–	–	esp. rough ground/grassland
Centaurea scabiosa L.		–	grassland & rough ground
Leondoton autumnalis L.		–	grassland

Context	4514	4515	
Feature	F.729	F.729	
Description	lower well	base of well	
Sample volume/litres	12	0.5	
Fraction examined	1/4	1/4	Ecology
Sonchus asper (L.) Hill		−	waste & cultivated ground
Lactuca c.f. serriola		−	waste & rough ground
Taraxacum agg.	−		rough grassland
Anthemis cotula L.		−	arable & rough ground, clay soils
Tripleurospermum inodorum L.		−	waste & cultivated ground
Senecio c.f. erucifolius	−		grassy places, banks, waysides
Alisma plantago-aquaticum L.	−		in/by ponds, ditches, canals
Juncus sp.	+		damp ground
Eleocharis c.f. palustris	+	+	damp ground
Cladium mariscus (L.) Pohl.	+		wet areas in fens, and by streams
small trilete Carex sp.	+	−	damp ground
large trilete Carex sp.		−	damp ground
mid Poaceae indet.	−		-
Poaceae indet. vegetative frags.	+++	+++	-
moss fragments	++		
twigs	++	+	
buds	+		
Charred plant remains			
straight, hulled Hordeum vulgare s.l. grain	2 ch		barley
Cladium mariscus (L.) Pohl.	1 ch		great fen sedge
vegetative Cladium mariscus (L.) Pohl	1 ch		great fen sedge leaves/stem
Waterlogged coleoptera (beetles)			
Nebria sp.	1		
Bembidion sp.	1		
Harpalus rufipes Deg.	1		Open country – apparently dominant ground beetle of open ground
Harpalus (Ophonus) sp.	1	1	Open country
Pterostichus (Poecilus) versicolor (Strm.)	1		Open fields (likes water)
Pterostichus melanarius (Ill.)	1		Open country – not too dry
Agonum dorsale (Pont.)	1		Open country – cultivated fields
Agonum sp.	1		moisture
Amara eurynota (Panz.)	1		Open country – cultivated fields, especially amongst weeds
Chlaenius tristis (Schal.)	1		bogs and fens, lake shores – lush vegetation
Megasternum boletophagum Marsh.	1		dung and decaying vegetation
Cercyon sp.		1	decaying organic matter
Orthoperidae indet.	1	1	wet vegetation
Proteinus brachypterus (F.)	1		fungi and decaying vegetation
Anotylus sp.	1		decaying organic matter
Platystethus sp.	1		dung/muddy banks
Lathrobium sp.	1		moisture
Xantholinus linearis (Ol.)	2		hay refuse
Philonthus spp.	2		decaying organic matter
Staphylinus sp.	1		
Aleocharinae gen. indet.	2		decaying organic matter
Cantharidae indet.	1		
Athous spp.	1		woodland margins
Scirtidae indet.	2		moisture
Cryptophagus spp.	4	2	decaying organic matter – especially in hay and barns
Stephostethus c.f. lardarius (Deg.)	2		rotting straw bales etc.

Context	4514	4515	
Feature	F.729	F.729	
Description	lower well	base of well	
Sample volume/litres	12	0.5	
Fraction examined	1/4	1/4	Ecology
Lathridius sp.	1	1	hay and straw refuse (mould feeders)
Anobium punctatum (Deg.)		1	woodworm or furniture beetle, partial to structural timbers
Ernobius sp.	1		wood
Tipnus unicolor (Pill.)	2	1	mainly synanthropic – found in barns in hay refuse, feeds in rotting wood
Ptinus fur (L.)	3	1	mainly synanthropic – stored products, granaries
Anthicus antherinus (L.)	2		hay and vegetation refuse
Aphodius spp.	2		dung
Phyllotreta vittula Redt.	2		pest on cereals – open country
Batophila rubi (Payk.)	2		On Rubus spp.
Psylliodes spp.	5		Cultivated fields
Bruchus sp.	1		Open country – legumes
Leperisinus orni Fuchs	1		associated with ash – found in broadleaved and pasture woodland
Apion (Aspidapion) aeneum (F.)	2		Malva sylvestris – dry weedy places
Apion spp.	12		open country
Phyllobius sp.	1		
Strophosoma spp.	2		
Sitona lepidus Gyll.	1		on clover (Trifolium spp.) waste places, grassland and agricultural soils
Hypera postica (Gyll.)	1		on clover (Trifolium & Medicago spp.)
Hypera sp.	1		open country
Ceutorhynchus contractus (Marsh.)	1		Brassicaceae, Sisymbrium spp. in winter found in grass tussocks
Ceutorhynchus spp.	7		
Waterlogged diptera (True Flies)			
Heleomyzidae		4	putrefying animal matter
Sepsidae		1	putrefying animal matter
Sphaerocaridae		3	putrefying animal matter
Scatopse notata		9	putrefying animal matter
c.f. Calliphoridae gen indet	1		Blow fly pupae (decaying animal matter)
Hemiptera			
Pentatomidae	2		
Diptera	2		

Table 5.20 Waterlogged remains from F729; insects identified by Dr Sarah Clark

knotweed (*Polygonum arviculare*), but occur in exceptionally low quantities. Black mustard seed has also been cultivated as food seasoning (Greig 1988), and it remains possible that the high numbers may represent small-scale cultivation in the vicinity of the well, or activities associated with use of the seeds. The aromatic shrub bog myrtle (*Myrica gale*) is also present as seeds. Bog myrtle grows upon wet, peaty soils in the fens and the seeds probably represent debris from cuttings which had been brought to the site. There are records of bog myrtle leaves being used as flavouring during brewing (Greive 1980), and the fruits were also recovered from a 10th–12th-century pit in Lincoln (Greig 1991).

Both insect and small faunal remains from *4515* are few, and the context appears to have been kept clear of most ecofactual material. The presence of a stone superstructure may have excluded surface debris, and the well itself may have been periodically cleaned. Of those insects present, the beetle remains strongly suggest a nearby building. Several taxa are specifically associated with decaying hay or straw, particularly *Cryptophagus* spp., *Lathridius* sp., *Tipnus unicolor* and *Ptinus fur*. One woodworm beetle, *Anobium punctatum*, is also present. A number of Dipteran pupae associated with putrefying animal matter have been recovered from *4515*. The larvae may have burrowed into this context from overlying *4514* in order to pupate, the overlying layer containing numerous trapped small fauna (*Small vertebrates*, p.99).

Overlying fill *4514* shows a rise in the range of plant and insect taxa, which may have corresponded with dereliction of the well. The

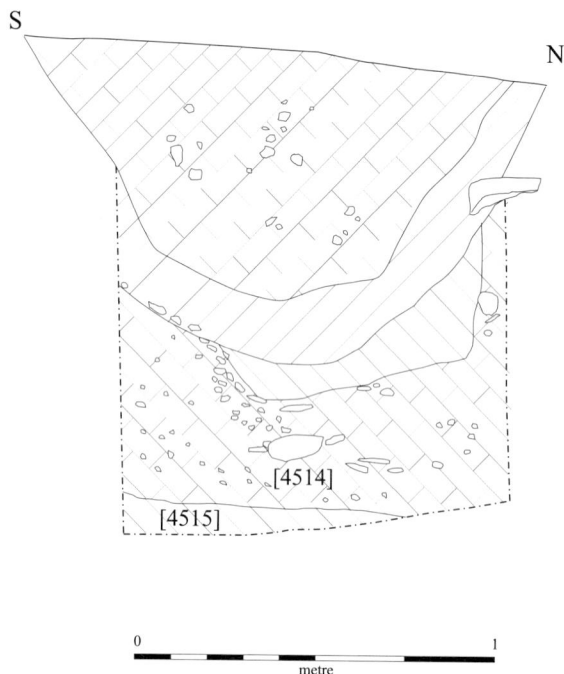

Figure 5.2 Section through well F729, Phase 11

most significant group of plants are those associated with wasteland. Nettles (*Urtica dioica*, *U. urens*), orache (*Atriplex patula/prostrata*), chickweed (*Stellaria media*) and broad-leaved dock (*Rumex obstutifolius*) all occur in abundance. Other significant taxa include mallow (*Malva sylvestris*), charlock (*Sinapis arvensis*) and black horehound (*Ballota nigra*). Although the range of taxa still suggest an open environment it was overgrown, as further attested by bramble (*Rubus* subgen. *RUBUS*). Plants of damp soils, including rushes (*Juncus* spp.), spike-rush (*Eleocharis* c.f. *palustris*) and true sedges (*Carex* spp.), are also frequent. Several seeds of hemp (*Cannabis sativa*) in *4514* could represent a cultivated or feral plant. There are good archaeobotanical and historical records of the growing of hemp for fibre, particularly in East Anglia, during the medieval period (Greig 1991; Bradshaw *et al*. 1981; Peglar 1993). The seeds from the well are few and appear to be debris from plants growing nearby, rather than from retting.

A diverse range of beetles have also been recovered from *4514*. A number of taxa associated with barns, straw or hay are still present, including *Xanotholinus linearis*, *Cryptophagus* sp., *Stephostethus* cf. *lardarius*, *Lathridius* sp., *Tipnus unicolor, Ptinus fur* and *Anthicus antherinus*. These types suggest the continuing presence and use of a nearby barn (perhaps Structure 29: Chapter 4, p.51). Many other taxa indicate the local environment as being open, although they are only represented by individuals. *Agonum dorsale*, *Amara eurynota*, and *Psyllides* spp. are associated with open cultivated fields, *Phyllotreta vittula* specifically with cereal crops. Such species may have been introduced to the well with hay or straw debris, or could represent cultivated fields nearby. The absence of waterlogged straw or hay waste itself suggests that the latter interpretation may be more apt.

Discussion

The botanical assemblage provides good Saxon and medieval evidence for farming activities on the fen-edge. Although some trends may be observed, they are subsumed within a broad pattern of charred remains which are largely unchanged during Periods II and III (late 7th–14th centuries).

Food plants

The majority of information regards cereal crops, which were exposed relatively frequently to charring conditions (Fig. 5.4). Other plant types such as fruits and vegetables are poorly represented but were probably also of importance. The abundance of certain plants in the assemblage reflects their frequency of exposure to charring conditions, and not directly their importance within the local economy.

During all examined phases wheat cereals are most significant, although there is a shift from hulled to free-threshing wheat types between the Roman and Mid Saxon contexts (Phases 3 and 5). The early remains from Phases 2 and 3 represent a different crop-processing stage and so any comparison with later phases should be treated with care. The charred remains from Phase 5 onwards represent primarily free-threshing cereals, with very similar processing sequences that are broadly comparable. The widest range of cereals occurs during the early 8th to mid-9th centuries (Phase 5) when charred free-threshing wheat, rye and barley grains are all well represented. Oats are difficult to confirm or disregard as a cultivated cereal from all phases due to the lack of speciable chaff, and their occurrence as both crops and arable weeds. From the mid-9th to the 14th–15th centuries (Phases 7–12) free-threshing wheat grain was increasingly abundant, whilst rye was less frequently charred.

The increasing medieval predominance of wheat suggests a selective emphasis towards cereals most suited to local arable conditions. Weed flora at the site (below, p.112) clearly indicate that crops were cultivated upon local heavy clay soils. These conditions would not favour rye, which flourishes upon well-drained light soils. The remains at West Fen Road support the observation by Murphy (1997) that although a similar range of crops are found at many earlier Saxon sites, each area rapidly developed its own range of crops suited to its needs and the local environment. Mid Saxon contexts at Brandon, Suffolk (Murphy 1994) contained large quantities of rye relative to grain, which corresponds well with the light sandy soils in this area. At Cottenham, Cambs (Mortimer 1998), the Late Saxon contexts included greater amounts of rye and barley than have been recovered at West Fen Road. The site was located on greensand above the River Great Ouse, and weed flora appeared to indicate local cultivation on these well-drained soils.

The re-appearance of spelt wheat during the 12th–13th centuries (Phases 9 and 10) is an interesting development. The cereal was of importance at West Fen Road during the Roman and Iron Age phases, but appears to have ceased cultivation during the Saxon period. Murphy (1997) notes the absence of spelt at many Mid Saxon sites in East Anglia, although it is present in some Late Saxon contexts at (for example) Springfield Lyons, Essex. There is debate as to the medieval role of hulled wheats in Britain. Two possibilities are that it was cultivated for animal fodder (Peña-Chocarro and Zapata-Peña 1998), or for certain wheat beers (Hillman 1982; Greig 1988). No indication of usage is provided by the low quantities recovered here.

Other cultivated resources are poorly represented. Celtic beans first occur in Roman contexts, but are particularly common in the Saxon phases. Neither peas nor lentils were recovered at West Fen Road, although both were recorded from contemporary phases at Cottenham (Mortimer 1998). A mineralised primitive plum stone in a 12th-century cess-pit is the only evidence of fruit. The abundant waterlogged black mustard seed in a 13th–14th-century well may indicate cultivation of the plant for seasoning purposes. Seeds of flax in several Late

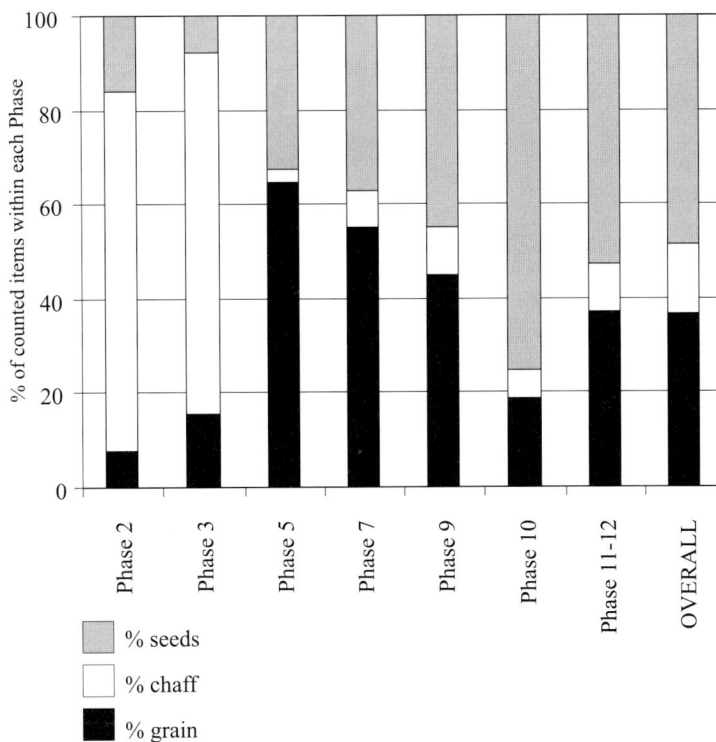

Figure 5.3 Summary of charred plant composition by phase

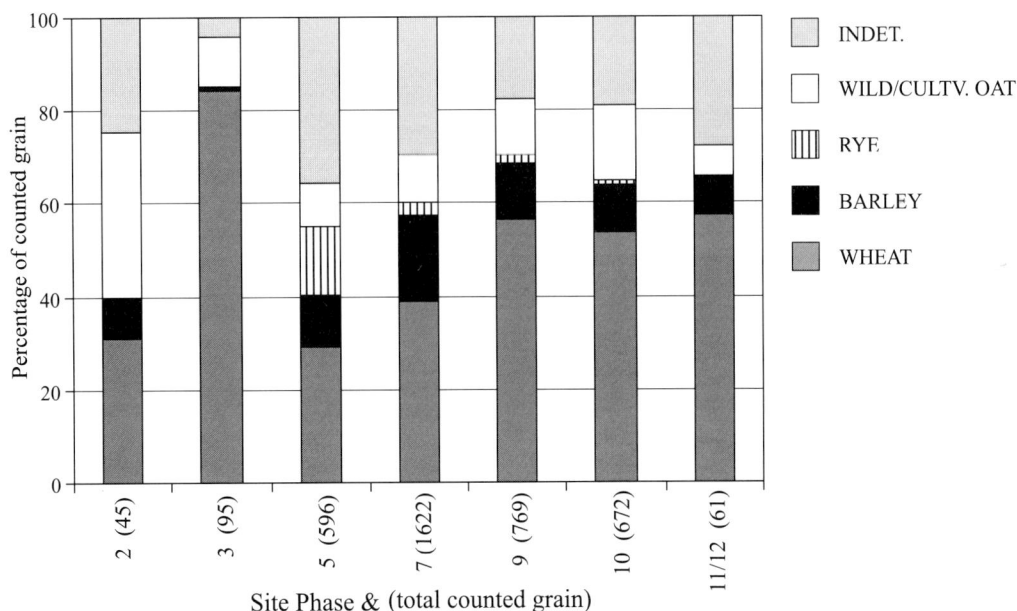

Figure 5.4 Summary of charred grain types by phase

Saxon contexts indicate its presence, although the plant may have been cultivated for fibre or food.

The variety of cereals and legumes corresponds well to types represented elsewhere in Saxon East Anglia (Murphy 1997), although the emphasis on free-threshing wheat appears to have been locally specific. A very similar range of crops was recovered from a 13th-century farm on clay soils at Stansted, Essex (Murphy 1990) and from West Cotton, Northants (Campbell 1994). There is therefore good evidence for the consumption of locally cultivated cereals at this fen-edge settlement.

Cultivation strategies
Charred seeds of the arable weed flora provide evidence for cultivation practices. The charred wild taxa clearly represent an admixture of sources, particularly in 12th- and 13th-century contexts when ash from sedge fuel also exists (Fig. 5.5).

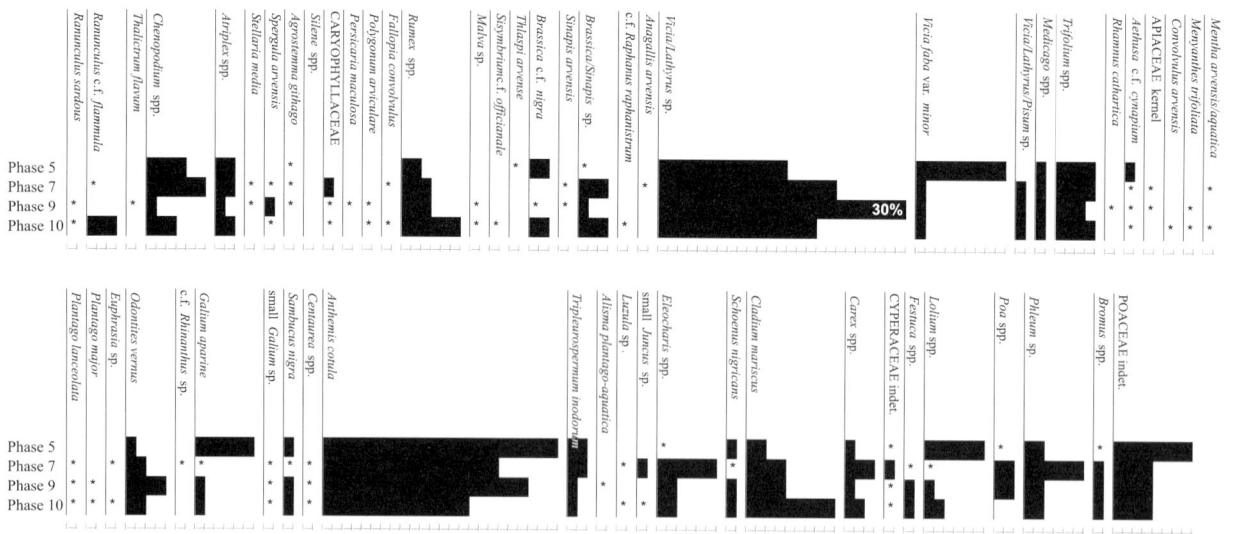

Figure 5.5 Summary of non-cereal taxa; each increment represents 1% of the count within a phase

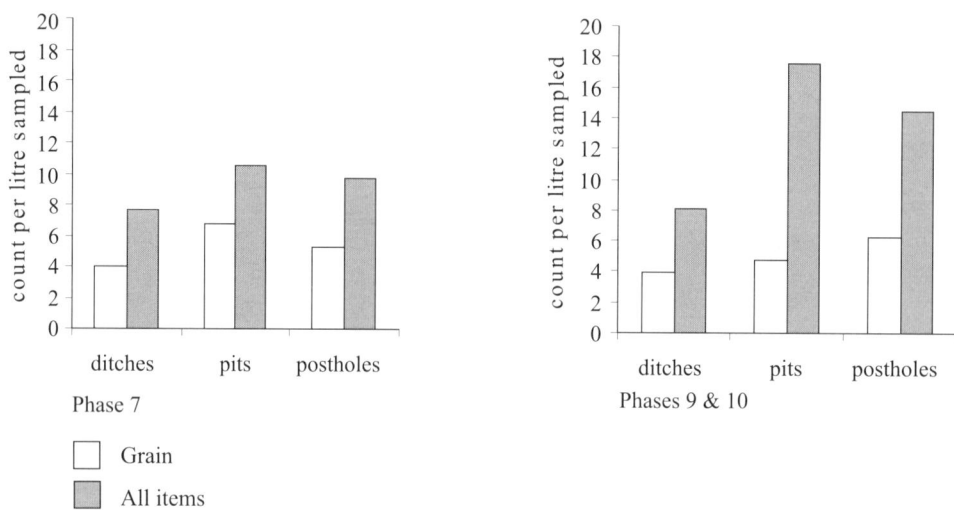

Figure 5.6 Summary of charred remains by feature type

Many of the taxa represent charred seeds of harvested weeds. This is not a direct representation of plants growing in cereal fields, but a transformation effected by harvesting method, crop-processing, and charring itself. One context, F1368 has been excluded from the calculations for Phase 10, since it represents a markedly different crop-processing stage. Most contexts are grain-rich with little chaff, and represent comparable products in which most seeds had been removed by threshing, winnowing and sieve-cleaning. The most frequent taxon, stinking chamomile (*Anthemis cotula*), is regarded as an indicator of heavy clay soils (Hanf 1983); this both reflects the local soils and suggests cereals were grown nearby. Another consistently represented weed, red bartsia (*Odontites vernus*), is characteristic of damp arable soils and suggests that some other wetland plants may be weeds of the cereal crops. Both common spike-rush (*Eleocharis palustris*) and true sedges (*Carex* spp.) do not increase notably in Phase 10 when sedge ash

(of *Cladium mariscus*) becomes significant, and their presence seems independent of this phenomenon. M. Jones (1984b) has suggested that spike-rush could tolerate damp arable conditions, particularly on field margins, and it has been recorded as such in experimental crops (Hinton 1991).

One particularly large group of weeds are the legumes, characteristic of nitrogen-poor soils where many of these species have an advantage over other plants. The most common types are of vetches and wild peas (*Vicia/Lathyrus* sp.), although both clovers (*Trifolium* spp.) and medicks (*Medicago* spp.) are also present. There appears a gradual increase in legumes through the medieval phases, and the 12th-century contexts (Phase 9) are particularly rich. One Phase 10 pit included numerous seeds of cultivated common vetch (*Vicia sativa* ssp. *sativa*) with a range of taxa characteristic of fallow land. The remains appear to be sieve-cleanings from cereals which had been grown as part of a crop-rotation system.

110

The high numbers of vetch/wild pea types noted in earlier phases may also be associated with use of legumes in a crop rotation system, rather than simply cultivation of nutrient-poor soils. The accompanying increase of docks (*Rumex* spp.) in Phase 10 is further good evidence for a crop-rotation system involving fallow; many docks thrive on disturbed, but not regularly ploughed, land.

Fenland resources

Although individual late 7th- to mid-12th-century contexts (Phases 5 and 7) comprise rich charred remains of great fen sedge leaves (*Cladium mariscus*), it is only during the 12th–13th centuries (Phases 9 and 10) that such contexts become numerous. A corresponding increase in the range (although not in the quantities) of wetland taxa occurs. Associated charred wetland plants include bog bean (*Menyanthes trifoliata*), common meadow-rue (*Thalictrum flavum*), water plantain (*Alisma plantago-aquatica*) and black bog-rush (*Schoenus nigricans*). There are good historical accounts for the use of great fen sedge as a fuel from the 17th century onwards (Rowell 1986), although the earliest records date to the 14th century (*ibid.*). The charred remains at West Fen Road indicate that the use of sedge fuel was common in post-Conquest times, and may have had Saxon origins. The increased use of sedge in the 12th–13th centuries could have been associated with changes in land tenure, or the limited availability of other fuels such as wood. Perhaps there was also increased appreciation for sedge as a fuel which burns rapidly, producing high temperatures ideal for ovens and kilns. The reality may well have comprised all these factors. Historical accounts also state that sedge was widely used for thatching and as ground-cover (Rowell 1986), although the rich charred remains appear to directly relate to its use as a fuel.

Contextual and spatial patterning of charred plant remains

The very complex stratigraphy encountered during excavation meant that it was impractical to carry out detailed spatial sampling. Two areas of Late Saxon activity (Phase 7) were intensively sampled, and these suggest that charred remains were associated with the post-built structures (above, p.105). The grain-rich contexts suggest food preparation activities, and so a possible domestic purpose for these structures.

Within the 12th–13th-century contexts (Phases 9 and 10) the character of the archaeological features themselves changes substantially, and most samples are now derived from pits. Two similar groups of large, squared pits were targeted for sampling, in Enclosure 16 (Phase 9) and Enclosure 6 (Phases 9 and 10). They vary markedly in terms of charred remains and show that a variety of deposition events created their fills. In order to broadly compare the Saxon and medieval evidence, the feature types have been summarised by charred composition (Fig. 5.6). No distinction has been made between ditches or pits associated with structures and those more distant, so the analysis is rudimentary. However, it is clear that substantial amounts of non-cereal remains are present in Phases 9 and 10, which are less common in Phase 7 contexts. The most significant amounts of non-cereal materials occur in Phase 9 and 10 pits and post-holes, and may be associated with the identified amounts of sedge ash. Greater amounts of

charred debris from crop-processing (weed seeds and chaff) are also present in these later phases. The increased presence of cereal chaff may denote a change in storage practices or the location of processing activities. It may be that crop processing was more displaced from the main settlement during the Saxon period but was brought closer to it in medieval times, leading to a rise in associated charred debris. Insect remains from the 13th–14th-century well F729 suggest barns were nearby at this date.

The local environment

The presence of few waterlogged contexts has provided only limited information on the local environment. Plant and insect macro-remains from the 13th–14th-century well F729 indicate open, rough grassland, with a nearby barn and possible arable land. The pollen recovered from a Late Saxon period context (*Pollen*, p.114) compares well to the contemporary charred weed flora. The numerous cabbage/charlock types (*Brassica/Sinapis* sp.) identified within both sources of evidence in particular support the interpretation that there was arable land nearby.

Conclusions

The charred remains overwhelmingly represent food-preparation activity at the site. There is no evidence of any large-scale processing of cereals or other plant resources. Threshing and winnowing may have been undertaken away from the site, perhaps in the fields. It is also possible that straw and chaff were regarded as resources, for example animal fodder and bedding, and protected from charring conditions.

The predominance of weeds characteristic of clay soils, combined with the emphasis on wheat rather than rye or barley, suggests that crops suited to the local conditions were favoured during both the Saxon and medieval periods. Both cultivated and wild plant resources appear to have been procured locally and not imported. There is good evidence for increased specialisation during the 12th–13th centuries: free-threshing wheat became a markedly predominant cereal, crop-rotation involving a vetch 'green manure' was undertaken, and fenland products were utilised in far greater quantities.

These changes suggest that the economic position of the settlement shifted during the medieval period, with respect to land rights or the need to raise capital. The specialisation reflects emphasis upon the cereal (wheat) which could thrive best on heavy clay soils, suggesting that some grain may have been produced to meet external demand. Sedge fuel (*Cladium mariscus*) may indicate that access to woodland had been curtailed or limited, whether by land rights, or simply depletion of local resources. Hundred Rolls for 13th-century Wicken, Ely, record areas of Commoners Land in the marsh. Within early 15th-century manorial records some areas are specifically described as sedge fen (Friday 1997, 193–4). The allocation of equivalent rights to fenland near West Fen Road may have facilitated the availability and use of sedge as a fuel.

In summary, the late 7th- to mid 12th-century arable activity at West Fen Road compares well to that associated with other contemporary settlements upon clay soils (*i.e.* Murphy 1990; Campbell 1994). Although the occasional sedge-rich context hints at the use of fen plants, these resources were incorporated within a strategy for subsistence that was focused upon clay soils, not the fenland. It was only during the 12th–13th centuries that both the diversity and intensity in use of fenland plant resources occurred. Not only was sedge frequently used as an oven or kiln fuel, but buckthorn and bog myrtle were brought to the site. At West Fen Road a truly 'fenland' economy with respect to plant resources was thus a 12th–13th-century phenomenon.

VI. Pollen
by Robert G. Scaife

Only three pollen samples were examined from the site, two of which relate to the Phase 3 occupation and one to the medieval period (further samples were destroyed by arson: see Chapter 1). Sub-samples of 1–2ml volume were prepared in the laboratory using standard procedures for the extraction of sub-fossil pollen and spores (Moore and Webb 1978; Moore *et al.* 1991). Pollen was generally very sparse and typical assessment counts of 100–150 grains per level (the pollen sum), plus all extant marsh/aquatic taxa and spores of ferns, were obtained with difficulty.

Taxonomy in general follows that of Moore and Webb (1978), modified according to Bennet *et al.* (1994) for pollen types and Stace (1997) for plant descriptions.

Ditch F1573 (*8575/8576*) Phase 3
Pollen was poorly preserved and sparse in this profile and consequently somewhat inadequate totals of *c.* 50 grains of dry land taxa (pollen sum) were counted for each level. However, two local pollen assemblage zones can be recognised in this sequence.

Zone 1. (48–28cm): Delimited high values of *Trifolium* type with higher percentage values of trees which include *Quercus* (to 38% in the basal level), *Fraxinus* (to 3%). Other trees include sporadic occurrences of *Betula, Pinus, Alnus,* and *Corylus* type. Herbs are, however, dominant throughout comprising the *Trifolium* type noted and dominant *Poaceae* (increasing to 50%). Cereal type (<5%) is present. Spores of ferns comprise monolete *Dryopteris* type with some *Pteridium aquilinum*. There are substantial numbers of derived/pre-Quaternary palynomorphs.

Zone 2. (28–4cm): Values of *Quercus* and *Trifolium* type are reduced, the latter to absence. *Poaceae* remains the dominant taxon increasing to 56%. There are also increases in *Lactucoideae* (to 28%) and in *Ranunculus* type, *Rumex, Scrophulariaceae* and *Centaurea scabiosa* type. There is also an increase in spores of *Pterdium aquilinum*.

Ditch F2051 (*8632*) Phase 3
Although there are some variations of the pollen in this profile, with values of *Quercus*, Chenopodiaceae and herb diversity being higher in the lower levels (below 20cm), these differences were not considered significant enough to warrant pollen zonation of this profile. Overall, herbs are dominant with high values of *Poaceae* (av. 40%), *Lactucoideae* (to 30%) and *Sinapis* type (22%) the latter being more important in the upper levels. The importance of Chenopodiaceae in the lower part of the sequence has been mentioned. Cereal pollen represents less than 5% of recorded palynomorphs. *Secale cereale* is of note at the top of the profile. Marsh/aquatic types are not abundant, but include *Typa angustifolia/Sparganium* and Cyperaceae (6%). Spores are consistent with *Pteridium aqilinum, Dryopteris* type and occasional *Polypodium vulgare*. Derived geological palynomorphs are abundant.

The generally inorganic sediments and the lack of peat in the profiles examined indicate that any pollen found may have had a complex taphonomy, coming from any one of several airborne, fluvial and colluvial sources. This is reflected in all of the profiles, which have large numbers of palynomorphs derived from the local geological bedrock. However, the contained pollen may provide evidence particularly of the local vegetation adjacent to these contexts. Sadly, pollen was sparse due to the alkalinity and the possible periodic drying-out and oxidation of the sediment, both of which are highly deleterious to pollen preservation.

Given that the section from ditch F1573 is of the earliest Romano-British phase, it is perhaps not surprising that trees and shrubs are more abundant in this period. *Quercus* (oak) was most important, and especially in the lowest level of the profile where values are higher than in any of the three sections examined. Other trees present in this period occur only sporadically. *Betula* (birch), *Pinus* (pine), *Alnus* (alder) and *Corylus* (hazel) are present but all are wind-pollinated, and as such are usually over-represented in the pollen spectra (Anderson 1970, 1973). Small totals here suggest they were not important locally. *Fraxinus* (ash), however, is markedly under-represented and even the small values in pollen zone 1 may indicate local importance. There is a progressive reduction in the main tree types (oak and ash) and this may indicate continued woodland clearance during the time span represented by the profile. Earlier in the late prehistoric period it is likely (on the basis of other regional data) that lime woodland with oak and hazel would have been important. Contrasting with this is the expansion of herbs, which are dominated by *Poaceae* (grasses) with *Trifolium* type (vetches) and *Lactucoideae* (dandelion types). Whilst the latter may also be enhanced through poor pollen preservation, these taxa are strongly indicative of local grassland/pasture. The sharp reduction in *trifolium* from 32cm remains unexplained but could relate to changes in immediately local fields, since pollen from this taxon is not likely to travel great distances in quantity. Percentages of cereal type indicate the use and growth of cereals but it is probable that this cultivation was not in proximity to the site. Furthermore, it is possible that this pollen could have come from secondary sources such as crop-processing (threshing and winnowing) liberating pollen trapped in the husks of the grain, or from domestic refuse including animal and human faeces.

In later Roman times, as represented by ditch F2051, there were few trees, with *Quercus* the only taxon with consistent presence, albeit with values less than 10% and also declining in the upper levels. There are only sporadic occurrences of other tree types from non-local growth — *Betula* (birch), *Pinus* (pine), *Alnus* (alder) and *Corylus* type (hazel and sweet gale). Herbs are dominant with *Poaceae* (grasses) and *Lactucoideae* (dandelion types), with *Plantago lanceolata* (ribwort plantain) suggesting dominance locally of pasture similar to that discussed for the earlier phase. Here, however, there are also substantial values of *Sinapis* type and stronger representation of cereal pollen (including *Secale cereale* — oats — at the top of the profile) and weeds which are typical of arable habitats. The latter includes, for example, *Polygonum aviculare* type (black bindweed) and Chenopodiaceae (goosefoots). The unusually high values of *Sinapis* type (*Brassicaceae*/charlocks) are interesting and it would be of great value to ascertain (from plant macrofossils/seeds) which plant this pollen comes from.

F2197 Phase 9 (Enclosure 11/18)
Counts of 100 grains per level were obtained except in the top sample (0–1cm). Pollen preservation was, however, poor in this top level, reflected by the small counts and the increasing abundance of *Lactucoideae* through the effects of differential preservation and destruction of thin walled/less robust grains. The main part of the profile is homogenous and no pollen assemblage zones were designated. The pollen spectra are characterised by high values of *Sinapis* type (to 48% at 16cm), Poaceae (to 37%) with expanding *Lactucae* and cereal type (to 7%). *Typha/Sparganium* and Cyperaceae are the only marsh/wetland taxa. Spores of ferns such as *Lactucoideae* become more important at the top of the profile, and this is also noted with spores of *Pteridium* and *Dryopteris* type. There are very large numbers of derived geological palynomorphs.

During the Late Saxon and medieval periods there were few trees, with only very small numbers of oak and sporadic alder. These values are substantially smaller than seen in the preceding Romano-British profiles. Grasses, dandelion types and charlocks are all important. Dandelion types may, however, reflect the poor pollen preservation in the uppermost/oxidised archaeological levels and thus differential preservation in favour of this taxon. As with the later Romano-British profile, the high percentages of charlocks is enigmatic. Such values are unusually high and this taxon is usually regarded as an indication of arable habitats (*i.e.* being an arable weed). The presence of cereal pollen (to 9%) and other weeds such as knotweed types and goosefoots suggest local arable cultivation.

Conclusions

In earlier Roman times the remaining woodland comprised oak and possibly ash, and suffered clearance. There is evidence of pastoral/grassland habitats, perhaps becoming more important. Small numbers of cereals show use but possibly not local growth in any quantity and may derive from secondary origins. By the later Roman period, there was little remaining oak woodland locally or at a distance. There was then strong evidence of pastoral habitats (segetal weeds especially charlocks) but also increased arable habitats with growth of cereals which include oats. During the Late Saxon/medieval period, there were smaller numbers of trees than in either of the preceding Roman period profiles. Only sporadic oak and hazel are represented, demonstrating a very open agricultural local landscape.

6. Discussion

I. Introduction

Chapter 2 outlined the prehistoric and Roman occupation and activity recorded by the CAU excavations to the south of West Fen Road: an intermittent Mesolithic/Neolithic and Bronze Age presence, enclosures and finds indicating intensive Iron Age activity nearby, and a heavily disturbed Roman enclosure complex within Area B. The pottery and building material suggest that a relatively low status rural settlement was in occupation throughout the Roman period, but with intensification in the 3rd and 4th centuries. Thereafter the site appears to have been abandoned during the 5th–7th centuries, prior to the establishment of a larger settlement in the Mid Saxon period, whose layout was partly determined by the pre-existing Roman enclosure ditches and earthworks, at least to the south of West Fen Road. The present chapter will discuss the evidence presented in Chapter 3 for the buildings and other archaeological features of Periods II and III, for the economic and environmental milieu of the site from the 8th century onwards, and for the developing role of West Fen Road as a routeway.

II. Archaeological features
(Figs 6.1–6.6)

The first impression to be gained from perusing the overall plan is of a site where the features are mostly ditches, an impression apparently confirmed by the context register where 66% of over 8000 recorded contexts relate to ditches, gullies and similar features. However, over a thousand contexts relate to pits and another thousand to structural elements such as post-holes and beam-slots. There are 250 contexts relating to layers and spreads, over a hundred to wells and ponds, and eighty to roads and paths (Fig. 6.1). There is evidence for 29 structures, with another nine conjectured, as well as for smaller-scale structural elements such as fence-lines, palisades and racks. At all periods (save the Early Saxon) from the Iron Age to the 14th century the site was occupied, and all activity phases bar Phase 3 (the Romano-British) featured clear evidence for domestic buildings. The main elements of the Saxon and medieval archaeology are discussed in broad terms by feature type, the Iron Age and Roman features having been discussed already in Chapter 2.

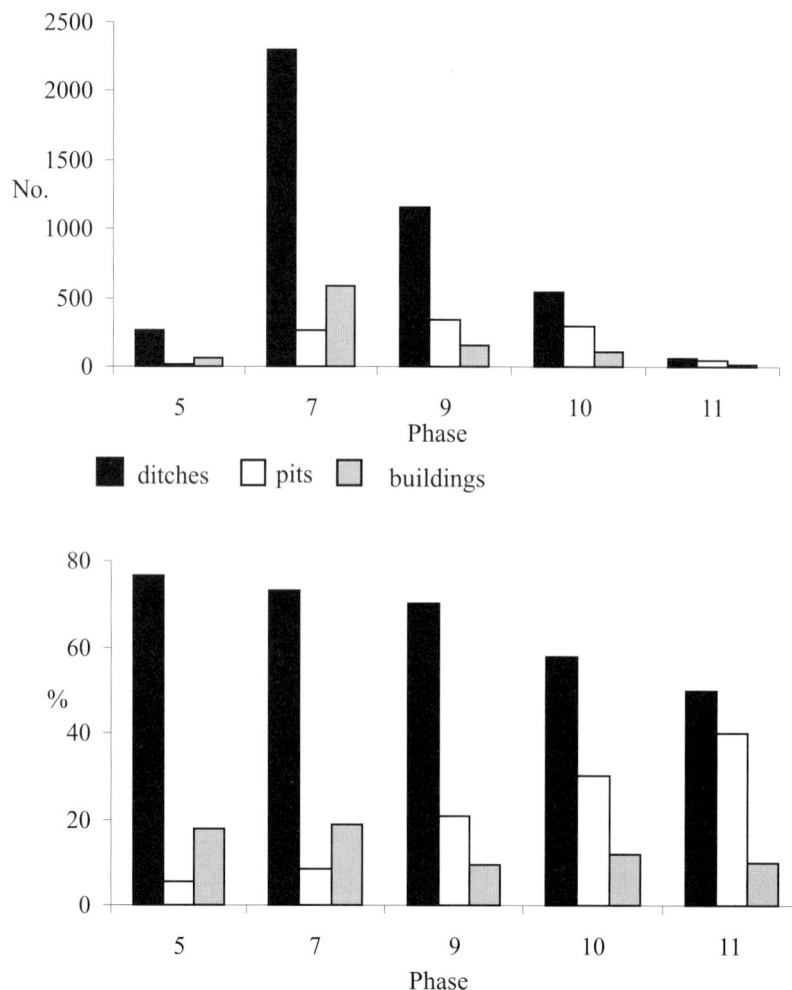

Figure 6.1 Number and percentage of contexts relating to feature types by phase

Phase / Enclosure	5 N/S	5 E/W	5 Sq. m	6 N/S	6 E/W	6 Sq. m	8 N/S	8 E/W	8 Sq. m	9 N/S	9 E/W	9 Sq. m	10 N/S	10 E/W	10 Sq. m	11 N/S	11 E/W	11 Sq. m	12 N/S	12 E/W	12 Sq. m
1	55	>60	3300	70	>40	2800	70	>35	2450	30	>30	900	30	>30	900						
2	80	>30	2400	90	>20	1800	75	>20	1500	55	>15	825	45	>15	675						
3	60	75	4500	75	50	3750	80	40	3200	85	80	6800									
4	55	55	3025	80	55	4400	85	55	4675	105	30	3150	100	30	3000						
5	60	55	3300	70	50	3500	70	40	2800	25	>20	500	25	>20	500						
6	50	>100	5000	50	>20	1000	60	>20	1200	75	>50	3750	70	>50	3500						
7	50	>80	4000	55	>75	4125	65	>30	1950												
8	75	135	10125																		
9				110	45	4950	110	55	6050	150	35	5250	60	50	3000						
10				55	50	2750	60	60	3600	60	50	3000	55	65	3575						
11				40	65	2600	40	>55	2200	50	85	4250	35	45	1575						
12				55	35	1925	90	40	3600	30	90	2700				35	75	2625			
13				55	55	3025	55	70	3850												
14				45	45	2025	45	>35	1575	55	>50	2750									
15							50	40	2000												
16							25	125	3125	35	100	3500	40	115	4600	40	115	4600			
17										155	70	10850	160	>100	16000	170	100	17000	205	115	23575
18										25	105	2625	30	>50	1500	65	55	3575			
19													70	120	8400	135	115	15525	165	115	18975
20													30	80	2400						
21																100	>100	10000	160	115	18400
			35650			**38650**			**43775**			**50850**			**49625**			**53325**			**60950**

Table 6.1 Table showing approximate dimensions of enclosures by phase (all in metres)

115

When discussing the size and depth of the features, it should be noted that all features were only recorded in detail below the level of the machine-stripped surface, and some were originally seen higher up in the soil sequence. In Area A, some features may have once been up to 0.40m deeper than recorded, and in Area B, 0.30m.

Enclosures and paddocks

A number of near-contemporary sites display evidence for major boundary ditches from the 7th century onwards. Flixborough (Lincs) featured a major ditched enclosure in its Phase 2 (late 7th–8th century: Loveluck 2001, 85), but not in later phases (*ibid.*, 108); the same is true of Catholme in Staffordshire (Losco-Bradley and Kinsley 2002). The latest phase at West Stow (Suffolk) also produced evidence for U-shaped enclosure ditches (West 1985, 54), although since these were dated by Ipswich ware they would appear to belong in the 8th century rather than the 7th. Before considering the ditches at West Fen Road in detail, it is worth pausing to consider their function. Many of the major ditches form the boundaries to enclosures. Approximate sizes for these enclosures are detailed in Table 6.1, and these were surprisingly consistent over time. Many of the enclosures were between 45m and 60m wide, and the occupied enclosures (as opposed to those taken up by paddocks or otherwise given over to agriculture) exhibit a similar range of sizes across the Saxon and medieval phases. From Phase 5 onwards, there is thus evidence for some degree of planning, and for continuity of use and occupation. Other British sites show similar evidence for Mid Saxon planned enclosures. At Goltho in Lincolnshire, the pre-manorial settlement featured large rectangular enclosures along the side of a trackway (Beresford 1987, 23). Cottam in East Yorkshire provides another good example of a relatively early ditched farmstead (Richards 1999), with a trapezoidal enclosure (the earliest associated find being a styca of AD 737) aligned on a trackway. Like West Fen Road it had been remodelled, probably in the early 9th century, with a more substantial ditched and banked enclosure; the earlier post-built halls were replaced (*ibid.*, 89). Further Late Saxon sites are known with similar features: examples include North Elmham Period III (Wade-Martins 1980), West Cotton (Selkirk 1987, 338–9), Wicken Bonhunt (Wade 1980, 100–2), Little Paxton (Addyman 1969, 67–8) and Wraysbury (Astill and Lobb 1989). Many of these land divisions occupy similar areas to those at West Fen Road, with a width of around 50m being common; these large enclosures contrast with the smaller crofts seen in the 11th-century phases at Barton Blount and Goltho, and which are a familiar feature of later medieval villages (Beresford 1975, 12–13; Astill and Lobb 1989, 83).

Many of the sites mentioned above are small in total area, however, and some display hints of higher-status occupation. Perhaps the best available parallel for West Fen Road, particularly for Phase 5, is the site at Riby Cross Roads, Lincolnshire (Steedman 1995), where an area of *c.* 2.3ha featured a number of occupied enclosures, together with at least one probable stock enclosure (though these enclosures tended towards oval shapes, in contrast to the more rectilinear bounded areas of West Fen Road). Another site which may compare well with the Late Saxon phase at West Fen Road is that at Yarnton in Oxfordshire: by AD 850 this featured timber halls lying within fenced

and enclosed areas, adjacent to animal enclosures, pens, paddocks, pits and wells (Allen *et al.* 1997, 126; Hey 2004). More locally, recently-excavated examples of enclosed sites are now known from Longstanton and Fordham, both in Cambridgeshire (Ellis and Rátkai 2001; Mould 1999). Reynolds (1999, 145) argues that there is a clear historical context for the introduction of such boundary features from the 7th century onwards. Ine's Laws contain a series of clauses which relate to the responsibilities of farmers for maintaining fences and enclosures: 'A ceorl's homestead must be fenced summer and winter.' Although these laws relate specifically to the West Saxon kingdom, Reynolds argues that they reflect more general concerns.

Ditches

These features are hard to distinguish temporally across the main phases of activity: only those of the Mid Saxon Phase 5 appear distinctive, being slight (with the exception of a single re-cut Roman boundary). They are shallow, U-shaped ditches with an average width of 0.70m and depth of 0.20m (Fig. 6.2). They are — or at least appear to be — discontinuous, although to some extent this might reflect truncation, either by the plough or by machine during the site stripping. The Mid Saxon settlement also made significant use of the earlier Roman banks and these probably marked the major boundaries of the enclosures, with the narrow ditches either acting as drainage runs alongside the earlier banks or marking internal divisions. It is doubtful whether ditches as slight as these, on heavy clay, would have provided significant site drainage, and their primary function must be seen as enclosure boundaries or sub-divisions, providing clear demarcation between land units rather than impervious barriers. The upcast from the ditches would have been used to create low banks; in order to be more than merely demarcation features, these would have needed reinforcement by hedging or fencing. There is no evidence for fencing along the ditch lines in the absence of any sign of deep earthfast posts, and so hedging may be more plausible.

The Phase 6 (later 9th–10th century) ditches fall into two size categories. Many remained slight, like those of Phase 5 (with an average width of 0.70m and depth of 0.30m), but others were larger and deeper (average width 1.60m, depth 0.53m: Fig. 6.3). Most of the smaller ditches marked internal divisions within enclosures and were much like those of Phase 5, except that they were more often continuous. The larger ditches generally marked the major enclosure boundaries. Most of these were on new alignments, disregarding the earlier Roman banks and often cutting across them, and this would have made it necessary for them to be more substantial. It is noteworthy that most of the larger ditches were aligned north–south, broadly following the local topography rather than cutting across it. As such, they would have acted as catchwaters rather than providing rapid drainage. Again, the ditched boundaries may all have been hedged, although the more substantial ditches and banks could have acted as effective barriers in themselves. The locations of the banks can be discerned by study of the ditch profiles and fill sequences, and of the positioning of re-cuts and later ditches. Some of the larger ditches had opposing steep and shallow edges; the steep side was generally that protected by bank-slip and away from the inside of the enclosure, while the shallower edge, within the enclosure, was more eroded.

Enclosure 5

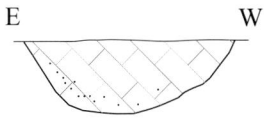

Enclosure 4

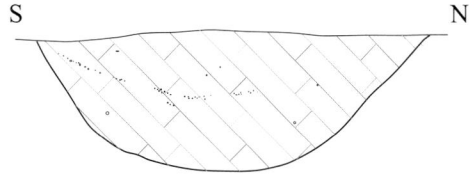

Ph5 F1617

Ph 5 F1489

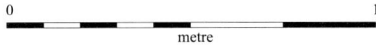

0   1
metre

Figure 6.2 Phase 5 ditch and gully sections

Enclosure 7   Enclosure 18

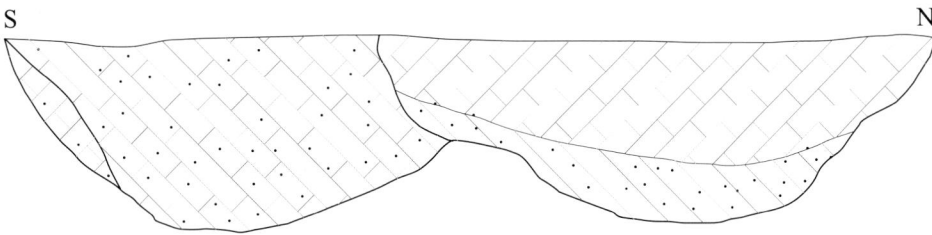

Ph6 F1777   Ph11 F1776

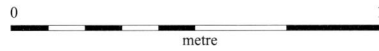

0   1
metre

Figure 6.3 Phase 6 ditch sections

Enclosure 5

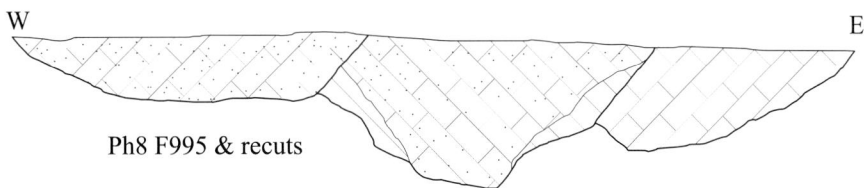

Ph8 F995 & recuts

Enclosure 4

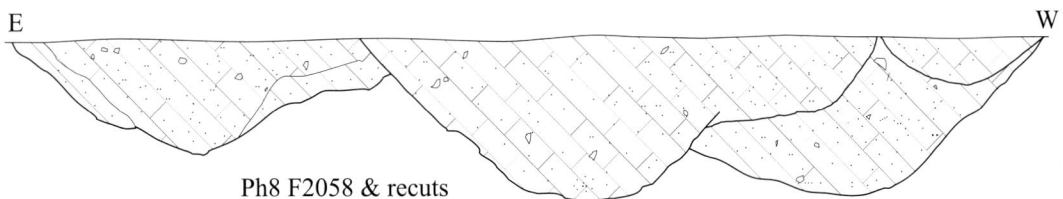

Ph8 F2058 & recuts

0   2
metres

Figure 6.4 Phase 8 ditch sections

117

Enclosure 7

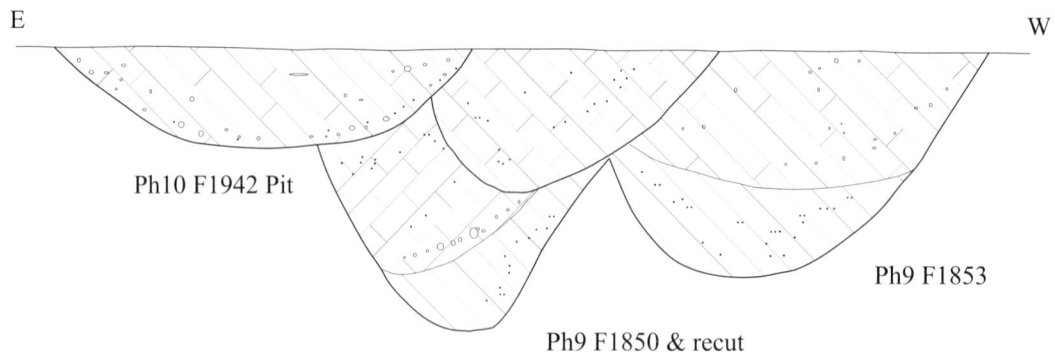

E   W

Ph10 F1942 Pit

Ph9 F1850 & recut

Ph9 F1853

Enclosure 20

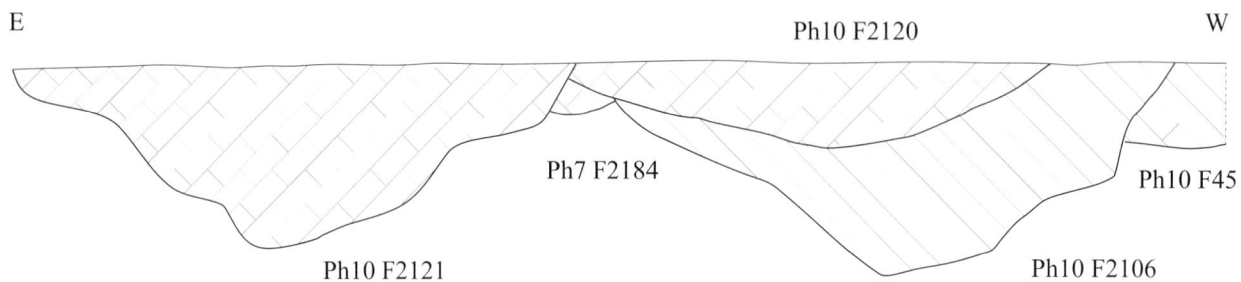

E   Ph10 F2120   W

Ph7 F2184

Ph10 F45

Ph10 F2121

Ph10 F2106

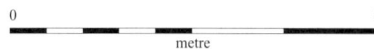

0   1
metre

Enclosure 20

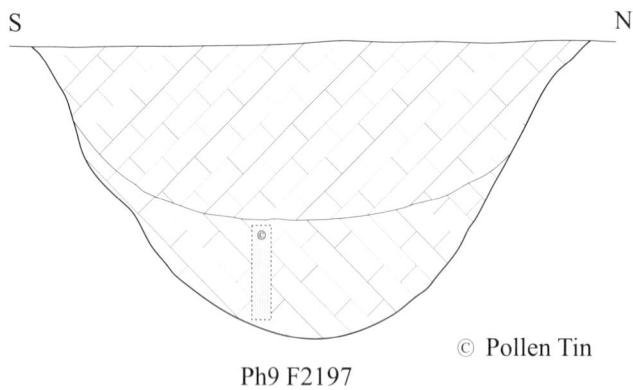

S   N

© Pollen Tin

Ph9 F2197

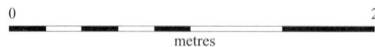

0   2
metres

Figure 6.5 Phase 9 and 10 ditch sections

Enclosures 5 & 19

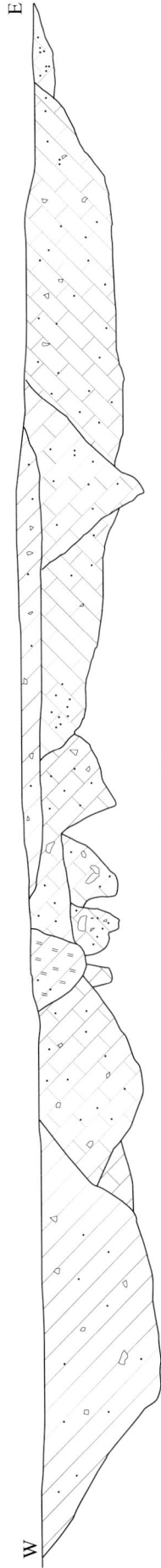

Ph12 F1012

Enclosure 12

Ph10 Pit F1338

Ph10 F1270

Ph10 F1338

Ph10 F1337

Ph9 F1345

metres

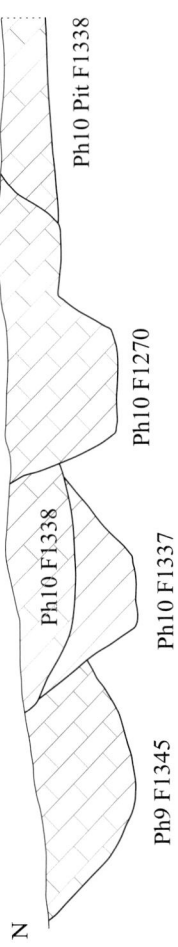

Figure 6.6 F1012 ditch section

119

Re-cutting or major cleaning of ditches almost always took place to one side of the original ditch — away from the bank, rather than cutting into the bank and bank slip.

Many areas saw very frequent re-cutting of ditch lines, in many cases amounting to re-digging of virtually new ditches on much the same line as earlier ones. These cannot represent simple restatement of a boundary or re-making of a hedgebank: a hedge, once established, will tend to increase in size and impenetrability rather than diminish. One motivation for this activity — and digging these ditches time and again through heavy clay would have been a major undertaking — must have been to channel water away from the enclosures. Judging by the amount of re-cutting evident in certain ditch lines, it seems that these ditches became infilled fairly rapidly.

Phase 8 (the later 10th–11th centuries) saw the excavation of further examples of smaller and larger ditches (Fig. 6.4). The former averaged 0.60m wide by 0.26m deep, the latter 1.43m by 0.46m. Once again all of the larger banks, and most of the larger ditches, were aligned north–south. The principal differences appear to be greater straightness and order in the layout of the enclosure boundaries, and the appearance of more permanent-looking double-ditched banks. In the previous phase the site plan had a very 'organic' look — the ditches curved and sinuous, the enclosures with rounded corners. This 'straightening-up' of boundaries must represent a deliberate act or acts, although it is difficult to understand to what purpose other than maximising the areas of the enclosures. The boundaries continued to be cut ever straighter through Phase 9, although this period also saw the development of a more open site landscape with fewer and larger enclosures. Narrow internal divisions persisted within the enclosures, and these retained the characteristic size and form of previous phases. While there was a slight increase in the overall size of the larger ditches, again, this is not thought to have been significant (Fig. 6.5). Most of the larger ditches cut in Phase 10 were re-cuts and realignments of earlier boundaries, or further shallow internal divisions.

During Phase 9, two pieces of land within Area A were taken out of settlement and turned over to the plough. Two sets of ditches within these areas appear to have been the hand-dug furrows of the original ridge and furrow strip system here. They aligned with the furrows that were recorded on the site prior to stripping, one group aligned north–south (Enclosure 14) and the other east–west (Enclosure 17). The former group were spaced 10m apart, the latter 9m. All of the component features were shallow, with steep-cut sides and flat bases; they were clearly hand-dug, and not simply the bases of later furrows. When originally dug they would have been up to 0.60–0.70m deep and (assuming that their edges continued at a relatively steep angle) perhaps 1.50m wide. Possible plough-turning areas — spreads of darker, disturbed subsoil containing intrusive later pottery — were seen at the eastern ends of two of those in Enclosure 17.

By Phase 10 the occupied area had contracted and large parts of the settlement land across Area B had been given over to agriculture, though there is no clear evidence that they had been ploughed and they may have been used as pasture. However, ploughing might have been a necessary preliminary to turning the deeply ditched settlement landscape to pasture, removing surfaces, dumps, hedges, building remains and other obstacles in the process. Area B had certainly seen ridge and furrow cultivation at some point in the medieval or post-medieval periods, but any associated earthworks had subsequently been removed by modern ploughing. A few narrow ditches were dug during Phase 10, mostly around the remaining structures, but the main ditched feature visible was now the massive boundary F1012 between Enclosures 19 and 21. This was not a single, wide ditch cut but the cumulative result of many successive re-cuttings along broadly the same line, culminating in a ditched zone c. 11–12m wide (Fig. 6.6), although there was never any one ditch of this width open at any one time. This sequence is thought to have begun in Phase 9, and redefinition continued through all succeeding phases. There was still a ditch here up to fifty years ago when Roger Cornwell, the farmer, remembers filling it in with his father. The unexcavated divide between Areas A and B — still a large ditch even after the development — is likely to have been a similar feature.

Gullies and slots

Within this category are included linear features that were not necessarily enclosure boundaries, were clearly other than ditches, or were too slight to deserve the designation 'ditch'. Some of these, while clearly 'structural', did not form any recognisable structures: those in Enclosure 1, Phase 8 and 9 for example, or those in Enclosure 9, Phase 6. These may have held fence posts, though their arrangements do not describe enclosed areas and they often intercut. Perhaps they represented 'one-sided' structures such as racks or wind-breaks. A few of the buildings (e.g. Structures 5, 6, 9 and 15) had shallow 'drip-gullies' along their long sides and occasionally around one end; occasionally there were fence-lines appended to these, some formed by simple post alignments but others with uprights set in deep, narrow palisade trenches (Structures 12 and 13). One of the large pit groups in Phase 9 (Enclosure 5) displayed what may have been a narrow excavated channel leading from a pond or well into the centre of the pit group.

Buildings

Twenty-nine structures were recognised during the CAU excavations, with a further nine conjectured. Twenty-seven (and five of those conjectured) dated to the Saxon and medieval periods. The majority appear to have represented domestic buildings or houses, with a few smaller sheds or barns. Most of the buildings have been regarded as domestic status on the basis of their size, and of the quantities of finds and the types of related archaeological features associated with them — for example, a post-hole building of 10m by 5m within a ditched enclosure associated with a well, a group of pits and a wide variety of contemporary artefacts has been regarded as domestic, as have later buildings with successive clay floors and separate cobbled areas. The earlier (Mid Saxon) buildings are harder to interpret as they are associated with few finds and had also been heavily disturbed by later activity.

Saxon buildings

All the Saxon buildings were timber-framed and most were of post-hole construction, although with some post-in-trench construction in the later phases and occasional slots for sill beams which were used

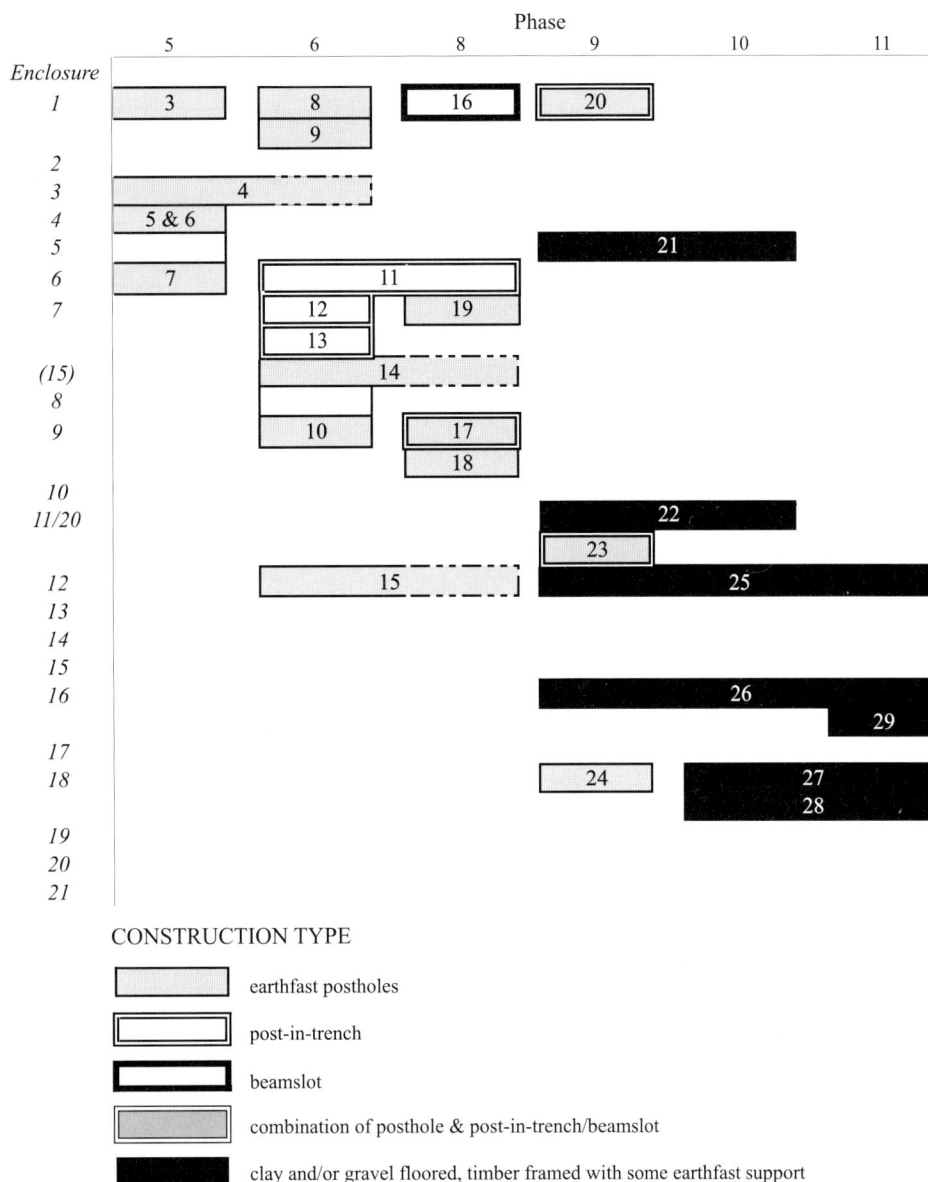

Figure 6.7 Building construction, dimensions and length of use

principally for internal divisions (Fig. 6.7). The earliest, Mid Saxon, domestic structures were small, no more than 8m in length and varying in width from 3m to 5m and were all of post-hole construction. The exception was a possible non-domestic structure, perhaps a barn, up to 12m long (Structure 3). Most of the smaller buildings had been replaced by the next phase, and only the small Structure 4 may perhaps have continued in use. The structures were on two principal alignments — either north-east to south-west or at right-angles to this — but varied slightly according to the alignments of their local enclosure boundaries. In only one case (Structures 5 and 6) had a building been rebuilt on the same site; all others, when replaced, were erected on fresh sites, though generally only a few metres away from their predecessor.

In Phase 6, the late 9th–10th centuries, the number, size and variety of buildings increased. The first post-in-trench buildings (Structures 11, 12 and 13) appeared, though post-hole construction continued. The post-hole buildings, whether domestic or non-domestic, were still generally small: the largest (Structure 8)

measured 10.50m by 5.00m, though beam-slots were also used in its construction. The probable non-domestic structures were smaller, and no more than 8.50m long. The post-in-trench buildings were somewhat larger than those of previous phases; although still no more than c. 5m wide they were up to 13m long (Structures 12 and 13). A small building in Enclosure 9, Structure 10, was just 3.50m square; it appeared similar to Structure 18 (Enclosure 9, Phase 8) and might have indicated the presence of a larger building to the north. Almost all the main structures were aligned north-east to south-west, with two set at right-angles to this, though again there were slight variations reflecting the alignments of surrounding ditches.

In Phase 8 a wide variety of construction techniques remained in use, with all three new buildings distinctively different in this regard: post-hole Structure 19 (replacing the large Structures 12 and 13), beam-slot Structure 16, and Structure 17 which used both post-hole and post-in-trench construction. The full size of the beam-slot building is not known although it was 5.50m wide, wider than any of the earlier buildings and perhaps a precursor to the medieval building types that follow. The two post-hole buildings were both relatively large, being 11m and 12m long and 4.5m and 5m wide. The structures' alignments remained much the same as in earlier phases, although those in the eastern part of the site tended to shift slightly towards north–south and east–west alignments. A small ancillary building (Structure 18), measuring 3m by 4m, was tucked in behind the southern end of the domestic Structure 17. It was similar in size and construction to Structure 10 in the previous phase, which it may have replaced. Clearly it was linked closely to the domestic structure, if not actually attached to it, and it may represent a cook-room, wash-room or privy.

Discussion

The Mid–Late Saxon buildings from West Fen Road fall within the size range already known from other contemporary sites and use similar constructional techniques. Mid Saxon buildings at Goltho, for example, were similarly all of post-hole construction (Beresford 1987), as were most of those at Staunch Meadow, Brandon, where sizes ranged from 4.20 x 2.80m to 15.50 x 7.50m (Carr *et al.* 1988). More recently, the discovery of a Mid–Late Saxon settlement at the Whitehouse Industrial Estate, Ipswich, revealed three Mid Saxon structures, employing a mixture of post-holes and beam-slots. The settlement plan shows that the post-hole arrangements here were not entirely regular, with variable distances between the posts and some 'weak' end walls (Nenk *et al.* 1996, 476–9). Some of the Goltho buildings also displayed the same poor alignment of post-holes as seen in the Phase 5 buildings from West Fen Road. Beresford (1987, 27) argued that the walls of the Goltho buildings were of either clay and wattle, or clay tempered with chopped straw; since clay would thus have completely surrounding the wall posts their poor alignment would have been of little consequence, while inferior timber could also have been used as the thick clay would have protected the wood. The wall-plate could also have been placed on top of the wall. Similar cob walling could have been employed here at West Fen Road. Perhaps the settlement's residents were constructing their own buildings in this manner, without assistance from the skilled carpenters whose work is evident at higher status sites in this period. In this case, might irregular structural post-hole alignment serve as an indicator of the settlement's relatively low status in this period, with buildings being serviceable but unsophisticated?

The later Saxon phases at West Fen Road displayed a greater variety of building types. Post-hole construction was still used for some structures, either partially or wholly, but sill-beam and post-in-trench methods were used also. This kind of variability is seen at other sites. At the higher-status Mid–Late Saxon settlement at Flixborough, for example, 7th–8th century buildings were mostly constructed using earthfast post construction, although sill-beam and post-in-trench methods were also used. By the early–mid 10th century, however, all of the buildings there had continuous trench foundations, and may have had more than one storey (Loveluck 2001, 83–90). Once again, the relatively late adoption of new constructional methods at West Fen Road may be an indicator of its humble status.

Medieval buildings
Activities involving structures ceased on the West Fen Road site, to all intents and purposes, after the 14th century. The excavations at Ely Forehill, however, revealed a building sequence from the 13th century onward, enabling parallels to be drawn between the two sites (Alexander 1998, 2003). Interpretation of buildings from an archaeological context is often hampered by the most common constraint of the archaeological record: that buildings rarely survive above foundation level. Where deeper stratified deposits did exist within the West Fen Road site, these too were subject to modern ploughing and/or recent disturbance. However, despite these limitations some broad trends can be identified, both in terms of materials used and construction techniques.

Wall construction
Earthfast posts, so common in the structures of the earlier periods, became rarer components of the main domestic buildings (Fig. 6.7). This is probably best illustrated by Structure 25: post settings around its periphery indicated that at least part of it had been constructed using earthfast posts, no doubt supporting a timber frame. In turn the majority of the post-settings were sealed by successive flooring events while few new post-settings appear to have related to the floors, suggesting that other forms of wall construction were being used. This is consistent with evidence from other medieval sites, where post-hole buildings are often replaced by other types of structure at the close of the 13th century (Clarke and Carter 1977; Atkin *et al.* 1985). At West Fen Road the relationship between the contemporary buildings Structure 27 and Structure 28 is interesting, since here two buildings of different construction lay side by side. The lack of post-settings within and around Structure 27 indicated the use of sills, while the rectangular post configuration of Structure 28 suggested that these held the main structural components of the building. Structure 27 in this case has been interpreted as the main domestic building, while Structure 28 is seen as a barn. Were the 'latest' techniques of construction deemed appropriate for a house, while older technology remained acceptable for a barn?

If the importance of earthfast posts diminished over time, then other kinds of upright support for walls must have been used. Timber beam-slots, while present within Structure 22 and Structure 26, may indicate internal divisions rather than representing external wall supports. At the Forehill site the most prevalent form of wall construction in the earlier phases — in other words, those contemporary with our later structures — was a sill or plinth supporting a timber frame superstructure (Alexander 1998, 2003). While positive evidence for sills was lacking at the West Fen Road site it is probable that these would have provided the foundations for most, if not all, of the later domestic buildings. This is hinted at by the collapsed limestone and flint footing within Structure 27; this represented the only evidence of masonry (however crude) used within the buildings. In the case of the early Forehill buildings, clay was the most common material used in the construction of sills, plinths or banks, while one instance of marl (clunch) construction was noted.

Although little evidence for walling survived it is assumed that clay, as at Forehill, was a major element within wall construction. Clay walling has been recognised at contemporary sites at Wisbech (Hinman

Phase 9

Phase 10

Phase 11

Grams per 10m sq.

· 1 - 10
· 11 - 20
• 21 - 40
• 41 - 80
• 81 - 160
● 161 - 320
● 321 - 640
● 641 - 1280
● > 1280

● Floor Tile

○ Roof Tile

Figure 6.8 Distribution of medieval roof and floor tile, in Phases 9, 10 and 11

2002) and Norwich (Atkin *et al.* 1985). To date, the largest corpus of excavated clay-walled buildings, in regional terms, comes from Norwich, where three types of walling have been recognised:

1. load-bearing walls up to eaves level;
2. clay packing between vertical structural timbers;
3. clay plinths supporting the base plate of a timber frame.

Any of these modes of construction could have been used at West Fen Road.

Evidence for timber superstructures is entirely lacking, although timber was probably a major component within all buildings of this period at West Fen Road. The surviving structural timbers at Forehill were all of oak, and this conforms with the general pattern exhibited by timber-framed buildings of this period (Alexander 2003, 146–7). While no timbers survived at West Fen Road, there is no reason to assume that the buildings do not fall into this pattern.

Roofs

It is assumed that most of the medieval buildings on the site were thatched. Great fen sedge would seem the most likely material, given its local availability and the lack of evidence for other thatching materials. Roof tile would have been a more expensive commodity, even in the later periods of occupation, and its infrequent presence suggests it was never a major component within the West Fen Road buildings. At Forehill, tile only occurs in quantities that suggest widespread usage or availability from the 15th century onwards. This implies only limited usage within Ely prior to this, and then possibly only within buildings of some status (Alexander 2003, 147). The pegged roof tile present at West Fen Road only appears within late contexts and even here was mostly incorporated within later surfaces, perhaps arriving on the site as hardcore (Fig. 6.8).

Floors

Clay was commonly used as a floor base throughout the duration of the occupation, chosen no doubt for its availability and damp-proofing qualities. However, the local grey/brown clay does not appear to have been used within the later buildings in unmodified form. All the clay floors within the late structures were rendered in a sandy yellow clay, quite distinct from the underlying natural material. Several hypotheses suggest themselves. One is that the clay was imported from elsewhere; another is that it was mixed, perhaps with sand, and prepared prior to the laying of the floor.

Gravel and cobbling were also used for internal surfaces, as in Structures 20, 21, 25 and 26. The differing properties of the surfaces within individual buildings possibly indicates different usages. In Structure 21 the surfaces were rendered in crushed erratic sandstone and sand, with small flint pebbles. Within Structure 26 the surface was carefully prepared using compacted small flints, probably rammed into place. The rougher flint surface within Structure 20, as well as the size of the building, might indicate that it had been a working building or outhouse. While gravel might have been used within the internal surfaces of Structure 25, these were later incorporated into a rougher yard surface covering much of the former building.

Hearths/ovens

No *in situ* hearth settings were present within any of the later medieval buildings: this was perhaps to be expected, given that hearths within the main rooms of buildings are unusual in the period in question (13th–14th century), when hearths were generally found in lean-tos or outhouses and rooms are presumed to have been heated by portable braziers (Atkin *et al.* 1985). The presence of braziers in the later phases of buildings may be inferred from scorched or burnt patches on the floors and spreads of ash amongst the floor deposits. Most of the later buildings displayed indications of at least possible brazier position. That brazier settings were indeed once present, although disturbed by later activity, is suggested by the presence of a quantity of fragmented square Ely tiles (Fig. 6.8). Many of the tiles were friable and appeared to have undergone heating or burning subsequent to their manufacture, suggesting their use in hearth settings. Small holes in many of the fragments suggest they were fixed in place, possibly with nails, either to the floor or to a wall as a hearth backing. No examples of this type of tile were recovered from the Forehill site, perhaps indicating a pre 13th-century *floruit*.

External surfaces

Gravel was the predominant material used for paths, yards and alleyways, particularly around Structures 27/28, Structure 25 and Structure 26. These surfaces varied in quality and build and suffered differing degrees of wear and later truncation. The most extensive surface, laid out around the pond and buildings within Enclosure 18, consisted mainly of rough gravel metalling, although in places there were signs of attempts to lay down a sandy bedding matrix prior to the spreading of the larger cobbles. The cobbles comprising the upper surface of the trackway within Enclosure 16 had also been set within a coarse sandy matrix, suggesting greater care in preparation. Elsewhere no attempts appear to have been made to provide bedding, with gravel spreads lain directly onto the clay subsoil.

Drains

Ditches and gullies surrounding properties no doubt channelled water away from the buildings. These aside, only two examples of possible timber-shuttered drainage channels were noted. These lay to the east of Structure 27 and to the west of Structure 26: significantly, perhaps, both were set within cobbled trackways. Timber drains running down one side of alleyways were a common feature on the Forehill site and appear to have been provided with each successive surface. Perhaps this was common practice and repeated here.

Building form

The lack of any clear wall lines, and the fact that some buildings were exposed only partially, means that many of the dimensions of the later structures are inferred from surviving floor areas, and from the limits of associated external features such as yards or trackways. All structures appeared rectangular in plan with no evidence of 'right-angled' annexes, although post positions outside the main structural areas possibly indicated 'lean-tos' or off-shoots. All the buildings fell within the ranges identified at sites elsewhere (Clarke and Carter 1977; Schofield 1997). Unfortunately, little can be said with

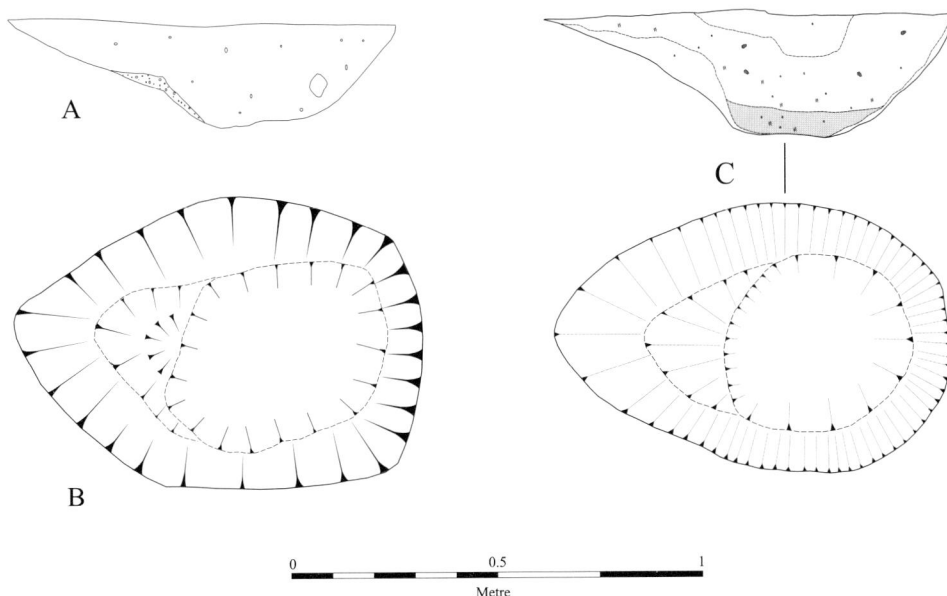

Figure 6.9 Plans and sections of boat-shaped pits
(a) section, F8, Denny End, Waterbeach; (b) plan, F2, Denny End, Waterbeach; (c) plan and section, F385, West Fen Road

regard to the height of the buildings, and about whether they contained upper storeys. Certainly the more substantial buildings could have supported a second floor, although even by this late period provision of upper rooms was by no means common. If upper space existed at all it would probably have been used for storage, rather than as living space.

Pits

The excavated area contained over 500 pits, the majority of which were excavated to some degree. The number of pits increased within each phase from Phase 5 onward, reaching a peak at Phase 10, despite the shrinkage of the area in use by that time and the apparent fall-off in settlement activity. Pits, often little considered in themselves, can prove highly informative on many aspects of life within a settlement, providing evidence for small-scale industrial activities, construction techniques, hygiene, the production, preparation and storage of food, and even sports and pastimes. It is crucial, however, that their function is ascertained. It is all too easy for archaeologists to refer to 'rubbish pits'. Even if pits were backfilled with 100% pure 'rubbish' at the end of their use-life (and very few, if any, ever were), this does not mean that their primary significance was as rubbish pits.

Very few Mid Saxon pits were recorded, and most of these were shallow and irregular. There is one example of a distinctive pit-type known from contemporary sites, however: the boat-shaped pit occurring in Enclosure 1 (Fig. 6.9C; F385, Fig. 3.1), which had one broad and one narrow end. The broad, flat, 'back' end is steep-sided and the narrow end shallower and tapering upwards. The dimensions of the pit are 2.00m x 1.30m x 55cm deep. It is of a type seen on other Early and Mid Saxon settlement sites in the region, and was clearly not initially dug as a rubbish pit, but for a specific and commonly required purpose. There are recent excavated examples at Denny End, Waterbeach (Fig. 6.9A–B) and at Cottenham, Cambs

(Mortimer 1996, 1998), both at sites on gravelly clay and Greensand subsoils. The Waterbeach and Cottenham examples are of the 6th and 8th centuries, that at West Fen Road dates to the 9th century. All of these features are virtually identical in form and size, and none contained large finds assemblages; their fills appear not to relate to the pits' original function. They also feature worn, redeposited or weathered natural at the lip of their shallow, pointed 'fronts'. These pits must have served a particular activity that was pursued widely but sporadically. Only two were recognised at West Fen Road, the other (in the same enclosure) dating to Phase 6. There is no evidence for linings, while their sub-circular bases appear to have been worn or cleaned out. The Phase 5 example contained a small but varied domestic waste assemblage in the backfill, but burnt and unburnt animal bone, fishbone, oyster shell and eggshell also occurred in the basal fill. Whether this material is *in situ* or represents secondary dumping is not known, but if it is *in situ* it may inform upon the pit's use; the distinctive fills in the bases of the pits may have been of different (earlier) date to the backfill material above.

Might these pits have been excavated as fattening pens for swine? This interpretative suggestion may at least succeed in encouraging debate about the particular functions that these, and other, earlier medieval pits may have had. While cattle and sheep, as domesticated herd animals, would have been a common sight in Mid Saxon settlements, pigs may have spent much of their lives at pannage in woodland nearby. When fresh (rather than dried or salted) pig meat was required, an animal might have been trapped within the wood and brought back to the settlement for fattening. Rather than being placed in a specially built secure pen, perhaps it was placed in one of these pits (hobbled if necessary), and the pit then covered over. Food scraps and other waste could then have been fed to the pig through a gap at the front of the pit and the immobile animal allowed to fatten, ready for slaughter and consumption when needed.

Phases 9 and 10 saw the appearance of distinctive groups of large, elongated oval or sub-rectangular pits (Fig. 6.10). There are three groups of between six and ten pits, and two smaller groups of two and four pits. These, by Phase 10, had developed into a specific 'type' characterised by their size and by vertical or slightly undercut edges, the latter suggestive of slumping and cleaning-out, and flat bases. They lay in groups, occasionally slightly intercutting; generally, where they cut earlier ditches, they did so only along their edges. The pristine nature of the sides suggested that they might have been timber lined, although no evidence for timber shuttering was evident. The pits appeared to have been rapidly backfilled after use, since the undercut/inclining sides have not collapsed. These pits, if lined, could have contained water or other liquid; water might have been supplied from nearby wells or ponds. All the pit groups lie downhill from wells at a distances of 10–40m; it is

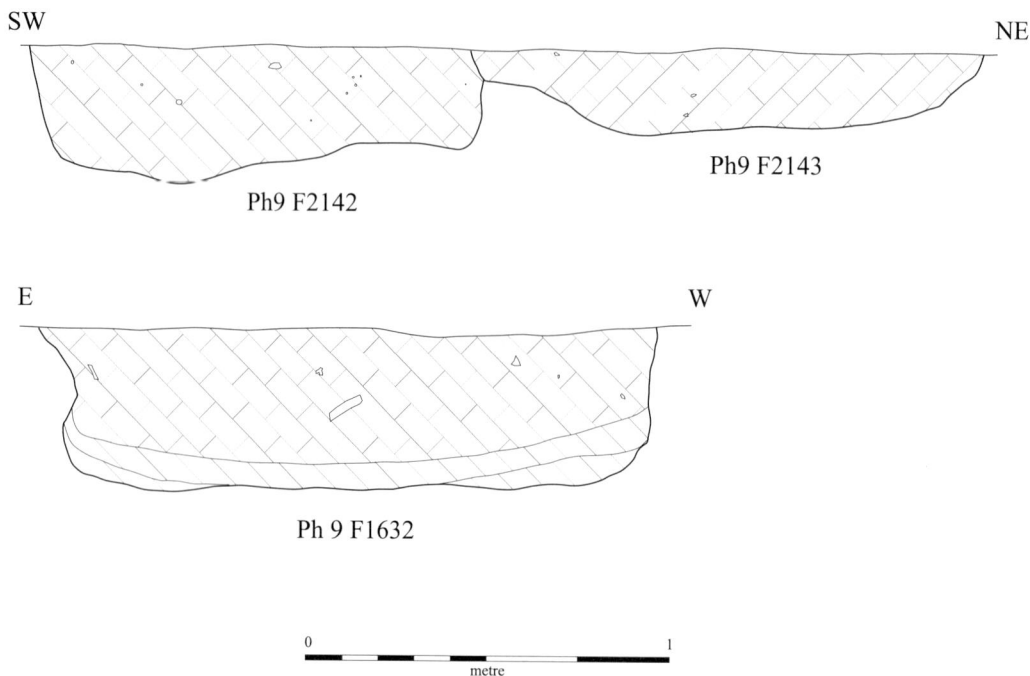

Figure 6.10 Sections of sub-rectangular, flat-bottomed pits

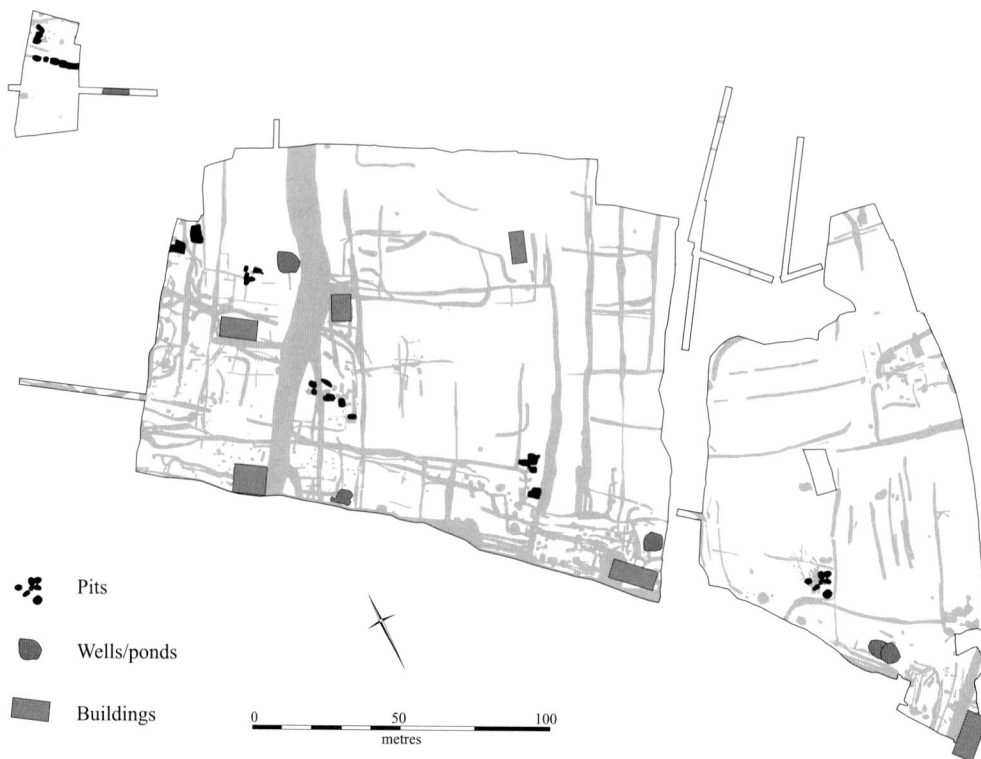

Figure 6.11 Medieval pit groups in relation to ponds/wells

126

possible that their function called for a constant supply of water.

By Phase 10 every occupied domestic enclosure contained a group of these pits; their nature suggests a specific function, and their frequency implies it was one that was common to all the properties (Fig. 6.11). It is hard to discern, however, as none of the environmental samples from their fills suggest any specific activity, nor did the pits contain finds indicating any specific use. They lay away from the domestic buildings, situated at the periphery or in corners of the enclosure compounds. Perhaps they were used for a processing activity involving a noxious smell, or other anti-social effect. Maybe they were retting pits used for soaking of flax or hemp for linen production, although it is difficult to see this being undertaken on such a small, 'cottage-industry' scale in the 12th and 13th centuries (cf. Leahy 2003, 62–4 for more information about the process). Since these pits did not appear until this general period, they are perhaps unlikely to be associated with an everyday practice such as cooking or washing. Either they were used in some semi-industrial process which, for economic or other reasons, was only pursued after the 12th century, or they relate to changes in the layout or use of the enclosures or to other changes or advances in technology or design. The most obvious technological transformation observable at Phase 9 is the shift in building technology from earthfast timber-framed construction to clay-floored sill-beam houses. An alternative interpretation for these pits, all of approximately the same size and cut deep into the clean sub-surface clay, would be as clay-quarries, each pit representing a successive re-flooring of a building. Support for this theory comes from Wraysbury which, like Little Paxton and Springfield Lyons, had pits close to residential areas that produced few finds (Astill and Lobb 1989, 84). Both Addyman (1969, 168–76) and Buckley and Hedges (1987, 28) argue that pits like these were dug for winning clay or gravel, and were then used subsequently as cess-pits.

Another major change observable in Phase 9 was the overall increase in the number of pits on the site, and particularly of those in the immediate vicinity of the domestic buildings. These were generally fairly small and relatively shallow, with uneven sub-circular or oval shapes (Fig. 6.12). They occasionally intercut; since they were often cut into the tops of earlier features, and occasionally gravel surfaces, they cannot have been quarry pits. They contained large finds assemblages, particularly of pottery, and appear to represent rubbish pits. Few pits interpreted as being dug for waste disposal appeared before this period, however, and it is unclear why they now emerged. With the growth in trade and in the accessibility of goods such as ceramics, ironwork etc., it is possible that there was now a greater need than before to separate communal and personal waste. The appearance of rubbish pits may also point to civic intervention, and coercion of residents into disposing of rubbish in a more controlled fashion: i.e. burying it, rather than letting it gather in middens. However, the idea of a population co-operating with centrally imposed rubbish-disposal disciplines should not be pushed too far. For whatever reason, back-plot disposal of rubbish appears to have become commonplace, here as well as within the core of Ely, from this period onward (as seen at Forehill and Broad Street: Alexander 2003, Cessford et al. forthcoming).

Another distinctive pit-type is recognisable from Phase 8 through to Phase 10. Occurring singly or in small groups, some are large and often ill-defined in plan, while others resemble short, fat ditch lengths. They are uniformly shallow — indeed, reduced to little more than

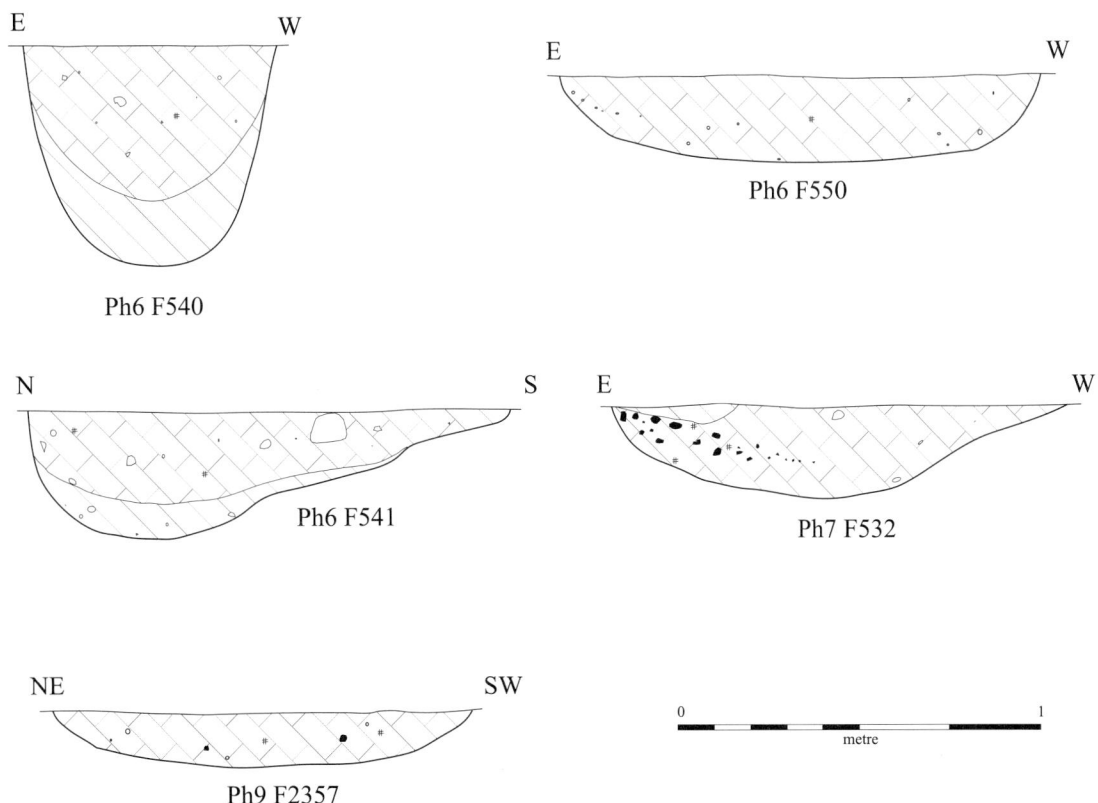

Figure 6.12 Other pit sections

127

slight hollows by truncation — and may be remnants of small localised quarries for clay for use in construction, for kilns or ovens, or for daub or cob walling. None of these applications would have required the cleaner, lower clay. Some of the larger, more amorphous examples could have been wallows.

Two possible storage-jar pits were recorded: one small example with the pot still in place, although shattered (F2385), and a second larger one (F2328). The larger example was circular and deep, with curving near-vertical sides and a narrowing flattish base (excavated under water and thus not clearly seen). The pottery assemblage of 115 sherds was principally from Thetford ware storage jars.

On thick heavy clay subsoil with no permeable layers beneath, cess pits will usually not function because there is nowhere for the liquid to drain, particularly in the autumn and winter months when the clay is swollen with groundwater. It is possible that human waste was collected for agricultural and industrial use, and possible examples of privies have already been discussed. However, two large, elongated Phase 9 pits in Enclosure 1 may have functioned as cess pits. Both were aligned north–south, lay parallel to each other twelve metres apart, and measured 3.50m by 1.00m with steep near-vertical sides. Both contained relatively large finds assemblages, principally of pottery, and both cut into an earlier, infilled ditch which ran east–west with the slope of the land. Clearly for a cess pit to function efficiently, liquid must drain to leave a relatively dry material that can break down. The positioning of these pits over earlier ditches may have been an attempt to utilise the relative free draining quality of the ditch fills, as opposed to the natural clays surrounding them — while the fill material would also have been relatively easy to excavate.

Ponds, wells and water supply

Few wells appear within the earlier period, only one Phase 5 feature being interpreted thus. Even this, it would appear, was not initially associated with domestic activity and may have provided water for animals, possibly within drier periods, when shallower ditches and gullies no longer held standing water. Even by Phase 8, there were only two recognised wells. Why there should be a general lack of wells in the earlier periods of occupation, while they become commonplace in medieval times, is not clear. There are several possible explanations. Either plentiful water which was considered potable could be collected from other on-site sources such as ditches and gullies, or water could easily be carried from a nearby stream or streams. While water from ditches and hollows might have sufficed for animals, it seems unlikely that it would have satisfied a household's needs.

Streams would certainly have run from the higher land of the Isle of Ely, from the springline at the junction of the Greensand and clay; where they were located at any one time, however, is difficult to gauge. Live streams still run along both the north and south boundaries of the site, to the south of West Fen Road and along the northern Greenfield boundary. Deposits interpreted as a relic stream channel recorded to the north of West Fen Road may indicate an ancient watercourse which was present throughout the whole prehistoric and medieval occupation history of the

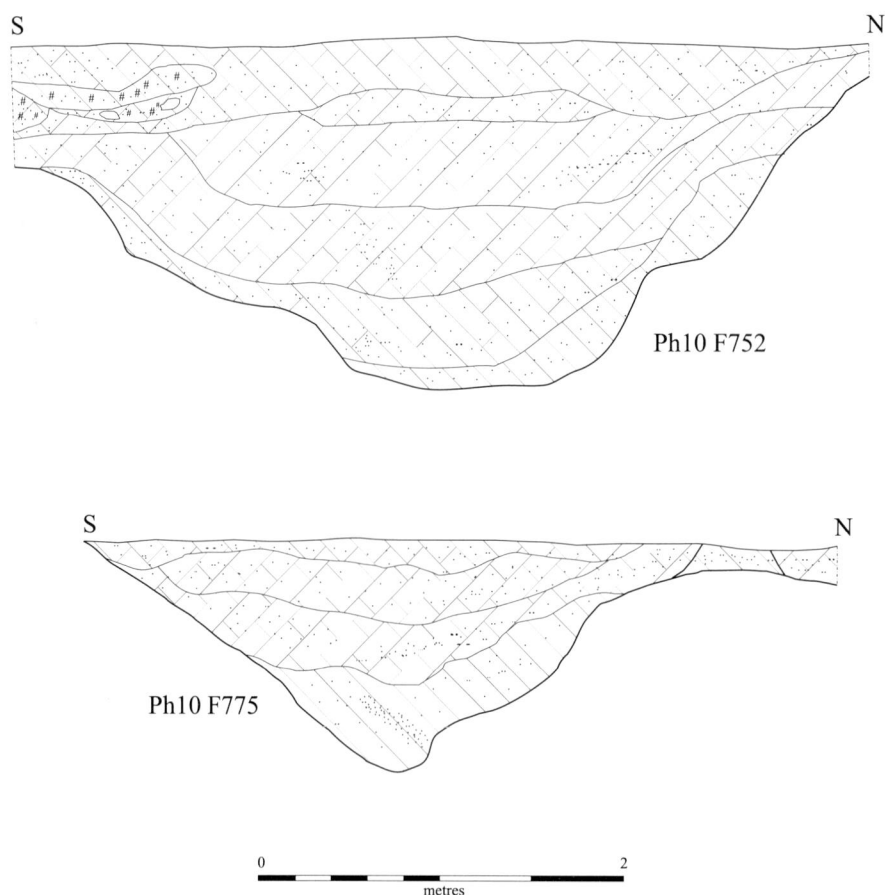

Ph10 F752

Ph10 F775

Figure 6.13 Well sections

128

site. Lying as it does along the base of the high land where it meets the low-lying skirt areas of the hill, it is in a location where a natural channel might have been expected to form. The extant southern stream is less well understood, and may only have been canalised along this approximate line when the settlement expanded to this southern boundary in the 12th century. Two of the Phase 9 wells were located along this southern side of the settlement, and may indicate a need for a more convenient water supply as the settlement and domestic buildings moved further away from the putative stream along West Fen Road.

This pattern, with the majority of wells located along the southern edge of the settlement, continued in later phases of the site's occupation. Two factors may have reinforced this tendency. First, that the increasing development of properties along the southern edge of the site would have required convenient individual water sources. Second, the natural stream running to the north of the site may have become inaccessible to these more southerly properties due to development and parcelling of land along the northern part of the site. While some of the wells might have been lined with timber or wattle hurdling, the lack of surviving waterlogged material meant that evidence for this was lacking. Most of the wells had wide upper cones, suggesting that only the lower parts of these, if any, were lined. An exception to this was provided by the late stone-lined well in Enclosure 16 (F729, Fig. 5.2). The effort expended on its construction may have represented an attempt at prolonging its life: three large wells had successively replaced one another within a relatively short period of time, perhaps indicating a relatively short life span for the three unlined wells nearby (Fig. 6.13). In the absence of wells, water may also have been obtained from ponds or the large tanks that appeared from the 12th century onwards, again mainly in the southern part of the site. These large features again cannot be interpreted more specifically than in terms of water storage. They may have supplied various activity areas, however, in particular the retting pits mentioned above. From Phase 10 onward, large ponds appeared, also chiefly along the southern periphery of the site.

Trackways
The Roman trackway in the southern part of the site formed the southern limit of the settlement in the Mid Saxon period, and may have survived as an access route up the hill. The major route across the western side of the island must have been that along West Fen Road itself (see below). To its south, however, we may gain a clear picture of the development of trackways through and alongside the CAU excavation site. While the Roman southern boundary was maintained during Phases 5 and 6 it was necessarily in use as a trackway, and an intra-site access developed along the back of the enclosures fronting West Fen Road. South of this, what were once open fields eventually become occupied, this southern shift necessitating the establishment of a trackway along the southern side of the site by at least the 11th century. The creation of the trackway appears to have coincided with the development of a series of properties and plots along its north side, and it was given a metalled surface sometime in the 13th century.

No evidence for any metalling of the early tracks survives and they were probably unsurfaced, since gravel spreads would have been evident in surrounding features and in slumping. Gravel metalling appears to have been preferred for the surfaces of the later trackways (Fig. 3.18). Four gravel pathways were recorded: two around Structures 27 and 28 (with the possible remains of a third leading off to the west), one skirting around Enclosure 12, and one running down the west side of the domestic building Structure 26 in Enclosure 16. All continued to the south beyond the limits of excavation, where they no doubt joined up with the (now metalled) Field Side trackway.

Throughout the occupation history of the settlement the trackways and enclosures were clearly designed, not only to define property boundaries, but also to control the passage of livestock. The longevity of most of the enclosures suggests that individual farmsteads lay within them, possibly with the property passing from one generation to the next. The exception to this was the system of paddocks recorded in the Late Saxon Enclosures 13 and 14; these were patently stock control areas with (in their earliest phase at least) access to the trackways, and appear to have been shared between the surrounding domestic enclosures. Enclosures of this kind have seldom been identified on Mid and Late Saxon sites, although they are common on medieval settlements.

III. Artefactual and ecofactual evidence

When considering the reliability of the finds and environmental evidence, the nature of the site and the circumstances of the excavation must be borne in mind, as outlined in Chapter 1. The later any feature, the more likely it is to contain a substantial amount of residual material. This can be seen clearly with the pottery, and must also be assumed to be the case for the small finds and animal bone.

Period II: Saxon

Production and subsistence
As discussed in Chapter 4, the site displays slight evidence for textile production, and related activities such as sewing, in this period (Fig. 6.14). A very small assemblage of worked stone, bone and metal artefacts indicates some on-site weaving and spinning, at least by Phase 7, and probably already in Phase 5: contexts of this latter phase produced a fragmentary clay loomweight, and two bone pin-beaters, indicating the use of a warp-weighted loom on the site. With regard to Late Saxon contexts, the recovery of a lead spindle whorl (weighing 53g) suggests that heavier fabrics were now being prepared for weaving on the site (Henry 1999). A double-pointed bone pin-beater, as well as a possible single-pointed example, suggest the use of both the warp-weighted loom and the vertical two-beam loom by this time. The absence of loomweights from this phase reflects the nature of the soil on the site: unfired clay is virtually undetectable on a site located on pure clay, and the Phase 5 example was only recognised during excavation because it had been fired. Finally, a bone needle shaft indicates some sewing activity. These finds, although a minute assemblage, do indicate that all stages of the domestic textile production process were carried out at West Fen Road during the Late Saxon period.

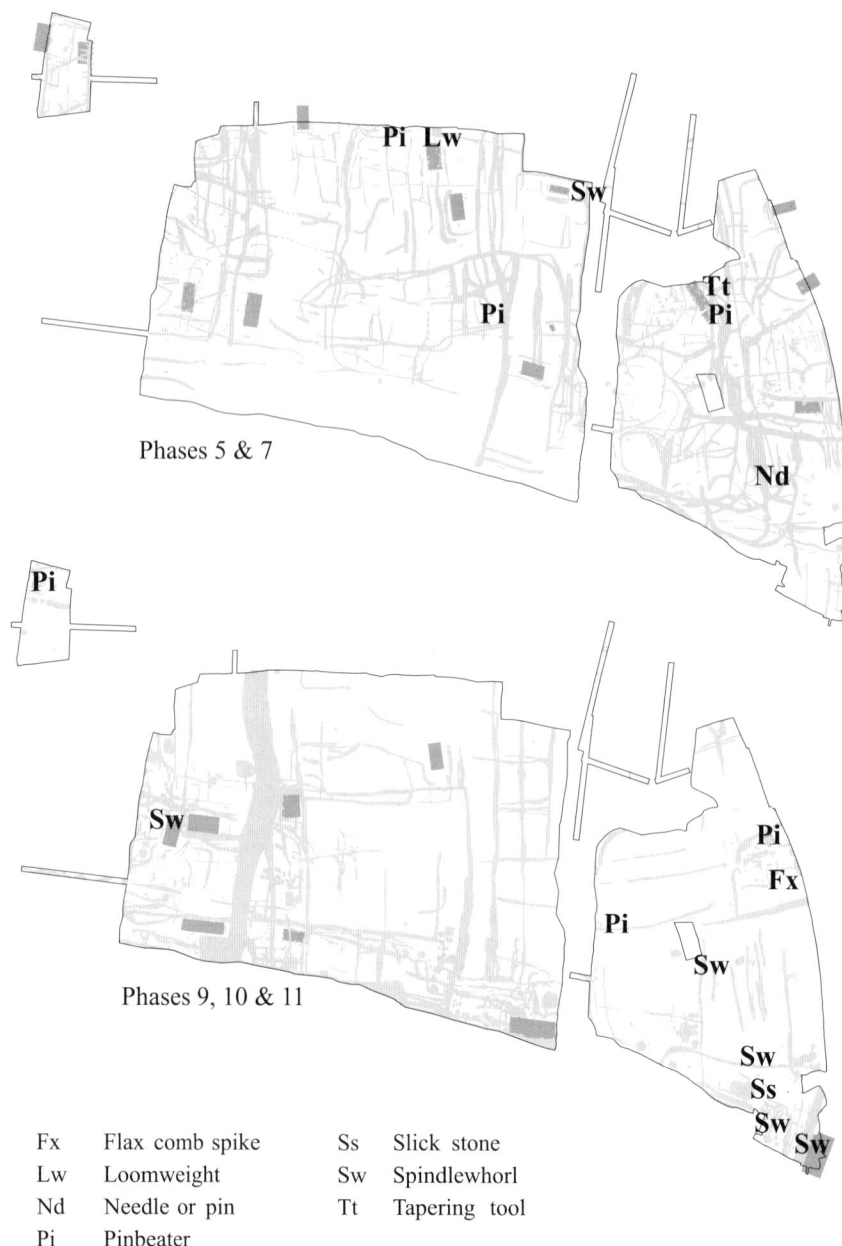

Phases 5 & 7

Phases 9, 10 & 11

Fx	Flax comb spike	Ss	Slick stone
Lw	Loomweight	Sw	Spindlewhorl
Nd	Needle or pin	Tt	Tapering tool
Pi	Pinbeater		

Figure 6.14 Distribution of weaving and textile equipment

While there is no evidence for pottery manufacture on site, there are some indications of small-scale iron-smithing, using charcoal as a fuel. Analysis of the slag indicates that hearth bottoms were varied in form; much of the slag was abraded and thought to derive from redeposited contexts. Two pieces of slag from a Phase 7 context appeared quite fresh; although no hammerscale was noted, pieces of tuyère were included. Slag was found in two distinct concentrations in Phase 7 contexts (Fig. 6.15), while hammerscale was also recovered in minute quantities from Mid–Late Saxon features nearby. This slight concentration of slag and hammerscale within the southern half of Enclosure 1 and Enclosure 12, suggests either the proximity of a small-scale metalworking area which had been disturbed by the time of excavation, or of a dump of material derived from this activity elsewhere. The very low quantities of both materials would probably indicate that the activity had not taken place on site, but perhaps at no great distance.

There is also a suggestion of small-scale bone- and antler-working on site: it seems unlikely that the small collection of perforated bones and a socketed point, mainly from Phase 6 and 7 contexts and all from the eastern half of the site, would have been imported to the site given the abundance of animal bone already available. The pinbeaters discussed above may also have been manufactured here. This suggestion is supported by evidence of saw marks on a small number of bones and sheep horn cores from Phases 5, 7 and 9.

In economic terms the main focus of the site appears to have been food production and its corollaries, leather and wool production. The animal bone assemblage indicates that sheep/goat and cattle were the predominant species in all phases. In the Mid Saxon period, sheep/goat was only slightly more common than cattle. This period also sees a peak in the number of pigs. Crabtree, studying bone from West Stow, argued that this indicated a strategy for the rapid establishment of an animal herd on a newly-founded

Grams per Context

·   1 - 10
·   11 - 20
●   21 - 40
●   41 - 80
●   81 - 160
●   161 - 320
●   321 - 640
●   641 - 1280
●   > 1280

0   50   100
metres

Figure 6.15 Distribution of slag in Phase 7

site (Crabtree 1990: indeed, at West Fen Road the proportion of pig is higher than that at West Stow). Later in the Saxon period sheep/goat and cattle become more numerous, suggesting a more typical Late Saxon producer economy. Even in the Mid Saxon phase, though, the numbers of pigs are insufficient to indicate a high-status site (Crabtree 1994) or, as has been suggested on this basis for Wicken Bonhunt, a specialist pig-producer site (Crabtree 1996). Indeed, the animal bone evidence reflects a localised subsistence strategy practised by the site's inhabitants. If surplus animals were being bred here they do not appear to have been killed and butchered on site: this aspect of food production is not archaeologically visible here.

Small numbers of horse bones (some with butchery marks), deer, rabbit, chicken, goose, duck, teal and woodcock also provide evidence for alternative food sources in the Saxon period. The low representation of wild bird bones, compared with other Mid–Late Saxon sites in East Anglia, should however be noted (cf. Crabtree 1996): the people of West Fen Road do not appear to have supplemented their diets by regular hunting of wild birds. Dogs, horses and cats were also evident in the animal bone assemblage from all Saxon (and medieval) phases; the relatively high recorded proportions of dog and horse bones are due to the numbers of articulated burials found. The ponies and small horses were probably primarily used for traction and transport (Hyland 1999), to judge from the pathologies recorded.

Low levels of fish remains were recorded from Saxon contexts, the majority of these being eel. While eel has been found in a majority (52%) of the contexts sampled the actual number of bones is very small, most samples containing single vertebrae. While it appears that eel were

a common food species, they hardly appear to have been abundant. Small amounts of herring were also found, along with lesser amounts of pike, cod, saithe, pollock and bream. Small amounts of shellfish are also in evidence in the Mid–Late Saxon period; oyster, cockle and mussel shell were recorded, as were snails, although these were not necessarily eaten.

Although heavily reliant on charred evidence from a small number of samples, the botanical assemblage from Phase 5 indicates that the arable focus of the site in the Mid Saxon period lay on free-threshing cereals, especially wheats (in contrast with the hulled wheats seen in the Iron Age and Roman assemblages, but entirely absent from sampled contexts of this phase). Small amounts of rye, oats and Celtic beans may also have been cultivated during this period. There are also some indications that great fen sedge was deliberately collected for fuel during this period — perhaps one of the only uses of fen resources, aside from the catching of eels, for which there is evidence prior to the 12th century. Common vetch may indicate that fodder was grown as part of a crop rotation scheme. All these factors might point to a widening of the subsistence strategy, but a continuing focus on crops that were suited to the local environment (wheat, rather than rye, for instance).

The Late Saxon (Phase 7) botanical evidence indicates broad continuity in subsistence strategy, with the continued dominance of free-threshing wheat and absence of hulled varieties, and small amounts of breadwheat and oats and moderate amounts of barley also indicated. An abundance of charred rye chaff from one Phase 7 context might support the suggestion that this plant was used as bedding in grain-drying kilns during this period. There is also evidence for flax (possibly being grown for its fibre),

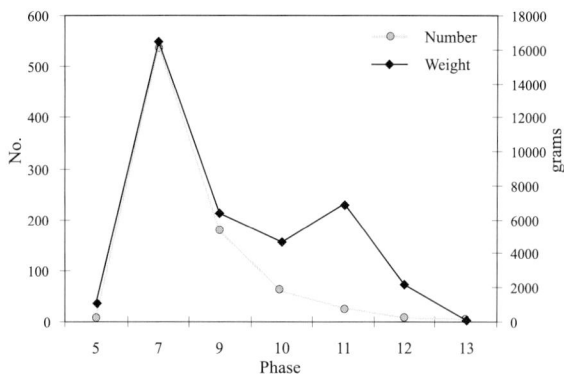

Figure 6.16 Lava quern by phase

Phase 7

Phase 9

Phases 10 & 11

Grams per context.
· 1 - 10
· 11 - 20
· 21 - 40
· 41 - 80
· 81 - 160
· 161 - 320
· 321 - 640
· 641 - 1280
· > 1280

Figure 6.17 Distribution of lava quern by phase

Celtic bean, and perhaps pea. One ditch from this phase produced numerous charred fragments of sedge, pointing to its use as fuel. Other collected wild food resources may have included hazelnuts and elderberries (although the latter could have reached the site through the use of scrub-wood as fuel). This botanical evidence contrasts with that typical of silt fen farming, which is characterised mainly by barley and breadwheat (Murphy 1993), and may therefore indicate that arable cultivation at West Fen Road was focused on the higher ground to north, east and south, rather than making use of the fenland to the west.

The weeds seen in these Mid–Late Saxon contexts, such as stinking chamomile, seem merely to indicate the farming of heavy clay soils, but the increase in wild legumes in Phase 7 may point to decreasing soil quality since these are characteristic of nitrogen-poor soils (and hence, perhaps, the use of vetch in crop rotation). Other weeds, such as fat hen, were also seen, however, and these favour nitrogen-rich soils; this may indicate that manuring was taking place in some areas. The charring of all cultivated and wild seeds (which led to their preservation) seemed to suggest that 'domestic' preparation was taking place. Threshing and winnowing may have taken place in the fields which, by the Mid Saxon period, appear to have extended considerably both to the south and north of the site. A millstone grit quern and numerous fragments of lava quern (which see a substantial peak in Phase 7, Fig. 6.16) indicate grinding of grain on site. The distribution of this lava quern (Fig. 6.17) indicated that broken fragments do not travel far from where they were once used, with clear concentrations observable around buildings.

Other indications of the environmental conditions in which this production was taking place come from the small vertebrate assemblage. In the Saxon period the site supported a wide variety of creatures, with common frog predominant but other amphibians and reptiles, such as grass snake, viper, common toad, bull frog and newts, also present. These suggest an environment of open, damp pasture and/or agricultural ground with drainage ditches and ponds.

Importation

One of the remarkable features of the site is its almost complete lack of any coinage. The single *sceatta*, recovered from one of the Phase 5 gullies surrounding Structure 4, is the only pre-Conquest coin recovered during the excavations. Unlike many of the other Mid to Late Saxon sites which have been discussed in the literature in recent years, this does not appear to have been

a site where any monetary trading was taking place (though the scale pan from a Phase 8 context may indicate the presence of someone involved in such trade).

Virtually all of the pottery seems to have been imported (as must the large quantities of lava quern), attesting to access to trade networks. There were no kilns or wasters indicating pottery production on the site and all of the identifiable sherds, with the exception of nine handmade pieces, were assigned to distinct types known to have been produced in quantity elsewhere — Ipswich ware, St Neots ware and Thetford ware. There is no known indigenous wheel-made pottery from the Isle of Ely until the medieval Ely wares began to be produced in the 12th

Figure 6.18 Plan showing density of Saxon pottery: (a) Ipswich ware and (b) Thetford and St Neots wares, both by 10m square

century. The Ipswich ware assemblage found on the site — one of the largest known outside Ipswich and London — mainly comprised small jars, with a small number of larger jars and pitchers and occasional Buttermarket-type bottles. This makes it a typical East Anglian assemblage of this kind and does not indicate any particularly high status for the site. Imported continental pottery, often associated with the wine trade, which tends to characterise inland high-status sites (and has been seen nearby in excavations at Ely Cathedral) is entirely absent in Period II (*cf.* the 10% of imported pottery from contemporary — and arguably high-status — Wicken Bonhunt: Wade 1980, 98). Even the locally imported pottery assemblage shows a lack of diversity. Stamford ware, in production — like Thetford and St Neots wares — throughout the Late Saxon

period, is all but absent, with just fifteen sherds within the contemporary Period II assemblage (0.37%). By comparison at Cottenham, a contemporary site on the mainland to the south-west, Stamford ware accounted for 2.7% of the assemblage, and at Brandon Road, Thetford — a far larger assemblage — for 3.8% (Mortimer 2000b; Dallas 1993). These higher figures would appear to be the norm and that at West Fen Road the exception, showing either difficulties of access or an inability to afford basic domestic items.

On-site activity

A number of artefacts seem to represent personal possessions. Two antler combs (one a single-sided composite and one a double-sided composite) came from

133

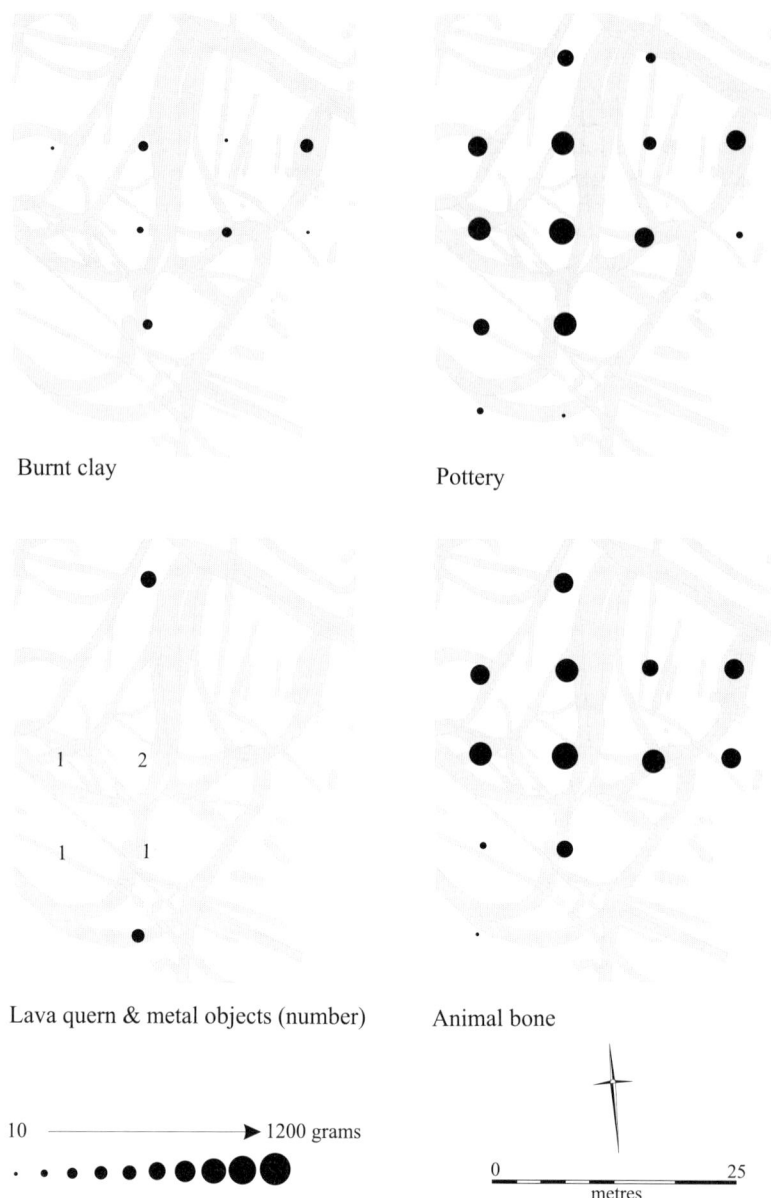

Figure 6.19 Plots showing character and extent of dumping in Phase 7 paddocks

Phase 5 contexts, and two further examples (both double-sided composites) from Phase 6. All these were found close to contemporary buildings. Another fragment of a double-sided composite comb from a Phase 10 context appears to fit more securely in a Mid Saxon date, and may be regarded as residual. A handled bone comb (unstratified) may also be of Mid–Late Saxon date. These were presumably all for grooming purposes, rather than associated with textile production.

A few items were for personal adornment. The only Saxon glass find, half a decorated blue glass bead from a Phase 6 context, may well have been a casual loss, as may a copper alloy dress-pin with polyhedral head from a Phase 5 context (along with another unstratified example of the same date), and a number of other metal artefacts from Phase 6 and 7 contexts. The latter included an iron buckle and strap-end, a hooked tag and an iron clip. (Two similar tags, a buckle and buckle-plate, the cloisonné enamel disc brooch, the copper alloy disc brooch with debased Borre style decoration, and the cast animal-head

strap-end from undated contexts also date to these phases.) Four knives came from Phase 7 contexts, and seven definite or possible whetstones confirm that metal implements were used (and sharpened) on site.

Other finds were more unusual. The possible stylus from a Phase 7 context may attest to links with the monastery or a higher-status household, though this suggestion must remain tentative. The rectangular bone mount from a Late Saxon context has been suggested to be an archer's wristguard, and is paralleled at a number of contemporary sites. It may be of interest that both of these items were found in the eastern part of Area A, possibly providing an indication of slightly 'higher-status' activity in Enclosure 1. The only other indications of weaponry on the site in this period were two iron arrowheads of Late Saxon or Saxo-Norman date, while the iron prick-spur and the bridle side-link bar from contexts of similar date denote equestrian activity. Three bone skates also came from Late Saxon contexts indicate the inhabitants' adaptation to winter conditions in the Fens. (A further example came from a Phase 10 context.)

Needless to say, caution is required when trying to characterise a site on the basis of its (incompletely excavated) finds assemblage, though the extensive use of metal-detecting both here and on the site to the north of West Fen Road offers a broader picture than might have been gained from hand collection alone. Astill and Lobb (1989, 88), discussing Late Saxon sites, argue that the quantity and range of finds alone do not appear to represent a guide to a site's status, since most Late Saxon sites are characterised by a dearth of material. They suggest that this phenomenon may be a general reflection of economic change during this period, or of a change in the way goods were circulated. Similarly, Loveluck (2001, 118–20) is quite right to warn against any simplistic equation between numbers of metalwork and coin finds with 'higher' or 'lower' status, especially when attempting to compare numbers of artefacts from Mid and Late Saxon phases of occupation (Mid Saxon phases at a variety of sites producing greater quantities than Late Saxon). However, at West Fen Road, there is little indication of elevated status in either the Mid or Late Saxon periods — compare the present site with (for example) Staunch Meadow, Brandon, Suffolk (Carr *et al.* 1988), a Mid Saxon site where excavations produced over 230 sherds of vessel glass, 234 bronze pins, around 60 bone implements, three styli, eight *sceattas* and a quantity of decorated metalwork in silver or gilt.

The excavations by Northamptonshire Archaeology to the north of West Fen Road have produced no evidence to contradict this picture, as they report a range of small finds comparable to those from the present site: a *sceatta*, three dress pins (two with polyhedral heads and one with a disc-shaped head) and a double-sided composite comb, along with a range of textile production artefacts including a possible heckle-tooth, fragments of annular loomweights, a ceramic spindle whorl and double-pointed pinbeaters. There were also 22 knives and a variety of structural fittings. More unusual finds included a fragment of a copper alloy page-turner (Mudd 2001). This evidence suggests that the part of the settlement to the north of West Fen Road saw occupation and activity of a similar nature to that to the south during the Mid Saxon period, despite the fact that no definite structures were identified there.

Waste disposal
The greatest part of any finds assemblage studied will derive from immediate waste disposal — the abandonment of used items, be they food waste, crocks, querns or building debris. Questions may arise concerning the manner of this abandonment — deliberately within pits or ditches, by direct or secondary middening, or by more 'casual' discard. In a community with limited income and resources, it is to be assumed that as much waste material as possible would have been recycled. Timbers from derelict structures would almost certainly have been re-used for as long as was possible and would then have become firewood. Food waste would have been fed to dogs and pigs; human waste may have been collected for use in industrial processes or as manure. In general, what remains for archaeologists to find is material which has no further practical use.

One factor that must be taken into account when looking at disposal practices within these enclosures is

Figure 6.20 Distribution of animal bone from the main domesticates in Phase 7

residuality. If, for example, a ditch shows a particularly high finds content over a part of its length it may not be clear whether deliberate dumping has taken place within it, or, alternatively, if it has cut through an area of earlier middening. With so many re-cut and intercutting ditches this becomes an even greater issue. One possible approach is to use the pottery from this period as a 'proxy' for all other rubbish: Fig. 6.18 shows the relative densities of pottery that was probably disposed of during the span of Phase 5 (Ipswich ware) and of Phases 6 and 8 (St Neots and Thetford ware), and appears to show a change in disposal practices between these two broad phases. In Phase 5, disposal clearly took place in close proximity to structures (mainly in nearby enclosure ditches). In the Late Saxon phases, however, while it appears that the enclosure ditches were still being used for disposal there were also areas where the remains of probable middens could be observed, perhaps suggesting a separation between different types, or quantities, of waste material.

The clearest midden area in Period II lay along the eastern edge of the 'paddocks' of Enclosures 13 and 14 in Phase 7. Here, mainly in the vicinity of Paddocks H and P, the upper fills of the later (Phase 8 and larger/later Phase 6) ditches were filled by a dark, organic 'midden-like' layer (Fig. 6.19). The finds assemblage from this layer is heavily pottery-oriented — nearly 50% of the material by weight — compared to the overall Phase 7 figure of 29%. There is only slightly less animal bone than the norm for

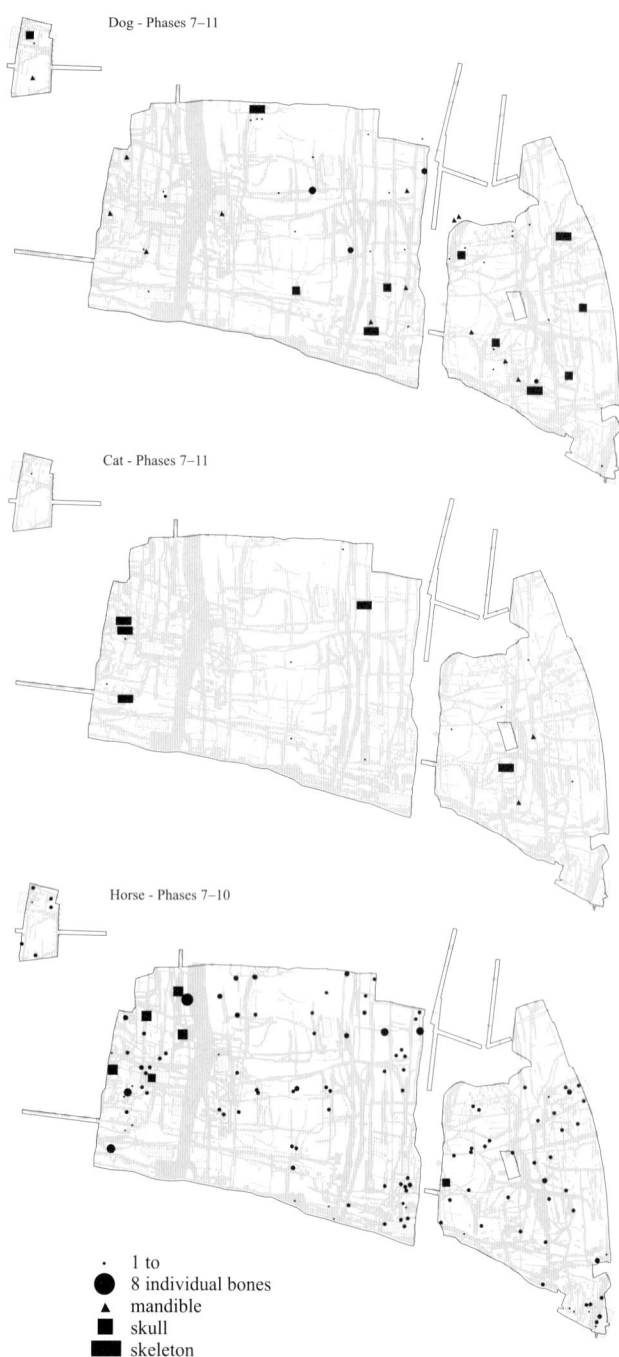

Figure 6.21 Distribution of dog, cat and horse bones in the main phases

Phase 7, but significantly less fired clay and lava quern. The lava quern, as suggested above, does not appear to have travelled far from its point of use and immediate discard. When looking at the locations of all quern fragments and other worked stone in Phase 7, in relation to contemporary structures and probable structures, there are clear 'halos' of discarded quernstone around many of the buildings, highlighting those in which crop processing or food preparation were taking place.

While the spread of cattle, sheep and pig bone is fairly even across the site (though with a definite concentration towards Area A: Fig. 6.20), a real concentration of horse bone (including two skulls) may be seen in the west of Area B, to the north of the structures in Enclosures 7 and 15. This concentration is seen to continue right through Phases 9 and 10, and includes five out of six horse skulls recorded from the site (Fig. 6.21). The concentrations of animal bone appear to fall into two categories: those in the immediate vicinity of contemporary structures, and those close to the edges of the enclosures. A study of the two bone concentrations within Enclosure 4 — one close to the possible structure, the other away from the structure within the enclosure's ditches — appears to show little real difference in the assemblages. Both contain similar-sized assemblages (220–250 pieces) from all four main domesticates, they have similar average bone weights (13–15g) and have roughly the same percentage of bones identifiable to species (41–44%), and there is no recognisable difference in the composition of the assemblages by skeletal element. It would appear, from this small study, that there is no *observable* difference between the collections. If a difference between them exists it may have been in the act of deposition, rather than the nature of the assemblage itself.

Period III: Saxo-Norman and medieval

Production and subsistence
Further evidence for textile manufacture is seen in this period (Fig. 6.14b). One double-pointed bone or antler pin-beater, and another probable example, from Phase 9 contexts may suggest the continued use of the warp-weighted loom (though these items may well have been residual); although this loom type disappeared rapidly from urban contexts after the middle of the 9th century, it persisted for much longer in rural and semi-rural contexts (Henry 1999). Two lead and two stone spindle whorls from this phase, and a lead and a decorated stone spindle whorl from Phase 10 contexts, provide some indication that this was becoming more of a specialist industry, with more standardised (and perhaps increasingly imported) equipment (*ibid.*); a fragmentary pair of iron shears from the same phase suggests the cutting of cloth on site. A black glass slick stone (of a type formerly known as a linen smoother) from a Phase 11 context indicate the finishing off or laundering of garments on site, as these are used to smooth cloth, especially garment seams (Walton Rogers 1997, 1745–9). The iron punch and band-type thimble from the same Phase 11 context seem to point to an additional type of activity on the site later on, perhaps using very heavy cloth or leather.

By the beginning of Period III, locally produced wheel-made pottery was beginning to become available. There are known kiln sites on the eastern side of Ely at

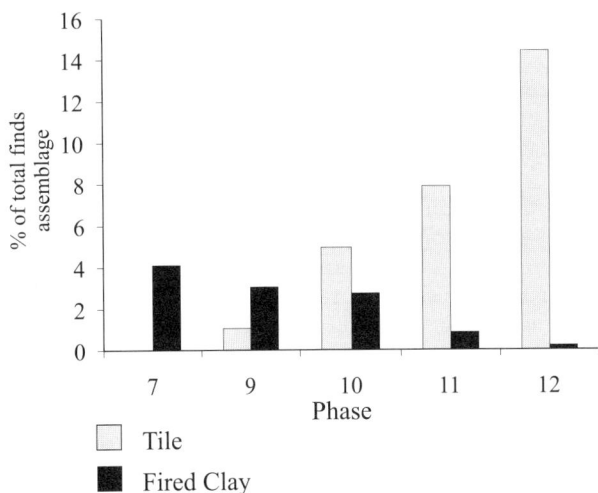

Figure 6.22 Chart showing tile and fired clay by phase, as a percentage of total finds assemblage

Potters Lane (Spoerry forthcoming), though the kilns themselves have not been excavated and there is no clear dating for their establishment. There is no evidence of pottery production either on the West Fen Road site or in the immediate vicinity, but this local and large-scale production very quickly increased the availability of pottery vessels (and thereby decreased their cost), and the amount of pottery on the site increased rapidly. Period III also saw the introduction of locally-made roof and floor tile. While small amounts were found in contexts of Phases 7 and 9, most pieces were almost certainly intrusive, though by Phase 9 (the 12th century) it is possible that the local pottery kilns were attempting to fire tile as well. It is during the span of Phase 10 (the 13th century) that both their production and use at Ely become clear; it is unlikely that the houses at West Fen Road would have been re-roofed in tile at any stage, however, and the relatively small quantities from the site may indicate their re-use, for example as hardcore. While it is possible that the floor tiles, which were also products of local kilns,

would have been used inside the buildings, at least by Phases 11 or 12, this was probably only in small numbers and around hearths. Many of the floor tiles recovered show signs of heavy burning.

Looking at the medieval tile and (all) fired clay as a percentage of the total finds assemblage by phase appears to show a divergent relationship, with tile increasing in quantity as fired clay decreases (Fig. 6.22). There will have been many reasons for this (not least the fact that tile fragments are considerably heavier than fired clay ones) but it is possible that a change in building techniques — a move away from wattle-and-daub buildings and increasing use of tiled hearths — was partly responsible.

The animal bone evidence reflects the increasing importance of wool production in the medieval economy, with a decline in slaughter of sheep/goat under two years, though cattle and sheep/goat remain the predominant species. As in the Saxon period, cattle were slaughtered at the optimum age for prime beef. Chicken, goose and duck bones are also seen, along with hare, deer and butchered horse bones (one of which from a Phase 12 context displayed skinning marks, possibly the work of a fellmonger). One dog sacrum from the latest medieval phase also displayed butchery marks; this may point to the processing of dog carcasses for fat (perhaps used in medicinal or cosmetic ointments or salves).

As in the pre-Conquest period, shellfish was a food resource, but this appeared to increase in importance during the 12th and 13th centuries; this is especially clear from the amounts of mussels and oysters consumed (Fig. 6.23). This reflects changes in diet, possibly due to changes in the availability of different foodstuffs, with greater access to sea resources being apparent. The fish assemblage also differed slightly from the preceding Saxon phases: while eel remained predominant the relative importance of marine fish, particularly herring, increased in the medieval period. Once again, this indicates a wider availability of traded goods (see Owen 2003, 66, for information about the vastly more varied diet in evidence at the monastic community, which was no doubt better-resourced). The eels were probably caught using basket traps or fine nets, and a lead fishing weight

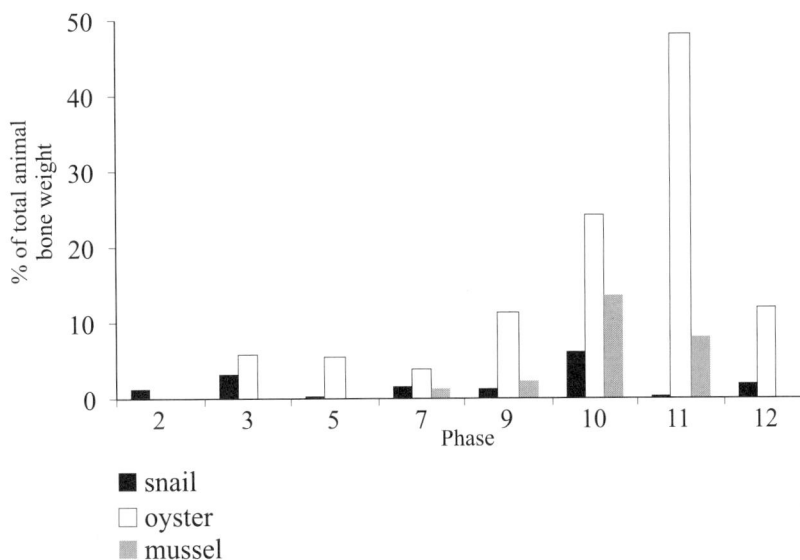

Figure 6.23 Chart showing shell as a proportion of animal bone weight by phase

137

from a Phase 9 context may provide some concrete evidence of this activity.

The Period III botanical assemblage again demonstrates continuity from the earlier phases. Free-threshing wheats predominated, with lower amounts of barley, rye and oats, but in the 12th–15th centuries low amounts of hulled wheats were also seen, and this represents a departure from earlier practice. Small amounts of Celtic bean and rounded pulses — perhaps peas or beans — suggest the cultivation of other resources; two plum stones from a cess-rich pit are the earliest recorded indications of the consumption of fruit (the stones having been eaten along with the fruit, as was common medieval practice). This period saw the earliest significant use of great fen sedge as a fuel (its association with cereal grain may suggest its use in bread ovens), indicating concerted exploitation of the fen environment for the first time. This is also evidenced by rush seeds (rushes perhaps being used for basketry or flooring) and buckthorn (from which dye could be extracted). This use of sedge as fuel in 12th–13th-century contexts predates the earliest records for this practice (Rowell 1986); its increasing use may reflect decreasing access to woodland (either through depletion, or perhaps through restriction of land rights to woodland and granting of land rights to sedge fen). Among the wild plants, the increasing incidence of clover and red bartsia point to increasingly nutrient-poor and damp soils.

Importation

Although there is evidence for an increase in the availability both of locally made and traded goods from the 12th century, imports are still very rare on the site. During the 12th and 13th centuries pottery was reaching the site from Stamford and Toynton (Lincs), Grimston and Blackborough End (Norfolk) and Lyveden (Northants), as well as from Essex and Yorkshire. The quantities of these wares, however, were remarkably small and the source for the vast bulk of the pottery was Ely itself. The commonest of the locally imported wares, an unglazed Blackborough End-type, forms only 2% of the Period III assemblage, while local Ely wares account for 90%. Only a single sherd of continental pottery was recovered from the site, a fragment of a Saintonge vessel from a Phase 10 (13th-century) context. As in the previous phase, very little coinage was recovered: just six coins span the 12th to the 16th centuries.

Activity

After Phase 7 it is unclear whether, or for how long, the importation and use of lava querns continued. With increased centralisation and control of the milling of cereals it seems unlikely that domestic milling would have continued on any large scale, and we might suggest that a mill controlled by the priory may have been implicated here. The number of fragments of lava quern recovered declined rapidly after Phase 9, but with this decline in numbers came a corresponding increase in the average weight of the fragments (Fig. 6.16). This may simply mean that the larger pieces of quern were surviving longer, and perhaps being picked up and re-used — in Phase 11 for example, over half were found re-used as cobbling within gravel surfaces. Looking at the locations of Phase 9 lava quern fragments by context

shows, in contrast to the distributions in Phase 7, less clustering around the contemporary structures (Fig. 6.17). In fact, the majority show little or no correlation between querns and buildings and it is possible that most or all of the lava is residual.

A small number of artefacts represent clothing and other personal possessions. Phase 9 contexts produced a hooked tag, and a possible dress-pin, along with five knives and a copper alloy buckle-plate, Phase 10 contexts produced five knives, a possible badge and a pair of shears, Phase 11 produced a lace-tag, a knife and some copper alloy wire, while Phase 12 contexts produced a dress pin with a wire-wound head. Unphased medieval objects from the site include three buckles, two buckle-plates and three strap-ends.

Other finds relate to animals and horse-riding activity. A distinctive early medieval horseshoe nail came from Phase 9, while a further horseshoe nail from Phase 10 and four horseshoes from Phase 11, along with an unphased harness pendant, mount and swivel, show that equestrian activity continued. A rumbler bell was probably once attached to livestock.

The small vertebrate assemblage suggests a less diverse population than in the preceding Saxon period; with the appearance of the house mouse for the first time, this suggests an intensification and increase in human activity on the site. The amount of hedging may also have reduced, suggesting an 'opening up' of the landscape. This suggestion is also supported by the Phase 9 pollen evidence, which shows a very open agricultural landscape. It is possible that this evidence points to a fundamental change in the nature of the settlement, from the rural Saxon occupation to a medieval settlement which, although apparently in decline, lay on the edge of an increasingly 'urban' community. Evidence from the lower and upper fills of the Phase 11 (14th-century) well F729 show its probable dereliction at this time, with a characteristic group of wasteland plants and an increase in the diversity of the small vertebrates associated with it, though beetle evidence suggests that barns were still in use in the vicinity. A number of items suggest a gradually increasing emphasis on security in the medieval period. A rotary key from Phase 9, a padlock and padlock key from Phase 10, a rotary key and hasp from Phase 11, and a loop-hasp for securing doors or shutters from Phase 12 all provide slight but consistent evidence for this trend. Wall-hooks from Phases 9 and 10 provide some evidence for internal fixtures. Whetstones were found in Phases 9, 10 and 11, and suggest knife-sharpening and other tool-use, while a mortar from a Phase 11 context indicates pounding, probably of food-related materials. The only evidence for weights and measures on the site is provided by a number of unphased medieval jetons and tokens.

Finally, a bone skate from a Phase 10 context and a bone sledge-runner from a Phase 11 context attest to the community's adaptation to winter conditions on the site. A 14th–15th century scabbard chape and an arrowhead from a Phase 9 context are the only indications of weaponry.

Waste disposal

The principal difference seen in the disposal of waste in this period from that seen earlier is the increase in the number of pits. While these pits may not necessarily have been dug primarily to receive rubbish they do contain dumped material, be it primary or secondary. The primary

Number of Sherds
per 10 metre square

- 10 - 20
- 21 - 50
- 51 - 100
- 101 - 200
- 200 plus

(a) Phase 9

(b) Phase 10

(c) Phase 11

(d) All Phases

- • Fineware sherd
- ● Import

Figure 6.24 Plots showing medieval pottery densities in Phases 9 to 11: (a) Ely wares in Phase 9; (b) Ely wares in Phase 10; (c) Ely wares in Phase 11; (d) Medieval glazed finewares

139

Cattle

Sheep/Goat

Pig

· 1 to
● 10 individual bones
■ Skull
▬ Skeleton

Figure 6.25 Distribution of animal bone from the main
domesticates in Phase 9

purpose of these pits is discussed elsewhere (see above). Because of the striking increase in the number of pits being dug within the occupied enclosures, and an equally dramatic decrease in the number of ditches, by Phase 10 practically the entire finds assemblage from the site comes from pits.

The directly occupied Enclosure 12 in Phase 10 provides a good example of this phenomenon, when seen in comparison to the unoccupied Enclosure 20 immediately to the west (Fig. 6.24). The pits in Enclosure

12 contained relatively small domestic assemblages which appear heavily dominated by ceramics (pottery and tile representing 82% of the assemblage by weight); these assemblages were far less mixed than those from the pits within Enclosure 20 to the west, where there was a higher proportion of other materials such as bone and slag. This is a pattern seen elsewhere, for example when comparing the domestic hinterland of Enclosure 16 to the dumps and pits in the non-domestic Enclosure 1. Assemblages from the former were dominated by ceramics (73% by weight), while the latter showed a more even spread of material including the semi-industrial lava quern, slag and burnt stone. It is possible that both primary domestic waste and that from other activities taking place at a distance from the buildings in separate enclosures was being disposed of in the immediate vicinity, leading to this contrast in the pit assemblages. One Period III dumping area has been identified in the western and northern part of Enclosure 1, mainly on the site of a small derelict building: it appears that this area had been abandoned by Phase 10. The accumulation seems to have been a straightforward dump of material intended for re-use as manure, rather than a true midden heap. The make-up of the assemblage is again more diverse than that of the contemporary pit groups around the structures. It is possible — particularly later in Period III, with the emphasis moving away from arable to pastoral farming — that small-scale middening for manuring the fields ceased to be a common practice.

The disposal of faunal remains in Phases 9 and 10 followed the pattern established in Period I (Fig. 6.25). There were dump areas both around and away from the buildings, though in Phase 9 it was only really the structures in Enclosure 7 that lay at the centre of a large concentration. It was in this area that the horse bones, and skulls, were found. The conjectured building to the east in Enclosure 4 lay at the centre of a wide swathe of dumped bone, occupying the same area, although more concentrated around the building, as that in the earlier phases (although residuality may be a factor here). By Phase 10, however, bone accumulations were confined to tight groups around the buildings themselves, and it is likely that the remainder of the area had been turned over to pasture by this time.

IV. The role of West Fen Road as a routeway

West Fen Road, which was certainly a routeway by the Mid Saxon period, is almost certainly of Roman or Iron Age origin. There are sites from both periods at West Fen Road: the Roman one is centred along it, while further excavated and crop-mark sites lie to the west. The distribution of Mid–Late Saxon settlement and attendant routeways around Ely shows a strong east–west emphasis, rather than the north–south one that might be expected given the distribution of the higher ground. The main east–west route came over the Stuntney Causeway (Fig. 6.26, J) from the east and continued across the island along the line either of West Fen Road or of West End/Fieldside, which runs parallel to the south (and marked the southern boundary of the Mid–Late Saxon settlement). The Norman motte also stands conspicuously on this cross-island route (Fig. 6.26, B). With little but fen to both east and west, and large expanses of high dry island to both north and south, this east–west axis only makes sense in the wider context of transport links. As an island in the fen

Figure 6.26 Plan of west Ely showing features and sites mentioned in the text

1 West Fen Road

2 Fieldside
2a track existing till Enclosure
2b earthwork track

3 West End

4 Beald Drove

5 Hurst Lane (Old Downham Rd)

6 Downham Road

7 St. John's Road

8 Cambridge Road

9 A10 bypass

A Ely Cathedral

B Cherry Hill (Motte & Bailey)

C St. Mary's Church

D Hospitals of St Mary's & St John's

E Modern Hospital - highest point in Ely

F Catchwater drain - 5 metre contour (except G)

G Earthwork/Enclosure

H Cropmarked silt/gravel island

I Cropmarked causeway

J Cropmarked channel

— to some extent in the Iron Age and Romano-British periods and increasingly so in medieval times — Ely's key transport links were by water, not road. Goods and people entered the island principally by boat, and this would have been the main factor not only in the layout of the main internal routes, but also in the siting of the settlements. The River Ouse today, on the eastern side of the city, is canalised and has been since the medieval period, but its main course once flowed much further out in the fen to the east. It is probable that this canalisation took place in the late 12th century after the foundation of the see of Ely (Fowler 1934, 22–3).

If, as discussed in Chapter 1, the main river access to the town from the east was probably of 12th-century origin, where did it lie before? The east–west axis of the early settlement, and the presence of possible settlement activity strung out along the low, wet western clays, must hold the answer. If it is assumed that the principal route into the island in the 8th–11th centuries was along this western side, it provides a reason for the existence of both West Fen Road itself and its attendant settlement — and for the demise of the latter once the canalised route to the east was established. West Fen Road, as its name suggests, leads directly into West Fen, a large embayment of deep fen with a spur of land to the north to Little Downham and the main bulk of the island lying to the south around Witchford and Witcham. The western side of the

embayment is partly blocked by the small island of Coveney, behind which lies the smaller Wardy Hill. Witchford sits on a stream exiting into West Fen from the large and landlocked Grunty Fen to the south. There are two possible ways by which river access could have been gained by heading west along West Fen Road: a causeway leading out across the fen to a river landing, or a road route further round the island to a location closer to the river. That a branch of the river ran across this north-western side of the island is in little doubt: the outflow from Grunty Fen has always had to exit through Witchford and West Fen, as it still does today, and West Fen itself is the catchwater for half the northern part of the island. A catchwater drain (Fig. 6.26, F) — in itself a major drainage undertaking, although its antiquity is unknown — follows the fen edge around the whole of West Fen, along the 5m contour.

At its western end, just beyond the excavation site, West Fen Road splits into three routes. A track called Hurst Lane (Fig. 6.26, 5) runs around the catchwater drain to the north to Little Downham; another, Beald Drove (Fig. 6.26, 4), follows the catchwater south towards Witchford; a third heads straight out towards the deepest part of the fen, below the 0m contour. Hurst Lane, now just a track, was once the main road from Ely to Little Downham. The current Downham Road appears to have been constructed around the middle of the 17th century:

141

while the late 17th-century 'Large Mappe of the Fennes' by Jonas Moore shows the current road leading to Downham, the earlier Speed map (1610) clearly does not. All other roads on the Speed map are shown and appear remarkably accurate, fitting well with the first 1830s Ordnance Survey maps and with modern maps. If the Downham Road had existed in 1610, it can be assumed that it would have been marked (Fig. 6.27).

At Little Downham there is a known later medieval hythe — Downham Hythe — linked into the river system by a canal called Sutton Lode (Hall 1996). It is also the site of one of the palaces of the Bishops of Ely. With the Ely–Downham road route running along West Fen Road, the Bishop's Palace and a later medieval hythe, Little Downham has to be a strong candidate for an original, pre-12th century landing place.

The alternative to this — the causeway — does not represent as simple an answer but is perhaps more intriguing. If the principal route lay to Little Downham, West Fen Road would not have needed to exist, as the road could have taken a more direct route, as the later one does. The main straight route across the island appears to be heading straight out into the fen with branches to north and south, to Downham and Witchford, representing subsidiary routes. Jonas Moore's map shows the two routes of West Fen Road and Fieldside coming out of the town and combining before heading out into the fen and coming to a halt, seemingly in the middle of nowhere, whereas the roads to Downham and Witchford are shown leading to their destinations. The western, post-medieval part of West Fen Road — the length that now heads out across the deeper fen to Coveney — is very straight, as modern Fen roads often are. The eastern section, as it heads off the island to the west of the site, is more sinuous, curving into a wide arc before it joins the modern straight road. This part of the road looks earlier, and aerial photographic evidence shows this arc continuing as a linear gravel or silt spread in the darker fen soil. This earlier road curves back on itself slightly, just to the north of the modern road and appears to end in a wider area of silt or gravel (Fig. 6.26, H). Immediately west of this small gravel island is the broad, dark crop-mark of an old river channel (Fig. 6.26, J): the channel that exits from Grunty Fen and flows up past the road, bending left and leaving West Fen between Coveney and the Little Downham spur. It is suggested that this could have been the main river transport link for the island, down West Fen Road, across a short causeway to a hythe on a channel, perhaps canalised, and thence to the wider river system. A possible point in favour of this idea is the positioning of Wardy Hill, tucked in behind the island of Coveney. The name Wardy Hill is of Saxon origin and means an island where a watch was

kept (Reaney 1943, 230). Wardy Hill sits in the Fen, at the point where the putative channel would have exited the island and would have been ideally placed to watch the approach to the island from the west and the river. Indeed, there is little else that could be watched from Wardy Hill, except a small part of the slope of the main island.

There is an intriguing earthwork feature immediately to the west of the site, at the bottom of the straight 'island' stretch of West Fen Road, as it enters the fen (Fig. 6.26, G). The catchwater drain is a sinuous feature as it follows the 5m contour, almost exactly, up from the south towards Witchford. When it reaches the area at the bottom of the site it diverts out into the Fen in a series of slightly arcing straight cuts, before returning to the line of the contour and winding up towards Little Downham. The area enclosed by this feature is approximately eight hectares. At the western side of the area there is a rectangular projection, the most conspicuous part of the earthwork, which juts out into the fen beyond. This area measures 100m by 50m, and there are high banks around both it and the straight stretch to the south. Beyond this, on the fen side, is a second right-angled ditch and bank (the bank now levelled but showing clearly on the 1830 map) which encloses almost the same area again. These earthworks sit astride the two east–west routes of West Fen Road and Fieldside, blocking off Fieldside completely (a shallow earthwork within the enclosure may mark its old course) and command the approach to the area from the fenward side. It appears to have been built for defence, to guard the approaches to the island from the fen along the causewayed stretch of West Fen Road. Its antiquity is unknown. It may have been a civil war defence: it can certainly be no later as the parish boundary of St Mary's, which includes the area of the West Fen Road settlement, follows the line of the catchwater drain and the earthwork exactly. A Second World War pillbox also occupies part of the earthwork, restating the theme of defence. If not of 17th-century origin it might date to the Anarchy, the period in the first half of the 12th century when Stephen and Matilda fought for supremacy. The Bishop of Ely at the time, Nigel, was heavily involved in this antagonism. To take the theme further (and a little into the realms of fantasy) Roger of Wendover, in his *Flores Historiarum*, states that 150 years after Hereward's death men still journeyed to see 'a wooden fortress in the fens, which the locals call Hereward's Castle'. Even 150 years later the Norman motte, if not still in use, would surely have been known for what it was. Whatever this other 'castle' was, however, nothing is known of it today.

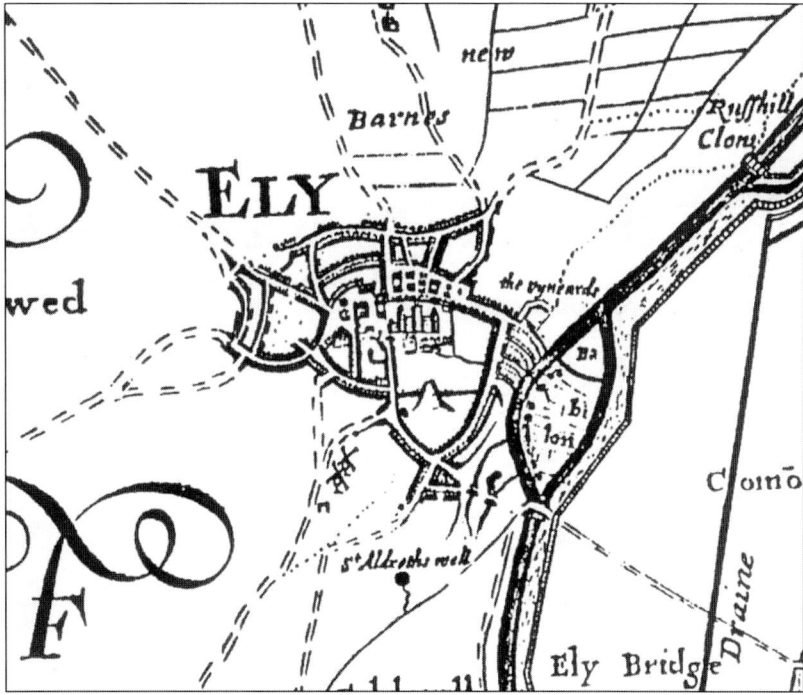

A

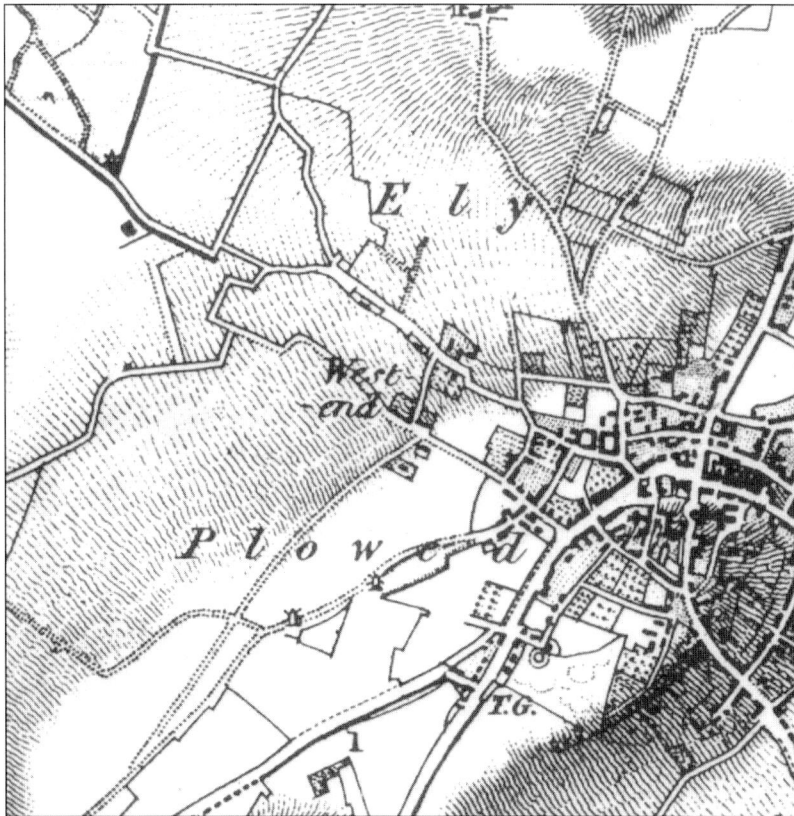

B

Figure 6.27 Ely road layouts: A – after Speed 1610; B – after 1st edn Ordnance Survey

7. Conclusions

I. Introduction

The Saxon and medieval settlement at West Fen Road is remarkable for several reasons. It joins a select body of sites of similar date to have been excavated on a comparable scale. Even so, the limits of the settlement have not been identified, except to the south. To the north it is assumed to have extended to the frontage of West Fen Road itself in the Late Saxon period, and the results of the excavations by Northamptonshire Archaeology show that it spanned the road prior to this; certainly it stretched further to the east and the west, to judge by the truncated enclosures apparent on the plans. In size, the excavated area considered in this report compares with those studied at Catholme, Staffs (Losco-Bradley and Kinsley 2002), Brandon Road, Thetford, Norfolk (Dallas 1993) and Yarnton, Oxon (Hey 2004). Its large artefactual assemblage (including over 20,000 sherds of pottery and 16,000 animal bones) and the number of stratigraphic relationships recorded have permitted detailed phasing of the site in a way that was impossible at (for instance) Catholme, despite some of the problems that were involved both in excavating the area and subsequently in phasing it.

West Fen Road is also one of the longest-lived Saxon to medieval settlements yet to be excavated on such a scale: from its establishment in the 8th century, it saw constant occupation until perhaps the early 15th century, although this declined from a peak in the 10th and 11th centuries. This continuity of occupation is further reflected in the surprisingly durable nature of the ditched enclosures: throughout many centuries, these plots of enclosed land remained in use, perhaps by the descendants of former occupants.

From the start, this was a secular rural settlement contemporary with the monastic centre for which Ely was famous; it seems possible that the settlement was even founded in order to provide food and services to the monastery. The site also offers the opportunity, not only to examine issues of continuity and change through the period of the Danelaw, but also right through the period of the Norman Conquest — a time at which the Isle of Ely played a pivotal role in contemporary religious and political life.

II. The establishment and development of the settlement
(Figs 7.1 and 7.2)

Fundamental to understanding any settlement site is an appreciation of why it is where it is, and the geographic, economic and political factors that created and sustained it. The Saxon settlement at West Fen Road appears to have been a *de novo* foundation, probably in the second quarter of the 8th century. This dating is suggested by the lack of handmade pottery and corresponding dominance of Ipswich ware in the earliest phase of the site, and a single

sceatta of 730–40. This was a time when widespread settlement shift is recorded in Eastern England. While there may have been an earlier Saxon predecessor along West Fen Road, within the core of the Romano-British site, this is only suggested by a handful of pottery sherds on these and the excavations to the north of the road (Mudd 2000). The low level of early pottery, and complete lack of contemporary features, suggest that any Early Saxon settlement would have been small-scale and limited to the roadside zone, since this was the only area that was not excavated.

The Mid Saxon settlement was partly laid out within the areas of Late Iron Age and Roman occupation, making use of some of the (presumably still visible) Romano-British enclosures. The Mid Saxon layout seen on the Ashwell Site was paralleled on the north side of the road. Although the excavations there by Northamptonshire Archaeology did not reveal unequivocal evidence for buildings, the range of the archaeological features and artefactual evidence was otherwise very similar: it may be argued that an extensive settled area extending to the north and south of the road was characterised by numerous sub-rectangular enclosures (Fig. 7.1). The extent of the Mid Saxon settlement to the north of the road makes it clear that this re-use is more by accident than design; the new settlement happened, in part, to occupy the earthworks of the former earthwork site, which itself was probably ranged along a road that was already in existence. The settlement enclosures excavated to the south of West Fen Road were the backs of plots fronting onto the road, and they extend further to the west than the main enclosures seen to the north of the road; as such, they represent a linear extension of the main settlement area. There was also a back route, running behind the more southerly enclosures, parallel to West Fen Road.

While part of the settlement was laid out within the confines of the Romano-British site, a new series of ditches was excavated to enclose at least six occupied areas, and probably more. These enclosures contained a number of domestic and non-domestic structures, along with other features such as pits. None of them were seen in their entirety and thus it is impossible to say whether all contained domestic buildings, though at least three of those that were seen did. To the south and west lay two large empty enclosures, perhaps used for the herding of animals. This system of enclosures may be paralleled at the excavated settlement at Catholme (Losco-Bradley and Kinsley 2002) and at that known from excavation and aerial photographs at Riby Crossroads (Steedman 1995), both of which may have been occupied from the 7th to the 9th centuries; other examples are known at Cottenham, Cambridgeshire (Mortimer 2000b), and at Brandon (Carr *et al.* 1988) and West Stow, Suffolk (West 1985) (Fig. 7.2; see Chapter 6 for further discussion).

How did this settlement relate to the documented monastic site? The double house for monks and nuns was founded at Ely in *c.* 673, on a new site said to lie a mile away from an existing settlement at Cratendune. As the

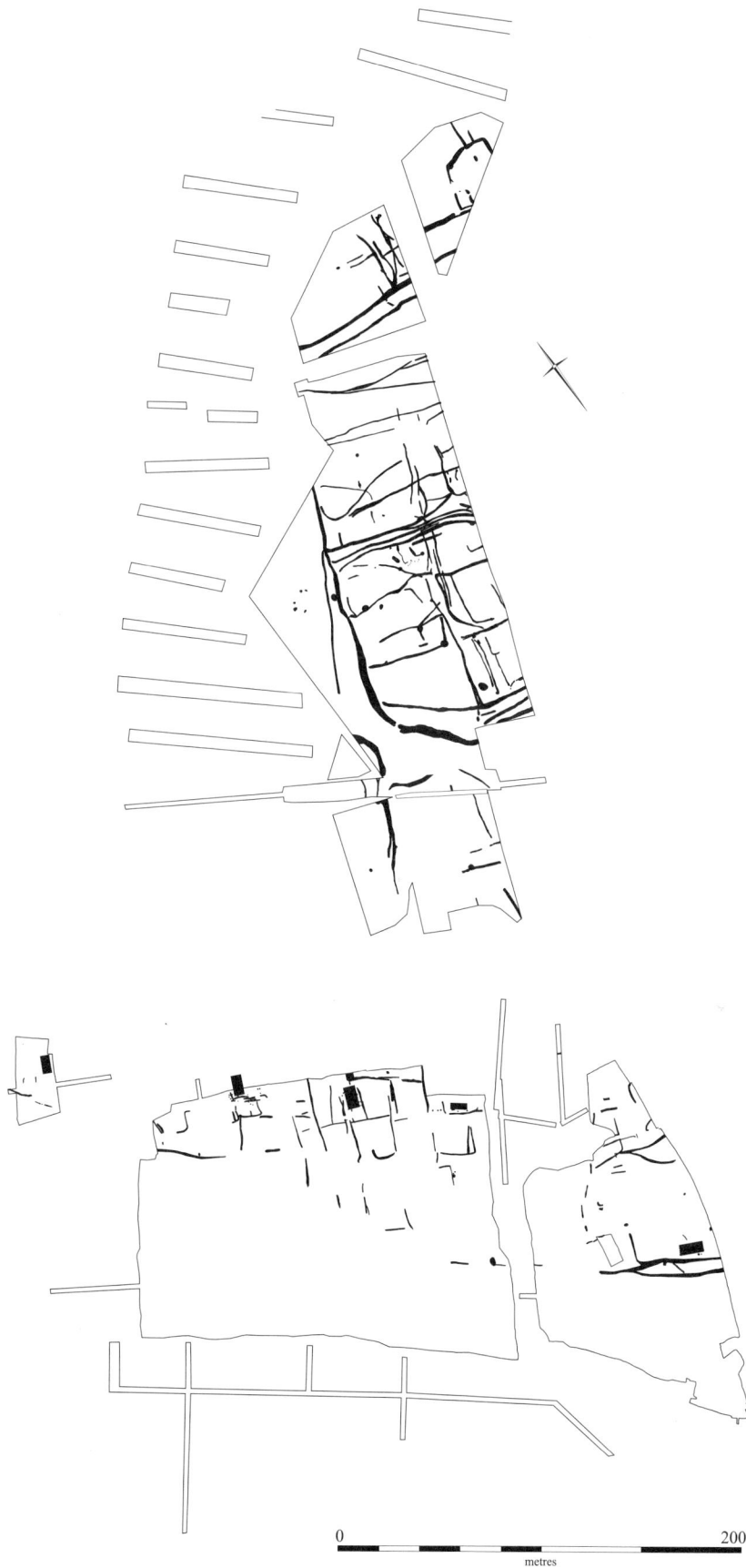

Figure 7.1 Overall Mid Saxon site plan, including excavations to the north of West Fen Road (Mudd 2000)

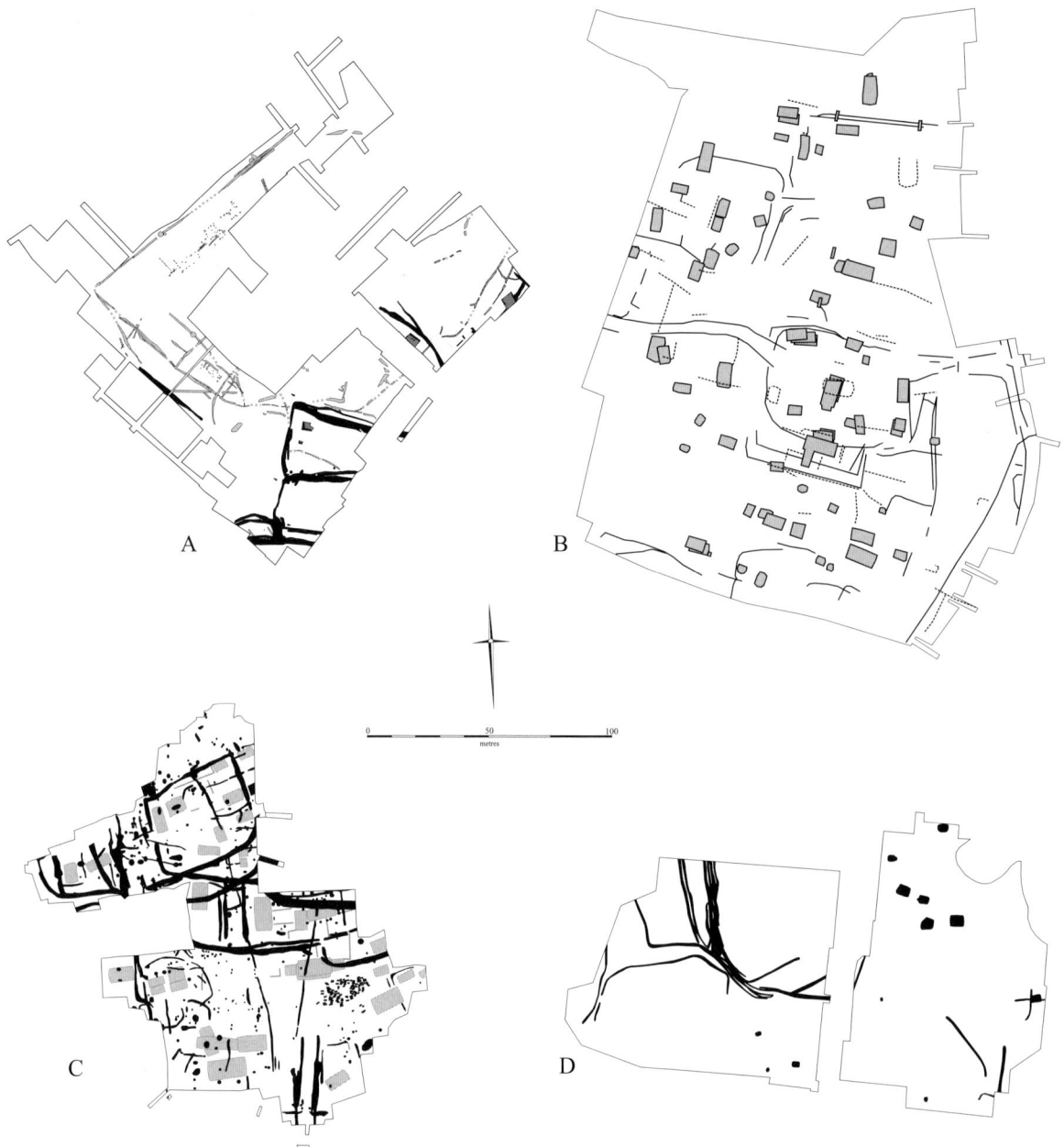

Figure 7.2 Other Mid Saxon sites considered in the text

A – Cottenham, Cambridgeshire (after Mortimer 2000b); B – Catholme, Nottinghamshire (after Losco-Bradley and Kinsley 2002); C – Brandon, Suffolk (after Carr *et al.* 1988); D – West Stow, Suffolk (after West 1985)

compiler of the *Liber Eliensis* records that ancient coins and objects were still being found on the site of the previous settlement (Blake 1962, 3–4), it is obvious that Cratendune cannot be located at West Fen Road. This area was still firmly in occupation at the time when *Liber Eliensis* was being compiled (between 1131 and 1174); furthermore, the excavations have produced no evidence of Saxon settlement prior to the 8th century. It is also stated that 'coins of many Kings' were found at Cratendune, making it probable that this site was intensively occupied in the Romano-British period. The identification of the site near Bedwell Hay Farm as Cratendune (Hall 1996) has been deemed unlikely (*The historical context*, p.4); the location of Cratendune thus remains uncertain.

It is suggested here that the land north and south of West Fen Road was part of the monastic estate at the inception of the settlement. The monastery — and later the abbey and then the bishop — would have acted as an overlord, and one with greater wealth and power than most. As the possible driving force behind the creation of the settlement, the location of Etheldreda's first monastery is worthy of detailed discussion here. Its whereabouts are subject to debate, and it was not necessarily located on the site of the current cathedral, although it is generally believed to have been so.

Etheldreda (also called St Aethelthryth and Audrey), the daughter of Anna, king of the East Angles, founded her double house for monks and nuns on a new site on high ground and the church was completed in 673. It is likely that this foundation would have become a focus for settlement, perhaps associated with the gradual or wholesale abandonment of earlier sites. The monastery itself is supposed to have been destroyed by Danes in 870,

146

and in 970 a Benedictine abbey was established. This was founded by Bishop Ethelwold on land granted by King Edgar (Blake 1962, 74–5), implying that Ely had become part of the royal estate and thus indicating a break with Etheldreda's monastic endowment. It has been argued that there is no direct link between Etheldreda's foundation and Ethelwold's, and that the origins of the lands and rights of the medieval church of Ely lie in King Edgar's charter of re-foundation (Miller 1951, 15).

While in the late 10th century it is probable that the Benedictine abbey would have been built in stone, the original 7th-century monastery would almost certainly have been of timber, even if it was added to and embellished in stone over the following two centuries. The site of the present cathedral (and probably the 10th-century abbey) was chosen partly because it lies on Greensand, which provides a good, solid foundation for large stone buildings. A 7th-century wooden church would not have needed to take this into consideration, since clay or sand subsoil would suffice. The cathedral lies at c. 19–20m OD; despite appearances from below this is not the highest part of the island, nor is it even the highest part of the area within Ely itself. Less than a kilometre to the south-west, overlooking the cathedral site, is a clay and sand hilltop reaching 26–27m OD, the highest point in the vicinity (Fig. 6.26, E). If height and visibility were of prime importance in the siting of a church, then this would have been an ideal location.

The hilltop in question lies at the south side of a parcel of land once occupied by the medieval hospitals of St John the Baptist and St Mary. At the north end of the area are medieval buildings believed to be the chapels of the two foundations. As David Hall (1996) has commented:

> They are rather odd because they were located very close together and amalgamated as early as 1240, whereas, elsewhere, most hospitals were being newly founded in the mid 12th century. Cobbett and Palmer have fully considered the site (1935). Cobbett discussed the architecture and identification of the three surviving medieval buildings. One of them has a carved tympanum that was variously thought to be either 8th century or late Norman in date. He speculated whether it was part of St Etheldreda's church. The historical sources were fully studied by Palmer; a hospital was first mentioned in 1169, but, as already noted, the two hospitals were amalgamated as St John's, in 1240.
>
> After the Dissolution, the site and buildings passed to Clare College, Cambridge, along with various muniments. A terrier of 1514 describes the arable land belonging to the hospital, being 97 acres scattered as strips in furlongs. A terrier of 1665 describes the 'manor place', orchards and closes adjoining with stone barn and other houses of office and one little tenement, in all extending to 20 acres. It then itemizes the open-field land. Twenty acres is a very large site for a medieval hospital, and may imply that the two hospitals occupied a special place, such as the main centre of the former settlement or possibly the site of the first monastery.

Henderson (1997, 217), commenting on the sculptural fragment, argued for an 8th-century date, and suggested that it may have decorated the inside or outside of the first stone church at Ely.

Wherever the first monastery was, the relationship between it and the settlement would certainly not have been an equal one: the settlement at West Fen Road appears to have been a provider of goods and services rather than a recipient. What, however, was the nature of the settlement at Ely in the Mid Saxon period?

First of all, there is some doubt about its extent. As well as the extensive remains at West Fen Road, occasional Mid Saxon features, or finds of Ipswich ware, have been identified at Chief's St., West End and St Mary's Lodge (Kenney 1999, 2002; Robinson 2000), further to the east at Lady Chapel and Walsingham House (Regan 2001; Hunter 1992), and at the base of the steep eastern slope at Broad St. (Cessford et al. forthcoming) (see Fig. 1.4 for locations). Excavations that have taken place immediately to the north of this strip at Upherds Lane, Chapel St. and Forehill, while showing evidence of Late Saxon activity, have produced no Mid Saxon finds or features (Taylor-Wilson 1992; Hinman 1996; Alexander 2003). Excavations to the south, at St. Johns Road, Green Field, and Potters Lane, have produced neither; the first-named produced only Iron Age evidence, the latter two medieval (Abrams 2000; Spoerry forthcoming). If the presence of occasional features and sherds of Ipswich ware can be taken as an indicator of settlement, this might suggest an extensive occupation area (though not necessarily one that was intensively occupied) stretching for at least 1.75km west (and possibly east) from the current city centre in the 8th and 9th centuries. How might such a settlement be characterised?

Ely was, categorically, not a *wic* site: comparison with the excavated areas of Hamwic and Lundenwic (Andrews 1997, Malcolm and Bowsher 2003) reveals nothing resembling the organised street and alley network, density and rapid replacement of buildings, or high proportion of imported goods seen on those sites. However, Blinkhorn (1999), through his study of Ipswich ware, has suggested that an 'economic boom' in eastern England in the second quarter of the 8th century was facilitated by the redistribution of goods from such developing *wic* centres. He postulates that some rural settlements began to produce a more specialised range of produce at this time, with the resultant surpluses allowing them to gain access to the emerging market. The laying out of the West Fen Road settlement (whatever its extent) may have played a part in this process. If this is the case, it is interesting that this appears to have occurred under monastic control, and this would seem to support Blair's (forthcoming) argument that directly exploited 'core areas' of territory emerged first on monastic estates. A key factor here must also have been the rapid development of a monetary economy in the first half of the 8th century (Metcalf 1984; Scull 2002).

A concept worth bearing in mind here is that of the 'monastic town'. In his study of Anglo-Saxon Oxfordshire, Blair (1998) lists a series of sites of known minsters that go on to develop urban characteristics in the later Anglo-Saxon period. At Eynsham, Bampton and Bloxham, for example, the core settlement of the ecclesiastical enclosure was enlarged by the addition of streets and house plots to accommodate the growing lay population (ibid., 119). Although this may not help us in our interpretation of the West Fen Road settlement as such, it does help to remove the argument from the confines of deciding whether or not such sites are 'proto-urban'.

It is worth remembering that our assumptions about the nature of urban and proto-urban life in Mid and Late Saxon England are biased by the results of excavations in the well-known *wic* sites at Southampton, York, London and Ipswich. There may have been a range of different settlement forms which are not so conducive to categorisation. Excavations at Steyning in West Sussex (Gardiner 1993; Gardiner and Greatorex 1997) have produced a now familiar picture of a small number of buildings set within large ditched enclosures. However, Steyning is described as a town in the Late Saxon period, and these large occupied enclosures have been found in a number of locations in and around the supposedly urban area. Gardiner and Greatorex (1997, 168–70) have raised the intriguing possibility that this pattern of enclosures represents the true nature of the Late Saxon small town: not intensively occupied and geared towards intensive craft production, like the main Saxo-Norman towns, but something rather different. As well as the concept of the 'monastic town', the idea of some settlements occupying an 'ambivalent' place between our notions of urban and rural conditions in the Late Saxon period may prove a flexible and productive one.

Certainly, the impression of Ely given by Domesday is one of a rural-type settlement (Hampson and Atkinson 1953, 34). Excavations within Ely city centre only reveal evidence for burgage plots from the 12th–13th centuries (Alexander 2003, Cessford *et al.* forthcoming). These show an intensification of activity on the eastern side of the island from the 12th century, and particularly the 13th–14th centuries. When the Ouse was canalised alongside the island's eastern side, it would have provided the incentive for a substantial shift in the focus of many of the town's activities. The construction of the new Norman cathedral in the late 11th century, again on the eastern side, and the subsequent establishment of a large market area and associated tenements in the Market Place just outside it (Robinson 1994, 6–7), would have been further pulls. It was in the 12th century that the intensity of occupation at West Fen Road began to diminish, with a central part of the site being given over to further paddocks and fields and some amalgamation of the previous enclosures. The number of structures did not really decrease, but there was the beginning of a major shift in actual occupation to the southern trackside. The consolidation of the West Fen Road settlement enclosures into larger, more 'productive', farms was almost certainly dictated by the Church authorities, possibly in a reorganisation of their holdings in the first decades of the new Norman order, with the drive to produce surplus crops for export and profit (see Owen 2003 for discussion of the economic demands of the monastic community).

This process continued through the 13th and 14th centuries, with increasing amounts of land at West Fen Road being given over to plough or pasture, and the consolidation of the domestic properties into three single farmsteads along the southern track set within large land-blocks of roughly equal size. The strip that the domestic enclosures occupy is narrow, no more than 50m wide, with the houses 10m back from the trackway. There is some evidence that such narrow occupied strips also fronted onto West Fen Road at this time: there are pit groups and domestic waste in Enclosure 6 in Phase 10 (13th century), suggesting that the earlier structure there had been re-built to the north along the roadside, while similar pits were seen at the back of Enclosure 2. However, there is no direct evidence for this occupation continuing beyond the 13th century. It is possible that here we see evidence of a major reorganisation of the bishop's holdings, with intensification of settlement between the new cathedral and the canalised Ouse and a corresponding decline in activity at West Fen Road.

Although generally the 13th century was an age of intensive farming and increased population, this trend reversed sharply in the early decades of the 14th century. There were harvest failures and livestock epidemics in 1315–22, and by the 1340s nearly 5000 acres had gone out of cultivation in Cambridgeshire, partly as a result of flooding (Miller and Hatcher 1978, 59–61). The Black Death, reaching Ely in 1349, would clearly have caused increased mortality and indirectly affected farming practices; much of the arable that remained was turned into pasture. Of the three farm units seen on at West Fen Road, the central one disappeared earliest, but all three were probably disused by the early part of the 15th century.

III. Conclusions

From its origins until its demise, the Saxon and medieval site at West Fen Road, Ely was part of a large settlement, possibly deliberately established as a food-producing site for the nearby monastery (whose location is not certain). Within shifting boundaries, its activities were geared towards crop and animal husbandry; any other production which took place on site appears to have been of a low-level, informal nature, such as occasional bone-working and small-scale metalworking or textile manufacture. Signs of any particular status are few: one *sceatta* from the Mid Saxon period, a possible stylus from the Late Saxon phase, and a few items of personal adornment represent the sum total for the pre-Conquest period. These tended to be concentrated in the higher, south-eastern corner of the site, and are perhaps an indication that the occupants of one or two of the farmsteads had slightly higher social aspirations, and perhaps greater available resources, than the rest of the settlement's inhabitants.

As is generally the case, the great events of history leave no trace for the archaeologist, and it is tempting to believe they had equally little impact on the majority of the populace at the time. Although the Danes are said to have burnt the monastery at Ely (Blake 1962, 54), this was probably a limited destruction; there is certainly no evidence of burning in phases of this date at West Fen Road, and it is unlikely that the settlement would have had anything to offer in the form of loot. The intensification of settlement on the site may have been a consequence of administrative changes brought about by the area's inclusion within the Danelaw, but is more likely to be a result of monastic activity or population change. This said, however, it is possible that the impact of the Danish incursion can be seen at West Fen Road. The large area of Mid Saxon settlement to the north of the road — perhaps three distinct phases of activity — was abandoned before the introduction of St Neots or Thetford ware around the last quarter of the 9th century. The monastery was sacked in 870 and it is possible that this event, directly or indirectly, was a root cause of this abandonment and the changes in land holding or organisation which it implies. Later on, the foundation of the Benedictine abbey at Ely in 970, and the subsequent establishment of an extensive estate on the Isle of Ely and beyond over the following 50 years, may have led to greater demands on the settlement, the inhabitants of which were presumably now dependants of the abbey.

Given the generally low status of the site, the Norman Conquest again appears to have wrought little immediate change on the West Fen Road settlement. Its inhabitants may, though, have experienced an increase in the burdens imposed on them by the feudal system, whereby all the abbey's dependants were reduced to the status of tenant (see Hampson and Atkinson 1953, 37). Indeed, the increasing exploitation of fen resources seen from the 12th century onwards may be a reflection of this (though would apparently contrast with the greater access to, for example, marine resources, which is seen at the same time; see King 1973 for a study of tenurial arrangements at Peterborough Abbey in the same period). Incidentally, it is interesting how little evidence there appears to be from West Fen Road for the exploitation of fen resources prior to this. Medieval chronicles document the varied fen resources available: for example, the Peterborough Chronicle of Hugh Candidus, written around 1150, stated:

> This marsh, however, is very useful for men; for in it are found wood and twigs for fires, hay for the fodder of cattle, thatch for covering houses, and many other useful things. It is, moreover, productive of birds and fish (quoted in Darby 1940, 21).

Darby (*ibid.*, 22–42) describes various other fen resources available, yet the environmental evidence from the West Fen Road site presented here shows how similar it was to contemporary lowland sites throughout its history, albeit with slight adaptations in the post-Conquest period.

After the Conquest, the volume of material culture recovered from the site does increase in quantity, but this probably says more about the generally higher availability and increased affordability of artefacts such as pottery and decorated metalwork, than it does about any changes to the social or economic status of the settlement. Despite its consistently poor material culture, this site was an integral part of Mid Saxon Ely, and its ability to produce surplus produce would have been fundamental to the continued functioning of the monastic settlement. The settlement was also part of Ely in the Late Saxon period, perhaps offering a new perspective on the organisation of the settlement at that time. With regard to the medieval period, the West Fen Road site may shed light on the relationship between an urban centre and its food-producing hinterland.

Appendix: Botanical evidence from Iron Age, Roman, Mid–Late Saxon and medieval contexts

	158	160	175	176	169	168	156	171	172	173	174
Sample	158	160	175	176	169	168	156	171	172	173	174
Context	6742	6973	7696	7697	8557	8559	6615	8575	8576	8579	8580
Feature	F.1503	F.1573	F.1514	F.1491	F.1573	F.1573	F.1461	F.1573	F.1573	F.2039	F.2039
Volume/ litres	2	2	8	10	8	7	6	10	10	10	10
Type	gully	ditch	gully	gully	ditch	ditch	pit	ditch	ditch	ditch	ditch
Site Phase	2	2	2	2	2	2	3	3	3	3	3
Cereals											
Hordeum vulgare sensu lato grain			1	2	1						1
Triticum aestivum sensu lato grain			1	6			1			4	
Triticum c.f. *spelta* grain							28				
Triticum spelta/dicoccum grain			5	1		1	24				1
Triticum sp. grain							22				
Triticum/Hordeum grain	1						1				
Avena sp. grain				9	4	3	2		2	6	
cereal indet. grain			2	6	1	1		2			1
Hordeum vulgare sensu lato rachis internode				2	3	1					
T. aestivum sensu lato rachis internode			1							1	
Triticum dicoccum Schubl. glume base			5	25	2	3					
Triticum dicoccum Schubl. spikelet fork				3	1						
Triticum spelta L. glume base	2		25	25	2		60				
Triticum spelta/dicoccum glume base	2		160	139	10	2	407				
Triticum spelta/dicoccum spikelet fork					2						
Avena sp. awn fragment			1		3	1	2				
Avena sp. lemma base							1				
cereal culm node						1	1			1	
Non-cereals											
Urtica dioica L.			1				1				
Corylus avellana L. (shell frags.)			1								
Chenopodium polyspermum L.					1	1					
Chenopodium ficifolium L.			1		2	1					
Chenopodium album L.			2	3		1					1
Chenopodium spp.				2	1						
Atriplex patula/prostrata							2				
Atriplex spp.			2			3					
Montia fontana ssp. *chondrosperma* (Fenzl) Walters				1							
Stellaria media (L.) Villars			3		1				1		
Persicaria maculosa Gray.			1	2	1						
Rumex crispus L.							2				
Rumex conglomeratus/obstutifolius/sanguineus							3				
Cochleria sp.				1							
small *Brassica* spp.					1						
Anagallis arvensis L.						6					
small *Potentilla* sp.							1				
Vicia faba L.										2	
small *Vicia/Lathyrus* sp. (<2mm)					1		6			1	
large *Vicia/Lathyrus* sp. (>2mm)			5								
Medicago lupulina L.						1					
small *Trifolium* spp. (<2mm)			2				3				
APIACEAE indet. kernel							1				
Plantago major L.							1				
Odontites vernus (Bell.) Dumort.			1				4				
Lapsana communis L.						1					
Crepis sp.						1					
Anthemis cotula L.							9				
Leucanthemum vulgare Lam.							1				
Tripleurospermum inodorum (L.) Schultz				1	1						
Luzula sp.							1				
Eleocharis c.f. *palustris* (L.) Roemer			1					1			
Cladium mariscus (L.) Pohl.			1			2					
Carex spp.				1		1					
CYPERACEAE indet.				1							
CYPERACEAE stems											
Festuca/Lolium sp.						3	2				
Poa annua L.					1						
Poa spp.						1					

Sample	158	160	175	176	169	168	156	171	172	173	174
Context	6742	6973	7696	7697	8557	8559	6615	8575	8576	8579	8580
Feature	F.1503	F.1573	F.1514	F.1491	F.1573	F.1573	F.1461	F.1573	F.1573	F.2039	F.2039
Volume/ litres	2	2	8	10	8	7	6	10	10	10	10
Type	gully	ditch	gully	gully	ditch	ditch	pit	ditch	ditch	ditch	ditch
Site Phase	2	2	2	2	2	2	3	3	3	3	3
Arrhenatherum elatius var. *bulbosum* (Gilib.) St-Amans		1									
Phleum c.f. *bertolonii* DC.					1						
Phleum sp.			1	4			2				
Poa/Phleum sp.			3			1					
Bromus spp.			3		1						
Bromus/Avena sp.			8								
medium POACEAE indet.							1				
POACEAE culm node		4									
Monocot. plant stems											
Monocot. plant basal culm node		9		1							
seed indet.					1		2				
parenchyma tissue											
large charcoal (>4mm)	++						+				
mid charcoal (2-4mm)	+++	–	++	+	+	–	++	+	–	+	++
small charcoal (<2mm)	+++	+	+++	+++	++	++	+++	++	++	++	+++
vitrified charcoal	++										

Table 5.11 Charred botanical evidence from Period I (Iron Age and Roman)

Cereals and non-cereals by sample (archaeobotanical remains)

	16	32	66	71	165	162	4	18	20	23	31	29	27	28	33	35	36	55	57	59	58	69	76	80	82	85	86
Sample	16	32	66	71	165	162	4	18	20	23	31	29	27	28	33	35	36	55	57	59	58	69	76	80	82	85	86
Context	1834	2223	2519	2642	7162	7163	1535	1864	2010	2113	2167b	2171	2172	2174	2218	2220	2248	2441	2455	2472	2477	2546	2708	2802	2861	2890	2891
Feature	F.385	F.543	F.591	F.629	F.1589	F.1589	F.340	F.426	F.447	F.491	F.520	F.523	F.534	F.526	F.540	F.541	F.549	-	F.578	F.583	F.585	F.601	F.567	-	F.678	-	-
Volume/litres	8	8	12	4	8	5	3	7	1	14	1.5	15	12	8	9	7	14	0.5	15	7	7	12	12	3	15	5	1
Type	lower pit	ditch base	pit	p-hole	pit	pit	ditch	later ditch	ditch	ditch	ditch base	ditch	ditch	ditch	cessy pit	pit	ditch	p-hole	pit	pit	ditch	pit	p-hole	p-hole	cessy ditch	p-hole	p-hole
Site Phase	5	5	5	5	5	5	7	7	7	7	7	7	7	7	7	7	7	7	7	7	7	7	7	7	7	7	7
Cereals																											
hulled, twisted Hordeum vulgare s.l. grain																1											
naked Hordeum vulgare sensu lato grain	1																										
hulled Hordeum vulgare sensu lato grain	1															3	1	2			1				9		
Hordeum vulgare sensu lato grain	41	3		15	5			8		5	2	7		3	1	111	5	2	11		8	10			2	5	
Triticum aestivum sensu lato grain			5	6	94	1		11	11	21	2	20	3	18	6	49	45	3	29	12	12	11	5		14	2	2
Triticum spelta/dicoccum grain									1																		
Triticum sp. grain	61		2		2	1			3	6				3	3	1	5	1	7		2	9				1	
Triticum/Hordeum grain	83			69	6	2			1	1		3		7	1	38	5		17		12	4	3			1	
Secale cereale L. grain					10	2		4			2					6	12								4	2	
Secale/Avena grain																	15										
Triticum/Secale grain	22				8									2	1	6	4		9		2		1				
Avena sp. grain	16	4		20	18	3		4				4		2	4	2			8	1	2	15	1	7	3	9	
cereal indet. grain	53		3	6	25			10		7		7		2	9	9	13		20	2	2	19	4	3	15	7	
6-row Hordeum vulgare s.l. rachis internode	1										1												1				2
Hordeum vulgare sensu lato rachis internode	2			1															1		6		1	3	4	1	
tetraploid Triticum aestivum s.l. rachis internode																											
hexaploid Triticum aestivum s.l. rachis internode							1		1								1			13							
T. aestivum sensu lato rhachis internode	5							1							1		6				5		4	4	2	6	
Triticum dicoccum L. glume base	2																										
Triticum spelta L. glume base									1																		
Secale cereale rachis internode																	39			2		1					
Hordeum/Secale sp. rachis internode																	3			1						1	
Avena sp. awn fragment	1																1						1		1	1	
Avena sp. lemma base																											
Avena sp. floret base																											
cereal culm node				1																1		1		1			
cereal basal culm node	6				2																1	3			1		
cereal indet. rhachis internode																	6								2		1
Non-cereals																											
Ranunculus c.f. flammula L.		1																				1					
Ranunculus sp.																						1					
Urtica dioica L.																											

152

Sample	16	32	66	71	165	162	4	18	20	23	31	29	27	28	33	35	36	55	57	59	58	69	76	80	82	85	86
Context	1834	2223	2519	2642	7162	7163	1535	1864	2010	2113	2167b	2171	2172	2174	2218	2220	2248	2441	2455	2472	2477	2546	2708	2802	2861	2890	2891
Feature	F.385	F.543	F.591	F.629	F.1589	F.1589	F.340	F.426	F.447	F.491	F.520	F.523	F.534	F.526	F.540	F.541	F.549	-	F.578	F.583	F.585	F.601	F.567	-	F.678	-	-
Volume/litres	8	8	12	4	8	5	3	7	1	14	1.5	15	12	8	9	7	14	0.5	15	7	7	12	3	12	15	5	1
Type	lower pit	ditch base	pit	p-hole	pit	pit	ditch	later ditch	ditch	ditch	ditch base	ditch	ditch	ditch	cessy pit	pit	ditch	p-hole	pit	pit	ditch	pit	p-hole	p-hole	cessy ditch	p-hole	p-hole
Site Phase	5	5	5	5	5	5	7	7	7	7	7	7	7	7	7	7	7	7	7	7	7	7	7	7	7	7	7
Corylus avellana L. (shell frags)																									2		
Chenopodium polyspermum L.																						1					
Chenopodium ficifolium								1				1	1														
Chenopodium album L.	2		9		2							1	1	5							1	14	1	3	2	1	
Chenopodium spp.			2		1																	4			1		
Atriplex patula/prostrata	4		1																								
Atriplex spp.	3						1	1														12			2		
CHENOPODIACEAE indet.																							1	1			
Stellaria media (L.) Villars								1															1		2		
Stellaria sp.																											
Spergula arvensis L.																											
Cerastium sp.																	1										
Agrostemma githago L.				1											1		1										
small CARYOPHYLLACEAE indet.							1																				
Fallopia convolvulus (L.) Á. Löve														1													
Rumex crispus L.				1	3														1			3					
Rumex conglomeratus/obstutifolius/sanguineus															1		1		1								
Rumex spp.				4	4																						
POLYGONACEAE indet.	1			5	5			1																	1		
Thlaspi arvense L.								1																			
Brassica c.f. nigra															1				1			1			5	1	
small Brassica spp.					1							2															
Sinapis arvensis L.										1						1											
Brassica/Sinapis sp.										1							2			1	1						
Vaccinium c.f. oxycoccos										1																	
Anagallis arvensis L.																											
Prunus/Crataegus sp. thorn																					-						
Crataegus monogyna						1																					
Vicia sativa L. type (<4mm)	12			5	5			6					1						9			4	1	2	1		
Vicia faba L.	2	1			25				2							1	2		1	1							
Lathyrus nissolia L.					4											2											
Lathyrus sp.							1																				
small Vicia/Lathyrus sp. (<2mm)	2				9				2	2				2		1	5			10			1	2	1		
large Vicia/Lathyrus sp. (>2mm)			4							3				4		1	6			2			2		6	3	
Vicia/Lathyrus/Pisum (>4mm)															1							3	1				
Medicago lupulina L.																	1		1				1			1	
Medicago spp.															1		3								1		
Medicago/Trifolium spp.					1												1			2					1		

153

Sample	16	32	66	71	165	162	4	18	20	23	31	29	27	28	33	35	36	55	57	58	59	69	76	80	82	85	86
Context	1834	2223	2519	2642	7162	7163	1535	1864	2010	2113	2167b	2171	2172	2174	2218	2220	2248	2441	2455	2477	2472	2546	2708	2802	2861	2890	2891
Feature	F.385	F.543	F.591	F.629	F.1589	F.1589	F.340	F.426	F.447	F.491	F.520	F.523	F.534	F.526	F.540	F.541	F.549	-	F.578	F.585	F.583	F.601	F.567	-	F.678	-	-
Volume/ litres	8	8	12	4	5	5	3	7	7	14	1.5	15	12	8	9	7	14	0.5	15	7	7	12	7	7	5	5	1
Type	lower pit	ditch base	pit	p-hole	pit	pit	ditch	later ditch	ditch	ditch	ditch base	ditch	ditch	ditch	cessy pit	pit	ditch	p-hole	pit	ditch	pit	pit	p-hole	p-hole	cessy ditch	p-hole	p-hole
Site Phase	5	5	5	5	5	5	7	7	7	7	7	7	7	7	7	7	7	7	7	7	7	7	7	7	7	7	7
small *Trifolium* spp. (<2mm)	4				6	1		10									2				1	3	1		6		
large *Trifolium* sp. (>2mm)					1																			1			
large legume cotyledon fragments					+++					-				+		+							+				
Linum usitatissimum L.	2			1				1																			
Aethusa c.f. *cynapium* L.																				2							
APIACEAE indet. kernel																	1				2						
BORAGINACEAE indet.																	1										
LAMIACEAE indet.																											
Mentha arvensis/aquatica L.																									1		
Plantago lanceolata L.								1							1												
Euphrasia spp.								1																			
Odontites vernus (Bell.) Dumort.					4			1	2	1				1			6		2					1	1	3	
c.f. *Rhinanthus* sp.	20				1			1																			
Galium aparine L.					1			1											1								
small *Galium* sp.																											
Sambucus nigra L.	1				2			1																		2	
Centaurea cyanus L.																											
Centaurea nigra L.								1																			
Centaurea sp.																											
Tanacetum vulgare L.	1																										
Anthemis cotula L.	27		1		43	1	1																1			8	
Anthemis/Tripleurospermum sp.													1														
Tripleurospermum inodorum (L.) Schultz	4				1	1		2									4				1	2		1	2		
small ASTERACEAE indet.				1	1	2															1						
large ASTERACEAE indet.																											
Luzula sp.														2													
small *Juncus* (<0.5mm)								1							1							1					
Eleocharis c.f. *palustris* (L.) Roemer								1							3				1		1	12			4		
Eleocharis sp.																											
Schoenus nigricans L.					2												1										
Cladium mariscus (L.) Pohl.	3				3			1		1	1						3		2		1	20				1	
vegetative *Cladium mariscus* (L.) Pohl.					++																—						
Carex c.f. *riparia* Curtis																						2					
Carex nigra type																						9					
large trilete *Carex* sp.																1						1					
small trilete *Carex* sp.																						3					
flat *Carex* sp.	1			1	1																						
Carex spp.	1				1			2						1		1	1										
CYPERACEAE indet.																			1			1			5	3	

154

	16	32	66	71	165	162	4	18	20	23	31	29	27	28	33	35	36	55	57	59	58	69	76	80	82	85	86
Sample	16	32	66	71	165	162	4	18	20	23	31	29	27	28	33	35	36	55	57	59	58	69	76	80	82	85	86
Context	1834	2223	2519	2642	7162	7163	1535	1864	2010	2113	2167b	2171	2172	2174	2218	2220	2248	2441	2455	2472	2477	2546	2708	2802	2861	2890	2891
Feature	F.385	F.543	F.591	F.629	F.1589	F.1589	F.340	F.426	F.447	F.491	F.520	F.523	F.534	F.526	F.540	F.541	F.549	-	F.578	F.583	F.585	F.601	F.567	-	F.678	-	-
Volume/litres	8	8	12	4	8	5	3	7	1	14	1.5	15	12	8	9	7	14	0.5	15	7	7	12	3	12	15	5	1
Type	lower pit	ditch base	pit	p-hole	pit	pit	ditch	later ditch	ditch	ditch	ditch base	ditch	ditch	ditch	cessy pit	pit	ditch	p-hole	pit	pit	ditch	pit	p-hole	p-hole	cessy ditch	p-hole	p-hole
Site Phase	5	5	5	5	5	5	7	7	7	7	7	7	7	7	7	7	7	7	7	7	7	7	7	7	7	7	7
CYPERACEAE stems				-	-																		+	+	-		
Festuca sp.																	2										
Festuca/Lolium sp.				2	2			2		1									1					1	1		
Lolium perenne L.																								1			
Lolium perenne/temulentum																								2			
Lolium c.f. temulentum L.	11																					1					
c.f. Lolium sp.	7																										
Lolium sp. rachis internode					1										1		4										
Poa pratensis L.					1		1	4																			
Poa spp.	1							2									1				1	1	1		3	3	
Glyceria c.f. declinata Breb.								2																			
Alopecurus sp.																	1										
Phleum pratense L.								2					2				1										
Phleum c.f. bertolonii DC.								1					1	1	1		1		1			6			1		
Phleum sp.	3																							5			
Bromus spp.						1				1										1	1	1					1
Bromus/Avena sp.																											
Hordeum c.f. murinum L.	4																										
small POACEAE indet.		1																	4	1		2	1	1	1		
medium POACEAE indet.	18				10			2									3					1	1				
large POACEAE indet.					1																		1				
POACEAE floret base													2		1												
POACEAE culm node																1				1		3					
POACEAE culm fragment								1					1		-	-					-	-					
nutshell indet. fragment																							-				
Monocot. plant stems																							+				
rootlet indet.																							+				
seed indet.				2		1		1			1			1	1	1	4		1	1	2	2	1		1		
seed head indet.																						1					
stem indet.				-						-											-						
leaflet indet.																											
bud indet.																											
bract indet.	-																						+				
Charophyte oogonium																				++							
moss fragment																											
charred concretion										+											-						
large charcoal (>4mm)	+	-	+	-	+	+	+	++	++	++	+	+	-	+	++	++	++	-	-	+	++	-	+	+	-	+	
mid charcoal (2-4mm)	++	+++	++	+	++	+	++	++	++	++	++	++	++	++	++	+++	+++	++	++	+++	++	++	++	++	-	++	++
small charcoal (<2mm)	++	+++	++	+	+++	+++	+++	+++	+++	+++	++	+	++	++	+++	+++	+++	+++	+++	+++	+++	+++	+++	+++	+++	+	+++
fungal sclerotia	-						-							++	++		++		+	+	+						
fungal thecae																											

Table 5.12 Charred botanical evidence from Period II (Mid to Late Saxon), I

155

Cereals

Sample	132	136	142	151	152	178	188	202	203	221	210	214	219	212	211	225	218	193	196
Context	4505	4809	5973	6017	6230	8113	8811	9615	9623	9629	9695	9727	9741	9765	9785	9821	9830	9847	9850
Feature	F.931	F.1090	F.1285	F.1303	F.1301	F.1914	F.2083	F.2588	F.2590	F.2593	F.2618	-	F.2619	F.2631	F.2638	F.2627	F.2649	-	-
Volume/litres	15	6	10	12	6	10	14	13	11	10	9	1	14	11	12	8	12	4	5
Type	pit	ditch	ditch	ditch	ditch	ditch	ditch	ditch	ditch	ditch	gully	p/h	ditch	ditch	ditch	ditch	ditch	p/h	p/h
Site Phase	7	7	7	7	7	7	7	7	7	7	7	7	7	7	7	7	7	7	7
hulled, twisted *Hordeum vulgare* s.l. grain		1																	
naked *Hordeum vulgare* sensu lato grain																			
hulled *Hordeum vulgare* sensu lato grain																	1		
Hordeum vulgare sensu lato grain		3	5	10	1	4	10	10	8	5	3	6	3	3	1	9	2	1	
Triticum aestivum sensu lato grain	1	2	53	43	3	4	15	5	9	7	3	35	1	14	16	61	4	4	8
Triticum spelta/dicoccum grain																			
Triticum sp. grain	2	2	1	14		3			10		1	6	1		9	7	4		
Triticum/Hordeum grain				35		5		8	6		2	15	5	5	12	2	1	7	1
Secale cereale L. grain									10		1								
Secale/Avena grain										1									
Triticum/Secale grain																			
Avena sp. grain		2	28	20		2	1		28	2	1		2	4	1	10		3	
cereal indet. grain	1	1	9	3		10	11	3	6	3	1	15	4	1	4			3	1
6-row *Hordeum vulgare* s.l. rachis internode				6															
Hordeum vulgare sensu lato rachis internode				5		1	1	2	1	1		1	1		1		1		
tetraploid *Triticum aestivum* s.l. rachis internode				1															
hexaploid *Triticum aestivum* s.l. rachis internode				5			1		4				1	3	3	8	2		
T. aestivum sensu lato rachis internode		2	2	5				2							5	6			
Triticum dicoccum glume base																			
Triticum spelta glume base																			
Secale cereale L. rachis internode			3	1								1			1				
Hordeum/Secale sp. rachis internode		1																	
Avena sp. awn fragment		3	1							1									
Avena sp. lemma base		2																	
Avena sp. floret base			1						2	1									
cereal basal culm node													1						
cereal indet. rhachis internode	1			1					1	1	1	1					1	1	

Non-cereals

	132	136	142	151	152	178	188	202	203	221	210	214	219	212	211	225	218	193	196
Ranunculus c.f. *flammula* L.											3								
Ranunculus sp.							1												
Urtica dioica L.				1														1	

156

	132	136	142	151	152	178	188	202	203	221	210	214	219	212	211	225	218	193	196
Sample	132	136	142	151	152	178	188	202	203	221	210	214	219	212	211	225	218	193	196
Context	4505	4809	5973	6017	6230	8113	8811	9615	9623	9629	9695	9727	9741	9765	9785	9821	9830	9847	9850
Feature	F.931	F.1090	F.1285	F.1303	F.1301	F.1914	F.2083	F.2588	F.2590	F.2593	F.2618	-	F.2619	F.2631	F.2638	F.2627	F.2649	-	-
Volume/litres	15	6	10	12	6	10	14	13	11	10	9	1	14	11	12	8	12	4	5
Type	pit	ditch	ditch	ditch	ditch	ditch	ditch	ditch	ditch	ditch	gully	p/h	ditch	ditch	ditch	ditch	ditch	p/h	p/h
Site Phase	7	7	7	7	7	7	7	7	7	7	7	7	7	7	7	7	7	7	7
Corylus avellana L. (shell frags)			6												1			1	
Chenopodium polyspermum L.			5	1													3		
cereal culm node																			
Chenopodium ficifolium		1		1				3	1	1	1		1	4	1				
Chenopodium album L.		1		2				1	3	1			1	2	1	1			
Chenopodium spp.																			
Atriplex patula/prostrata		1											1						
Atriplex spp.													2					1	
CHENOPODIACEAE indet.																			
Stellaria media (L.) Villars													1		1				
Stellaria sp.														1					
Spergula arvensis L.																			
Cerastium sp.																			
Agrostemma githago L.		1					1		1		1		2	1					
small CARYOPHYLLACEAE indet.		1																	
Fallopia convolvulus (L.) Á. Löve		1																	
Rumex crispus L.													1		1	1		1	1
Rumex conglomeratus/obstutifolius/sanguineus								3	3		3			2			2		
Rumex spp.				1					1	1			1						
POLYGONACEAE indet.								3											
Thlaspi arvense L.								1											
Brassica c.f. nigra								1											
small Brassica spp.																			
Sinapis arvensis L.				1									3	2			2		
Brassica/Sinapis sp.																			
Vaccinium c.f. oxycoccos							1						1		1		1	1	
Anagallis arvensis L.								—											
Prunus/Crataegus sp. thorn																			
Crataegus monogyna Jacq.			2					1	1	1					1	1			
Vicia sativa L. type (4mm)						1		1	1		2	1		3	4	5		1	2
Vicia faba L.				16				7	26	3				1	3	3			
Lathyrus nissolia L.																			
Lathyrus sp.			3	1				2	2				1	1	2				
small Vicia/Lathyrus sp. (<2mm)		1									1					1			2
large Vicia/Lathyrus sp. (>2mm)																			
Vicia/Lathyrus/Pisum (>4mm)																			
Medicago lupulina L.																			
Medicago spp.																			
Medicago/Trifolium spp.																			

157

Sample	132	136	142	151	152	178	188	202	203	221	210	214	219	212	211	225	218	193	196
Context	4505	4809	5973	6017	6230	8113	8811	9615	9623	9629	9695	9727	9741	9765	9785	9821	9830	9847	9850
Feature	F.931	F.1090	F.1285	F.1303	F.1301	F.1914	F.2083	F.2588	F.2590	F.2593	F.2618	-	F.2619	F.2631	F.2638	F.2627	F.2649	-	-
Volume/litres	15	6	10	12	6	10	14	13	11	10	9	1	14	11	12	8	12	4	5
Type	pit	ditch	ditch	ditch	ditch	ditch	ditch	ditch	ditch	ditch	gully	p/h	ditch	ditch	ditch	ditch	ditch	p/h	p/h
Site Phase	7	7	7	7	7	7	7	7	7	7	7	7	7	7	7	7	7	7	7
small *Trifolium* spp. (<2mm)		2		1	.			3	1	3	2	1	1	2			1		1
large *Trifolium* sp. (>2mm)		-		-			-		-										
large legume cotyledon fragments															+				
Linum usitatissimum L.						2													1
Aethusa c.f. *cynapium* L.																1			
APIACEAE indet. kernel									1							1			
BORAGINACEAE indet.				1									1						
LAMIACEAE indet.													1						
Mentha arvensis/aquatica				1					1					1					
Plantago lanceolata L.									1					1					
Euphrasia spp.							1		2				1			3			
Odontites vernus (Bell.) Dumort.							1											1	
c.f. *Rhinanthus* sp.																			
Galium aparine L.										1						2	1		
small *Galium* sp.									1					1					
Sambucus nigra L.																			
Centaurea cyanus L.																			
Centaurea nigra L.																			
Centaurea sp.																1			
Tanacetum vulgare L.																			
Anthemis cotula L.			4	12		4	5	8	10	1	2	1	3	2	5	5	1	1	2
Anthemis/Tripleurospermum sp.							1	1	1										
Tripleurospermum inodorum (L.) Schultz				3															
small ASTERACEAE indet.				1						1			1		1				1
large ASTERACEAE indet.								1							2				
Luzula sp.																			
small *Juncus* (0.5mm)			1					1	1		3		8	13			12	1	
Eleocharis c.f. *palustris* (L.) Roemer																			
Eleocharis sp.								1	1										
Schoenus nigricans L.								1	1										
Cladium mariscus (L.) Pohl.				1			1	2	3	1			1	2	1		2		
vegetative *Cladium mariscus* (L.) Pohl.				+++									-						
Carex c.f. *riparia* Curtis																			
Carex nigra type											1								
large trilete *Carex* sp.				1															
small trilete *Carex* sp.													1	2					
flat *Carex* sp.									1				1				1		
Carex spp.																			
CYPERACEAE indet.	1																		

158

Table 5.13 Charred botanical evidence from Period II (Mid to Late Saxon), II

	132	136	142	151	152	178	188	202	203	221	210	214	219	212	211	225	218	193	196
Sample	132	136	142	151	152	178	188	202	203	221	210	214	219	212	211	225	218	193	196
Context	4505	4809	5973	6017	6230	8113	8811	9615	9623	9629	9695	9727	9741	9765	9785	9821	9830	9847	9850
Feature	F.931	F.1090	F.1285	F.1303	F.1301	F.1914	F.2083	F.2588	F.2590	F.2593	F.2618	–	F.2619	F.2631	F.2638	F.2627	F.2649	–	–
Volume/litres	15	6	10	12	6	10	14	13	11	10	9	1	14	11	12	8	12	4	5
Type	pit	ditch	ditch	ditch	ditch	ditch	ditch	ditch	ditch	ditch	gully	p/h	ditch	ditch	ditch	ditch	ditch	p/h	p/h
Site Phase	?	?	?	?	?	?	?	?	?	?	?	?	?	?	?	?	?	?	?
CYPERACEAE stems	–		+																
Festuca sp.				3			1				2			1					
Festuca/Lolium sp.														2					
Lolium perenne L.																			
Lolium perenne/temulentum																			
Lolium c.f. temulentum L.																			
c.f. Lolium sp.																			
Lolium sp. rachis internode																			
Poa pratensis L.		1		1		1			1									1	
Poa spp.															2	3			
Glyceria c.f. declinata Breb.																			
Alopecurus sp.																			
Phleum pratense L.		1		8		5	1	6		1	1		2	3	1	1	1		2
Phleum c.f. bertolonii DC.		2	2																
Phleum sp.			1	1		1	1			1			3	1		2	2		1
Bromus spp.		1	1																
Bromus/Avena sp.																			
Hordeum c.f. murinum L.							1				2		1				1	1	1
small POACEAE indet.											2		1						
medium POACEAE indet.								2					1	2			1	1	1
large POACEAE indet.				2															
POACEAE floret base									2						1		–		
POACEAE culm node		2	2	3															
POACEAE culm fragment		+	+	+++															
nutshell indet. fragment																			
Monocot. plant stems				+															
rootlet indet.				3															
seed indet.		1		+				2			1				2				3
seed head indet.				+															
stem indet.				+															
leaflet indet.		++		–							–								
bud indet.			–																
bract indet.							1												
Charophyte oogonium				1												+	1		
moss fragment				–												+++			
charred concretion	–	–		–	–	–	–	–	–	–	–		–	–	–			–	–
large charcoal (4mm)	–	+	–	+++	–	–	–	–	+	–	+	++	–	–	+		++	++	+
mid charcoal (2–4mm)	+	+++	++	+++	–	+	–	++	++	++	++	+++	+++	+++	+++	+	+++	++	++
small charcoal (2mm)	++	+++	++	+++	–	++	++	+++	+++	+++	+++	+++	+++	+++	+++	+++	+++	+++	+++
fungal sclerotia																			
fungal thecae																			

159

Cereals

	10	14	22	60	51	37	63	97	?	147	164	177	184	181	204	201	206	61
Sample	10	14	22	60	51	37	63	97	?	147	164	177	184	181	204	201	206	61
Context	1638	1812	2027	2191	2207	2230	2490	3314	5515	6202	7570	8846	8870	9169	9635	9637	9673	2309
Feature	F.306	F.2328	F.467	F.537	F.539	F.546	F.579	-	F.1178	F.1357	F.1684	F.2097	F.2210	F.2226	F.2596	-	F.2613	F.547
Volume/litres	12	5	10	13	15	6	12	8	10	5	5	14	14	8	10	4	10	14
Type	wall slot	deep pit	pit	pit	pit base	pit	pit	pit	pit	pit	pit	pit	pit	ditch	pit	p/h	pit	pit
Site Phase	9	9	9	9	9	9	9	9	9	9	9	9	9	9	9	9	9	10
hulled, twisted *Hordeum vulgare* s.l. grain				2												1		
hulled *Hordeum vulgare sensu lato* grain			1	1		1							2		6	2		
Hordeum vulgare sensu lato grain	7	1	14	4	1	10	1	3	3	4	20		4	2		2	1	3
Triticum aestivum sensu lato grain	23		109	30		40	25	14		41	17		27	13	6	12	5	7
Triticum spelta/dicoccum grain			3					1										
Triticum sp. grain	6	2	28	2		3	8	6		5	9	1	2	5				28
Triticum/Hordeum grain	4		2	11		1		1	2	9			6	4		4	4	3
Secale cereale grain											1						1	
Secale/Avena grain																		
Triticum/Secale grain				2		1		2		3			1					
Avena sp. grain	7		32	5		7		4		8	9		8	3	2	3	1	4
cereal indet. grain	4		10	5		6	4	4		11	26		8	4	1	2		7
Hordeum vulgare sensu lato rachis internode	20														1	1		
Hordeum vulgare sensu lato awn frag.	2																	
tetraploid *Triticum aestivum* s.l. rachis internode																		
hexaploid *Triticum aestivum* s.l. rachis internode	1	1	1			1				3			2				4	
T. aestivum sensu lato rhachis internode	3		3	1	9	1	1			2	8		3	1		2	3	
Triticum dicoccum (Schubl) glume base																		
Triticum spelta glume base											2							
Triticum c.f. *spelta* spikelet fork											15							
Triticum spelta/dicoccum glume base			1								46							
Triticum spelta/dicoccum spikelet fork					1													
Secale cereale L. rachis internode																		
Avena sp. awn fragment	14	1	3	2	1					1	1					1		
Avena sp. floret base	1																	
cereal culm node	1		2								2			1				
cereal basal culm node																		
cereal indet. lemma base															1			
cereal indet. rhachis internode	3					1			1									

160

Non-cereals

	61	206	201	204	181	184	177	164	147	?	97	63	37	51	60	22	14	10
Sample	61	206	201	204	181	184	177	164	147	?	97	63	37	51	60	22	14	10
Context	2309	9673	9637	9635	9169	8870	8846	7570	6202	5515	3314	2490	2230	2207	2191	2027	1812	1638
Feature	F.547	F.2613		F.2596	F.2226	F.2210	F.2097	F.1684	F.1357	F.1178	-	F.579	F.546	F.539	F.537	F.467	F.2328	F.306
Volume/litres	14	10	4	10	8	14	14	5	5	10	8	12	6	15	13	10	5	12
Type	pit	pit	p/h	pit	ditch	pit	pit	pit	pit	pit	pit	pit	pit	pit base	pit	pit	deep pit	wall slot
Site Phase	10	9	9	9	9	9	9	9	9	9	9	9	9	9	9	9	9	9
Ranunculus sardous Crantz.					1									1				
Ranunculus sp.				1														
Thalictrum flavum L.																1		
Corylus avellana L. (shell frags)																3		
Chenopodium polyspermum L.																		2
Chenopodium ficifolium Sm.																		
Chenopodium album L.	1		1			1												1
Chenopodium spp.		1		1				3						1		2		
Atriplex patula/prostrata					1	1							3			1		
Atriplex spp.				1														
CHENOPODIACEAE indet.	3														1	2		1
Stellaria media (L.) Villars																	1	
Spergula arvensis L.		2	1						2									
Agrostemma githago L.		1																
Silene c.f. vulgaris																		
Silene nutans/latifolia																		
small CARYOPHYLLACEAE indet.												1						
Persicaria maculosa Gray.										1								
Polygonum aviculare L.													1					
Fallopia convolvulus (L.) Á. Löve																		
Rumex acetosella L.													1	1			1	12
Rumex crispus L.	3							1										
Rumex conglomeratus/obstutifolius/sanguineus		1	3			2						6	1			1		
Rumex spp.	3												1					
POLYGONACEAE indet.																1		
Malva neglecta Wallr.	1																	
Malva sp.																1		
Sisymbrium c.f. officianale																		
Thlaspi arvense L.																		
Lepidium sp.			1															
Brassica c.f. nigra						1										1		
Brassica rapa/nigra				2														
small Brassica spp.	4																	
Sinapis arvensis L.				2														3
Sinapis arvensis L. capsule fragments					1													
Brassica/Sinapis sp.			1			1						3	1		2	1		1

161

	10	14	22	60	51	37	63	97	?	147	164	177	184	181	204	201	206	61
Sample	10	14	22	60	51	37	63	97	?	147	164	177	184	181	204	201	206	61
Context	1638	1812	2027	2191	2207	2230	2490	3314	5515	6202	7570	8846	8870	9169	9635	9637	9673	2309
Feature	F:306	F:2328	F:467	F:537	F:539	F:546	F:579	-	F:1178	F:1357	F:1684	F:2097	F:2210	F:2226	F:2596	-	F:2613	F:547
Volume/litres	12	5	10	13	15	6	12	8	10	5	5	14	14	8	10	4	10	14
Type	wall slot	deep pit	pit	pit	pit base	pit	pit	pit	pit	pit	pit	pit	pit	ditch	pit	p/h	pit	pit
Site Phase	9	9	9	9	9	9	9	9	9	9	9	9	9	9	9	9	9	10
c.f. *Raphanus raphanistrum* L.	1																	
BRASSICACEAE indet.			1															
small *Potentilla* sp.				1														
Potentilla c.f. *anserina*																		
Rosa sp. sepal base (disc)															1			
Prunus spinosa L.																		
Prunus domestica L.																		
ROSACEAE indet.																		
Vicia c.f. *cracca* L.			3															
Vicia c.f. *hirsuta* (L.) Gray			1				1											
Vicia sativa L. type (<4mm)	9				8													
Vicia faba L.	1										3		1					
Lathyrus c.f. *pratensis* L.			1															
Lathyrus nissolia L.			2								2							
Lathyrus sp.																		1
small *Vicia/Lathyrus* sp. (<2mm)	1		73	3		5	5	3	1	5			6	3	4	4	2	6
large *Vicia/Lathyrus* sp. (>2mm)	2	1	35	2		9	3	3		4	5		2	4	3	1	3	2
Vicia/Lathyrus/Pisum (>4mm)	1			1	4				1						1	1		
Medicago lupulina L.			5															
Medicago spp.	2		4															
Medicago/Trifolium spp.															1			
small *Trifolium* spp. (<2mm)	8		4		2		1			1	1		2	3	4			1
large *Trifolium* sp. (>2mm)																1		
large legume cotyledon fragments			++	+			+ ++			+			-	+				
Rhamnus cathartica L.											2							
Aethusa c.f. *cynapium* L.	1					1					2							
Apium sp.										1	1							
APIACEAE indet. kernel																		
Solanum nigrum L.																		
Convolvulus arvensis L.																		
Menyanthes trifoliata L.															1			
Myosotis sp.																		
BORAGINACEAE indet.																		
Mentha arvensis/aquatica																		
LAMIACEAE indet.					1													
Plantago lanceolata L.															2			
Plantago major L.					1										1			
immature *Plantago* sp.																		
Euphrasia spp.																		
Odontites vernus (Bell.) Dumort.	1		5		6	1				2	2		1	2	1	3	1	1

Sample	10	14	22	60	51	37	63	97	?	147	164	177	184	181	204	201	206	61
Context	1638	1812	2027	2191	2207	2230	2490	3314	5515	6202	7570	8846	8870	9169	9635	9637	9673	2309
Feature	F.306	F.2328	F.467	F.537	F.539	F.546	F.579	-	F.1178	F.1357	F.1684	F.2097	F.2210	F.2226	F.2596	-	F.2613	F.547
Volume/litres	12	5	10	13	15	6	12	8	10	5	5	14	14	8	10	4	10	14
Type	wall slot	deep pit	pit	pit	pit base	pit	pit	pit	pit	pit	pit	pit	pit	ditch	pit	p/h	pit	pit
Site Phase	9	9	9	9	9	9	9	9	9	9	9	9	9	9	9	9	9	10
c.f. Rhinanthus sp.										1								
Galium aparine L.										1	1							
small Galium sp.				1														
Sambucus nigra L.			2		1	1								1				
Dipsacus fullonum L.																		
Carduus tenuiflorus/crispus																		
Cirsium c.f. arvense (L.) Scop.																		
Carduus/Cirsium sp.																		
Centaurea scabiosa L.																		
Centaurea nigra L.		1																
Centaurea sp.																		
Centaurea sp. kernels																		
Lapsana communis L.																		
Anthemis cotula L.	17	7	34	13	25	1	9			10	7		10	8	2	16	5	10
Tripleurospermum inodorum (L.) Schultz	1	1	1								1				1			
small ASTERACEAE indet.																		
large ASTERACEAE indet.																		
Alisma plantago-aquatica L.															2			
small Juncus (<0.5mm)																		
Lemna sp.	1																	
Luzula sp.																		
Eleocharis c.f. palustris (L.) Roemer	4		5							1			2	1	6			
Eleocharis sp.			2															1
Schoenus nigricans L.			1	1		1									4			1
Cladium mariscus (L.) Pohl.	2		7	1	8	2	1			1	2		4	1	2	1		3
vegetative Cladium mariscus (L.) Pohl.			++		+	+								+	+++			–
Carex c.f. remota																		
large trilete Carex sp.																		
small trilete Carex sp.		1	2	1											1			2
flat Carex sp.					1										1			
Carex spp.	2																	
CYPERACEAE indet.			1	–						–								
CYPERACEAE stems			+							7	++							
Festuca sp.				1							1					1		1
Festuca/Lolium sp.			2							2	1		2	1				
Lolium perenne L.			2		3								1					
Lolium perenne/temulentum																		
Lolium c.f. temulentum L.																		
c.f. Lolium sp.																		
Lolium sp. rachis internode																		
Vulpia c.f. bromoides																		

Table 5.17 Charred botanical evidence from Period III (medieval), I

	10	14	22	60	51	37	63	97	?	147	164	177	184	181	204	201	206	61
Sample	10	14	22	60	51	37	63	97	?	147	164	177	184	181	204	201	206	61
Context	1638	1812	2027	2191	2207	2230	2490	3314	5515	6202	7570	8846	8870	9169	9635	9637	9673	2309
Feature	F.306	F.2328	F.467	F.537	F.539	F.546	F.579	-	F.1178	F.1357	F.1684	F.2097	F.2210	F.2226	F.2596	-	F.2613	F.547
Volume/litres	12	5	10	13	15	6	12	8	10	5	5	14	14	8	10	4	10	14
Type	wall slot	deep pit	pit	pit	pit base	pit	pit	pit	pit	pit	pit	pit	pit	ditch	pit	p/h	pit	pit
Site Phase	9	9	9	9	9	9	9	9	9	9	9	9	9	9	9	9	9	10
Poa spp.	7		1		3		2			1					4		3	
Agrostis sp.																		
Phleum pratense L.	1																	
Phleum c.f. bertolonii DC.	2		1	3	2					4				2		1		1
Phleum sp.			1								1							
Poa/Phleum sp.			1		1					1	2							
Bromus spp.					1	1												
thin Bromus sp																		
Bromus/Avena sp.			1				2				1							
flattened POACEAE indet.					1													
small POACEAE indet.		1			2													
medium POACEAE indet.				1	2										2			
large POACEAE indet.			4		1		1						1	1	2		2	3
POACEAE floret base					1	3	1									3		
POACEAE culm node	5				1						1		1		1			
POACEAE culm fragment										–		–			–			
nutshell indet. fragment			1		1													
Monocot. plant stems			–					++										
rootlet indet.	–	–																
seed indet.	2		1	1		2	4		2	1				2				1
stem indet.			–			–												
leaflet indet.										–			–					–
bud indet.			–									–						
bract indet.																		
Charophyte oogonium															1			
moss fragment																		
charred concretion																–		
large charcoal (>4mm)	–	+	++	+	+	+	+	–	+	++	–	–	+	+	++	+	+	++
mid charcoal (2–4mm)	++	++	+++	+	++	++	+++	+	+	+++	++		++	+	+++	+++	+++	+++
small charcoal (<2mm)	+++	+++	+++	+++	+++	+++	+++	++	++	+++	+++	+	+++	+++	+++	+++	+++	+++
vitrified charcoal			–															
fungal sclerotia	+		+				+											++
fungal thecae																		+++

164

Cereals

	56	101	103	127	144	148	166	182	205	209	208	96	119	161
Context	2461	3321	3324	3590	5983	6238	7733	9233	9649	9751	9753	3267	3565	7130
Feature	-	F.752	F.774	-	F.1292	F.1368	F.1452	F.2275	F.2601	F.2621	F.2622	F.751	-	F.1012
Volume/litres	10	12	6	12	12	10	15	12	10	12	10	12	14	3
Type	posthole	well base	cessy pit	floor	pit	pit	pit	pond	pit	pit	pit	well	over floor	ditch
Site Phase	10	10	10	10	10	10	10	10	10	10	10	11	12	12
hulled, twisted Hordeum vulgare s.l. grain							1							
hulled Hordeum vulgare sensu lato grain	5						2				1			
Hordeum vulgare sensu lato grain	7	7	2	9	2	7	16	1		12	1	2		3
Triticum aestivum sensu lato grain	83	17	3	1	7	79	43	7	13	3	3	21	2	3
Triticum spelta/dicoccum grain					1									
Triticum sp. grain	5	6			2	2	40	5	3		3	2	2	5
Triticum/Hordeum grain	2		3		4	4	17	3	2		4	2		1
Secale cereale grain						3	2							
Secale/Avena grain				2		2								
Triticum/Secale grain						2			2		1	1		
Avena sp. grain	2	5		13	1	48	32			3		1	3	
cereal indet. grain	21	9	1	9		17	4	3	2	4	1	11	2	
Hordeum vulgare sensu lato rhachis internode	1	3		3			5		1			2	1	
Hordeum vulgare sensu lato awn frag.							1							
tetraploid Triticum aestivum s.l. rachis internode											1			
hexaploid Triticum aestivum s.l. rachis internode	13					86	2	1		3	4	4		
T. aestivum sensu lato rhachis internode			1	6		6	1		2	1	3	3	3	
Triticum dicoccum Schubl. glume base						6								
Triticum spelta glume base														
Triticum c.f. spelta spikelet fork														
Triticum spelta/dicoccum glume base	1					2	1							1
Triticum spelta/dicoccum spikelet fork														
Secale cereale rhachis internode						1	1			1				
Avena sp. awn fragment				1		9	4		1			1	1	
Avena sp. floret base														
cereal basal culm node						3	11				7			
cereal culm node		1					1			1				
cereal indet. lemma base	3						1						1	

Sample	56	101	103	127	144	148	166	182	205	209	208	96	119	161
Context	2461	3321	3324	3590	5983	6238	7733	9233	9649	9751	9753	3267	3565	7130
Feature	-	F.752	F.774	-	F.1292	F.1368	F.1452	F.2275	F.2601	F.2621	F.2622	F.751	-	F.1012
Volume/litres	10	12	6	12	12	10	15	12	10	12	10	12	14	3
Type	posthole	well base	cessy pit	floor	pit	pit	pit	pond	pit	pit	pit	well	over floor	ditch
Site Phase	10	10	10	10	10	10	10	10	10	10	10	11	12	12
cereal indet. rhachis internode		1				4			1					
Non-cereals														
Ranunculus sardous Crantz.														
Ranunculus sp.														
Thalictrum flavum L.				1			17							
Corylus avellana L. (shell frags)										1	1			
Chenopodium polyspermum L.									1					
Chenopodium ficifolium Sm.								1						
Chenopodium album L.				1					1			1		
Chenopodium spp.							4				2		1	
Atriplex patula/prostrata							1				4			
Atriplex spp.				1		2	5							
CHENOPODIACEAE indet.			1			1	1				1	1		
Stellaria media (L.) Villars														
Spergula arvensis L.									2					
Agrostemma githago L.						1								
Silene c.f. vulgaris						3								
Silene nutans/latifolia						2								
small CARYOPHYLLACEAE indet.							3					1		
Persicaria maculosa Gray.						1								
Polygonum aviculare L.						7	2				1			
Fallopia convolvulus (L.) Á. Löve						2	3							
Rumex acetosella L.														
Rumex crispus L.	1	1		2		1088	1				1		3	
Rumex conglomeratus/obstutifolius/sanguineus						8								
Rumex spp.			1						1				1	
POLYGONACEAE indet.		1	1			24	9		1					
Malva neglecta Wallr.														
Malva sp.							1							
Sisymbrium c.f. officianale														
Thlaspi arvense L.						1								
Lepidium sp.				1										
Brassica c.f. nigra	1					2	11				1			
Brassica rapa/nigra										1				
small Brassica spp.		2		2								1		
Sinapis arvensis L.												1	1	
Sinapis arvensis L. capsule fragments						++						1		

166

Sample	56	101	103	127	144	148	166	182	205	209	208	96	119	161
Context	2461	3321	3324	3590	5983	6238	7733	9233	9649	9751	9753	3267	3565	7130
Feature	-	F.752	F.774	-	F.1292	F.1368	F.1452	F.2275	F.2601	F.2621	F.2622	F.751	-	F.1012
Volume/litres	10	12	6	12	12	10	15	12	10	12	10	12	14	3
Type	posthole	well base	cessy pit	floor	pit	pit	pit	pond	pit	pit	pit	well	over floor	ditch
Site Phase	10	10	10	10	10	10	10	10	10	10	10	11	12	12
Brassica/Sinapis sp.	1					2	4		1		1	1		
c.f. *Raphanus raphanistrum* L.													–	
BRASSICACEAE indet.														
small *Potentilla* sp.														
Potentilla c.f. *anserina*							1							
Rosa sp. sepal base (disc)						–						–		
Prunus spinosa L.		1												
Prunus domestica L.		1	2 m				2							
ROSACEAE indet.							2							
Vicia c.f. *cracca* L.														
Vicia c.f. *hirsuta* (L.) Gray														
Vicia sativa L. type (>4mm)						262								
Vicia faba L.	2	2	1			2	2				3			
Lathyrus c.f. *pratensis* L.	1													
Lathyrus nissolia L.														
Lathyrus sp.			1									1		
small *Vicia/Lathyrus* sp. (<2mm)	15		1			29	14		1	1	1	4	4	
large *Vicia/Lathyrus* sp. (>2mm)	19	5	2	5	2		5		3	3	2			
Vicia/Lathyrus/Pisum (4mm)	2			1		1			1		4			
Medicago lupulina L.											1	3	1	
Medicago spp.							3		2			2		
Medicago/Trifolium spp.					1	1	1			1		2		
small *Trifolium* spp. (<2mm)	2	2		3	1	13			2					
large *Trifolium* sp. (>2mm)													5	
large legume cotyledon fragments	+		–		+	+++	+	+				++	1	
Rhamnus cathartica L.														
Aethusa c.f. *cynapium* L.														
Apium sp.														
APIACEAE indet. kernel						2								
Solanum nigrum L.							1							
Convolvulus arvensis L.						3								
Menyanthes trifoliata L.							2							
Myosotis sp.			1 m			2								
BORAGINACEAE indet.														
Mentha arvensis/aquatica							1							
LAMIACEAE indet.							1							
Plantago lanceolata L.						1	1				1			
Plantago major L.				1										
immature *Plantago* sp.						1								
Euphrasia spp.							2							

167

Sample	56	101	103	127	144	148	166	182	205	209	208	96	119	161
Context	2461	3321	3324	3590	5983	6238	7733	9233	9649	9751	9753	3267	3565	7130
Feature	-	F:752	F:774	-	F:1292	F:1368	F:1452	F:2275	F:2601	F:2621	F:2622	F:751	-	F:1012
Volume/litres	10	12	6	12	12	10	15	12	10	12	10	12	14	3
Type	posthole	well base	cessy pit	floor	pit	pit	pit	pond	pit	pit	pit	well	over floor	ditch
Site Phase	10	10	10	10	10	10	10	10	10	10	10	11	12	12
Odontites vernus (Bell.) Dumort.	4	1	1	2	2	3	2		1	1			1	
c.f. *Rhinanthus* sp.	1											1		
Galium aparine L.						35	6							
small *Galium* sp.				1		1								
Sambucus nigra L.	1						3							
Dipsacus fullonum L.							2							
Carduus tenuiflorus/crispus						6								
Cirsium c.f. *arvense* (L.) Scop.						1								
Carduus/Cirsium sp.						1								
Centaurea scabiosa L.						6								
Centaurea nigra L.						5							1	
Centaurea sp.	1			1		1								
Centaurea sp. kernels						15								
Lapsana communis L.						1								
Anthemis cotula L.	13	2	2	5	2	558	38		2		2	8	2	5
Tripleurospermum inodorum (L.) Schultz			1	2	1	2	5					2	1	
small ASTERACEAE indet.					1	1	1					1		1
large ASTERACEAE indet.						2								
Alisma plantago-aquatica L.														
small *Juncus* (0.5mm)						1								
Lemna sp.						1						++ u		– u
Luzula sp.						1								
Eleocharis c.f. *palustris* (L.) Roemer							2		1		1	2	2	
Eleocharis sp.							4							
Schoenus nigricans L.	3						1							
Cladium mariscus (L.) Pohl.	7	1				10	38		1					
vegetative *Cladium mariscus* (L.) Pohl.	+++	+		1	-	+	+++		++	3	+++	3	4	
Carex c.f. *remota*	1						1							
large trilete *Carex* sp.							1							
small trilete *Carex* sp.						1	2			1	2	1	1	
flat *Carex* sp.						2								
Carex spp.						1	1							
CYPERACEAE indet.						-								
CYPERACEAE stems		++		+								+		
Festuca sp.				4		4	3					3	1	
Festuca/Lolium sp.				2									-	
Lolium perenne L.														
Lolium perenne/temulentum														
Lolium c.f. *temulentum* L.														
c.f. *Lolium* sp.	1	2					2							

	56	101	103	127	144	148	166	182	205	209	208	96	119	161
Sample	56	101	103	127	144	148	166	182	205	209	208	96	119	161
Context	2461	3321	3324	3590	5983	6238	7733	9233	9649	9751	9753	3267	3565	7130
Feature	-	F.752	F.774	-	F.1292	F.1368	F.1452	F.2275	F.2601	F.2621	F.2622	F.751	-	F.1012
Volume/litres	10	12	6	12	12	10	15	12	10	12	10	12	14	3
Type	posthole	well base	cessy pit	floor	pit	pit	pit	pond	pit	pit	pit	well	over floor	ditch
Site Phase	10	10	10	10	10	10	10	10	10	10	10	11	12	12
Lolium sp. rachis internode						1								
Vulpia c.f. *bromoides*							1							
Poa spp.		1				19	5					3	2	1
Agrostis sp.		1											1	
Phleum pratense L.		1												
Phleum c.f. *bertolonii* DC.	1			1			1		2					
Phleum sp.					1								1	1
Poa/Phleum sp.						2			2					
Bromus spp.						9	4				1	1		
thin *Bromus* sp.														
Bromus/Avena sp.														
flattened POACEAE indet.										1				
small POACEAE indet.			1			6	5			1				
medium POACEAE indet.	1	1				1	9		1			1		1
large POACEAE indet.							2							
POACEAE floret base							1							
POACEAE culm node	2					5			1			2		
POACEAE culm fragment				++				−					+	
nutshell indet. fragment														
Monocot. plant stems														
rootlet indet.														
seed indet.	2		1			9	21		1			1		
stem indet.						+	+							
leaflet indet.							−							
bud indet.					−		−							
bract indet.					1							−		
Charophyte oogonium												−u		
moss fragment						+	+					−		
charred concretion					−			+						
large charcoal (4mm)	+	++	+	+	+	+	+	−	+		++	−		−
mid charcoal (2–4mm)	+++	++	+	+	++	+++	++	+	+++	++	+++	−	+	+
small charcoal (2mm)	+++	+++	+++	+++	+++	+++		+++	+++	+++	+++	++	++	++
vitrified charcoal														
fungal sclerotia	+				−	+						−		−
fungal thecae	−						++							

Table 5.18 Charred botanical evidence from Period III (medieval) contexts, II

169

Bibliography

Primary sources

BL Cotton Claudius C XI. 1417 survey of Ely

BL Cott. Tib. Bii (British Library). 1222 survey of the manors of the bishop of Ely.

BL Cott. Vesp. A19, fos 61–98. 1417 survey of Ely.

BL Harley 329. 1417 survey of Ely.

CLC. Acc. 1985/5, Box 3/2 (Clare College, Cambridge). Map of Clare College property in Little Downham.

CRO 515 (Cambs. County Record Office). Ely St Mary's Open Field Inclosure Map 1844.

CUL EDR D10/1/1. Rental of Ely Barton 1436–7.

CUL EDR D10/1/2. Rental of Ely Barton 1440–1.

CUL EDR G3/27. 1251 survey of the manors of the bishop of Ely.

PRO C66/401. 1417 survey of Ely

Published sources

Abrams, J., 2000 — *Iron Age Settlement and Post Medieval Features at 36b St. Johns Road, Ely: an archaeological evaluation.* Cambridgeshire County Council Archaeological Field Unit Rep. No. 187

Abrams, J., 2002 — *Medieval Occupation Features at 2 West End, Ely: An Archaeological Excavation.* Cambridgeshire County Council Archaeological Field Unit Rep. No. 203

Addyman, P.V., 1964 — 'A Dark Age settlement at Maxey, Northants', *Medieval Archaeol.* 8, 20–73

Addyman, P. V., 1969 — 'Late Saxon settlements in the St Neots area, II', *Proc. Cambridge Antiq. Soc.* 62, 59–93

Alexander, M., 1997 — *Excavations at the Old Bishops Palace, Ely.* CAU Report No. 215

Alexander, M., 1998 — *Excavations at Forehill, Ely: Post-Excavation Assessment and Updated Project Design.* CAU Report No. 282

Alexander, M., 2003 — 'A medieval and post-medieval street frontage: Investigations at Ely Forehill', *Proc. Cambridge Antiq. Soc.* 92, 135–82

Allen, T., Hey, G. and Miles, D., 1997 — 'A line of time: approaches to archaeology in the Upper and Middle Thames Valley, England', *World Archaeol.* 29(1), 114–19

Anderberg, A., 1994 — *Atlas of Seeds and Small Fruits of Northwest-European Plant Species with Morphological Descriptions. Part 4. Resedaceae–Umbelliferae.* Stockholm: Swedish Museum of Natural History

Anderson, S.T., 1970 — 'The relative pollen productivity and pollen representation of north European trees, and correction factors for tree pollen spectra', *Danm. Geol. Unders.* Ser I, 196

Anderson, S.T., 1973 — 'The differential pollen productivity of trees and its significance for the interpretation of a pollen diagram from a forested region', in Birks, H.J.B. and West, R.G. (eds), *Quaternary Plant Ecology.* Oxford: Blackwell

Andrews, P., 1995 — *Excavations at Redcastle Furze, Thetford, 1988–9.* E. Anglian Archaeol. 72

Andrews, P., 1997 — *Excavations at Hamwic: Vol. 2, Excavations at Six Dials.* CBA Research Report 109, London

Armitage, P. and West, B., 1987 — 'Faunal evidence from a late medieval garden well of the Greyfriars, London', *Trans. London Middlesex Archaeol. Soc.* 36, 107–36

Armitage, P.L. and Clutton-Brock, J., 1976 — 'A system for classification and description of horn cores of cattle from archaeological sites', *J. Archaeol. Sci.* 3, 329–48

Astill, G. and Lobb, S.J., 1989 — 'Evaluation of prehistoric, Roman and Saxon deposits at Wraysbury, Berkshire', *Archaeol. J.* 146, 68–134

Atkin, M., Carter, A. and Evans, D.H., 1985 — *Excavations in Norwich 1971–8. Part II,* E. Anglian Archaeol. 26

Backhouse, J., Turner, D.H. and Webster, L. (eds), 1984 — *The Golden Age of Anglo-Saxon Art.* London: British Museum Publications

Baker, P., 2002 — *The Vertebrate Remains from Six Saxon Sites in the Lincolnshire and Norfolk Fenlands (Saxon Fenland Management Project).* English Heritage, Centre for Archaeology Reports, 46/2002

Barthel, H.J., 1969 — 'Schlittknochen oder Knochen Geräte?', *Alt-Thuringen* 10, 205–28

Bass, W.M., 1992 — *Human Osteology: A Laboratory and Field Manual.* Columbia: Missouri Archaeological Society, Inc.

Becker, C., 1990 — 'Bemerkungen über Schlittknochen, Knochenkufen und ähnliche Artefakte, under besonderer Berücksichtigung der Funde aus Berlin-Spandau', in Schibler, J. Sedlmeier, J. and Spycher, H. (eds), *Festschrift für Hans R. Stampfli.* Berlin

Beebee, T. and Griffiths, R., 2000 — *Amphibians and Reptiles.* London: Harper Collins

Beijerinck, W., 1947 — *Zadenatlas der Nederlandsche Flora.* Wageningen: Veenman and Zonen

Bellamy, B., 1983 — 'Medieval pottery kilns at Stanion', *Northamptonshire Archaeol.* 18, 153–61

Bennet, K.D., Whittington, G. and Edwards, K.J., 1994 — 'Recent plant nomenclatural changes and pollen morphology in the British Isles', *Quaternary Newsletter* 73, 1–6

Beresford, G., 1975 — *The Medieval Clay-land Village. Excavations at Goltho and Barton Blount.* Society for Medieval Archaeology Monograph No. 6, London

Beresford, G., 1987 — *Goltho. The Development of an Early Medieval Manor c. 850–1150.* Engl. Heritage Archaeol. Rep. No. 4, London

Berggren, G., 1969 — *Atlas of Seeds and Small Fruits of Northwest-European Plant Species with Morphological Descriptions. Part 2. Cyperaceae.* Stockholm: Swedish Natural Science Research Council

Berggren, G., 1981 — *Atlas of Seeds and Small Fruits of Northwest-European Plant Species with Morphological Descriptions. Part 3. Saliaceae–Cruciferae.* Stockholm: Swedish Museum of Natural History

Biddle, M. (ed.), 1990 — *Object and Economy in Medieval Winchester.* Winchester Studies 7ii, Oxford (2 vols)

Blair, J., 1988 — 'Introduction: from Minster to Parish Church', in Blair, J. (ed.), *Minsters and Parish Churches. The Local Church in Transition 950–1200,* 1–19. Oxford: Oxford University Committee for Archaeology

Blair, J., 1998 — *Anglo-Saxon Oxfordshire.* Stroud: Sutton Publishing

Blair, J., forthcoming — *The Church in Anglo-Saxon Society*

Blake, E.O., 1962 — *Liber Eliensis.* London: Royal Historical Society

Blinkhorn, P.W., 1990 — 'Middle Saxon pottery from the Buttermarket Kiln, Ipswich', *Medieval Ceramics* 13, 12–16

Blinkhorn, P.W., 1999 — 'Of cabbages and kings: production, trade and consumption in Middle Saxon England', in Anderton, M. (ed.), *Anglo-Saxon Trading Centres and their Hinterlands. Beyond the Emporia*, 4–23. Glasgow: Cruithne Press

Blinkhorn, P.W., in press a — *The Ipswich Ware Project: Ceramics, Trade and Society in Middle Saxon England,* Medieval Pottery Res. Group Monograph

Blinkhorn, P.W., in press b — *Middle Saxon Pottery from the Lady Chapel, Ely*

Boardman, S. and Jones, G., 1990 — 'Experiments on the effects of charring on cereal plant components', *J. Archaeol. Sci.* 17, 1–11

Boessneck, J., 1969 — 'Osteological differences between sheep (*Ovis aries*) and goat (*Capra hircus*)', in Brothwell, D. and Higgs, E. S. (eds), *Science in Archaeology*, 2nd edition, 331–58. London: Thames and Hudson

Bourdillon, J. and Coy, J.P., 1980 — 'The animal bones', in Holdsworth, P. (ed.), *Excavations at Melbourne Street, Southampton, 1971–76*, 79–121. CBA Res. Rep. 33, London

Bradshaw, R.H.W. et al., 1981 — 'New fossil evidence for the past cultivation and processing of hemp (*Cannabis sativa L.*) in eastern England', *New Phytologist* 89, 503–10

Brodribb, A.C.C., Hands, A.R. and Walker, D.R., 1972 — *Excavations at Shakenoak Farm, near Wilcote, Oxfordshire. Part III: Site F.* Oxford: Exeter College

Brothwell, D., 1981 — *Digging Up Bones.* London: British Museum (Natural History)

Bryant, G.F. and Steane J.M., 1969 — 'Excavations at the deserted medieval settlement at Lyveden', *J. Northampton Mus. and Art Gall.* 5, 3–50

Buckley, D. and Hedges, J., 1987 — *The Bronze Age and Saxon Settlements at Springfield Lyons, Essex: an interim report.* Essex County Council Occasional Papers 5

Buckton, D., 1986 — 'Late 10th- and 11th-century *cloisonné* enamel brooches', *Medieval Archaeol.* 30, 8–18

Buikstra, J.E. and Ubelaker, D.H. (eds), 1994 — *Standards for Data Collection from Human Skeletal Remains.* Arkansas Archaeological Survey, Research Series No. 44, Fayetteville

Bushnell, G.H.S. and Hurst, J.G., 1953 — 'Some further examples of sgraffito ware from Cambridge', *Proc. Cambridge Antiq. Soc.* 46, 21–6

Campbell, G., 1994 — 'The preliminary archaeobotanical results from Anglo-Saxon West Cotton and Raunds', in Rackham, J. (ed.), *Environment and Economy in Anglo-Saxon England*, 65–82. York: Council for British Archaeology

Carr, R.D., Tester, A. and Murphy, P., 1988 — 'The Middle-Saxon settlement at Staunch Meadow, Brandon', *Antiquity* 62, 371–7

Cessford, C., Alexander, M. and Dickens, A., forthcoming — *Between Broad Street and the Great Ouse: Waterfront archaeology in Ely*, E. Anglian Archaeol.

Clark, J. (ed.), 1995 — *Medieval Finds from Excavations in London: 5, The Medieval Horse and its Equipment c. 1150–c. 1450.* London: Museum of London

Clarke, H. and Carter, A., 1977 — *Excavations in King's Lynn 1963–1970.* Society for Medieval Archaeology Monograph Series No. 7, London

Coad, J.G. and Streeten, A.D.F., 1982 — 'Excavations at Castle Acre Castle, Norfolk, 1972–77', *Archaeol. J.* 139, 199–227

Cobbett, L., 1934 — 'A Saxon carving found at Ely', *Antiq. J.* 14, 62–3

Cobbett, L. and Palmer, W. M., 1935 — 'The hospitals of St John the Baptist and St Mary Magdalene at Ely, and the remains of Gothic buildings still to be seen there at St John's Farm', *Proc. Cambridge Antiq. Soc.* 36, 58–108

Cohen, A. and Serjeantson, D., 1996 — *A Manual for the Identification of Bird Bones from Archaeological Sites*, revised edition. London: Archetype Publications Ltd.

Cowie, R., Whytehead, R.L. and Blackmore, L., 1988 — 'Two Middle Saxon occupation sites: excavations at Jubilee Hall and 21–22 Maiden Lane', *Trans. London Middlesex Archaeol. Soc.* 39, 47–164

Crabtree, P., 1990 — *West Stow: Early Anglo-Saxon Animal Husbandry.* E. Anglian Archaeol. 47

Crabtree, P., 1994 — 'Animal exploitation in East Anglian villages', in Rackham, J. (ed.), *Environment and Economy in Anglo-Saxon England*, 40–54. CBA Res. Rep. 89, London

Crabtree, P., 1996 — 'Production and consumption in an Early complex society: animal use in Middle Saxon East Anglia', *World Archaeol.* 28(1), 58–75

Crummy, N., 1983 — *The Roman Small Finds from Excavations in Colchester 1971–9.* Colchester Archaeol. Rep. 2, Colchester

Crummy, N., 1988 — *The Post-Roman Small Finds from Excavations in Colchester 1971–85.* Colchester Archaeol. Rep. 5, Colchester

Cunningham, C.M., 1982 — 'Medieval and post-medieval pottery', in Drury, P.J. (ed.), 'Aspects of the origins and development of Colchester Castle', *Archaeol. J.* 139, 358–80

Dallas, C., 1993 — *Excavations in Thetford by B.K. Davison between 1964 and 1970.* E. Anglian Archaeol. 62, Gressenhall

Darby, H.C., 1934 — 'The fenland frontier in Anglo-Saxon England', *Antiquity* 8, 185–201

Darby, H.C., 1940 — *The Medieval Fenland.* Cambridge University Press

Darby, H.C. and Miller, E., 1948 — 'Political history', *VCH Cambridgeshire*, 2.

Davis, S.J.M., 1991 — *Faunal Remains from the Late Saxon–Medieval Farmstead at Eckweek in Avon: 1979–1989 Excavations.* Ancient Monuments Lab. Rep. No. 35/91

Davis, S.J.M., 1992a — *A Rapid Method for Recording Information about Mammal Bones from Archaeological Sites.* Ancient Monuments Lab. Rep. No. 19/92

Davis, S.J.M., 1992b — *Saxon and Medieval Animal Bones from Burystead and Langham Road, Northamptonshire: 1984–1987 Excavations.* Ancient Monuments Lab. Rep. No. 71/92

Dickman, C.R. and Doncaster, C.P., 1987 — 'The ecology of small mammals in urban habitats I: populations in a patchy environment', *Journal of Animal Ecology* 56, 629–40

Dickman, C.R., and Doncaster, C.P., 1989 — 'The ecology of small mammals in urban habitats II: demography and dispersal', *Journal of Animal Ecology* 58, 119–27

Dobney, K. and Reilly, K., 1988 — 'A method for recording archaeological animal bones: the use of diagnostic zones', *Circaea* 5(2), 79–96

Dobney, K.M., Jaques, S.D. and Irving, B.G., 1996 — *Of Butchers and Breeds: report on vertebrate remains from various sites in the City of Lincoln.* Lincoln Archaeol. Stud. No. 5

Dunning, G.C., 1961 — 'A medieval pottery inkstand from Byland Abbey', *Medieval Archaeol.* 5, 307

Edmonds, M., Evans, C. and Gibson, D. 1999 — 'Assembly and collection: lithic complexes in the Cambridgeshire Fenlands', *Proc. Prehist. Soc.* 65, 47–87

Egan, G., 1998 — *The Medieval Household. Daily Living c.1150–c.1450*, Medieval Finds from Excavations in London 6, London

Egan, G. and Pritchard, F., 1991 — *Dress Accessories c.1150–c.1450. Medieval Finds from Excavations in London 3*, London

Ellenburg, H., 1988 — *Vegetation Ecology of Central Europe*, 4th edition. Cambridge University Press

Ellis, P. and Rátkai, S., 2001 — 'Late Saxon and medieval village remains at Longstanton, Cambridgeshire: Archaeological excavations at Home Farm 1997', in Ellis, P., Coates, G., Cuttler, R. and Mould, C. (eds.), *Four Sites in Cambridgeshire. Excavations at Pode Hole Farm, Paston, Longstanton and Bassingbourn, 1996–7*, 62–103. Brit. Archaeol. Rep. Brit. Ser. 322 (=BUAFU Monograph Series 4)

Ellis, S.E., 1969 — 'The petrography and provenance of Anglo-Saxon and medieval English honestones, with notes on some other hones', *Bulletin British Museum (Natural History)* 2.3, 135–87

Elsdon, S.M., 1993 — *Iron Age Pottery in the East Midlands: a handbook.* Nottingham: University of Nottingham, Department of Classics and Archaeology

Evans, C. and Hodder, I., forthcoming — *The Haddenham Project II: Marshland Communities and Cultural Landscape.* McDonald Institute Research Series, Cambridge

Evans, C. and Knight, M., 2000 — *Investigations at Hurst Lane, Ely, Cambridgeshire: Integrated assessment and updated project design.* English Heritage/CAU, Cambridge

Evans, C., 1992 — 'Commanding gestures in lowland: the investigation of two Iron Age ringworks', *Fenland Research* 2, 16–26

Evans, C., 1997 — 'Hydraulic communities: Iron Age enclosure in the East Anglian Fenlands', in Gwilt, A. and Haselgrove, C. (eds), *Re-constructing the Iron Age*, Oxbow Monograph 71, 216–27

Evans, C., 2002 — 'Metalwork and "cold claylands": pre-Iron Age occupation on the Isle of Ely', in Lane, T. and Coles, J. (eds), *Through Wet and Dry: Proceedings of a conference in honour of David Hall*, 33–53. Lincolnshire Archaeol. Heritage Rep. Ser. No. 5/WARP Occ. Pap. 17

Evans, C., 2003a — *Power And Island Communities: Excavations at the Wardy Hill Ringwork, Coveney, Ely.* E. Anglian Archaeol. 103, Cambridge Archaeological Unit

Evans, C., 2003b — 'Britons and Romans at Chatteris: Investigations at Langwood Farm, Cambridgeshire', *Britannia* 34, 175–264

Evans, C., Knight, M. and Webley, L., forthcoming — 'An island prehistory: Iron Age settlement, poverty and Romanization on the Isle of Ely', *Proc. Cambridge Antiq. Soc.*

Evans, J., 2001 — 'Material approaches to the identification of different Romano-British site types', in James, S. and Millett, M. (eds), *Britons and Romans: advancing an archaeological agenda*, 26–35. CBA Research Report 125, London

Evison, V., 1956 — 'An Anglo-Saxon cemetery at Holborough, Kent', *Archaeologia Cantiana* 70, 84–141

Evison, V., 1957 — 'A group of late Saxon brooches', *Antiq. J.* 37, 220–2

Faulkner, L. (ed.), 1997 — 'Sedgeford historical and archaeological research project, 1996: first interim report', *Norfolk Archaeol.* 42, 532–5

Fell, C., 1953 — 'An early Iron Age Settlement at Linton, Cambridgeshire', *Proc. Cambridge Antiq. Soc.* 46, 31–42

Foreman, M., 1991 — 'The bone and antler', in Armstrong, P., Tomlinson, D.G. and Evans, D.H. (eds.), *Excavations at Lurk Lane, Beverley, 1979–82*, Sheffield Excavation Reports 1, 183–96. Sheffield

Foreman, M., 1992 — 'Objects of bone, antler and shell', in Evans, D.H. and Tomlinson, D.G. (eds.), *Excavations at 33–35 Eastgate, Beverley, 1983–86*, Sheffield Archaeological Reports 3, 163–74. Sheffield

Fowler, G., 1934 — 'Fenland waterways past and present. South level district. Part II', *Proc. Cambridge Antiq. Soc.* 34, 2–33.

Friday, L. (ed.), 1997 — *Wicken Fen: The making of a wetland nature reserve.* Colchester: Harley

Gallois, R.W., 1988 — *Geology of the Country around Ely.* London: HMSO

Gardiner, M. and Greatorex, C., 1997 — 'Archaeological excavations in Steyning, 1992–95: Further evidence for the evolution of a late Saxon small town', *Sussex Archaeol. Collect.* 135, 143–71

Gardiner, M., 1990 — 'An Anglo-Saxon and medieval settlement at Botolphs, Bramber, West Sussex', *Archaeol. J.* 147, 216–75

Gardiner, M., 1993 — 'The excavation of a late Anglo-Saxon settlement at Market Field, Steyning, 1988–9', *Sussex Archaeol. Collect.* 131, 21–67

Garmonsway, G.N., 1972 — *The Anglo-Saxon Chronicle.* London

Gibson, D., 1995 — *Excavations at West Fen Road, Ely, Cambridgeshire.* CAU Report No. 160

Gibson, D., 1998 — *An Archaeological Desk-Top Assessment of the Land between St John's Road and West Fen Road Ely.* CAU Report No. 272

172

Gidney, L.J., 1996 'The cosmetic and quasi-medical use of dog fat', *Newsletter of the Osteoarchaeological Research Group* 11, 8–9

Gleed-Owen, C.P., 2001 *Further Archaeozoological Work for the Pool Frog Species Recovery Programme*, English Nature, Unpublished Report

Grant, A., 1982 'The use of tooth wear as a guide to the age of domestic animals', in Wilson, B., Grigson, C. and Payne, S. (eds), *Ageing and Sexing Animal Bones from Archaeological Sites*, Brit. Archaeol. Rep. Brit. Ser. 109, 91–108

Greig, J.R.A., 1988 'Plant resources', in Astill, G. and Grant, A., *The Countryside of Medieval England*, 108–27. Oxford: Blackwell

Greig. J.R.A., 1991 'The British Isles', in van Zeist, W. *et al.* (eds.), *Progress in Old World Palaeoethnobotany*, 299–334. Rotterdam: A.A. Balkema

Grieg, S., 1933 *Middelalderske Byfund fra Bergen og Oslo.* Oslo

Grierson, P. and Blackburn, M., 1986 *Medieval European Coinage with a Catalogue of the Coins in the Fitzwilliam Museum, Cambridge I. The Early Middle Ages (5th–10th centuries).* Cambridge University Press

Grieve, M., 1980 *A Modern Herbal.* Harmondsworth: Penguin

Guido, M., 1978 *The Glass Beads of the Prehistoric and Roman Periods in Britain and Ireland.* Rep. Res. Comm. Soc. Antiq. London 35

Guido, M., 1999 *The Glass Beads of Anglo-Saxon England, c. 400–700.* Rep. Res. Comm. Soc. Antiq. London 56

Gurney, D. (ed.), 1996 'Archaeological finds in Norfolk 1995', *Norfolk Archaeol.* 42, 387–96

Haldenby, D., 1992 'An Anglian site on the Yorkshire Wolds. Part II', *Yorkshire Archaeol. J.* 64, 25–39

Hall, D., 1996 *The Fenland Project Number 10: Cambridgeshire Survey, The Isle of Ely and Wisbech*, E. Anglian Archaeol. Rep. 79, Cambridgeshire County Council

Hall, D., 2001 'Medieval pottery from Forehill, Ely, Cambridgeshire', *Medieval Ceramics* 25, 2–21

Hampson, E.M. and Atkinson, T.D., 1953 'City of Ely', *VCH Cambridgeshire*, 4

Hanf, M., 1983 *The Arable Weeds of Europe.* Ludwigshafen: BASF Aktiengesellschaft

Harcourt, R.A., 1974 'The dog in prehistoric and early historic Britain', *J. Archaeol. Sci.* 1, 151–75

Healey, R.H., 1969 'Bourne Ware', *Lincolnshire Hist. Archaeol.* 4, 108–9

Healey, R.H., 1975 *Medieval and Sub-Medieval Pottery in Lincolnshire*, unpublished M. Phil. thesis, University of Nottingham

Henderson, I., 1997 'Anglo-Saxon sculpture', in Hicks, C. (ed.), *Cambridgeshire Churches*, 216–32. Stamford: Paul Watkins

Henry, P., 1999 'Development and change in late Saxon textile production: an analysis of the evidence', *Durham Arch. J.* 14–15, 69–76

Herrmann, J., 1962 *Köpernick. Ein Beitrag zur Frühgeschichte Gross-Berlins.* Deutsche Akademie der Wissenschaften zu Berlin, Schriften der Sektion für Vor- und Frühgeschichte 12, Berlin

Hey, G., 2004 *Yarnton: Saxon and Medieval Settlement and Landscape.* Oxford: Oxford Archaeology

Heywood, V.H., 1978 *Flowering Plants of the World.* Oxford University Press

Higbee, L., 1998 'Animal bones', in Mortimer, R., *Excavation of the Middle Saxon to Mediaeval Village at Lordship Lane, Cottenham*, Cambridgeshire. CAU Report 254

Hill, J.D., 1995 *Ritual and Rubbish in the Iron Age of Wessex: a study in the formation of a specific archaeological record.* Brit. Archaeol. Rep. Brit. Ser. 242, Oxford: Tempus Reparatum

Hill, J.D., Evans, C. and Alexander, M., 1999 'The Hinxton Rings — A Late Iron Age cemetery at Hinxton, Cambridgeshire, with a reconsideration of northern Aylesford-Swarling distributions', *Proc. Prehist. Soc.* 65, 243–74

Hillman, G., 1981 'Reconstructing crop husbandry practices from charred remains of crops', in Mercer, R.J. (ed.), *Farming Practice in British Prehistory*, 123–162. Edinburgh University Press

Hillman, G., 1982 'Evidence for spelt malting at Catsgore', in Leech, R., *Excavations at Catsgore 1970–1973: a Romano-British village*, 137–140. Bristol: Western Archaeological Trust

Hinman, M., 1996 *Late Saxon and Medieval Features at Chapel Street, Ely: An archaeological evaluation at the site of the old health centre.* Cambridgeshire County Council Archaeological Field Unit, Report No. 750

Hinman, M., 2002 *Deeply Stratified Medieval and Post-Medieval Remains at Market Mews, Wisbech.* Cambridgeshire County Council Archaeological Field Unit Rep. No. 156

Hinton, M.P., 1991 'Weed associates of recently grown *Avena Strigosa* from Shetland, Scotland', *Circaea* 8(1), 49–54

Hofland, L.H., 1969 'De benen schaatsen', *Westerheem* 18, 125–7

Holbrook, N. and Bidwell, P., 1991 *Roman Finds from Exeter.* Exeter City Council

Holdsworth, P.E., 1976 'Saxon Southampton: a new review', *Medieval Archaeol.* 20, 26–61

Holdsworth, P.E., 1980 *Excavations at Melbourne Street, Southampton, 1971–6*, CBA Res. Rep. 33, London

Holmes, E.F., 1988 *Sewing Thimbles.* Finds Research Group AD 700–1700, Datasheet 9

Holton-Krahenbuhl, A., 1988 'Excavations at the Paddock, Ely, Cambs', *Proc. Camb. Antiq. Soc.* 77, 119–23

Holton-Krayenbuhl, A., 1997 'The infirmary complex at Ely', *Archaeol. J.* 154, 294–8

Hope-Taylor, B., 1977 *Yeavering: An Anglo-British Centre of Early Northumbria.* London: HMSO

Horton W., Lucas G. and Wait G.A., 1995 'Excavation of a Roman site near Wimpole, Cambs, 1989', *Proc. Cambridge Antiq. Soc.* 83, 31–74

Huggins, R.M., 1972 'Monastic grange and outer close excavations, Waltham Abbey, Essex, 1970–72', *Essex Archaeol. Hist.* 4, 30–127

Hunter, J.P.C., 1992   *Archaeological Investigations at Walsingham House, Ely, 1991.* CAU Report No. 62

Hurst, J.G., 1956   'Saxo-Norman pottery in East Anglia: Part I. St Neots Ware', *Proc. Camb. Antiq. Soc.* 49, 43–70

Hurst, J.G., 1957   'Saxo-Norman pottery in East Anglia: Part II. Thetford Ware', *Proc. Camb. Antiq. Soc.* 50, 29–60

Hurst, J.G., 1958   'Saxo-Norman pottery in East Anglia, Part III. Stamford Ware', *Proc. Camb. Antiq. Soc.* 51, 37–65

Hurst, J.G., 1976   'The pottery', in Wilson, D.M. (ed.), *The Archaeology of Anglo-Saxon England*, 283–348 London: Methuen

Hyland, A., 1999   *The Horse in the Middle Ages.* Stroud: Sutton

Jackson, D.A. and Dix, B., 1987   'Late Iron Age and Roman settlement at Weekley, Northants', *Northamptonshire Archaeol.* 21, 41–94

Jackson, R.P.J. and Potter, T.W., 1996   *Excavations at Stonea, Cambridgeshire, 1980–85.* London: British Museum Press

Jaques, D. and Dobney, K., 1996   *Vertebrate Remains From Excavations at Tower 10, City Walls, York: Technical Report 96/28.* Unpublished report from the Environmental Archaeology Unit, York

Jenner, A. and Vince, A., 1983   Hertfordshire Glazed Ware, *Trans. London Middlesex Archaeol. Soc.* 34, 151–70

Jennings, S., 1981   *Eighteen Centuries of Pottery from Norwich*, E. Anglian Archaeol. 13

Jessop, O., 1996   'A new artefact typology for the study of medieval arrowheads', *Medieval Archaeol.* 40, 192–205

Jones, G., 1984   'Interpretation of archaeological plant remains: ethnographic models from Greece', in van Zeist, W. and Casparie, W.A. (eds.), *Plants and Ancient Man*, 43–61. Rotterdam: A.A. Balkema

Jones, M., 1981   'The development of crop husbandry', in Jones, M. and Dimbleby, G. (eds.), *The Environment of Man: the Iron Age to Anglo-Saxon period*, Brit. Archaeol. Rep. Brit. Ser. 87, 95–127

Jones, M., 1984a   *The Ecological and Cultural Implications of Carbonised Seed Assemblages from Selected Archaeological Contexts in Southern Britain.* Unpublished D. Phil. thesis, University of Oxford

Jones, M., 1984b   'The plant remains', in Cunliffe, B., *Danebury: an Iron Age hillfort in Hampshire, volume 2. The excavations 1969–1978, the finds*, 483–95. London: Council for British Archaeology

Kaufman, D., 1998   'Measuring archaeological diversity: an application of the jackknife technique', *American Antiquity* 63(1), 73–85

Kendrick, T.D., 1938   *Anglo-Saxon Art to AD 900.* London: Methuen

Kenney, S., 1999   *Anglo-Saxon and Medieval Deposits at 2 West End, Ely: An Archaeological Evaluation.* Cambridgeshire County Council Archaeological Field Unit Rep. No. 164

Kenney, S., 2002   *Roman, Saxon and Medieval Occupation at the former Red, White and Blue Public House, Chief's Street, Ely.* Cambridgeshire County Council Archaeological Field Unit Rep. No. 195

Keynes, S., 2003   'Ely Abbey, 672–1109', in Meadows, P. and Ramsay, N. (eds), *A History of Ely Cathedral*, 3–58. Woodbridge: Boydell Press

Kilmurry, K., 1980   *The Pottery Industry of Stamford, Lincs. c. AD 850–1250.* Brit. Archaeol. Rep. Brit. Ser. 84

King, E., 1973   *Peterborough Abbey, 1086–1310: a study in the land market.* Cambridge University Press

Knight, M., 1999   *An Archaeological Evaluation of Land off West Fen Road, Ely, Cambridgeshire.* CAU Report No. 309

Lauwerier, R. and Van Herringen, R., 1998   'Skate and prickers from the circular fortress of Oost-Souburg, the Netherlands (AD 900–975)', *Envir. Archaeol.* 3, 121–6

Layard, N., 1908   'Bone skates and skating skates', *East Anglian Miscellany* 2, 74

Leah, M., 1994   *The Late Saxon and Medieval Pottery Industry of Grimston, Norfolk: Excavations 1962–92*, E. Anglian Archaeol. 64

Leahy, K., 2003   *Anglo-Saxon Crafts.* Stroud: Tempus

Leahy, K. and Paterson, C., 2001   'New light on the Viking presence in Lincolnshire: the artefactual evidence', in Graham-Campbell, J., Hall, R., Jesch, J. and Parsons, D.N. (eds), *Vikings and the Danelaw*, 181–202. Oxford: Oxbow

Lethbridge, T.C. and Tebbutt, C.F., 1933   'Huts of the Anglo-Saxon period', *Proc. Cambridge Antiq. Soc.* 33, 133–5

Lloyd, N., 1925   *A History of English Brickwork.* H. Greville Montgomery (reprinted 1990, Antique Collectors' Club)

Losco-Bradley, S. and Kinsley, G., 2002.   *Catholme. An Anglo-Saxon Settlement on the Trent Gravels in Staffordshire.* Nottingham: Department of Archaeology

Loveluck, C., 2001   'Wealth, waste and conspicuous consumption. Flixborough and its importance for mid and late Saxon settlement studies', in Hamerow, H. and MacGregor, A. (eds), *Image and Power in the Archaeology of Early Medieval Britain*, 78–130. Oxford: Oxbow

Lucas, G., 1997   'Prehistoric, Roman and post-Roman pottery', in Price, J., Brooks, I.P. and Maynard, D.J. (eds), *The Archaeology of the St Neots to Duxford Gas Pipeline*, Brit. Archaeol. Rep. Brit. Ser. 255, 49–88

Lucas, G., forthcoming   *Excavations at Vicar's Farm, West Cambridge*

Lucas, R., 1993   'Ely bricks and roof-tiles and their distribution in Norfolk and elsewhere in the sixteenth and eighteenth centuries', *Proc. Cambridge Antiq. Soc.* 82, 157–62

Mabey, R., 1996   *Flora Britannica.* London: Sinclair-Stevenson

MacDonald, K.C., 1992   'The domestic chicken (*Gallus gallus*) in sub-Saharan Africa: a background to its introduction and its osteological differentiation from indigenous fowls (*Numidinea and Francolinus sp*)', *J. Archaeol. Sci.* 19, 303–18

MacGregor, A., 1975   'Problems in the interpretation of microscopic wear patterns: the evidence from bone skates', *J. Archaeol. Sci.* 2, 385–90

MacGregor, A., 1976   'Bone skates: a review of the evidence', *Archaeol. J.* 133, 57–74

MacGregor, A., 1982 — *Anglo-Scandinavian Finds from Lloyds Bank, Pavement and other Sites*, Archaeology of York 17/3, London

MacGregor, A., 1985 — *Bone, Antler, Ivory and Horn. The technology of skeletal materials since the Roman period.* London: Croom Helm

MacGregor, A., 1995 — 'Roman and early medieval bone and antler objects', in Phillips, D. and Heywood, B., *Excavations at York Minster. Volume I: From Roman Fortress to Norman Cathedral*, 414–27. London: HMSO

MacGregor, A. and Bolick, E., 1993 — *A Summary Catalogue of the Anglo-Saxon Collections (Non-Ferrous Materials) in the Ashmolean Museum, Oxford.* Brit. Archaeol. Rep. Brit. Ser. 230

MacGregor, A., Mainman, A.J. and Rogers, N.S.H., 1999 — *Craft, Industry and Everyday Life: Bone, Antler, Ivory and Horn from Anglo-Scandinavian and Medieval York*, Archaeology of York 17/12, London

Malcolm, G. and Bowsher, D. with Cowie, R., 2003 — *Middle Saxon London. Excavations at the Royal Opera House 1989–99*, MOLAS Monograph 15, London

Malim, T. and Hines, J., 1998 — *The Anglo-Saxon Cemetery at Edix Hill (Barrington A), Cambridgeshire*, CBA Res. Rep. 112, London

Malim, T., 1993 — 'An investigation of multi-period cropmarks at Manor Farm, Harston', *Proc. Cambridge Antiq. Soc.* 82, 11–54

Maltby, M., 1979 — *Faunal Studies on Urban Sites: The animal bones from Exeter 1971–1975.* Exeter Archaeol. Rep. Vol. 2

Mann, J.E., 1982 — *Early Medieval Finds from Flaxengate, 1: Objects of antler, bone, stone, horn, ivory, amber and jet,* Archaeology of Lincoln 14-1, London

Margeson, S., 1993 — *Norwich Households. Medieval and Post-Medieval Finds from Norwich Survey Excavations 1971–78,* E. Anglian Archaeol. 58

Margeson, S. and Williams, V., 1985 — 'The artefacts', in Ayers, B., *Excavations within the North-East Bailey of Norwich Castle, 1979,* E. Anglian Archaeol. 28, 27–48

Markham, G., 1681 — *A Way To Get Wealth*

Masser, P., 2000 — *Archaeological Evaluation at West Fen Road, Ely: the Cornwell Bungalow Site.* CAU Report No. 373

Masser, P., 2001 — *Archaeological Excavations at West Fen and St John's Roads, Ely, Cambridgeshire: The Trinity and Runciman Lands. Assessment Report.* CAU Report No. 432

McCarthy, M.R. and Brooks, C.M., 1988 — *Medieval Pottery in Britain AD 900–1600.* Leicester University Press.

Medieval Pottery Research Group, 1998 — *A Guide to the Classification of Medieval Ceramic Forms*, Medieval Pottery Research Group Occasional Paper 1

Meindl, R.S. and Lovejoy, C.O., 1985 — 'Ectocranial suture closure: a revised method for the determination of skeletal age at death based on the lateral-anterior suture', *American Journal of Physical Anthropology* 68, 57–66

Metcalf, D., 1984 — 'Monetary circulation in southern England in the first half of the eighth century', in Hill, D. and Metcalf, D. (eds), *Sceattas in England and on the Continent. The seventh Oxford symposium on coinage and monetary history.* Brit. Archaeol. Rep. Brit. Ser. 128, 27–69

Miles, D., 1984 — *Archaeology at Barton Court Farm, Abingdon, Oxon*, CBA Res. Rep. 50, London

Miller, E. and Hatcher, J., 1978 — *Medieval England — Rural Society and Economic Change 1086–1348.* London: Longman

Miller, E., 1951 — *The Abbey and Bishopric of Ely.* Cambridge University Press

Moffett, L., 1994 — 'Charred cereals from some ovens/kilns in Late Saxon Stafford and the botanical evidence for the pre-*burgh* economy', in Rackham, J. (ed.), *Environment and Economy in Anglo-Saxon England*, 55–64. York: Council for British Archaeology

Moore, P.D. and Webb, J.A., 1978 — *An Illustrated Guide to Pollen Analysis.* London: Hodder and Stoughton

Moore, P.D., Webb, J.A. and Collinson, M.E., 1991 — *Pollen Analysis*, 2nd edition. Oxford: Blackwell Scientific

Mortimer, R., 1996 — *Excavation of a Group of Anglo-Saxon Features at Denny End, Waterbeach, Cambridgeshire.* CAU Report No. 164

Mortimer, R., 1998 — *Excavation of the Middle Saxon to Medieval Village at Lordship Lane, Cottenham, Cambridgeshire.* CAU Report No. 254

Mortimer, R., 2000a — *Excavations at Bloodmoor Hill, Carlton Colville, Suffolk: An Interim Report.* CAU Report No. 386

Mortimer, R., 2000b — 'Village development and ceramic sequence: the Middle to Late Saxon village at Lordship Lane, Cottenham, Cambridgeshire', *Proc. Cambridge Antiq. Soc.* 89, 5–33

Mould, C., 1999 — *Hillside Meadow, Fordham, Cambridgeshire. Archaeological Investigations 1998. Post-Excavation Assessment and Research Design.* Birmingham University Field Archaeology Unit Project No. 565

Mudd, A., 2000 — *West Fen Road, Ely, Cambs. Interim progress report on excavations to March 2000.* Northamptonshire Archaeology

Mudd, A., 2001 — *West Fen Road, Ely. Post-excavation assessment and updated project design.* Northamptonshire Archaeology

Murphy, E.M., 2001 — 'Medieval and post-medieval butchered dogs from Carrickfergus, Co. Antrim, Northern Ireland', *Environmental Archaeol.* 6, 13–22

Murphy, P., 1985 — 'The cereals and crop weeds', in West, S., *West Stow. The Anglo-Saxon Village*, E. Anglian Archaeol. 24, 100–8

Murphy, P., 1990 — *Stansted Airport, Essex: Carbonised Plant Remains.* Ancient Monuments Lab. Rep. 129/90

Murphy, P., 1993 — 'Anglo-Saxon arable farming on the silt fens — preliminary results', *Fenland Research* 8, 75–8

Murphy, P., 1994 — 'The Anglo-Saxon landscape and rural economy: some results from sites in East Anglia and Essex', in Rackham, J. (ed.), *Environment and Economy in Anglo-Saxon England*, 23–39. York: Council for British Archaeology

Murphy, P., 1997 — 'Environment and economy', in Glazebrook, J. (ed.), *Research and Archaeology: a framework for the Eastern Counties, 1. Resource Assessment*, E. Anglian Archaeol. Occ. Pap. 3, 54–5

Nenk, B., Margeson, S. and Hurley, M., 1996 — 'Archaeology in Suffolk', *Proc. Suffolk Inst. Arch. Hist.* 38(4), 457–86

O'Connor, T., 1982 — *Animal Bones from Flaxengate, Lincoln c. 870–1500*. Archaeology of Lincoln 18(1). London, Council for British Archaeology

O'Connor, T., 1989 — *Bones from Anglo-Scandinavian Levels at 16–22 Coppergate.* Archaeology of York 15(3), London: Council for British Archaeology

Oosthuizen, S., 1998 — 'The origins of Cambridgeshire', *Antiq. J.* 78, 85–109

Orton, C., 1998–9 — 'Minimum standards in statistics and sampling', *Medieval Ceram.* 22–23, 135–8

Ottaway, P., 1992 — *Anglo-Scandinavian Ironwork from Coppergate*, Archaeology of York 17(6), London: Council for British Archaeology

Owen, D., 2003 — 'Ely 1109–1539: priory, community and town', in Meadows, P. and Ramsay, N. (eds), *A History of Ely Cathedral*, 59–75. Woodbridge: Boydell Press

Palmer, R., 1996 — 'A further case for the preservation of earthwork ridge and furrow', *Antiquity* 70, 426–40

Palmer, R., 1998 — *Land off West Fen Road, (centred TL530805), Ely, Cambridgeshire: Aerial Photographic Appraisal.* Air Photo Services Report 1998/16

Palmer, W.M., 1936 — 'Enclosures at Ely, Downham and Littleport. AD 1548', *Trans. Cambs. Hunts. Antiq. Soc.* 5, 369–84

Payne, S., 1973 — 'Kill-off patterns in sheep and goats: the mandibles from Asvan Kale', *Anatolian Studies* 23, 281–303

Payne, S., 1985 — 'Morphological distinction between the mandibular teeth of young sheep *Ovis* and goats *Capra*', *J. Archaeol. Sci.* 12, 139–47

Payne, S., 1987 — 'Reference codes for wear states in the mandibular cheek teeth of sheep and goats', *J. Archaeol. Sci.* 14, 609–14

Payne, S. and Bull, G., 1988 — 'Components of variation in measurements of pig bones and teeth, and the use of measurements to distinguish wild from domestic pig remains', *Archaeozoologia* 2, 27–66

Peglar, S.M., 1993 — 'The development of the cultural landscape around Diss Mere, Norfolk, U.K., during the past 7000 years', *Review of Palaeobotany and Palynology* 76(1), 1–47

Pelling, R. and Robinson, M., 2000 — 'Saxon emmer wheat from the upper and middle Thames Valley, England', *Enviro. Archaeol.* 5, 117–19

Peña-Chocarro, L. and Zapata-Peña, L., 1998 — 'Hulled wheats in Spain: history of minor cereals', in Jaradat, A.A. (ed.), *Triticeae III*, 45–52. New Delhi: Oxford and NBN

Piper, P.J., forthcoming — *The Rodents, Reptiles and Amphibians: A Palaeoecological and Taphonomic Study of the Micro-Faunal Remains Recovered from Archaeological Sites.* Unpublished D. Phil. thesis, University of York

Postan, M.M., 1975 — *The Medieval Economy and Society.* London

Powell, A., 2002 — 'The animal bone', in Foreman, S., Hiller, J. and Petts, D. (eds), *Gathering the People, Settling the Land: The Archaeology of a Middle Thames Landscape, Anglo-Saxon to Post-Medieval* (data held on CD). Oxford: Oxford Archaeological Unit

Pritchard, F., 1991 — 'Small finds', in Vince, A.G. (ed.), *Finds and Environmental Evidence*, Aspects of Saxo-Norman London II, 120–278. London: London and Middlesex Archaeological Society

Pryor, F., 1984 — *Excavation at Fengate, Peterborough, England: The fourth report.* Northamptonshire Archaeological Monograph 2/Royal Ontario Museum of Archaeology Monograph 7, Leicester/Toronto

Radley, J., 1971 — 'Economic aspects of Anglo-Danish York', *Medieval Archaeol.* 15, 37–57

Reaney, P.H., 1943 — *The Place-Names of Cambridgeshire and the Isle of Ely*, English Place-Name Society Vol. XIX. Cambridge University Press

Regan, R., 2001 — *Excavations South of The Lady Chapel, Ely Cathedral, Cambridgeshire. Assessment Report.* CAU Report No. 419

Regan, R. and Evans, C., 1998 — *The Archaeology of Colne Fen: Site I.* CAU Report No. 273

Regan, R. and Evans, C., 2000 — *The Archaeology of Colne Fen: Sites III and IV.* CAU Report No. 398

Regan, R., 2000 — *The Archaeology of the Green Land Site, Isle of Ely.* CAU Report No. 351

Reynolds, A., 1999 — *Later Anglo-Saxon England. Life and Landscape.* Stroud: Tempus

Richards, J.D., 1999 — 'Cottam: an Anglian and Anglo-Scandinavian settlement on the Yorkshire Wolds', *Archaeol. J.* 156, 1–110

Riddler, I.D. and Walton Rogers, P., forthcoming — 'The small finds', in Parfitt, K., Corke, B. and Cotter, J., *Excavations off Townwall Street, Dover, 1995–6*, Canterbury Archaeological Trust Occasional Papers, Canterbury

Riddler, I.D., 1988 — 'Late Saxon or late Roman? A comb from Pudding Lane', *London Archaeol.* 5, 372–4

Riddler, I.D., 1990a — 'Saxon handled combs from London', *Trans. London Middlesex Archaeol. Soc.* 41, 9–20

Riddler, I.D., 1990b — 'Eine Stielkamm aus Haithabu', *Berichte über die Ausgrabungen in Haithabu* 27, 177–81

Riddler, I.D., 1991 — 'The worked bone and antler', in Fasham, P.J. and Whinney, R.J.B. (eds), *Archaeology and the M3*, 45–50. Hampshire Fld Club Archaeol. Soc. Monogr. 7, Gloucester

Riddler, I.D., 1993 — 'Saxon worked bone objects', in Williams, R.J. (ed.), *Pennyland and Hartigans. Two Iron Age and Saxon Sites in Milton Keynes*, 107–19. Buckinghamshire Archaeol. Soc. Monogr. Ser. 4, Aylesbury

Riddler, I.D., 1997 — 'Combs with perforated handles', *Archaeol. Cantiana* 117, 189–98

Riddler, I.D., 2001 — 'The small finds', in Gardiner, M. (ed.), 'Continental trade and non-urban ports in Middle Anglo-Saxon England: Excavations at *Sandtun*, West Hythe, Kent', *Archaeol. J.* 158, 228–52

Riddler, I.D., 2004 — 'Production in Lundenwic: antler, bone and hornworking', in Leary, J., *Tarbehrt's*

Lundenwic: Archaeological Excavations in Middle Saxon London. PCA Monograph, London, 145–8

Riddler, I.D., forthcoming a
'The small finds', in Pickard, C., 'Excavations at the National Portrait Gallery, London', *Trans. London Middlesex Archaeol. Soc.*

Riddler, I.D., Trzaska-Nartowski, N.T.N. and Hatton, S., forthcoming
An Early Medieval Craft: Antler and Boneworking from Ipswich Excavations 1974–1994, E. Anglian Archaeol.

Rigold, S., 1978
'The St Nicholas or 'Boy Bishop' tokens', *Proc. Suffolk Inst. Archaeol. Hist.* 34(2), 87–101

Robinson, B., 1994
Ely City Centre Redevelopment: An archaeological desk-top study. Cambridge County Council Archaeological Field Unit Report No. 108

Robinson, B., 1998
Note in *Medieval Archaeol.* 42, 119

Robinson, B., 2000
Saxon and Medieval Occupation at St Mary's Lodge, Ely: A recording brief. Cambridgeshire County Council Archaeological Field Unit, Report No. 171

Roes, A., 1963
Bone and Antler Objects from the Frisian Terp Mounds. Haarlem: Tjeenk Willink

Rogers, N.S.H., 1993
Anglian and other Finds from Fishergate. Archaeology of York 17/9, London

Rogerson, A. and Ashley, S. J., 1985
'A medieval pottery production site at Blackborough End, Middleton', *Norfolk Archaeol.* 39(2), 181–9

Rogerson, A. and Dallas, C., 1984
Excavations in Thetford 1948–59 and 1973–80, E. Anglian Archaeol. 22

Rogerson, A., 1995
A Late Neolithic, Saxon and Medieval Site at Middle Harling, Norfolk, E. Anglian Archaeol. 74

Rowell, T.A., 1986
'Sedge (*Cladium mariscus*) in Cambridgeshire: its use and production since the 17th century', *Agr. Hist. Rev.* 34, 140–8

Rulewicz, M., 1958
'Wczesnoredniowieczne zabawki i przedmioty do gier z Pomorza Zachodniego', *Materialy Zachodnio-Pomorskie* 4, 303–54

Rulewicz, M., 1994
Rybowstwo Gdanska na tle Osrodków Miejskich Pomorza od IX do XIII Wieku. Gdansk Wczesnoredniowieczny 10, Gdansk

Schofield, J., 1997
'Urban housing in England', in Gaimster, D. and Stamper, P. (eds), *The Age of Transition: The Archaeology of English Culture 1400–1600*, Society for Medieval Archaeology Monograph 15 (Oxbow Monograph 98)

Scull, C., 2002
'Ipswich: Development and contexts of an urban precursor in the seventh century', in Hardh, B. and Larsson, L. (eds), *Central Places in the Migration and the Merovingian Periods*, 303–16. Uppakrastudier 6 (Acta Archaeologica Lundensia Series 8 No. 39). Stockholm: Almqvist and Wiksell International

Selkirk, A., 1987
'West Cotton', *Current Archaeol.* 106, 337–9

Sellwood, L., 1984
'Objects of bone and antler', in Cunliffe, B. (ed.), *Danebury Excavation Report Volume 2*, 371–8. CBA Res. Rep. 52, London

Semenov, S.A., 1964
Prehistoric Technology. London: Cory, Adams and Mackay

Sherley-Price, L., 1968
Bede: A History of the English Church and People. London

Silver, I.A., 1969
'The ageing of domestic animals', in Brothwell, D. and Higgs, E. (eds), *Science in Archaeology*, 283–301. London: Thames and Hudson

Simoons, F.J., 1994
Eat Not This Flesh. University of Wisconsin Press

Smith, C., 1998
'Dogs, cats and horses in the Scottish medieval town', *Proc. Soc. Antiq. Scotl.* 128, 859–85

Spence, C., 1990
Archaeological Site Manual. London: Museum of London

Spoerry, P., forthcoming
A Late Medieval Pottery Kiln Dump at Potters Lane, Ely, 1995

Stace, C., 1997
New Flora of the British Isles, 2nd edition. Cambridge University Press

Stafford, P., 1985
The East Midlands in the Early Middle Ages. Leicester University Press

Stallibrass, S., 1982
'The faunal remains', in Potter, T.W. and Potter, C.F., *A Romano-British Village at Grandford, March, Cambridgeshire*, 98–122. British Museum Occasional Papers 35, London

Steane, J.M., 1967
'Excavations at Lyveden', *J. Northampton Mus. and Art Gall.* 2, 1–37

Steedman, K., 1995
'Excavation of a Saxon site at Riby Cross Roads, Lincolnshire', *Archaeol. J.* 151, 212–306

Steel, D.G. and Bramblett, C.A., 1988
The Anatomy and Biology of the Human Skeleton. Texas: A and M University Press

Stenberger, M., 1961
'Uppsala: Das Gräberfeld bei Ihre im Kirchspiel Helvi auf Gotland. Der wikingerzeitliche Abschnitt', *Acta Archaeologia* 32, 1–134

Stenberg-Tyrefors, B. and Johansson, B. M., 1993
'Ben med tydliga spar av att vara bearbetade', *Populär Arkeologi* 11, 4–7

Taylor, D. and May, J., 1996
'Other bone and antler artefacts', in May, J., *Dragonby. Report on Excavations at an Iron Age and Romano-British Settlement in North Lincolnshire*, 349–64. Oxbow Monograph 61, Oxford.

Taylor-Wilson, R.H., 1992
Archaeological Investigations at Upherds Lane, Ely, Cambridgeshire. CAU Report No. 75

Tempel, W.-D., 1972
'Unterscheide zwischen der Formen der Dreilagenkämme in Skandinavien und auf den friesischen Wurten von 8. bis 10. Jahrhundert', *Archäologisches Korrespondenzblatt* 2, 57–9

Tusser, T., 1557
A Hundreth Good Pointes of Husbandrie

Ulbricht, I., 1984
Die Verarbeitung von Knochen, Geweih und Horn im mittelalterlichen Schleswig. Ausgrabungen in Schleswig, Berichte und Studien 3, Neumünster

van Vilsteren, V.T., 1987
Het Benen Tijdperk. Gebruiksvoorwerpen van been, gewei, hoorn en ivoor 10,000 jaar gelden tot heden. Drents Museum

van Wijngaarden-Bakker, L.H., 1981
'Mesheften, kaardenkammen en glissen', in *Bodemonderzoek in Leiden*, 61–6. Leiden

Von den Driesch, A. and Boessneck, J., 1974
'Kritische Anmerkungen zur Widerristhöhenberechnug aus Längenmaßen vor- und frühgeschichtlicher Tierknochen', *Säugetierkundliche Mitteilungen* 22, 325–48

Von den Driesch, A., 1976 — *A Guide to the Measurement of Animal Bones from Archaeological Sites.* Peabody Museum Bulletin 1, Cambridge Mass., Harvard University

Wade, K., 1980 — 'A settlement site at Bonhunt Farm, Wicken Bonhunt, Essex', in Buckley, D.G. (ed.), *Archaeology in Essex to AD 1500*, 96–102. CBA Res. Rep. 34, London

Wade-Martins, P., 1980 — *Excavations in North Elmham Park 1967–1972*, E. Anglian Archaeol. 9

Wait, G.A., 1985 — *Ritual and Religion in Iron Age Britain*, Brit. Archaeol. Rep. Brit. Ser. 149

Walton, P., 1991 — 'Textiles', in Blair, J. and Ramsay, N. (eds), *English Medieval Industries*, 319–54. London

Walton Rogers, P., 1997 — *Textile Production at 16–22 Coppergate*, Archaeology of York. The Small Finds 17/11, London

Waterman, D.M., 1959 — 'Late Saxon, Viking and early medieval finds from York', *Archaeologia* 97, 59–105

West, B., 1983 — 'A note on bone skates from London', *Trans. London Middlesex Archaeol. Soc.* 33, 303

West, S.E., 1963 — 'Excavations at Cox Lane (1958) and at the Town Defences, Shire Hall Yard, Ipswich (1959)', *Proc. Suffolk Inst. Archaeol.* 29, 232–303

West, S.E., 1985 — *West Stow. The Anglo-Saxon Village*, E. Anglian Archaeol. 24

West, S.E., 1998 — *A Corpus of Anglo-Saxon Material from Suffolk*, E. Anglian Archaeol. 84

White, K.D., 1970 — *Roman Farming*. London: Thames and Hudson.

Whittaker, P., 1996 — *Archaeological Recording of Bays 5–9, South Choir Aisle, Ely Cathedral, Cambridgeshire.* CAU Rep. No. 180

Wild, J.P., 1970 — *Textile Manufacture in the Northern Roman Provinces.* Cambridge University Press

Wilson, D.M., 1964 — *Anglo-Saxon Ornamental Metalwork 700–1100.* London: British Museum Publications

Young, C.J., 1977 — *Oxfordshire Roman Pottery*, Brit. Archaeol. Rep. Brit. Ser. 43

178

Index

East Anglian Archaeology

is a serial publication sponsored by ALGAO EE and English Heritage. It is the main vehicle for publishing final reports on archaeological excavations and surveys in the region. For information about titles in the series, visit **www.eaareports.org.uk**. Reports can be obtained from:

Phil McMichael, Essex County Council Archaeology Section
Fairfield Court, Fairfield Road, Braintree, Essex CM7 3YQ

Reports available so far:

No.1, 1975 Suffolk: various papers
No.2, 1976 Norfolk: various papers
No.3, 1977 Suffolk: various papers
No.4, 1976 Norfolk: Late Saxon town of Thetford
No.5, 1977 Norfolk: various papers on Roman sites
No.6, 1977 Norfolk: Spong Hill Anglo-Saxon cemetery, Part I
No.7, 1978 Norfolk: Bergh Apton Anglo-Saxon cemetery
No.8, 1978 Norfolk: various papers
No.9, 1980 Norfolk: North Elmham Park
No.10, 1980 Norfolk: village sites in Launditch Hundred
No.11, 1981 Norfolk: Spong Hill, Part II: Catalogue of Cremations
No.12, 1981 The barrows of East Anglia
No.13, 1981 Norwich: Eighteen centuries of pottery from Norwich
No.14, 1982 Norfolk: various papers
No.15, 1982 Norwich: Excavations in Norwich 1971–1978; Part I
No.16, 1982 Norfolk: Beaker domestic sites in the Fen-edge and East Anglia
No.17, 1983 Norfolk: Waterfront excavations and Thetford-type Ware production, Norwich
No.18, 1983 Norfolk: The archaeology of Witton
No.19, 1983 Norfolk: Two post-medieval earthenware pottery groups from Fulmodeston
No.20, 1983 Norfolk: Burgh Castle: excavation by Charles Green, 1958–61
No.21, 1984 Norfolk: Spong Hill, Part III: Catalogue of Inhumations
No.22, 1984 Norfolk: Excavations in Thetford, 1948–59 and 1973–80
No.23, 1985 Norfolk: Excavations at Brancaster 1974 and 1977
No.24, 1985 Suffolk: West Stow, the Anglo-Saxon village
No.25, 1985 Essex: Excavations by Mr H.P.Cooper on the Roman site at Hill Farm, Gestingthorpe, Essex
No.26, 1985 Norwich: Excavations in Norwich 1971–78; Part II
No.27, 1985 Cambridgeshire: The Fenland Project No.1: Archaeology and Environment in the Lower Welland Valley
No.28, 1985 Norfolk: Excavations within the north-east bailey of Norwich Castle, 1978
No.29, 1986 Norfolk: Barrow excavations in Norfolk, 1950–82
No.30, 1986 Norfolk: Excavations at Thornham, Warham, Wighton and Caistor St Edmund, Norfolk
No.31, 1986 Norfolk: Settlement, religion and industry on the Fen-edge; three Romano-British sites in Norfolk
No.32, 1987 Norfolk: Three Norman Churches in Norfolk
No.33, 1987 Essex: Excavation of a Cropmark Enclosure Complex at Woodham Walter, Essex, 1976 and An Assessment of Excavated Enclosures in Essex
No.34, 1987 Norfolk: Spong Hill, Part IV: Catalogue of Cremations
No.35, 1987 Cambridgeshire: The Fenland Project No.2: Fenland Landscapes and Settlement, Peterborough–March
No.36, 1987 Norfolk: The Anglo-Saxon Cemetery at Morningthorpe
No.37, 1987 Norfolk: Excavations at St Martin-at-Palace Plain, Norwich, 1981
No.38, 1987 Suffolk: The Anglo-Saxon Cemetery at Westgarth Gardens, Bury St Edmunds
No.39, 1988 Norfolk: Spong Hill, Part VI: Occupation during the 7th–2nd millennia BC
No.40, 1988 Suffolk: Burgh: The Iron Age and Roman Enclosure
No.41, 1988 Essex: Excavations at Great Dunmow, Essex: a Romano-British small town in the Trinovantian Civitas
No.42, 1988 Essex: Archaeology and Environment in South Essex, Rescue Archaeology along the Gray's By-pass 1979–80
No.43, 1988 Essex: Excavation at the North Ring, Mucking, Essex: A Late Bronze Age Enclosure
No.44, 1988 Norfolk: Six Deserted Villages in Norfolk
No.45, 1988 Norfolk: The Fenland Project No. 3: Marshland and the Nar Valley, Norfolk
No.46, 1989 Norfolk: The Deserted Medieval Village of Thuxton

No.47, 1989 Suffolk: West Stow: Early Anglo-Saxon Animal Husbandry
No.48, 1989 Suffolk: West Stow, Suffolk: The Prehistoric and Romano-British Occupations
No.49, 1990 Norfolk: The Evolution of Settlement in Three Parishes in South-East Norfolk
No.50, 1993 Proceedings of the Flatlands and Wetlands Conference
No.51, 1991 Norfolk: The Ruined and Disused Churches of Norfolk
No.52, 1991 Norfolk: The Fenland Project No. 4, The Wissey Embayment and Fen Causeway
No.53, 1992 Norfolk: Excavations in Thetford, 1980–82, Fison Way
No.54, 1992 Norfolk: The Iron Age Forts of Norfolk
No.55, 1992 Lincolnshire: The Fenland Project No.5: Lincolnshire Survey, The South-West Fens
No.56, 1992 Cambridgeshire: The Fenland Project No.6: The South-Western Cambridgeshire Fens
No.57, 1993 Norfolk and Lincolnshire: Excavations at Redgate Hill Hunstanton; and Tattershall Thorpe
No.58, 1993 Norwich: Households: The Medieval and Post-Medieval Finds from Norwich Survey Excavations 1971–1978
No.59, 1993 Fenland: The South-West Fen Dyke Survey Project 1982–86
No.60, 1993 Norfolk: Caister-on-Sea: Excavations by Charles Green, 1951–55
No.61, 1993 Fenland: The Fenland Project No.7: Excavations in Peterborough and the Lower Welland Valley 1960–1969
No.62, 1993 Norfolk: Excavations in Thetford by B.K. Davison, between 1964 and 1970
No.63, 1993 Norfolk: Illington: A Study of a Breckland Parish and its Anglo-Saxon Cemetery
No.64, 1994 Norfolk: The Late Saxon and Medieval Pottery Industry of Grimston: Excavations 1962–92
No.65, 1993 Suffolk: Settlements on Hill-tops: Seven Prehistoric Sites in Suffolk
No.66, 1993 Lincolnshire: The Fenland Project No.8: Lincolnshire Survey, the Northern Fen-Edge
No.67, 1994 Norfolk: Spong Hill, Part V: Catalogue of Cremations
No.68, 1994 Norfolk: Excavations at Fishergate, Norwich 1985
No.69, 1994 Norfolk: Spong Hill, Part VIII: The Cremations
No.70, 1994 Fenland: The Fenland Project No.9: Flandrian Environmental Change in Fenland
No.71, 1995 Essex: The Archaeology of the Essex Coast Vol.I: The Hullbridge Survey Project
No.72, 1995 Norfolk: Excavations at Redcastle Furze, Thetford, 1988–9
No.73, 1995 Norfolk: Spong Hill, Part VII: Iron Age, Roman and Early Saxon Settlement
No.74, 1995 Norfolk: A Late Neolithic, Saxon and Medieval Site at Middle Harling
No.75, 1995 Essex: North Shoebury: Settlement and Economy in South-east Essex 1500–AD1500
No.76, 1996 Nene Valley: Orton Hall Farm: A Roman and Early Anglo-Saxon Farmstead
No.77, 1996 Norfolk: Barrow Excavations in Norfolk, 1984–88
No.78, 1996 Norfolk:The Fenland Project No.11: The Wissey Embayment: Evidence for pre-Iron Age Occupation
No.79, 1996 Cambridgeshire: The Fenland Project No.10: Cambridgeshire Survey, the Isle of Ely and Wisbech
No.80, 1997 Norfolk: Barton Bendish and Caldecote: fieldwork in south-west Norfolk
No.81, 1997 Norfolk: Castle Rising Castle
No.82, 1998 Essex: Archaeology and the Landscape in the Lower Blackwater Valley
No.83, 1998 Essex: Excavations south of Chignall Roman Villa 1977–81
No.84, 1998 Suffolk: A Corpus of Anglo-Saxon Material
No.85, 1998 Suffolk: Towards a Landscape History of Walsham le Willows
No.86, 1998 Essex: Excavations at the Orsett 'Cock' Enclosure
No.87, 1999 Norfolk: Excavations in Thetford, North of the River, 1989–90
No.88, 1999 Essex: Excavations at Ivy Chimneys, Witham 1978–83
No.89, 1999 Lincolnshire: Salterns: Excavations at Helpringham, Holbeach St Johns and Bicker Haven
No.90, 1999 Essex:The Archaeology of Ardleigh, Excavations 1955–80
No.91, 2000 Norfolk: Excavations on the Norwich Southern Bypass, 1989–91 Part I Bixley, Caistor St Edmund, Trowse
No.92, 2000 Norfolk: Excavations on the Norwich Southern Bypass, 1989–91 Part II Harford Farm Anglo-Saxon Cemetery